FRENCH DRAMA
OF THE INTER-WAR YEARS
1918–39

FRENCH DRAMA
OF THE
INTER-WAR YEARS
1918–39

by

Dorothy Knowles, M.A.

Docteur ès Lettres en Sorbonne
Officier d'Académie

GEORGE G. HARRAP & CO. LTD
London · Toronto · Wellington · Sydney

First published in Great Britain 1967
by GEORGE G. HARRAP & CO. LTD
182 High Holborn, London, W.C.1

Composed in Linotype Juliana and printed by
Western Printing Services Ltd, Bristol
Made in Great Britain

PREFACE

THE twenties and thirties in Paris were fruitful years for the drama. They were also exciting years, when a host of young writers and young producers, breaking with the traditions of the pre-1914 stage, came up with new themes, new dramatic techniques, and new production methods, to suit the new times and new audiences. These years threw up new names which have since graced play-bills the world over. It is doubtful whether some of the most successful of present-day Parisian playwrights, be it Jean-Paul Sartre, or Samuel Beckett, or Eugène Ionesco, would ever have captured the attention of the general public, or would ever even have thought of writing for the theatre, had it not been for the *avant-garde*, or Studio theatre movement, that prepared the way for them. It was one of the five original *avant-garde* producers, Charles Dullin, who first staged a play by Sartre, *Les Mouches*, in 1943, and Camus owed his first success in the Paris theatre, *Caligula* (1945), to Jacques Hébertot, who was associated with the Studio theatre movement throughout the whole inter-war period. As for the "anti-theatre" of the fifties, had it not been for the liberalizing of traditional dramatic conceptions by the playwrights of the inter-war years, it is questionable whether such completely free forms could have come into being at all—in France at any rate.

To establish a hard and fast classification of the products of these years of continuous experimentation in the Studio theatres, or workshops (*ateliers*), to use Dullin's term, would be an impossible task, but the discerning playgoers were conscious of a pattern that emerged before their eyes. They knew that if they went to such and such a theatre they would very likely see a play that interested them, even if they did not like it, and that the production would follow certain lines. If they wished to see a play by a particular author they knew in which theatres to look for it. It is this pattern, its emergence, its crystallization, and, to a certain extent, its dissolution and its replacement by another, that this book attempts to describe. Many playwrights, conveniently, take their places easily in the pattern and do not change them. Others do not, and I have had to decide how best to fit them in. Was it necessary to divide up their work? But to do so would be to ignore the general inspiration of a given writer and the total contribution which he made to the dramatic movement by virtue of it, so I have kept each dramatist's plays together whenever possible. A further problem is presented by the fact that the theatrical movement did not come to a stop with the war in 1939, nor was it the declaration of war that heralded the end of the phase through which it had passed; it was clearly ready for a change before the war. Certain playwrights, particularly the younger ones who emerged in the thirties, continued to write after the war ended, and some are still writing, often in the same vein. Should no account be taken of their later works? Should the extension into the second post-war period of the pre-war pattern be ignored? The view taken here is that the aftermath of the movement is a part of it and must be followed into the very different general situation of the late forties and the fifties.

Though the *avant-garde* movement is the most exciting and the most significant, it constitutes, quantitively, only a small part of the theatrical production of the time, and it must be placed alongside the run-of-the-mill theatrical entertainments, "le théâtre digestif du Boulevard", or after-dinner comedy, if its originality is to be appreciated.

Nowadays the clear distinction between the "Boulevard" and the Studio theatres, which existed thirty years ago, has been obscured. Jean Vilar registered this fact in January 1965 in the *Nouvelles littéraires*. It is now possible to produce a play by Félicien Marceau in between a play by Sartre and a play by Genêt in a Boulevard theatre. The explanation lies in the fact that the original *avant-garde* movement has invaded the Boulevard. Meanwhile a new distinction has come into being, the distinction between theatre-land on the one hand and the *centres dramatiques* and popular theatres on the other. These latter are now in the same position of antagonism to easy box-office appeal that was occupied by the *avant-garde* of the thirties. They constitute a new *avant-garde* of the present day, and have learnt much from the *avant-garde* described in this volume.

For Studio theatre plays, the theatre and the date of the first production are given. The name of the producer follows the name of the theatre when the producer's name is not permanently connected with that theatre. Only the year of the production is given for less important plays.

For Boulevard theatre plays, normally only the year of the production is given.

Important revivals are indicated and also significant English productions.

D.K.

CONTENTS

International—Théâtre du Peuple 1937—Henri
Ghéon and the Compagnons de Notre-Dame—Henri
Brochet and the Compagnons de Jeux—Léon Chan-
cerel and the Comédiens Routiers—*Attempts at
Tragedy*: Albert Boussac de Saint Marc—Saint-
Georges de Bouhélier—Paul Demasy—Philippe Fauré-
Frémiet—Paul Raynal—*The Chronicle Play*: Paul Fort
—*The Verse Play*: François Porché.

ILLUSTRATIONS

I

The Theatres and Producers

*The national theatres—The Boulevard theatres—
—The Studio theatres: Jacques Copeau—Charles Dullin
—Louis Jouvet—Georges Pitoëff—Gaston Baty—
Antonin Artaud—Jean-Louis Barrault—René Rocher
—Les Escholiers—La Petite Scène—Art et Action.*

BETWEEN the two wars there were three distinct types of theatre in Paris, the national theatres, the Boulevard theatres, and the Studio theatres. The most famous of the Studio theatres were founded and directed by Jacques Copeau and by the Cartel des Quatre, which consisted of Charles Dullin, Louis Jouvet, Gaston Baty, and Georges Pitoëff. It was in their theatres that most of what was new and worthwhile was created. The rôle of the principal national theatre, the COMEDIE-FRANÇAISE, or Théâtre Français (the terms are synonymous), as an educational institution and museum of national culture prevented it then, as it does now, from opening its doors to young playwrights. In the first decade and a half after the Armistice realism and non-conformist tendencies in morals did not find favour with its audiences. On the other hand, these same audiences were quite prepared to tolerate a Célimène or a Ruy Blas well past their prime. When the works of the new generation were occasionally staged the choice fell on plays by Paul Raynal, Paul Géraldy, and Charles Vildrac, not Henri Lenormand or Jean-Jacques Bernard or even Edouard Bourdet, who, ironically enough, was to become the director of the theatre in 1936. The budget was tight and risks could not be taken. Even the casting of plays became difficult because members of the company, forced to supplement their earnings by film work or by accepting engagements in the provinces or abroad (their contracts did not allow them to perform elsewhere in Paris), were often not available for a production. Some

of the best actors, Pierre Fresnay, Jean Marchat, Marie Bell, left the
Comédie altogether, cheerfully paying, out of infinitely superior
earnings on the Boulevard, the indemnity required for their release
from the national theatre.

Direct intervention by the State in the affairs of the theatre was,
and still is, unusual. The same was true of the second national
theatre, the Odéon, now called the Théâtre de France. In the
latter theatre there was intervention in 1962 over the proposed
production of Armand Salacrou's *Boulevard Durand*; at the Comédie-Française in 1933 there was intervention when the Action
Française profited by the political slant given to *Coriolanus* in
René Piachaud's adaptation in order to demonstrate against the
Government, and the Government unwisely countered by appoint-
ing the Director of Public Safety in the place of Emile Fabre as head
of the national theatre! Within a few days it had to recall Emile
Fabre.

In 1936 the Government undertook a complete reorganization of
the Comédie, in order to clear away the cobwebs which it was
accused of allowing to gather. It appointed Edouard Bourdet director, in place of Emile Fabre, and arranged for him to have the assis-
tance of four producers from the experimental theatres—Jacques
Copeau, whose name had already been put forward in 1929 by cam-
paigners for the reform of the Comédie, Dullin, Jouvet, and Baty.
These men were responsible for a certain rejuvenation of the
classics, and battle was joined by the critics over their interpretation of certain plays. They also presented some new authors, such
as Henri Lenormand, championed by Baty, and Jean Giraudoux,
whose sole producer was Louis Jouvet. The stock of the Comédie
rose, and also its takings. The director, Edouard Bourdet, combined
the knowledge of a skilled administrator with that of a successful
craftsman of the theatre.

From 1922 to 1930 the ODEON was under the direction of the
actor-producer Firmin Gémier, who had had ample experience of
both experimental and commercial theatres. His declared aim was
to bring the Odéon up to date because, like the Comédie-Française,
the Odéon was a drama museum. The Odéon was also known as a
family theatre and a scholastic theatre catering for the Latin
Quarter. This was a handicap; the audiences of students and
middle-class "regulars" were not prepared to follow Gémier along
avant-garde lines, and much preferred Labiche and Alexandre

Dumas. As he himself was not an experienced classical actor, he did little to renew the classical repertory; instead he introduced modern works by Henri Lenormand, Jean-Jacques Bernard, and others who had not managed to get a hearing at the Comédie-Française. He sought to modernize the staging as well as the programmes, but financial worries dogged him. The theatre was inadequately subsidized, and by 1929 the members of the company were looking, like those of the Comédie-Française, towards the lucrative Boulevard. In 1930 the Odéon passed under the sole management of Paul Abraham, who had shared it with Gémier since 1925 at Gémier's request.

The term BOULEVARD THEATRE is used of those theatres which are solely or mainly commercial enterprises. Not all are situated on the boulevards. They include many small theatres, known as *bon-bonnières*, which seat only two or three hundred spectators and are, for the most part, *de luxe* establishments designed to suit the after-dinner audience which is prepared to go to the theatre only at nine o'clock. The plays are usually in three short acts, with long intervals to be spent in the foyer and bar. They are performed by five or six exquisitely groomed or gowned actors and actresses, who must include at least one well-known star.

The "Boulevard" also includes the Théâtre Sarah-Bernhardt, the Châtelet, the Porte-Saint-Martin, all particularly suited, by their size, to spectacular performances. To these may be added the newer Théâtre Pigalle, which has remarkable staging facilities but has never been a success. After the war it became a cinema.

Some of the older Boulevard theatres, like the Théâtre de Paris, attempt to combine good theatre with profit-making, and have sandwiched a number of the more literary plays between ordinary commercial productions; Marcel Pagnol's *Marius* was one of these. A few, such as the Théâtre des Arts, the Mathurins, the Théâtre Montparnasse, the Comédie des Champs-Elysées, have become at times the homes of *avant-garde* producers and of theatre groups.

JACQUES COPEAU was the first of the new generation of *avant-garde* producers. He was a man of letters, whose particular concern was dramatic criticism, and he was so scandalized by the commercialization of the theatre of the Banquet Years ("la belle époque", 1900–14), and by the obvious divorce between literature and the stage, that he founded the Vieux-Colombier (1913), with the aid of the writers grouped around the *Nouvelle Revue française*.

The exclusion of professional men of the theatre from this enterprise gave a clue to his intentions. He deliberately situated his theatre away from the Boulevard, in a quiet quarter on the Left Bank. His plan was to attract an audience of students, writers, and artists. Two of the future directors of the Cartel were in his company, Charles Dullin and Louis Jouvet, who acted as his assistant producer. The programme consisted of French and foreign classics interspersed with good plays of the preceding thirty years. The Vieux-Colombier was, in short, an "Art Theatre".

The term "Art Théâtre" had been used in 1907 by Goldberg in a plan which he had drawn up for Valmy-Baysse, who had founded the Nouveau Théâtre d'Art in 1906, but it was not used. André Rouveyre published the substance of the plan in Le Mercure de France, 1927 (September 1st and 15th), where he maintains that the real architect of the Vieux-Colombier was, in fact, Goldberg and not Copeau. Copeau merely carried out, admittedly, in almost every detail, the basic idea of the plan.

Before the theatre opened in the autumn of 1913 the company spent the summer rehearsing at Limon, in the *département* of Seine-et-Marne, and performing exercises of all kinds with a view to cultivating physical and mental versatility. In addition to Jouvet and Dullin the company included Valentine Tessier, Blanche Albane (the wife of Georges Duhamel), Suzanne Bing, and Romain Bouquet. Copeau had deliberately avoided calling in established actors, so as to be able to build up a harmonious and disciplined group. Nevertheless, in spite of Copeau's scheme whereby an actor who had taken a leading part in one production should take a very minor one in the next, stars did emerge, but the enthusiasm of the members of the company was such that attractive offers could not lure them away.

Copeau's public was just as enthusiastic, but it was very "select" and "exclusive", and an audience of snobs was not at all what Goldberg had had in mind; on this point Copeau, at least at the outset, was at variance with the original project, which states: "The new Art Theatre must concern itself with democracy, but it must educate the people and give it healthy fare and not an intellectual hash . . . For that reason the Art Theatre must get in touch with the People's Universities and the Labour Exchanges and put a number of seats at their disposal, cheap." Other seats were to be allocated to schools, colleges, and the like. In this way the theatre could create a large democratic audience without having recourse to "popular drama", and at the same time it could safeguard the freedom and integrity of dramatic art. Copeau's audience was not at all a popular one. However, in his *Souvenirs du Vieux-Colombier*, published in 1931, he declared that he had never pleaded for an austere art form accessible only to an *élite* and that, on the contrary, the theatre could only develop properly through contact with a wide public and in a form which must be called "popular". In fact, his influence was limited to a narrow, but influential, circle.

As far as the programme of his first season is concerned—and there were no others before the war—few plays by contemporary writers were billed, though there was a production of *L'Echange* by Paul Claudel. The style of the production was new at the time; a single tree in the foreground, with a backcloth representing the sky, focused attention on the movement of the actors and their gestures. It is a setting which *Waiting for Godot* has made familiar.

In 1915, after visiting Gordon Craig in Florence, Copeau and Suzanne Bing started up a school of acting for young professional and amateur actors and children. His work as a dramatic critic had convinced Copeau of the cultural and technical incompetence of many successful actors of the first decade of the century, and he deplored the total sacrifice of teamwork to the cult of the star. In 1917 Copeau went on an artistic mission to the United States, where he gave lectures and play-readings, then, after returning to Paris to re-form his company with Dullin and Jouvet, who had been released from the army, he ran a two-year season of the Vieux-Colombier in New York. At the beginning of 1920 the Vieux-Colombier reopened in Paris, where it became an inspiration to other companies which were also formed to combat "commercialism in the theatre".

On Copeau's return from New York the Association des Amis du Vieux-Colombier financed alterations to the stage and auditorium. Wings and backcloth were replaced by a permanent architectural setting consisting of an arch supporting a balcony which was reached by steps. Access to the stage was through two ordinary doors in the wall, both on one side, but this was a matter of chance. Copeau had a proscenium added to the stage, with steps leading up from the auditorium. Footlights were dispensed with and lateral lighting was introduced. Sets in the usual sense were not used, but only a few single props, which were not necessarily authentic but chosen so as to evoke the desired impression of the scene of the action. Lucien Dubech[1] recalls the setting of Emile Mazaud's little play, *La folle Journée*, for which a suburban landscape was needed. André Antoine,[2] he says, would not have failed to reproduce lines of chimney-pots and mildewed walls, but Copeau merely hung up an electric light bulb in a tree. As Copeau himself would have put it, "a stylized element replaces the accumulation of details . . . which detract from the dramatic action".[3] In *La Mort de Sparte*, by Jean Schlumberger, the townsfolk are anxiously awaiting the arrival of King Cléomène; he unrealistically appears, over the portico, symbolizing in an expressive manner that he is the last hope of the people.

These examples illustrate what was fundamental in Copeau's reform of staging. His standpoint was the opposite of Antoine's, who, in the 1880's, had got rid of convention and aimed at realism of detail. Instead of realism Copeau deliberately aimed at reminding his audience that they were at the theatre. He preferred a "picture interpreted by the intelligence" to a "photographic image", an impression to a description. Such a theory led inevitably to stylization in setting and acting, and a strong family resemblance between the various productions resulted. A school of staging had come into being, the effects of which were to be seen not only in the work of Dullin and Jouvet but also of others who had little contact with Copeau. Another producer, Georges Pitoëff, working alone, carried to its utmost limit the principle of simplification in staging, though without any suggestion of systematization. Long-established producers like Firmin Gémier were also influenced, and one young producer, Gaston Baty, gave proof of the vitality of the new doctrine by his strong reaction against it.

Copeau's guiding principle was that the staging of a play includes the movements and gestures, the sound of voices and even silences, in short, everything which constitutes the "spectacle", and it was the producer's task to bring all these elements into harmony with each other. By this work of co-ordination the producer takes part in the creation of the work of art, but he also remains a critic, and his place is outside the work. The ideal would be for the poet to be his own producer but not for the producer to imagine himself as a poet. It was through Copeau that the Paris public first saw plays staged on the principle of one mind conceiving the whole of the artistic and technical operations required to bring a written text to life, though the limited public of the Théâtre d'Art and the Œuvre in the 1890's had enjoyed a modest foretaste of this sort of production. Antoine, too, had considered the problem of harmonizing the various elements of a production.

Copeau was, of course, not unaware of the work of Adolphe Appia, Georg Fuchs, Max Reinhardt, Stanislavsky, and Meyerhold, in addition to that of Gordon Craig. Craig's influence on him was particularly strong. For his theory of lighting Copeau was indebted to Appia and even reproduced in the programmes of the Vieux-Colombier a passage from Appia's *Die Musik und die Inscenierung*. The actor being the essential factor in any setting, Appia considered that the lighting should be so devised as to throw the actor's person and movements into relief, thereby adding a third dimension, and that the structure of the setting itself should show up his attitudes and gestures. Lighting had an active part to play, it should not be reduced merely to making a vertical backcloth visible.

Out of this school of staging began to emerge a school of drama. In a pamphlet of the Vieux-Colombier (1923–24) Copeau pointed out that his manner of staging the classics had brought them to life again and enabled them to become a source of inspiration to young playwrights. Régis and Veynes dedicated their satire *Bastos le hardi* to Copeau in these words: "Had it not been for his theatre this play would never have been written; let him take the credit for it." Yet Copeau's choice of modern plays was disappointing. He was under pressure from the group of the N.R.F., several members of which made a not very successful attempt to write for the theatre they had helped to found. Good plays written by others were, however, submitted to him, and it is inexplicable that Copeau should have let plays like *Knock ou le triomphe de la médecine* (Jules Romains) and *Martine* (Jean-Jacques Bernard) slip through his fingers. Those authors whom he did stage all got the impression that he wished to remodel their works entirely.

When Copeau reopened the theatre in 1920 he also reopened the school. School and theatre were, in his opinion, one and the same thing; no renewal of the theatre was possible unless one began at the beginning—that is to say, with the establishment of a school. Even the theatre public had its "school"; its teachers were Copeau, Jouvet, and Georges Chennevière, who gave public lectures on various aspects of the theatre, literary and technical, from the time of its origins. The school proper undertook the formation of actors, technicians, producers, and even playwrights. "The 1921–22 phase which includes the founding of the school", Copeau wrote in 1921, "is quite as important as, if not more important than, the 1913–14 phase which is the founding of the theatre, the 1919–20 phase which consists of its re-establishment after the war, and the 1920–21 phase which saw the building up of a public for the theatre."[4] The school, which was directed by Jules Romains until 1923, gave the actors a solid general culture and a wide variety of technical training. Three famous clowns, the Fratellini Brothers, were brought in to teach them a freedom of movement with which the realistic, or "hands-in-the-pocket", actor was quite unfamiliar. Copeau also called upon Jean Dorcy, a teacher of mime and acrobatics, not to resuscitate Greek mime as such nor the miming of the *commedia*, but to develop the art of mime as part of the literary actor's technique. In 1923 Etienne Marcel Decroux joined Copeau's school and began to work with Dorcy. He acted more or less unclad and with his face covered by a mask. He had been interested in sculpture, and after working with Dorcy had the idea of sculpture in motion. The technique of the Noh play was also studied. All this training was aimed at producing the complete actor, master of *all* the means of expression at a man's command and not merely of two or three. In 1925 Decroux joined Charles Dullin's school, where he met a new recruit, Jean-Louis Barrault, in 1931.

From 1923 Copeau devoted most of his attention to the school, then suddenly in 1924, without any apparent reason, he closed the Vieux-Colombier. The material difficulties which he alleged were not a sufficient explanation; the theatre had always paid its way and in any case it was not intended as a commercial enterprise. The reason was in Copeau himself or in the company. It is known that there had been certain disagreements between Copeau and Dullin and Dullin had left to work with Firmin Gémier in 1918. In 1922 Jouvet too left, regretfully, it would seem. In the artistic field there was, however, no divergence of opinion between Jouvet and Copeau; disagreement had been over practical issues, and when Copeau abandoned the Vieux-Colombier he handed over part of his company, sets, and repertory to Jouvet, making him his material heir as well as his spiritual heir.

Together with those disciples who were prepared to follow him in retreat, Copeau withdrew to Pernand-Vergelesse, in Burgundy, where he trained them specially in the art of improvisation, attempting a type of modern *commedia dell'arte*. In 1913 Copeau had declared war on the commercial theatre, which had deprived playwrights with real literary talent of contact with the public. In 1924 he appeared to consider that literary drama was moribund and that only farce held out any hope for the future. Given such a conception of theatre, the actor becomes the focal point, and he has to be taught how to mime, improvise, invent, untrammelled by any text. As a result, Copeau found himself criticized for attempting to form interpreters of Sophocles and Racine by teaching them first to "bleet like sheep", and for using methods applicable only to farce. The Copiaus, as the group was then called, performed farces and "diversions" at harvest and vintage celebrations in Burgundy, and improvised scenes, dances, and miming found their way into the text which had been learned. In *L'Illusion*, adapted by Copeau from Corneille in 1928, the "presentational" method of acting, involving a complete disregard for stage realism and the frank acceptance of the actor as an actor or entertainer, was used. The offshoot of Les Copiaus, La Compagnie des Quinze, directed by Copeau's nephew, Michel Saint-Denis (1931–34), inherited this tradition from Copeau and maintained it throughout its existence.

Copeau's belief in the salutary influence of farce and of the *commedia* is expressed in his comments in the programmes of the Vieux-Colombier. In the programme of *Les Fourberies de Scapin* (1920) he declared that he aimed at a purely theatrical presentation so as to get back to an old tradition which, if revived, would help to renew the whole of dramatic art. "Those who mock me by calling me a 'Jansenist' are little aware of my passionate interest in good farce. Just give me time to train actors capable of performing farce and to set my fellow-producers gradually on the road which leads out of the hornets' nest of literature towards broader horizons and richer sources." Molière sets the scene of his play in Naples. Copeau added "but the action takes place on a bare wooden trestle platform", the function of which, he explained, is to throw the actor's movements into relief without the attention being distracted by settings. To repeat one of Copeau's favourite stories about the comment of a stage-hand at the Vieux-Colombier: "There is no scenery and so you can see the words." In discussing this same production Copeau himself said: "The text alone matters"; it was a cardinal principle of Copeau's that a production should be conceived in terms of the text alone. Molière's farce was

accompanied by a *Prologue improvisé* on the lines set down by
Nicolo Barbieri, the Beltrame of the *commedia*, and his name was
quoted in the programme. Critics viewed with alarm the path that
Copeau was taking in his professed respect for the text; it was only
a question of time, they thought, before Scaramouche, Harlequin,
and other stock characters of the *commedia* would be cutting
capers upon his stage. Such was not, however, Copeau's intention,
but the choice of *Turandot*, by Carlo Gozzi (February 2nd, 1923),
was an acknowledgment of his debt, and his productions of Musset
and Marivaux gave ample proof of the influence of the *commedia*
upon him. Even Copeau's choice of modern plays was dictated by
his particular notion of drama and by the training he had given to
his company.

On Copeau's achievements one might well quote Charles Dullin:

> I am happy to state here that without Jacques Copeau, with-
> out his refusal to compromise and without his alleged calvinism,
> enterprises like ours could not survive three months under
> present conditions. Jacques Copeau has cleansed the stage; he has
> brought back the predominance of the mind over the machine
> and of true culture over literary veneer; he has gathered together
> a public which is an *élite* and it now comes to our performances.

In 1934 Copeau planned to take over a Boulevard theatre and
do for the general public what he had already done for the *élite*
who had attended the Vieux-Colombier. The plan came to nought,
but in 1936–37 he staged Paul Raynal's *Napoléon unique*, in
which he played the part of Fouché, and André Obey's play on
Don Juan at the Porte-Saint-Martin, but neither Raynal, Obey, nor
Copeau could hold the public of the old Boulevard of the east end of
Paris. Claude Berton, writing in *Lumière* (February 2nd, 1937), said:

> The days of the first efforts of the Vieux-Colombier to which
> one went as one would to Mass are over. Years have passed. The
> problems of life and therefore those of the theatre have changed.
> Nowhere is there a return to the methods of the past, to a
> simplified material set-up, and to a dwarfing of dramatic visions
> under the direction of a dictatorial producer ... the era of the
> all-powerful producer is over.

Copeau's other activities include two Shakespeare productions in
Paris, the production of an anonymous sixteenth-century mystery
play, *Santa Uliva*, in the Cloister of Santa Croce in Florence, in

1933, and of Rino Alessi's *Savonarola* on the Piazza della Signoria, in 1935, with rhythmic crowd movements which proved quite a sensation. He also took the title-rôle in Henri Ghéon's *La Vie profonde de Saint François d'Assise* at the Théâtre des Champs-Elysées, in 1926, and collaborated with Ghéon in his production at Chartres, in 1927, of *Le Triomphe de Notre-Dame de Chartres*. In 1943 he produced his own play, *Le Miracle du pain doré*, in the courtyard of the Hospice de Beaune, and three years later published *Le petit Pauvre, François d'Assise*. These activities were doubtless inspired by Copeau's conversion to Roman Catholicism in the middle-twenties and also by his changed conception of what constituted true theatre and a real theatre public. Such productions were forerunners of those organized by Jean Vilar in 1947, in the courtyard of the Palais des Papes, in Avignon.

In May 1940 Copeau was nominated general manager of the Comédie-Française, but resigned a year later because of a clash with the Occupation authorities over his son's activities in the Resistance movement. He died in October 1949.

L'Atelier, sometimes referred to as "the Vieux-Colombier of the Right Bank", was founded by CHARLES DULLIN in 1922. It began as a school in 1921, and its members lived and worked together in the Touraine much as Copeau's company had done at Limon in 1913, and it gave performances in the provinces before taking over the Théâtre Montmartre, which it renamed L'Atelier.

Dullin's experience was already rich and varied when he formed the school; he had learned his profession the hard way, performing in little local theatres. He had acted in old-fashioned melodrama which, he said, taught him that there existed a complete art called "theatre". He also acted in realistic plays on the Théâtre Libre pattern and later spent two years at the Odéon under André Antoine's direction, but was never converted to realism, which he stigmatized as commonplace, conventional, and even harmful, because it excluded every element that went to make real theatre. When he founded his first theatre, the Théâtre de la Foire at Neuilly (1908), he attempted instead to revive the tradition of the *commedia dell'arte*. At the Vieux-Colombier Copeau encouraged him to work on these lines, and during the war Dullin tried out more fully the art of improvisation on a given theme in rapidly organized performances behind the lines. Not that Dullin wished in his theatre to emulate an art form which had had its time; he saw it rather as a means of helping the actor to develop his individual talents and his own personality and also acquire a mastery of what he looked upon as a plastic art, the art of bodily movement and expression.

It was in 1911 that Dullin made his name as an actor, playing Smerdiakov in *Les Frères Karamazov*, an adaptation by Jacques Copeau and Jean Croué, played at the Théâtre des Arts, then under Jacques Rouché's management. When Rouché withdrew in 1913 Dullin joined Copeau and his newly formed company at the Vieux-Colombier, but he left in 1918 to work with Firmin Gémier, acting for him at the Cirque d'Hiver, in 1919, in his experimental popular theatre. He followed Gémier when the latter went to the Comédie-Montaigne, and he undertook the management of Gémier's School of Dramatic Art. His association with Gémier is particularly interesting in view of the disclosure, in 1952, of the existence of a project drawn up by Dullin in 1937, at the request of a Cabinet Minister, Jean Zay, but which had been consigned to oblivion by a change of government. In this project Dullin envisages the development of a popular theatre movement and the creation throughout France of a number of "artistic centres", such as have, in fact, gradually come into existence since 1945, under the name of *Centres dramatiques* and are now Government-sponsored. Some of his theoretical proposals with regard to the repertory and to theatre architecture remind one of the solutions Jean Vilar was to adopt when faced with the real practical problems of running a National Popular Theatre some fifteen years later. Dullin proposed *Le Cid* as an obvious choice of play; Vilar actually opened with this play. Dullin proposed the recruitment of a new theatre audience independent of the existing one; Vilar went out to the working-class suburbs of Paris to give his first performances. Dullin's preoccupation with the idea of a popular theatre was clearly behind his unsuccessful application, made in the same year as the one in which he drew up his project, for the lease of the Théâtre Sarah-Bernhardt, a municipal theatre which could provide a large number of cheap seats. When, finally, in 1941 he obtained the lease of the theatre, called Théâtre de la Cité during the German occupation, his small but faithful audience of shop and office workers and students, which had been ever ready to patronize the productions of "le père Dullin", was quite lost in the vast auditorium. Nor did they, as Dullin had confidently expected they would, prove to be the natural leaders of a new dramatic movement. Dullin had clearly failed in his attempt to establish a true popular theatre, and he abandoned the Théâtre de la Cité in 1947. His last triumph before a Paris audience was in 1947–48 at the Théâtre Montparnasse-Baty, then under Marguerite Jamois's management, when he produced Armand Salacrou's *L'Archipel Lenoir* there. He died on December 11th, 1949, while planning to put on in the same theatre Balzac's *La Marâtre*, which he had produced in Lyon earlier that year.

From the outset Dullin's temperament had inclined him towards a conception of theatre much more comprehensive than that generally held in France in the first decades of the century. He aimed at a "complete spectacle" formed of all the different elements which the theatre can command: poetry, movement, and even dancing, music, colour, settings, costumes, and also architecture. His performance of *Volpone* (1928) was a good example of what such a conception could achieve. One of his first productions at the Atelier was Francis de Miomandre's translation of Jacinto Grau's *El Señor de Pigmalión*; it had a close affinity with the *commedia* and at the same time recalled the ballet *Coppélia*. His production of Alexandre Arnoux's *Huon de Bordeaux* a month later seemed also to be inspired by ballet, so strong was the emphasis on the plastic element. Dullin had placed even stronger emphasis on the plastic element in an earlier production of Arnoux's mimo-drama *Moriana et Galvan*, before he went to the Atelier; it was easy to incline it towards ballet as the text is so slight. Even Balzac's realistic *Mercadet ou le faiseur* was given a purely theatrical presentation by Dullin. His pink and yellow setting, like a candy-shop, and his ballet of creditors and servants were the product of fantasy. In Dullin's hands the play became, in 1936, a sort of operetta without music, having, as its component parts, farce, satire, and poetry. In this form it obtained a success such as it had never had in previous presentations, which had always been realistic. Countering the judgment of adverse critics, Dullin declared, quite unabashed: "The moment a performance does not square with ordinary reality they cannot understand." Life and colour were similarly imparted to André Obey's adaptation of *King Richard III*. The battle scenes were mimed and danced to the rhythmic beat of drums and the clash of arms, and Dullin, as the royal hunch-back, made a striking entry into the field, bent double beneath the weight of an enormous lance.

Music-hall provided Dullin with further inspiration, and he gave a performance entitled *L'Atelier Music-Hall*. It consisted of Georges Pillement's *Cyprien ou l'amour à dix-huit ans*, three parodies by Marcel Achard of Sacha Guitry, Paul Géraldy, and Mouézy-Eon entitled *Pour dire, je vous aime*, together with dances, mime, and some recitations by Dullin of poems by Laforgue, Verlaine, and Villon. This experiment, Dullin's article, "Pourquoi je fais du Music-Hall", published in *L'Intransigeant* (June 10th, 1923), and a subsequent lecture at the Collège de France, caused a storm to break over his head. He was accused of wanting his actors to be gymnasts, tightrope walkers, mimes, and even clowns, and of believing that clowns could save the declining art of drama. In his apostolic frenzy, said the critics, Dullin made the pupils in his school imitate animals, doubtless in order to impart to them a greater versatility! After such hard words and the public's cat-calls Dullin waited thirteen years before turning again to music-hall, then for the main part in *Le Camelot* he engaged Georgius, one of the outstanding figures of the music-hall and *café-concert*. In an explanatory article entitled "De la comédie italienne aux grands comiques de café-concert", published in *Le Journal* on September 27th, before the first night, Dullin wrote:

> Except for the greatest amongst them, stage actors of both comedy and tragedy have always sacrificed acting to the text ... It was therefore natural that I should think of him [Georgius, whom he saw as descending from Harlequin] to act a *modern Italian comedy* like *Le Camelot* by Roger Vitrac. I would add that, from the very first rehearsals, Georgius seemed to me to have always belonged to the Atelier. The reason is that the Atelier also has many points in common with the *commedia dell'arte*.

However, the experiment proved conclusively that there was a vast difference between farce of the funfair or the music-hall and farce of the theatre proper, or the real *commedia*, and that although the *commedia* belonged to the anti-literary tradition it was, in fact, writers and not actors who had brought it back to the modern stage.

The Japanese theatre reinforced the inspiration which Dullin had got from the *commedia*. He admired the careful training given to the Japanese actors and the fact that they were not formed in the school of the "frightful natural".

The Japanese actor sets out from the most meticulous realism, his synthesis is achieved through his very need for truth. For us the word "stylization" immediately evokes a kind of stultified aestheticism, a colourless and docile rhythmical pattern; for him stylization is direct, eloquent and more expressive than reality itself.[5]

The Japanese actors' use of the mask, like that of the actors of the *commedia dell'arte*, impressed him, and he attributed to it the extreme expressiveness of their body movements. He introduced the mask into the training of his own actors, and used masks in his production of Jean-Paul Sartre's *Les Mouches*, in 1943.

Dullin envisaged a Western theatrical art as complete and all-embracing as the Oriental. Guidance, as well as texts, could also, he believed, be obtained from the ancient Greeks, Shakespeare, and Molière. It was his firm conviction that the theatre should take us away from routine existence and create an atmosphere of "fantasy"; that a play should be a living dream. His Atelier was therefore intended by him not only as a school for actors but also for playwrights, who were to be helped to the realization that the theatre is not an image of ordinary reality but a world apart, governed by its own special laws. Modern playwrights were not much to his taste, but those whose works he did produce, like Armand Salacrou at his début, Jules Romains with *Musse*, Marcel Achard with his circus play *Voulez-vous jouer avec moâ?*, which has a hint of poetry in it, clearly viewed the theatre in a similar light. It is, however, characteristic of Dullin that he tended to ask modern playwrights, even writers like Jean Cocteau, for adaptations of old and new masterpieces written in other tongues, rather than for original works. Aristophanes, Calderón, Cervantes, George Farquhar, Goldoni, Evreinov, were all to be seen at the Atelier, and Dullin was the first to stage Pirandello in France; he began with *Il piacere dell'onestà* (1922), in an adaptation by Camille Mallarmé, and followed it up with Benjamin Crémieux's adaptations of *Così è (se vi pare)* and *Tutto per bene*. Whatever he staged, Dullin always had a profound respect for the text. According to Salacrou, who had personal experience of Dullin's method of work, a *mise en scène* for Dullin was not a *mise en place*, nor even an artistic *mise en place*, but a deep understanding of the characters.

The story of the Atelier is one of continuous struggle, very often

for mere existence. The desk on which the white-faced Mercadet
leaned when his creditors appeared for the last time was, Dullin
confessed in his *Souvenirs*, symbolic of his own desk, but Balzac
saved the day for him that time. To quote Salacrou, "Charles Dullin
said to me: 'The bailiff came to the house this morning. He was
very embarrassed and said, Please excuse me, Monsieur Dullin, I am
very sorry indeed but here I am again.' "[6]

With his impeccable productions of Jules Romains and Marcel
Achard, Jean Sarment and Fernand Crommelynck, Jean Cocteau
and Jean Giraudoux, and not least of Molière, LOUIS JOUVET worked
for a smart Parisian public, a moneyed public, between the two
wars. Yet he began his career as actor and producer in theatrical enterprises which were at the opposite pole, being aimed at the working-class and lower middle-class. It was in 1909, while pursuing his
pharmaceutical studies, that Jouvet linked forces with the Groupe
d'Action d'Art, which had been trying since 1907 to familiarize the
"popular" public with the works of writers like Flaubert, Laforgue,
and Verlaine, and sought, by performing in such centres as the
Popular University of the Faubourg St Antoine and in the provinces, to introduce this public to the work of Balzac as well. The
group staged *Le Faiseur* and a dramatic version, by Jouvet, of *Le
Colonel Chabert*. Subsequently, in an equally short-lived venture at
the old Théâtre du Château d'Eau, in a popular quarter of Paris,
he attempted, along with Camille Corney, to pursue the policy of
"popular culture" with dramatic performances at popular prices,
thus heralding the work done today in the *centres dramatiques* or
Paris suburbs like Aubervilliers and Saint-Denis. In 1951, when he
died, the wheel had turned almost full circle: Jouvet had been nominated Inspector of these centres and, two days before his sudden
death, had discussed with the Ministry of Fine Arts his desire to
run a provincial centre himself at St Quentin, because he had come
to the conclusion that the future of the theatre lay with them and
not with the managers of the Paris theatres.

In the meantime, partly as a result of working alongside Copeau
at the Vieux-Colombier, Jouvet had come to believe in the possibility of renewing the conventional realistic drama of the time
by means of fixed types, on the lines of those of the *commedia
dell'arte*. This influence was reinforced by personal timidity, which
made him look back with regret at the time when the actor played
under a comic or tragic mask. Sir Andrew Aguecheek, the doctor

in Molière's *La Jalousie du barbouillé*, one of the five doctors in *L'Amour médecin*, and Jules Romains's burlesque professor Trouhadec, are character rôles with which Jouvet made his reputation in the early years, though, ironically enough, it was Jules Romains who helped to draw him away from such rôles by requesting him to play Knock with no disguise or make-up of any kind and with only a pair of spectacles.

On leaving the Vieux-Colombier Jouvet formed his own company and settled in at the Comédie des Champs-Elysées (1923), where for two years his productions alternated with those of the Georgian actor-producer Georges Pitoëff, who ranged through Ibsen, Shaw, Wilde, Pirandello, and Tolstoy. Jouvet was little concerned with foreign plays, whether at the Comédie, where he stayed for ten years, or afterwards at the Athénée, though *Au grand large*, Sutton Vane's *Outward Bound*, proved a considerable success in 1926–27. Nor did he stage many plays belonging to the traditional French repertory, apart from Molière's *L'Ecole des femmes*, *Tartuffe*, and *Don Juan*, which he acted at the age of sixty, presenting a hero who was completely blasé and who opted for evil in the hope of provoking a reaction from the heavens, even if it were to bring only a punishment. Jouvet's interest lay with the younger French playwrights, though he turned his attention to them only after they had been produced elsewhere. The two exceptions are Jean Giraudoux, whose work occupied him so exclusively from 1928 onward that he had little time to look for other dramatic talent until after Giraudoux's death, and Jean Genêt, who was introduced to him by Cocteau. Genêt's play *Les Bonnes*, which he staged in 1947, set Jouvet thinking about certain metaphysical problems which worried him greatly after his return to France following his four years' tour of South America and Mexico during the Second World War.[7] He accepted with alacrity to produce Sartre's *Le Diable et le bon Dieu* after he had read the first act and had been told by Sartre that in the second act Gœtz was to turn over to Good. He did not count on a further possible development in a third act, and, when he received the complete text, proceeded with the production much against his will, turning frequently to the Church for assurance about the existence of an after-life. Then, as if to purge the "sin" of the production, he feverishly prepared a play adapted by Pierre Bost from Graham Greene's novel *The Power and the Glory*, and reserved for himself the rôle of the priest, which he felt in need of playing. He died during rehearsals, before the play could be staged.

Jouvet disliked the design of modern theatres and preferred the medieval and the Elizabethan stage to the circumscribed space of the Italian stage, which he referred to as the "boîte à images, boîte d'illusion". For a time along with Copeau he had placed his faith in an "architectural stage", though he maintained that the idea had not been taken far enough by them since they had endeavoured to use it in a theatre which differed little in form from any other theatre. Until a different type of theatre was devised one might, he thought, act with profit in the streets. Like Copeau, he favoured simplicity in staging because a simple setting is the most suggestive. Settings, he held, should look like settings, even when they were conceived on realistic lines; the audience should feel that it was at the theatre. In his production of L'Ecole des femmes the strangely tall and narrow house, with garden walls which opened and shut, flower-beds on wheels, which ran out to the footlights and back, according to the scene of the action, and four unlit chandeliers, which hung on thick red silk cords from a blue sky, was clearly a stage décor, though the chandeliers might well have constituted an oblique reference to Molière's time. The décor was by Christian Bérard, who also undertook other décors for Jouvet. For Don Juan Jouvet turned to Braque.

Conscious artistry and perfect finish were the hallmark of every one of Jouvet's productions. His sets were sophisticated. He restored the footlights, which Copeau had abandoned. One could say that his productions were selfconscious or consciously theatrical. His company boasted of some of the best actors and actresses in Paris and included several from the Vieux-Colombier, who came to him in 1924, when Copeau closed the theatre and handed over to him its properties and repertory. The permanency of the company made it possible for Jouvet to develop a style and degree of perfection in technique such as only Les Copiaus and Les Quinze had achieved. Yet the actor necessarily took second place to the text, and Jouvet struggled, by means of extended rehearsals and long hard work, to help the actor "soak himself in the text" and achieve such technical mastery that the text "came to the fore of its own accord", to quote the testimony of one of the troupe, Jean Meyer.[8]

Jouvet was particularly sensitive to the quality of the language of a text, and his treatment of a Cocteau or Giraudoux play showed this clearly. In *Prestiges et Perspectives du théâtre français* (1945) he states that great drama is, in the first place, good writing. Of *Amphitryon 38* he said that the story had, in fact, already been treated seventy-five times, not thirty-eight, adding that it is not the choice of the story, the theme, nor even the action of the play that counts, but the language and everything that is suggested by the language, that a writer's originality is to be found in his style, and that the actor's art is to speak, to "breathe" the text (Jouvet uses the phrase "respirer un texte") in such a way that it can be momentarily confounded with the writer's "creative breath". It was the better to throw into relief language like Giraudoux's, which was not familiar to a theatre audience, that Jouvet demanded of the members of his troupe a static type of acting. He further demanded of them a kind of incantation and even verbal orchestration of the text. The consequent slowing-up of the rate of speech allowed for the full effect of the text, both auditory and emotive. The aim of the theatre, according to Jouvet, is not to make something understood, but to make it felt. The culminating point of Jouvet's work along these lines was reached in the last scenes of *Ondine*, where progressively lowered lights threw the element of sound into ever greater relief, with the words almost ceasing to be the vehicle of thought. True, the tonality of the voices added "depth", a further dimension beyond those of space, but this was an extreme case, a limiting case, and Jouvet could go no further without disrupting the unity which he had so far achieved by successfully blending the various elements that go to make up a theatre production.

In his last projected production before his death, Jouvet, a disciple of Copeau and Stanislavsky, made a complete *volte-face* and envisaged for *La Puissance et la gloire* a type of acting with which one was to become familiar in the performances of the Theatre of the Absurd (Ionesco, Beckett, Adamov). In an interesting letter to Pierre Renoir,[9] who was to act with him in this "cold-epic" play, he explained that there was something in it akin to what Brecht called "theatre of alienation"; it was non-affective drama which called more for a judgment, an acceptance of a responsibility, and involvement in the action, than for mere participation in the feelings expressed, or "communion" with the characters or with actors who had managed to get inside the characters and be identified with them. Jouvet, who had been so completely a man of his time, would, in this instance, have been in advance of his time had he lived to carry out his intent.

Outside the theatre Jouvet became widely known because of the number of films in which he appeared. In 1932 he made *Topaze* and *Knock* for Marcel Pagnol. He made a second version of *Knock* in 1950 with Guy Lefranc. He appeared in Julien Duvivier's *Carnet de bal* (1936), *La Fin du jour* (1938), *La Charette fantôme* (1939) and *Un tel Père et fils* (1940), in Jean Renoir's *Les Bas-fonds* (1935) and *La Marseillaise* (1937), in Marcel Carné's *Drôle de drame* (1937) and *Hôtel du nord* (1938), Pabst's *Le Drame de Shanghaï* (1938), Clouzot's *Quai des orfèvres* (1947), and some twenty other films.

GEORGES PITOEFF was essentially a producer of foreign plays, and he staged for the Paris public the works of a great many playwrights of other countries which otherwise they might never have seen, or provided new interpretations of works they already knew. "Your theatre is the true League of Nations", said Georges Duhamel. Four of Duhamel's plays were among the seventy French plays Pitoëff also produced. These seventy French plays constituted about a third of his total repertoire and include a few classics such as *Le Mariage de Figaro* and *La Dame aux camélias*. His preference, however, went to writers of idealistic plays, particularly Maurice Maeterlinck or Paul Claudel, and writers of poetic plays, particularly *avant-garde* writers like Fernand Crommelynck, Jules Supervielle, and Jean Cocteau. He was also drawn to writers who expressed the disquiet of the First post-World War generation—Jean Anouilh, who owed his first real successes in the theatre to him, Henri Lenormand, whom he made known as a dramatist and whose work he played more frequently than that of any other French writer. He also staged occasional plays by Jean-Jacques Bernard, Charles Vildrac, and Stève Passeur, choosing those which had a romantic flavour, as well as plays by more purely literary men, Drieu de la Rochelle, Maurice Martin du Gard, and André Gide.

When he installed his company in the Comédie des Champs-Elysées in 1922 Pitoëff had already worked as a producer in Geneva for seven years. His contact with the theatre, in fact, dated from his early youth in Tiflis, where he was born in 1884, and where his father directed the State theatre. Furthermore, he had worked in Moscow, along with Meyerhold and Bakst, under the direction of Vera Kommissorievskaya. After Vera Kommissoriev-

Œdipe, roi de Thèbes. Producer: Gémier

Coll. Rondel, Biblio. de l'Arsenal

Le Simoun. Producers: Gémier and Baty

The Vieux-Colombier in 1912

Coll. Rondel, Biblio. de l'Arsenal

The Vieux-Colombier in 1919

skaya's death he had joined a company formed by her sister and had acted Shakespeare, Molière, Musset, Ibsen, Tolstoy, all over Russia and Siberia. It was doubtless this early experience which made him long for a wider audience than the ordinary "bourgeois" Parisian audience, and he expressed his belief, in 1936, that the renewal of the theatre depended on the renewal of the public.[10]

When in Moscow, Pitoëff had become acquainted with the various ideas then afoot for revolutionizing the theatre, such as the use of perfume for certain acts and the distribution of flowers to the spectators. He came temporarily under the influence of Stanislavsky, but then reacted against him, declaring that the theatre should get beyond the appearance of the action to its essence. He claimed that his views were confirmed by Stanislavsky's later productions of The Cherry Orchard, which had not progressed from the first one. In 1912, when The Three Sisters was to be seen in Moscow, in a strictly realistic mise en scène of Stanislavsky's, Pitoëff was staging it with four velvet curtains, two screens, two lamps, and a few chairs, in his own theatre in St Petersburg (1912–14). He again used curtains for Oscar Wilde's Salomé, in which a raised platform covered with white satin was reached by steps with black velvet treads and white satin risers, providing a contrast with the black velvet curtains at the back of the stage. Again, in Lenormand's Le Mangeur de rêves, he used long pieces of coloured ribbon stretched against a background of black velvet curtains to indicate a room or the blue Mediterranean sea. Such a simplification of setting did not result from the will to simplification of an artist who was an ascetic, as appears to have been the case with Copeau, nor did it result from a formula or system. Indeed, of the producers of his time, Pitoëff was the least inclined to develop a "manner" peculiar to himself; he approached each play with a completely open mind and looked to the text to inspire the elements of the setting which could best express its nature. However, one must add, armed with certain facts provided by his biographers, that aesthetic asceticism must have suited the state of his finances.

In Pitoëff's view there were as many types of setting as there were plays, and it is the idea at the centre of the play which should determine the mise en scène, the sole function of which is to bring this idea out clearly. It was he, naturally, who decided just what that idea was. In Shaw's Saint Joan, for example, he insisted on taking Joan's conviction of being sent from God as central. He brushed aside all Shaw's irony and fastened on the idea of saintliness. The theory is set out in Pitoëff's *Notre Théâtre* (1949); it does not need any literary or historical criticism, being guided by the *metteur en scène*'s intuition. Having decided that the "idea" is saintliness, the *metteur en scène* chooses a setting reminiscent of an altarpiece, a triptych formed of an arch in the centre and a half-arch on either side. About a year after this production Pitoëff, writing in *Le Temps* (August 24th, 1925), stated that for him the problem of production of any one play was to give scenic form to the "secret truths", the "invisible forces", contained in the play, that this "secret truth" must be detached and made perceptible to the senses by the invention of a form or mode of setting which can give it concrete existence; imagination, continuing the creative work of the author, can itself create a new sensual world, and this faculty had inspired another type of setting at the very moment when realistic settings had firmly conquered the stage. The realistic and non-realistic points of view on staging were flippantly put later in a brief exchange between the founder of realistic staging in France, André Antoine, and Georges Pitoëff—"But where on earth can you find bedrooms without ceilings?" "At the theatre, of course, Monsieur Antoine." And in 1932, when he produced Schnitzler's *Reigen* (*La Ronde*), for the actress's sumptuous bedroom he set a small platform on the stage in one corner and enclosed it on two sides, forming the same angle as the back and side of the full stage, with two low walls; a rich piece of drapery trailed from the bed on the platform, forward towards the footlights on to the stage proper. When dealing with a realistic play Pitoëff rarely respected the ordinary laws governing everyday life and everyday things. Not that he attempted to get away from the reality represented by the text. On the contrary, he concentrated on it until the indispensable elements of the desired setting, certain pieces of furniture or particular objects, rose, as it were, to the surface of his consciousness, to the exclusion of all others. Reality was transposed, idealized, to the point of making the real more intensely real.

Another important influence on Pitoëff, apart from those to which he had been subjected in his own country, was that of Jacques Dalcroze. He became acquainted with his work when he visited Hellerau in 1911. From then onward the search for rhythm, when ordering the various elements of a production, became basic in his work. Pitoëff placed the actor—that is to say, the character incarnate—at the centre of the production, and considered that a *décor* was useless if it did not help to put the character across to the public. He was himself a good actor, and his acting was particularly successful in portraying an unsettled frame of mind, whether it was in Chekhov, Gorky, and Tolstoy or in Lenormand and Anouilh. French critics considered his Hamlet to be unrivalled by any purely French actor's. Unfortunately his voice, hoarse and harsh, and his strong accent, limited the number of parts he could play. He was fully aware of his shortcomings in this direction and, at a dinner given in his honour after his first success in Paris, when Paul-Napoléon Roinard thundered in a wine-befuddled speech, "Et qui s'occupe de la langue française?" Pitoëff whispered to his neighbour, Lenormand, "Moi! Je la massacre."[11]

His wife, Ludmilla Pitoëff, whom he had met in Paris, though she too was born in Tiflis, had a pleasing voice and accent. She also had a striking presence, despite the fact that she was slight and frail. From her lessons with Paul Mounet she had learned the value of simplicity in acting. Her willowy form and her earnestness made her completely convincing in poetic parts; as a seagull who had once been a woman she would hang longingly over a bowl of goldfish, struggling against the unwomanly desire to plunge her head into it;[12] her Joan of Arc was all purity and transparent fervour. No interpretations of any one rôle could have been more different than were Ludmilla Pitoëff's and Sybil Thorndike's of Shaw's heroine,[13] and, given Pitoëff's eccentric interpretation of the play, this is not unexpected. Ludmilla's complete prepossession with the part inspired her husband, together with René Arnaud, to write a very non-Shavian "dramatic document", *Le vray Procès de Jeanne d'Arc*, using the verbatim report of the trial. Certain contemporaries of the Pitoëffs, such as Lenormand, attributed to her playing of Saint Joan a religious crisis which drew her away from writers who had interested her so far and preoccupied her with Paul Claudel. Claudel's *L'Echange* remained one of Ludmilla's favourite plays, and when Pitoëff died in 1939 he was working on *Le Père humilié*. Interest in Claudel as a dramatist was growing at the time, and this fact could also explain Ludmilla Pitoëff's choice of *L'Annonce faite à Marie* and *L'Otage*, during the war, for playing in America and Canada. Her last rôle before she died near Paris, in 1951, was that of Charlotte Brontë in *Survivre*, by Michel

Philippot. Pitoëff's last rôle was Stockmann. He performed it knowing that the effort would hasten his death, but he felt like a man
with a mission.

The whole trend of Pitoëff's work was to disengage the theatre
from ordinary experience, to idealize and generalize it. It was
sometimes naïve, but its radical simplicity of approach encouraged
French metteurs en scène to rethink the principles of their art, and
its influence was in this respect beneficial for the whole of the next
generation of playgoers.

The term "total theatre" has recently become a fashionable one
in English theatre criticism. All GASTON BATY's work is based on this
concept, which he carried to the extreme in an ill-advised attack on
"His Majesty the Word" (Sire le Mot) in 1920. This outburst led
to his being accused of using the text as a mere pretext for stage
decoration and of his being looked upon as "Theatre Enemy Number 1", to quote the critic Lucien Dubech. Baty always vehemently
denied the accusation, and the playwrights whose plays he produced agreed with him in refuting it. "I could testify to the fact
that with him [Baty] the text retains its prime importance in the
hierarchy of theatrical values", wrote Henri Lenormand.[14] Baty
attempted to define his own position when he said: "As a reaction against the French tradition which is both Cartesian and
Jansenistic, I try to serve the theatre according to Saint Thomas."[15]
Saint Thomas did not separate man from nature; he did not exclude
the beasts from some special domain reserved for men; all creatures
have a relationship with God. And so, said Baty, all creatures have
the right to be included in drama, which is a universe in miniature.
Inanimate objects and the elements must be included also. Factories,
ships, mountains, and also the great forces of nature, sun, sea,
wind, fog, all may play their part in moulding human characters
and therefore should be physically represented on the stage whenever they come into play. And beyond the physical world are invisible presences which surround man, while before him lies the
mystery of death and the Beyond. For such drama the traditional
methods of staging were manifestly inadequate; the spectator had
to be made physically aware of these things, and this meant calling into play all the possible means of expression. "Painting, sculpture, the dance, prose, verse, song, music, these are the seven chords
stretched side by side on the lyre of drama."[16] These seven arts are
complementary to each other, each making the contribution which

it alone can make, whereas with Wagner several arts merely express the same theme.

Baty also tried to carry his attack into the opponents' camp, though it must be said he charged at windmills. He would have it that the theatre had so far tried to describe men living outside time and space, in a world of Calvinists and Jansenists, who despised the body and were blind to art and beauty. The influence of Cartesianism was equally catastrophic for the drama. Jansenism and Cartesianism together produced French classical drama, which appealed only to the mind, in contrast to the Mystery play, which had attempted to appeal to the heart. Drama was reduced to the characters, and the characters were reduced to their intelligence. This was strange literary criticism, but Baty had the bit between his teeth. As far as the Romantic formula was concerned he saw little difference between it and the Classical formula; where the Classics talked of reason, the Romantics talked of feelings and colour, but neither reached a true and full concept of the art of the theatre; both were circumscribed within their literary tradition; for both, the theatre was a verbal art; both were slaves of "Sire le Mot". Not, as has already been stated, that Baty despised the spoken or written word. He likened the dramatic text to the solid core of the fruit, the centre round which the other elements were organized. In the theatre the text plays the part reserved to words in ordinary life: words directly express ideas, and indirectly express feelings and sensations in so far as the intelligence can analyse them. But whatever defies analysis can find no expression in words, and it is the function of the staging—decoration, music whether verbal or instrumental, lighting, costume, gesture—to go on from the point where words themselves leave off and help to present an integral, or total, vision of the world in an integral, or total, drama. Thomism had provided Baty with a philosophy in which mind and matter are closely integrated, but this idea of the integration of mind and matter, of character and background (in the theatre that means character and setting), which leads away from idealism, can lead also to the aesthetics of Flaubert, in which the relation between the individual and the milieu is so intimate. Another step and Baty would have reached the Goncourt brothers. His Thomism is difficult to distinguish from philosophical naturalism and might well have brought him to the aesthetic naturalism of André Antoine's Théâtre Libre, had it not included all nature and not only society, had it not demanded the "spirit" as well as the "clay", to use Melchior de Vogüé's term, when he was distinguishing between the naturalism of the Russians and the French. Baty appeared, in fact, to be going over ground which had already been trodden in the novel between *Madame Bovary* and de Vogüé's *Roman russe*, and his choice of Dostoievsky's *Crime and Punishment*, which he adapted for the stage some three years before he adapted *Madame Bovary*, would seem to be indicative of this development. In Baty's opinion Antoine had inaugurated a new era in the theatre, initiating the revolt against the "Cartesian" stage and the hypertrophy of the verbal element. He had shown that the actor was not alone on the boards, that he was surrounded by objects of all kinds, and that these objects existed alongside man and were part of him. When he thought he was merely applying naturalism to the theatre Antoine was, in fact, linking up with the Thomist current, which, for Baty, meant liturgical drama, the medieval theatre, Shakespeare, and Calderón. The achievements of the Théâtre Libre on the production side were remarkable; unfortunately the playwrights were clinging to a formula which those on the production side were rapidly invalidating. Baty envisaged the creation of a new theatre, which, without repeating the medieval or Greek theatre, would be based on the same principles.

These ideas of Baty's are to be found mainly in a series of essays published between 1917 and 1921 and grouped under the highly significant titles of *Le Masque et l'encensoir* (1926) and *Vie de l'art théâtral, des origines à nos jours* (1932). The latter work was written in collaboration with the art critic René Chavance. Unlike Dullin, Jouvet, and Pitoëff, Baty was not an actor and had spent several years on theatre research before undertaking any productions himself. He was familiar with the ideas of Gordon Craig, Adolphe Appia, and Georg Fuchs, and had watched Fritz Erler and Max Reinhardt at work in Germany. In 1909, in Paris, he had seen Diaghilev's Russian Ballet, and in 1910–13 had observed the work of Jacques Rouché at the Théâtre des Arts. He had also followed Copeau's experiment at the Vieux-Colombier. Because he was not an actor, Baty tended to displace the actor from his central position on the stage and see in him one of the many elements constituting "total drama".

Baty's first contact with the theatre was through the marionettes of the Théâtre Joly, in Lyon. He remained interested in them throughout the rest of his life; he had his own marionette theatre, the Théâtre Billembois, and wrote for it. His first work in the field of production was done in 1919 as Firmin Gémier's assistant in the Cirque d'Hiver, in Gémier's audacious experiment in popular theatre. In 1921 Baty formed his own company, Les Compagnons de la Chimère—not the cruel sphinx of ancient mythology but the bird-woman of folk-tales of the north. In 1923, after a year's costly stay in La Baraque de la Chimère, which the company built in Boulevard Saint-Germain, Baty did the main part of his work in the exiguous Studio des Champs-Elysées, and then, from 1930 to 1943, in the old Théâtre Montparnasse, to which he gave his name. Given his "anti-Cartesianism", Baty favoured works in which non-human elements played an essential part and needed to be given physical representation on the stage. Henri Lenormand could offer him these. The expressionist play, which demands the co-operation of the other arts and is written with stage performance in mind, was particularly to Baty's taste, and Jean-Victor Pellerin as well as Lenormand provided the texts. Baty also used expressionist techniques where one would least expect it—for example, in his own adaptation of *Madame Bovary*, in which a chorus of "Belles" reveals Emma's romantic dreams. Baty was less concerned, as he stated in the programme, with the story of events than with the drama which was enacted in the heart of this *bourgeoise* tormented by romantic dreams. This explains the real magnificence of the set representing the box at the provincial theatre attended by Emma, which, seen without rose-coloured spectacles, would be ordinary and uninspiring. In another scene a happy Emma talks with her lover in a sunlit arbour in full flower, whereas later, when she takes arsenic in despair in the same arbour, the light is wan and every leaf and flower has withered. The pictorial quality of these settings is characteristic of Baty's productions as a whole.

Baty's repertory is constituted by escapist plays of all kinds, because Baty saw himself in the rôle of a "marchand d'oubli", whose task was to open the way to a more significant life beyond the superficialities of everyday existence. This outlook made him hostile to topicality of any kind and to all forms of "committed" drama. When the flow of modern escapist plays began to dry up Baty escaped into the past with plays by Molière, Marivaux, Musset, Shakespeare, Goethe. These productions were controversial because they sought to suggest to the audience a way of looking at the work;

Baty's *Macbeth*, for example, had a strongly religious bias. So, too, his adaptation of *Madame Bovary* and his original dramatic work *Dulcinée*, written round one detail in Cervantes' *Don Quixote*. The moderate success of this supreme attempt at total drama was a keen disappointment to Baty who, become author as well as producer, seemed to be emulating the creative artist imagined by Gordon Craig. Despite the qualities of the production, Baty as a playwright had, himself, fallen victim to "Sire le Mot".

Baty's last work was done at Aix-en-Provence, where he helped to set up, in 1951, the new *Centre dramatique*, also called La Comédie de Provence. Feeling himself out of tune with the "committed drama", and with the less select Paris audiences of the early post-war years (he called them a "crowd", not an audience), he determined to seek out what he considered to be the unspoilt public of the provinces and, since his choice fell on Aix, to renew the theatrical tradition of Provence, with which he was acquainted through his work with Gémier at the Cirque d'Hiver. Because of ill-health, he was able to give little more than moral support to the work of the *Centre*. He died the following year, in 1952.

In 1927, Baty, Dullin, Jouvet, and Pitoëff had grouped themselves into a Cartel in order to proclaim the similarity of their aims, give each other moral and material support, and unite the audience they were gradually building up instead of dividing it among themselves. They published their manifesto in the first number of *Entr'-acte* (1927–34), the official organ of Jouvet's theatre, which followed the tradition of the short-lived *Cahiers du Vieux-Colombier* (1920–21). *Correspondance* (1922–23) was the official publication of the Atelier, and *Le Bulletin de la chimère* (1922–23) and *Masques* (1926–33) those of Baty's theatre.

With his demand for a new form of "total" dramatic art and his antagonism to "Sire le Mot", ANTONIN ARTAUD, poet, actor, producer, author, and also theoretician of the theatre, would seem, at first sight, to have reached much the same conclusions about the theatre's scope and the use of the means at its disposal, as Baty himself. But whereas Baty sought to renovate the theatre while working within the accepted mould, Artaud, critical of Western civilization as a whole, envisaged the theatre as a magical operation, a ritual ceremony carried to such a degree of frenzy as to modify the spectators' lives as well as those of the actors. In an important text, *Le Théâtre et la peste*, he defined the aim and essence of the theatre by comparing the theatre with an epidemic of plague: both drain abscesses collectively, both force men to drop their masks and see themselves as they are, both constitute a crisis ending in a cure or in death.

Artaud's career as an actor began in 1920 at the Œuvre, with Lugné-Poë, but Dullin's ideas and methods were more to his taste, particularly the improvisation and the training he gave in the Japanese actor's art of acting without having recourse to any accessories. Yet later, in 1927, when he and Roger Vitrac were running the very controversial Théâtre Alfred Jarry (1927–29),[17] he wrote disparagingly of Dullin's contribution to the reform of the theatre, of Pitoëff's (with whom he had worked in 1923), of Jouvet's, and of Gémier's. His own ideas took shape in 1931 after seeing the actors of the Bali theatre at the Colonial Exhibition in Paris. Earlier, in 1922, he had seen a group of Cambodian dancers in Marseille. His theatrical doctrine is set out in a series of essays, letters, and manifestos dating from 1931–36 and published in 1938 under the collective title Le Théâtre et son double. The book was reissued in 1944, two years before Artaud was released after seven years in mental homes. The circumstances surrounding its reissue in 1944 gave the book considerable publicity, and it is perhaps significant that the movement represented by the work of men like Ionesco, Beckett, Genêt, and Adamov (first manner) got under way in the theatre some five years after it reappeared. It is significant, too, that Roger Blin, who has been involved in the production of plays by these writers, was associated with Artaud in his second theatrical venture, the Théâtre de la Cruauté (1935). So, too, was Jean-Louis Barrault, who was influenced by him to the point of not knowing, as he himself said, how deeply he was indebted to him for some of his ideas. But Artaud, who had watched him rehearsing with the actors for the Théâtre de la Cruauté, would not accept Barrault's proposal to enter into any real collaboration with him because of fundamental differences between them, despite the superficial similarity.

The Théâtre de la Cruauté, of which the sole production was that of Artaud's own version of the Cenci story, offered a practical illustration of his dramatic theories. The Peter Weiss-Peter Brook Marat-Sade spectacle at the Aldwych Theatre, London, in 1964, was in the same line, and, since Sade believed in the amorality of human nature, Artaud might well have chosen him as a fit subject for his Théâtre de la Cruauté, all the more so as Sade was a favourite figure with the Surrealists to whose group Artaud had once belonged. Cruelty, according to Artaud, means rigour, unflagging application, unrelenting determination, irreversible decisions. It is an appetite for life; it is not a matter of bloodshed and murder.

In Les Cenci, a "theatrical text" which, Artaud said, arose in his mind in concrete fashion as he wrote, he attempted to carry out the idea of a theatre which was a pure, autonomous creation like to that realized by the Balinese, with their fusion, in a perspective of hallucination and fear, of dance, song, and pantomime. In his writings he constantly contrasts Oriental theatre, in which all creation comes from the stage, with Occidental theatre, which he defines as a branch of literature, a sonorous species of language, a performed text, as "purely verbal theatre, knowing nothing of what makes theatre—namely, everything that is in the air of the stage, that is measured and circumscribed by the air, that has density in space: movements, shapes, colours, vibrations, attitudes, screams". The stage is a physical and concrete place which demands to be filled, and to be made to speak its own concrete language, which is directed towards the senses and is independent of the spoken word. This language is truly theatrical only in so far as what it expresses is outside the scope of articulated speech. Architecture, lighting, setting, as well as music, gestures, pantomime, and the human voice are elements of this language. Besides its conceptual content, articulated speech has a sound value, an affective value, and should be manipulated as if it were a plastic substance. Like the Oriental theatre, the theatre of the West should turn words into incantation, extend the voice and use its vibrations and its qualities, thus making of the voice, in the sonorization of the spectacle, one element of the whole, together with music and sounds of all kinds. Artaud refused to accept the Western theatre's "enslavement to the text", and sought to return to the notion of a unique language half-way between gesture and thought, to a new physical language based no longer on words but on signs, and which would act directly on the human organism. Gestures would have the same weight as words, and attitudes a deep symbolic signification. It was a question of creating a "metaphysics of speech, gesture and expression" in order to banish from the stage psychology and "human interest". It was a question of manifesting external forces making the whole of nature re-enter the theatre;

"space thundering with images and crammed with sounds speaks too". It was a question of bringing about the total involvement of the spectators in the spectacle: the two closed worlds of stage and auditorium should go; the dramatic action should take place in the midst of the spectators and flow all around them. It is in this spirit that a number of experiments have since been carried out. JEAN-LOUIS BARRAULT's first theatrical venture, after four years' apprenticeship with Dullin, was *Autour d'une mère* (1935), a "mimo-drama" based on William Faulkner's *As I lay dying*. Like Artaud's *Les Cenci*, which preceded it by one month, it cut across current theatre practice and was a striking revelation of the power of physical gesture. Artaud said of it—with approval—that it was "organized in relation to the stage and *on* the stage and had no existence apart from the stage". The performance moved forward from the breaking-in of a wild horse, mimed by Barrault, and the death agony of the mother, who looked like a Mexican totem. At the last minute Barrault had to take over the part of the mother, and his controlled breathing, tuned to the rasp of a saw with which the son, acting on his mother's orders, was making the coffin, was certainly productive of terror and fear. After the mother's body had stiffened in death she rose up to walk among those still alive. Her two lyrical speeches and two short explanatory passages were the only words spoken during the two hours of the performance.

Barrault's first production proper was *Numance*, which he adapted himself from Cervantes' *Numancia*. It was politically committed and was intended as a "gesture of solidarity" with the Spanish republicans. The text was accompanied by miming and ballet-like crowd movements. Barrault's debt to Decroux and Artaud was evident. The 1937 production was an enormous success and is still remembered in Paris, even though a revival in 1965, with a text by Jean Cau, was a failure. Barrault claimed the subject to be of continual topicality, but this did not prove to be the case and the success of 1937 was thus shown to have been, partly at any rate, due to the intellectual atmosphere of 1937. It must be added, however, that Barrault's miming effects and visual drama no longer made the impact that they had made thirty years earlier. Times had changed and Barrault had stood still. In 1937, however, all this was new and exciting. From Cervantes' work Barrault had culled what he has called "a ballet of man against man and against nature", a vast, rhythmic pattern of words and gestures.[18] It was suited to large-scale production, and one may note that in the Roman theatre at Orange in 1965, before a huge audience, it had a success which was not repeated at the Théâtre de France in the October of that year.

Barrault's third production was *Hamlet*, Jules Laforgue's parody, together with *La Faim*, adapted by Barrault from Knut Hamsun's novel. It followed on from *Numance* in 1939 and was Barrault's first attempt at "total theatre"—that is to say, at transmitting life to the theatre by the "*total* use of the whole scale, the complete palette of the human being". Understood in this way, "total theatre" posed the problem of the re-education of the actor of the West in order to make him, in Artaud's terms, an *athlète affectif*.

In 1940 Barrault entered the Comédie-Française, at Copeau's request, in order to play *Le Cid*. He produced Claudel's *Le Soulier de satin* there, and also Gide's adaptation of *Antony and Cleopatra* (1945). Into this play he introduced three mimed scenes, making of the carousel at sea a silent ballet which worked up to a striking crescendo of movement, of the battle of the galleys a mime executed by three figures at the prow of a ship, and three "dancers" (Barrault, Decroux, and Jacques Charron), who suggested the unhurried movement of the galleys by their slow-motion twists and turns and the sound of waves against the ships' sides by their glissades; and of the land battle a sort of Pyrrhic dance by two soldiers using stylized cuts and thrusts and circling movements. Two years before this, in the film *Les Enfants du paradis*, Decroux and Barrault as Jean-Gaspard Deburau and his son, Charles, the famous white-faced pierrots of the Funambules in the early nineteenth century, devised some remarkable mime sequences. When the two men performed together again, in 1945, Gordon Craig[19] greeted the performance as a revelation in theatrical technique, the "creation of an alphabet—the A.B.C. of Mime". But whereas Decroux envisages mime as the sole means of giving the actor a complete training in the use of his body, thus enabling him to devise acting in full harmony with the spirit of the text of the play, Barrault maintains that there is a visible language, a significant form of bodily movement, *le geste*, which should accompany the spoken language, and should at times be consistent with it, at other times at variance. *Le geste*, like the spoken language, has its own syntax and metre, which must be learned, so different is this "transposed" bodily movement from ordinary movement. The spoken word is a form of expression using physical means, the muscles of the throat and chest, as against those of the spinal column, which are called into play in *le geste*. Gesture and speech being physically related, the passage from the one to the other presents no difficulty. Surveying the whole of his productions between 1935 and 1949 in his book *Réflexions sur le théâtre*, Barrault describes them as extending from what he calls *le geste pur* at one end of a rainbow to *le verbe pur* at the other, from *Autour d'une mère* and *La Faim* to *Partage de midi* with *Antoine et Cléopâtre* and *Numance* at the topmost point of the arc.

In *Nouvelles Réflexions sur le théâtre*, in a chapter dealing with his production of Claudel's *Christophe Colomb*, Barrault defines his position with regard to the question of "total theatre". It is essentially the position of an actor, unlike that of Gaston Baty, a non-actor producer.

In 1946 the Compagnie Madeleine Renault—Jean-Louis Barrault was formed and opened at the smart Marigny Theatre. In 1959 it was invited to go to the State theatre, the Odéon, which was renamed Théâtre de France. The first production was Claudel's *Tête d'Or*. Later came Giraudoux, a revival of *The Trial*, adapted by Gide and Barrault from Kafka, and Ionesco, *Rhinocéros* and *Le Piéton de l'air*. The lines on which Barrault has worked have remained constant throughout.

These are the men, from Copeau to Barrault, who, in addition to bringing about great changes on the production side, provided a platform and a public for a new generation of dramatists, few of whom would otherwise have managed to make their way into the ordinary established theatres. Jean Giraudoux is the classic example. Some other producers were also very active. RENE ROCHER, director of the Odéon from 1942 to 1944, did much between the two wars to familiarize the Boulevard theatre public with the type of play put on in the *avant-garde* theatres, as, for example, when he staged Henri Lenormand's *Asie* at the Théâtre Antoine. A large number of irregular dramatic groups also contributed to the success of the new drama. According to *Comœdia* (October 26th) there were actually some forty-five societies in Paris in 1927, though only five hired regular theatres for their productions. The long-established Escholiers was the most interesting, as many of the plays they staged (they gave only two performances of a play) later made their way into Boulevard theatres, the Comédie-Française, the Odéon, and some of the best actors in Paris started their careers in these productions. Another long-lived company, La Petite Scène, had its own theatre from 1930; it was in a converted barn in rue Falguière. The curious "theatre laboratory", Art et Action, had its own premises in rue Lepic. It was not unlike the Lamda Theatre Club in London, which Peter Brook directed, in 1964, in an experimental programme entitled "The Theatre of Cruelty". Art et Action, originally called Art et Liberté (1914–1918), was run by a number of actors grouped round a former actress of the Comédie-Française, Madame Lara. They experimented before invited audiences in unusual forms of drama, which they called "Improvised Theatre", "Book Theatre", "Chamber Theatre" (for a work like Dante's Divine Comedy, 1931, judged too intimate for normal production in a theatre; in an unusual presentation the spectators' attention, perhaps one should say readers' attention, was concentrated on the text by the avoidance of exits and entrances of the actors, whose presence was indicated only when their participation was required; auditory and visual impressions reinforced the effect of the text). There was also "University Theatre" (1933), based on texts on the University syllabus, but the group was not well advised in attempting, for example, a confrontation of the metaphysical system of Leibniz and Voltaire's refutation of it in Candide, since dramatic exercises could bear little relation to scholarly exegesis. Earlier in 1926, in staging Diderot's Le Neveu de Rameau, it had been better inspired, because of the intrinsic dramatic qualities of Diderot's dialogue, qualities which have since been exploited by the actor Pierre Fresnay in a regular theatre, the Œuvre (1964). It did pioneering work also in producing some of the surrealist plays of the 1920's.

NOTES

1. La Crise du théâtre, 1928, pp. 162–163.
2. Founder of the Théâtre Libre, 1887.
3. Encyclopédie française, vol. 17, Section B, December 1935, "La Mise en scène", by Jacques Copeau.
4. L'École du Vieux-Colombier, p. 36, Cahiers du Vieux-Colombier, No. II, 1921.
5. Souvenirs et notes de travail d'un actor, 1946, p. 60.
6. Arts, September 10th–16th, 1953.
7. Jouvet left Paris in 1941 after being forbidden to perform Jules Romains and Giraudoux, declared to be "anti-cultural", and being required to play Schiller and Goethe.

8. *Les Lettres françaises*, August 24th–30th, 1961.
9. Ibid.
10. *Notre Théâtre*, by G. Pitoëff, 1949, p. 31.
11. *Les Pitoëff, souvenirs*, H.-R. Lenormand, 1943, p. 49.
12. Lenormand's *La Folle du ciel*.
13. See Lenormand's description of the performances of both actresses in his book *Les Pitoëff, souvenirs*, pp. 121–125, and John Palmer's in *Studies in the Contemporary Theatre*, 1927.
14. *Les Pitoëff, souvenirs*, p. 189.
15. *Revue de Paris*, August 15th, 1935, "Gaston Baty", by F. Porché.
16. "Les Sept voix de la Lyre", *Bulletin de la Chimère*, March 1922, No. 11.
17. Conscious of the rapid development of cinema techniques, this enterprise aimed at using "purely theatrical means" to get rid of the conventional psychology, the literature, and the artifice of the conventional stage, and allow drama to become a transcription of immediate experience. *Œuvres Complètes*, 1961, vol. II, "Le Théâtre Alfred Jarry et l'Hostilité publique".
18. *Le nouvel Observateur*, October 27th–November 2nd, 1965.
19. *Arts*, August 3rd, 1945.

II

Studio Theatre: Cocteau and Company, Intelligence Unlimited

Jean Cocteau—Fernand Crommelynck—Emile Mazaud —René Benjamin—Léon Régis and François de Veynes—Jules Romains—Roger Vitrac—Raymond Roussell—Georges Ribemont-Dessaignes—Ivan Goll —Robert Desnos.

THE intelligentsia of the twenties affected, in public at any rate, a certain lack of high seriousness. The work of one of the most engaging personalities of modern French literature, JEAN COCTEAU, illustrates this very clearly. As a man of letters he is distinguished by his versatility. In the domain of the theatre alone his talent is all-embracing: ballet, drama, stage technique, all have been matter for experimentation, and never once has Cocteau exploited the success of any single type of theatrical work. In addition to being a playwright he was also an actor and a producer, and as such was an outstanding example of an all-round man of the theatre. He came into the public eye before the 1914–18 war; the following ditty, inspired by this picturesque figure, was sung in the café-concerts:

> Tout ce qu'il y a de plus beau,
> La Vénus de Milo,
> La Belle Otéro,
> Le petit Cocteau.

His work in the theatre dates, however, from after the war. It is the product of an extremely alert and intelligent mind and completely defies classification, though in most of it the intention to burlesque is apparent. His first work, a ballet, *Le Dieu bleu*, which he com-

posed in collaboration with F. de Madrazzo, was performed at the
Châtelet in May 1912, with music by Reynaldo Hahn and
costumes by Bakst. Then came *Parade*, with music by Erik Satie,
settings by Picasso, and choreography by Massine; it was performed by the Ballets Russes at the Châtelet on May 18th, 1917.
One of the first modern ballets, it arose out of the intimate collaboration, under Diaghilev's attentive eye, of writer, musician,
painter, and dancer. The work was intended to "stagger"[1] the public, as Cocteau's comparison of the ballet with Picasso's cubist
paintings implied. As if Cubism did not suffice, traces of Dadaism
were also to be found in the work. The strangely built-up costumes
invented by Picasso for the European Manager and the New York
Manager were specially "staggering" and looked like a couple of
"skyscrapers". Nevertheless, the performance was not as revolutionary as had been intended, as the "suggestive noises", such as
factory whistles, the tapping of typewriters, the hum of dynamos,
which were to have accompanied Satie's score, had had to be very
much simplified because of technical difficulties. The first performances[2] provoked an outcry all the same, the audience mistaking
for a music-hall show what was actually the artistic transposition
of a music-hall show. Cocteau himself considered *Parade* to be a
tiny window giving a glimpse of what the contemporary theatre
should be like. *Le Bœuf sur le toit ou The Nothing Doing Bar*
(Comédie des Champs-Elysées, February 21st, 1920), a burlesque
with movements, set to the music of Darius Milhaud, was a further
work conceived by Cocteau, but executed by several different types
of artists all working together. This *pantomime-farce*, named after
the artistic cabaret in the rue Boissy d'Anglas, where it was performed, had the co-operation of the clowns, the Fratellini Brothers.
By resorting to the methods and personalities of the circus, Cocteau,
as he said in his preface, aimed at infusing new life into farce. He
also used masks and positions revealed by the slow-motion camera.

Another attempt on the part of Cocteau to create a new comic
medium is to be found in *Les Mariés de la Tour Eiffel*,[3] performed
by the Swedish Ballet at the Théâtre des Champs-Elysées on June
18th, 1921. A work of art, according to Cocteau, is the commonplace transfigured by poetry, so he takes as his subject a wedding-
party at the photographer's on the Eiffel Tower on the fourteenth
of July. Poetry must be looked for, not in the exotic but in the
familiar. Poetry rids us of the habit of looking without seeing,

contracted in our life-long contact with reality. Poetry makes us see the world with new eyes. In his preface to the play, where he explains his conception of the theatre, Cocteau also declares his aim of substituting *une poésie de théâtre*, which he compares with a ship's rigging, for *la poésie au théâtre*, likened by him to fine lace, invisible from a distance. His imagery, he tells us, is not to be found in the text but in the action of his play; ready-made expressions come, as it were, to life, ideas materialize. None of the numerous actors speaks. They dance and mime their rôles. Two human gramophones speak in their place and comment on their movements. The wedding-group is to be photographed, but the camera is out of order. That morning, when the photographer had said to a client: "Quite still please and you'll see the dicky-bird", out had stalked an ostrich which had remained at large in the tower. The camera is still out of order when the photographer endeavours to get a picture of the wedding-group. A bathing beauty from Trouville emerges from the camera, then a child (a future victim of the next war) who greets the newly-weds as father and mother, a lion which devours the General who, believing it to be a mirage, has not taken cover. When all these, including the ostrich, are got back into the camera the photographer can take the wedding-photo. The group strikes the stilted attitude typical of the occasion, and a picture dealer, mistaking it for a Primitive, buys it for one billion francs. The General, who is regurgitated from the camera because he is indigestible, takes up his stand in the picture, to the future delight of the dealer because, as Gramophone Number Two explains, "In a work of art unnoticed details are always coming to light." Cocteau claimed that in this facetious play he had built a machine for transmitting poetry to the stage, but that not even his admirers had understood his intention, since they had seen in *Les Mariés* a farce, a satire, everything except what he had intended them to see —namely, the plastic expression of poetry.

Cocteau learned much from Diaghilev and Stravinsky, with whom he worked, just as, through his association with writers like Guillaume Apollinaire, painters like Picasso, and musicians like Erik Satie, he became acquainted with new art forms. Acknowledging his debt to Satie and Picasso, Cocteau said that whereas the influence of a writer sometimes induces literary mannerisms, the "amazing discipline of freedom" enforced by Satie or Picasso militated against any such effect.

Antigone (Atelier, December 20th, 1922),[4] the next of Cocteau's works to be performed, opened a new phase in his dramatic output, for though he still collaborated with other artists, it was to a lesser extent. In Les Biches,[5] Le Train bleu,[6] and Le pauvre Matelot,[7] which followed, he contented himself with supplying the scenario or book out of which others were to create the ballet or opera.

Antigone, in which he followed Sophocles closely, except in one detail where he added a negative to Créon's final statement that he feared that the old laws would, after all, have to be followed, was a tragedy in three acts with music by Honegger for harp and oboe. The chief interest of the production lay in the attempt to enhance the text by new elements of beauty in staging, chiefly by the use of masks. The setting itself was by Picasso. With regard to the text, Cocteau declared that he had "adapted Antigone to the rhythm of the times". His adaptation of Antigone was to have much the same relation to Sophocles as an aerial view of Greece would have to the country itself, a number of beauties would disappear, others would be thrown into greater relief, and there would be unusual shadows and angles. Such was Cocteau's theory of composition as expounded in the preface, though for Charles Dullin, who took the part of Créon, Antigone was like a pencil copy of a painting. Cocteau, the better to bring out the dramatic and human interest, had condensed Sophocles' text. At the same time he had indulged in an independent exercise in style.

. In Roméo et Juliette, written in 1918 but performed only on June 2nd, 1924, at the Soirées de Paris,[8] Cocteau had already applied the same method of contraction. He aimed at bringing out the eternal aspect of the drama, pared of all incidental or local matter. Described by Cocteau as a "pretext in 5 acts and 23 tableaux for a choreographic production", Roméo et Juliette was essentially a ballet. The actors in black, with collars, gloves, and faces providing the sole touches of colour, moved against a black velvet background with deliberate rhythmic movements rehearsed to music which was afterwards suppressed. Characters were directed to walk or run without, however, moving forward; certain sections, such as the opening of Act V, were mimed, servants crossed the stage carrying a long strip of black material to indicate the passing of the night, and, after they had crossed, the morning light was to be seen shining through the windows. Many other similar technical or symbolic devices were used to replace the lyrical passages in

Shakespeare's play. The published text contains some indications for staging and acting, but no complete record of this artistic polygraph exists.

Oedipus Rex, with music by Stravinsky, is an opera-oratorio adapted from Sophocles by Cocteau according to the same principles of concentration, and then translated into Latin by J. Daniélou, so that it could be treated purely as phonetic material. It was first performed by the Diaghilev Ballet Company at the Théâtre Sarah-Bernhardt on May 20th, 1927.[9] From this work he took Œdipe-Roi, and later, in June 1937, directed its production at the Théâtre Antoine. In 1962 the Lyon festival opened in the ancient Roman theatre at Fourvière with a remarkable performance of a new version by Cocteau of Œdipe-Roi. It was described as a "lyrical tragedy" with music by Maurice Thiriet, and all the arts were called upon to play their part; in addition to choral singing and tragic recitative, mime and dance were interspersed among the spoken lines. This was just twenty years after the work was actually completed, and unfortunately for Cocteau this delay has prevented the work from being recognized as one of the first attempts at "total theatre".

Cocteau's first original play is Orphée (Théâtre des Arts-Pitoëff, June 5th, 1926).[10] It contains elements seen in his previous work and links up with his surrealist film Le Sang d'un poète (1931) and his film Orphée (1950). Once again Cocteau borrows his subject, but this time he renews it completely, using the legend to examine the relationship between the poet and his inspiration, and to meditate on death and the mystery of time. Orphée and Eurydice, a very modern couple, are in love but bicker constantly. Orphée, attired in a pullover and flannel trousers, gives all his attention to his horse Pégase, who taps out messages to him. This excites Eurydice's jealousy. Heurtebise, a glazier of no fixed abode, whose head is surrounded by a halo formed by the sun's reflection on the sheets of glass he carries on his back, is the couple's guardian angel, but he loses Eurydice's confidence when she sees him float in mid-air: "I thought you were of the same species as myself, but you are like the horse", she says. After Eurydice has licked a poisoned envelope, death, in the guise of a smart woman attired in evening dress and a cloak, comes to perform a surgical operation on her so as to liberate life, in the form of a dove, from her body. She comes through a mirror, the gateway to the other world (because we see ourselves grow old in our mirrors): this is in accordance with Cocteau's theory of imagery in action, not in words; he uses the same image in the two films already mentioned. But Death leaves her gloves behind, and Orphée, putting them on, passes through the mirror to take them back to her in Hades and ask for Eurydice in return. After losing his wife a second time, Orphée sacrifices his future as a poet, and life itself, to rejoin her. The play ends with the very down-to-earth police inspector floundering about in a magic world, trying vainly to reduce it to ordinary logic. This is by no means Cocteau's best play, but in it is to be found the first expression in the theatre of his constant preoccupation with the problem of poetic creation, which he presents as a descent into Hell and an embrace of Death, followed by a glorious resurrection.

The film *Orphée*, based on the same myth, is very different from the play. It probes more deeply than either the play or the film *Le Sang d'un poète* into the question of the artist and his destiny. If in this first film, as Cocteau says, he played the theme with one finger only, he orchestrated it in the film *Orphée*. By 1950 it was no longer the poet and his inspiration which interested Cocteau but the source of that inspiration. For this reason the Princess, the incarnation of everything which transcends the human predicament, becomes the central figure of the film. She fascinates Orphée, who seeks to rejoin her in death without a thought for Eurydice. The film has a different setting from the play; the references to the German occupation and the French Resistance movement are obvious throughout.

Another theme running through the film is the problematic existence of free will. It is the main theme of *La Machine infernale* (Comédie des Champs-Elysées-Jouvet, April 10th, 1934).[11] A secondary theme is the existence of an endless hierarchy, with the implied impossibility of discovering who issues the orders originally: "The gods have their gods. We have ours. They [men] have theirs. It is what is called infinity", says Anubis, the jackal. In this rehandling of the Oedipus story Cocteau's Sphinx believes that she spared Œdipe freely, but her gesture was not a free one because Œdipe *had* to live in order to fulfil the oracle. In the film *Orphée* Cocteau leaves one in doubt as to whether the Princess brings about the death of Orphée and Eurydice of her own accord or whether her apparent freedom of action is not a mere illusion. The fact remains that the nameless beings in command do not undo her work. Free will, according to Cocteau in *La Fin du Potomak* (1939), is God's alibi, it allows God to set traps for man without having to shoulder any responsibility for them. Orphée is caught in a trap, and possibly also the Princess.

In *La Machine infernale* Cocteau is not concerned with the struggle of man against implacable destiny, but with the devilish cunning with which the heartless gods had constructed the most perfect of "infernal machines for the mathematical annihilation of a human being". Cocteau here points an accusing finger at the gods, just as he had in the Prologue to *Œdipe-Roi*, where the chorus (a single actor) accuses the gods of setting traps for man with the senseless cruelty of the young. Such an attitude to the gods is not that of Sophocles but rather that of Gide's Œdipe (*Œdipe*, 1922), who protests against the "base treachery of god". In Cocteau's play, although the victims emerge bruised and mangled, the ultimate failure of the infernal machine to destroy them is indicated in the closing lines, which forecast the lasting renown that is to be theirs.

Like Gide's Œdipe, Cocteau's hero is adventurous and uses the oracle's evil prophecy as an excuse to leave the home of his supposed parents in order to satisfy his "thirst for the unknown". Like Gide's Œdipe also, he is arrogant and ambitious, and this, together with his inability to see that he is measuring himself against some force stronger than himself, makes him walk into the trap set for him by the devilish gods. The hints, or "signes d'intelligence et de politesse", which they give him for their greater amusement go unnoticed; he, like Jocaste, remains blissfully unperceptive, counting for good luck what is, in fact, his undoing.

The "signes d'intelligence" allow for the free use of dramatic irony from the very beginning of the play. In the first act, which is reminiscent of *Hamlet*, with its ramparts guarded by soldiers and the nightly apparition of the ghost of Laius, returning, not to demand revenge, but to give warning, the scarf which catches on everything and nearly strangles Jocaste a number of times, and also the brooch "qui crève l'œil de tout le monde", are all stern warnings for the spectator, but pass unnoticed by the intended victims of misfortune.

In the second act it is a child who asks: "This lady is the Sphinx, isn't she?" whereas his mother, and later Œdipe, chat with the Sphinx without having any inkling of her real identity. In the third act Œdipe's fate is foreshadowed by his momentary loss of sight when he seeks to read his future in Tirésias's blind eyes. Further-more, such actions as Jocaste's, when she rocks the cradle on which the sleeping Œdipe has rested his head, or phrases like "petite mère chérie" and "gros bébé" uttered when the two are dropping with sleep, and also Œdipe's description of his feelings for Jocaste in his interview with Tirésias, throw into relief their fundamental mother-and-son relationship. The strong Freudian element which is present in these unintentional gestures and utterances and in the dreams which pursue Œdipe and Jocaste on their wedding-night, during moments of fitful slumber, adds a further dimension to what might have remained sardonic hints by the gods.

The second act, containing Œdipe's encounter with the Sphinx, forms the core of the play because it introduces the theme of free will on which the play is based. Not only does the Sphinx believe she has spared Œdipe of her own free will, but Œdipe fondly imagines that by leaving the court of Corinth he will give the lie to the oracle; he has, in fact, contributed to its fulfilment. Later in his conversation with Tirésias, in the third act, he congratulates himself on having succeeded, and asks why the gods would have led him into the nuptial chamber if his wedding with Jocaste dis-pleased them. "Do you claim to be able to solve the problem of free will in a single minute?" exclaims Tirésias.

In the fourth act, when the drama has been played out and this "roi de jeux de cartes", as he is called by the Voice which intro-duces each act, learns the awful truth, he becomes at last a real man. In the final moment of this act Jocaste's ghost, invisible to all but Œdipe and the equally blind Tirésias, returns to direct her son's faltering feet, and she counts the steps for him as she had done for herself in the first act, closing the circle, as it were. This image of the mother guiding her newly-found child through life is both powerful and moving, though it may be criticized as detract-ing from the legendary rôle of Antigone.

The second act contains other interesting ideas. The Sphinx, who is the goddess Némésis, is represented at first as a beautiful girl sickened by her rôle of slaughterer of men and longing to love and be loved. She changes before the audience's eyes into the fearsome winged Sphinx of men's imagination, to show that she is master of the situation. Cocteau here gives visual form to the idea that the gods always assume the form that men's imagination gives them. In this form she reduces the fatuous Œdipe to utter helplessness with the verbal gymnastics of her spells, so different from the familiar language used elsewhere in the play and the topical slang of the soldiers in the first act.

In this act too, Cocteau, using the image of a single pinprick making an endless number of holes in a piece of material that has been folded several times, gives a definition of his conception of time. There is no reason why the Sphinx, a goddess, should seek sudden and petty revenge for Œdipe's failure to respond to her love, because the revenge can be amplified by the use of the huge machine of time. *La Machine infernale* is a highly significant play, and Cocteau knew it. "Up to now," he said to the Paris Press, "my plays have been mere exercises, or, like *Orphée*, 'spectacles' of a rather special nature ... I am making my real debut in the theatre with *La Machine infernale*." With this poetic play in prose, Cocteau took his place beside those writers like Jean Giraudoux, who believed that the theatre was as much the province of the true man of letters as the novel or the poem. For Cocteau language is not merely a vehicle for the communication of ideas or the meaning of events, it has a creative rôle to play. It is with the rhetoric of spells and the monotonous repetitions of popular incantations that the Sphinx spins an invisible thread to bind Œdipe hand and foot: "bouclé comme la mer ... un fil qui te ligote avec la volubilité des arabesques folles du miel qui tombe sur du miel". "Et je parle, je travaille, je dévide, je déroule, je calcule, je médite, je tasse, je vanne, je tricote, je natte, je croise, je passe, je repasse, je noue et dénoue et renoue ..." And on and on she goes until Œdipe, powerless, cries out in anguish: "Laissez-moi! Grâce!" In contrast there is a refreshing conversation between two soldiers: "Ma décision est prise", says the young soldier, "je vais m'inscrire pour aller au Sphinx." "Et la frousse?" asks his companion. "Quelle frousse?" "La frousse quoi ... la frousse! ... toi pauvre petit soldat de deuxième classe ..."

But even in *La Machine infernale*, where he deliberately exploits the resources of language for the benefit of the stage, Cocteau does not neglect the more usual scenic elements. Stage technique here is as important as in Cocteau's less exclusively literary works; there is the transformation of the winged Sphinx, the materialization of Œdipe's dreams on his wedding-night, Jocaste's maternal action in rocking the cradle on which Œdipe, in his troubled sleep, has laid his head.

Working still in the domain of myth and legend, no longer Greek but Celtic, Cocteau wrote *Les Chevaliers de la Table Ronde* (Œuvre, October 14th, 1937).[12] The castle of the king, Artus, is in the grip of the illusionist Merlin. Galaad *le très pur*, the poet, destroys the illusion, thereby bringing unhappiness and even death to some of the inmates. Artus finds the truth particularly unpalatable, but nevertheless prefers it to continued happiness based on illusions. When the third act begins Artus's suspicions are already aroused about Lancelot and Guenièvre, and the tragic course taken by his jealousy is revealed by an interesting technical device: the audience hears a conversation of the lovers as the king in his jealousy imagines it, and at the same time sees Artus's tortured reactions, which lead to his killing Lancelot. Ginifer, Merlin's familiar spirit, who appears successively as Guenièvre, Galaad, and Gauvain, is another interesting invention. He is the lie made flesh and constitutes the pivot of the play. As he always remains his own uncultured self, whatever physical form he may adopt, he supplies a comic element, but the false image which he gives of these three characters greatly distresses the victims of the deception. The scene in the second act, when a brazen-faced "Guenièvre" mocks Lancelot and boldly proclaims her love for another, is a telling example. Here the tragic and the comic are more closely allied than anywhere else in the play. There is also a good deal of magic, a talking flower, strange journeys through the air, and, in the second act, an invisible devil who partners Lancelot at chess. This is clearly a play by an expert, not profound but technically interesting.

It is not only in the domain of myth and fantasy that Cocteau seeks his subjects. A modern series opens with *La Voix humaine* (Comédie-Française, February 17th, 1930),[13] written just after *Orphée*. This one-act monodrama with one character is another of Cocteau's defiant experiments, a "pretext for an actress", a "solo for a human voice". The single character, a woman who has been abandoned by her lover, talks to him for the last time on the telephone, and, in her words and the silences which follow, the drama of the separation, with the emptiness it brings, is played out, and the perfidy and annoyance of the invisible and inaudible lover are revealed. It was intended to be a demonstration of the potentialities of a single human voice, to show how unworthy modern realistic acting had become of Racine and Molière.

The series of modern plays of which the matter is the interplay of human affections, and which derive none of their interest from mere scenic effects, is continued by *Les Parents terribles*,[14] first performed on November 14th, 1938, at the Ambassadeurs. Cocteau had been made temporary director of this theatre by the Municipal Council of Paris, but had to resign after an argument with the Council and the Ministry of Education over an ill-advised invitation sent to Paris schools by the star Alice Cocéa. The play was transferred to the Bouffes-Parisiens, where it had a successful run. It was revived at the Gymnase on October 23rd, 1941, but was banned by the Occupation authorities after German troops had thrown teargas bombs in the auditorium. It was revived again on February 8th, 1946, when it was clear that what had been an *avant-garde* play had become a very great Boulevard success. In the preface to *La Machine à écrire* Cocteau states that *Les Parents terribles* was a tragedy which touched the masses on the raw by its attack on the disorders of a decadent *bourgeoisie*. It was this attack which provoked the early violent opposition to the play. Such an attack actually ran counter to Cocteau's own theory that a playwright must not take sides, but must concentrate on achieving "style", though not "fine writing". It is a powerful play and Cocteau's best.

Cocteau made another interesting statement regarding this play in an interview reported in the *Œuvre* (October 11th, 1938). "I was the first playwright", he said, "to take an intense interest in settings and to proclaim that a text was only a pretext for creating settings and showing them off on a lavish scale. I put on *Antigone*, *Roméo*, *Orphée*, and *La Machine infernale* for the sake of the setting, for the pictorial framework, in short for everything which now seems to me to be irrelevant . . . I have written this play solely for the sake of the actors. Nothing shall occur to distract the spectator's attention from the acting, or from the text. There shall be nothing in the setting which is not absolutely necessary, not a chair which has not some special function. There will be no cigarettes, no telephone, no maids, no accessories to fill up any gap, or any silence . . . The theatre must be more real than reality, more real than life. It is life intensified and concentrated." In a subsequent interview reported in the *Figaro* of November 8th, 1938, Cocteau said that when he wrote *Les Parents terribles* he was in a small hotel in Montargis, where he had no books except *Britannicus* and *Le Misanthrope*. The repeated reading of these plays inspired him with a desire to emulate the artistic economy of Racine and Molière.

"It seems to me that I must make every single gesture a cog in the machine, as it were, and never admit any expression of feeling which is purely decorative for fear of unnecessary elaboration." This economy of concentration, according to Cocteau, removes the possibility of even momentary relaxation of the spectator's nerves. The actor is the instrument by which the playwright magnetizes his audience.

Cocteau was here putting forward the classical notion according to which all concrete details must be subordinated to the theme. The merely accessory is irrelevant. Emphasis is laid on the work of the author and of the actor, and there is no place for "business", such as the use of the telephone. For his characters Cocteau did not envisage any "monolithic" creations, such as Corneille's Horace or Rodrigue, but rather characters subject to dual or multiple enthusiasms and conflicting emotions, in a manner more typical of Racine. "Two of the rôles", Cocteau writes, "create the balance of the order and of the disorder which motivate the play. The young man whose disorder is pure, and his aunt whose order is not pure." Here, in a very different setting, Cocteau treats the theme already developed in Les Chevaliers de la Table Ronde— namely, the establishment of a new order after truth has been brought to light. Here, too, appears the theme, later to be exemplified in Hans and the Cardinal in Bacchus, of the purity of the disorder of the impulsive mind and the impurity of the order of the calculating mind. For Michel, a spoilt child and a mother's boy, order is established only after his mother's death, which he unwittingly brings about in his desire to escape her jealous affection. This mother, a slovenly creature who spends the day amid piles of dirty linen, going to and fro in a dressing-gown covered with cigarette burns, between her unmade bed and an untidy dressing-room, is a powerful force of disorder, albeit pure. Her well-groomed but embittered sister Léo, the only really grown-up person in the play, brings truth to light and order—a new order—into the home at the price of her sister's suicide, which she does nothing to prevent. Whether her feelings for her sister's husband, her ex-fiancé, in any way affect her attitude it is hard to say; in any case, Léo herself does not know, nor does she care to know. The whole action, which moves forward inexorably to the mother's death, is set in motion by the son's failure to return home one night. In an admirable first act the characters face up to reality for the first time in twenty years, and say what they have on their minds. The father learns that he and his son have the same mistress, but the situation, current in Boulevard comedy, here has a poignancy not to be found on the Boulevard. The second act shows the attempt of the father, in his monstrous egoism, and of the mother, in her monstrous possessiveness, to prevent the son's engagement to the girl. The third act is given to the torment of the mother, who cannot accept to share her son with any other. Her passion, as absolute as any child's —there is not the slightest hint of any subconscious incest in her attitude—raises her to the level of a figure of tragedy. She is like one possessed. Beside her, Léo, statuesque, stands like destiny itself. There is no mistaking the Greek inspiration of the play despite the "Boulevard" elements, to which Cocteau himself drew attention by making the father compare himself to a character in a Labiche play. Little wonder that the critics of the first performance referred to the flat of the Atrides, spoke of beslippered Labdacides, and conjured up the shades of Clytemnestra, Electra, Jocasta, and Creon. *Les Parents terribles* is a tragedy, but in it the characters bellow out their passions without classical restraint, and when Michel learns that his father is his rival he throws himself upon a pile of dirty linen on the floor in a fit of jealous rage. In 1948, with the complete text as a scenario and almost the same cast as he had had in the stage production, Gabrielle Dorziat, Jean Marais, and Yvonne de Bray, who had inspired the play but whose part had been taken by Germaine Dermoz because of her illness, Cocteau undertook the difficult task of making a film from his play. In the film he limits himself to the two settings used in the play, but his camera picks out significant objects and gestures for their visual as well as for their psychological value, and the film is far from being "canned theatre"; it is a fine example of the art of the cinema.

In *Les Monstres sacrés*,[15] which was staged on the Boulevard at the Théâtre Michel on February 17th, 1940, Cocteau took up the challenge of the Boulevard on its own ground and wrote a first-rate play both by Boulevard and literary standards, though he declares that the play was written with no thought for the literary element, but only for the actors and their rôles. The theme is the inability to separate real life and the stage, common among many of the great figures of the stage. Here the "sacred monsters" are a famous married couple of uncertain age. The young actress, Liane, is a budding "monster", a mythomaniac. Too inexperienced yet to have been given an important part in any stage play, she attempts to play one in the life of this couple. The "sacred monsters", for their part, strike many dramatic attitudes while playing the drama of their own lives, before they finally come down to earth.

The character of the mythomaniac reappears in Cocteau's "poison-pen" drama *La Machine à écrire*, aimed, as he says, at the decadent *bourgeoisie* of the "terrible feudal provinces" of France, before the German victory of 1940, particularly its hypocrisy. Despite the reference to the provinces, despite the plot which gives the play every appearance of a thriller, Cocteau's main concern is with the family. Within the four walls of the home its members pace round and round, as though devouring each other. They also devour two other characters who do not belong to them: the woman who had loved the father and is now under the spell of the son, and the detective, "uncle" Fred, who gets caught up personally in the drama of the family. The play dates from 1939 but was not staged until April 29th, 1941, as Jean Marais was not available; its run at the Théâtre Hébertot was cut short by the Government on the grounds that it was a libel on French provincial life.[16] The showing of Clouzot's poison-pen film, *Le Corbeau*, was stopped on similar grounds. In its presentation of French provincial life the film scores over the play, but there is a Pirandellian element in the play which does not enter into the film. For various reasons three of the characters falsely confess to the authorship of the anonymous letters and end up convinced of the truth of their confession. Truth and falsehood, reality and imagination, become so intermingled as to be indistinguishable. Even the spectator is baffled. The first two acts are technically brilliant, but the play tails off in a melodramatic third act, in which the culprit appears to be arbitrarily designated so as to allow the curtain to fall.

The war did not affect Cocteau's output. In 1941 he wrote *Renaud et Armide*, which was performed at the Comédie-Française on April 13th, 1943, and revived in the Salle-Luxembourg on November 23rd, 1948. Referred to by Cocteau as a "romantic tragedy" because of its attempt to combine the romantic and classical traditions, *Renaud et Armide*, written in alexandrines, is, more strictly speaking, a love poem. Its fairy-tale characters are hardly those of tragedy. Cocteau's inspiration is not here dramatic but musical, and the work appears as an interesting experiment in purely verbal opera.

Musical form seems to have dictated the composition of the romantic drama *L'Aigle à deux têtes* (Théâtre Hébertot, December 20th, 1946).[17] Cocteau sees the play as a fugue, with the Queen and her would-be assassin forming the two themes, which are announced one after the other in separate acts, before they are brought together in the final act. The play is a further defiant experiment on Cocteau's part. A true man of the theatre, he viewed with dismay the disappearance, in the theatre of his time, of the "sacred monsters of the stage" like Sarah Bernhardt and Lucien Guitry, and he attributed it to the cinema, with its youthful stars and essentially subdued acting. With the great actors had disappeared the great rôles, and the theatre had been devitalized. Racine had written great rôles as well as great plays, and this was the challenge which Cocteau attempted to take up in *L'Aigle à deux têtes*, after referring, in *Les Monstres sacrés*, to the current lack of good plays with great parts. The play finished, he entrusted the two main parts, both exhausting, to Edwige Feuillère and to Jean Marais, whose full-blooded and vigorous Néron (*Britannicus*), at the Comédie-Française, had come nearest to the creations of Mounet Sully and the other "sacred monsters" of the stage. Without Edwige Feuillère and Jean Marais, Cocteau would not, he says, have dared to put on his play. In 1948 he made a film of the play, using the same cast as he had had in the stage production. But whereas *Les Parents terribles* is a film in its own right, and first-rate, *L'Aigle à deux têtes* is no more than a photographed play, to which has been added sequences presenting picturesque mountain gallops and stately castle balls.

In *L'Aigle à deux têtes* Cocteau takes up the threads of *Les Monstres sacrés* and of *La Machine à écrire*. His heroine presents an extreme case of mythomania, and plays a part throughout in all sincerity. Unable to create a work of art, she tries to become a work of art herself, to "be a tragedy". Cocteau reveals the source of his inspiration in a preface which also serves as a detailed commentary on the play. The play has all the trappings of a melodrama, assassins, spies, poisons, storms, and dumb servants, and closes with the dramatic death, on the stage, of the two main characters. It earned for Cocteau the dubious title of the "Victor Hugo of the eighth *arrondissement*"—the centre of smart, luxurious taste. Nevertheless, in this melodrama Cocteau poses once again the problem of free will. Was the fate of Cocteau's Queen ordained by the gods, or had she forged her own destiny? Unlike Œdipe, who unwittingly executes what the oracle had foretold, the heroine of this play decides the whole course of her life, even to her death, which she resolves to suffer by the hand of the anarchist Stanislas, her would-be assassin, whom she has grown to love. There is, however, a lingering suggestion in the play that the Queen's decisions may, after all, be the workings of fate.

After *L'Aigle à deux têtes* Cocteau once again turned his attention to the ballet, and in 1946 produced, in close collaboration with the dancer and choreographer Jean Babillé, the *mimodrame*, or dumb-show performance, *Le Jeune homme et la mort* (Théâtre des Champs-Elysées, June 25th). In the "choreographic tragedy", *Phèdre* (Opéra, June 14th, 1950), Cocteau limited his participation to the development of the theme and the designing of the costumes and sets. He returned to drama in 1951 with *Bacchus*, his only remaining stage play of importance. It was performed by Barrault at the Théâtre Marigny on December 20th, 1951, and followed close on Jean-Paul Sartre's *Le Diable et le bon Dieu*. Both plays utilize much the same setting—Germany of 1523—though to very different ends. Cocteau's theme is an individual's lone fight against tyranny, whatever its source, and the inevitable failure of such a fight. *De la difficulté d'être bon* or *De la difficulté de rester libre* or *De la difficulté d'être*, Cocteau suggested, harping back to his essay published in 1947, as fitting subtitles for his play. Hans is mistakenly considered to be the village idiot and is chosen for the part of Bacchus by lay and ecclesiastical authorities, who fear the possible outcome of the five-yearly harvest-festival *mascarade*, because of political unrest and religious dissension. Once elected, Hans throws aside his protective mask of idiocy and seeks to institute, during his seven days of absolute power, a reign of goodness and of justice. At the heart of the play is the discussion between Hans, Cocteau's "primitive mystic" who refuses to believe in a supervisory God and proclaims the autonomy of men and the need for love on earth, and the Cardinal, who, with the blinkers of dogma severely limiting his vision, is intent only on saving the Church. Interesting as this scene is, it illustrates the fact that the play is, for the most part, more dialectical than dramatic. As a stage-play it cannot compare with *La Machine infernale* and *Les Parents terribles*. However, it provoked much more discussion than either of these, to a certain extent because it was contemporary with *Le Diable et le bon Dieu* and Thierry Maulnier's *Le Profanateur*, two plays in which the hero, like Hans, claims the right of freedom of action unfettered by any particular ideology or the abusive power of the Church. Cocteau always had to face up to bitter criticism, but François Mauriac's open letter on *Bacchus*, published in the *Figaro littéraire* in December 1951, was grossly unfair; Sartre termed it "inadmissible". It attacked Cocteau in his private life and attributed to him personally the opinions of his hero Hans. It was to Cocteau's politically-minded Cardinal and somewhat ludicrous Bishop that Mauriac took exception. He maintained that only the presence of an "authentic saint" or a "true Christian" among the characters would have shown that Cocteau was attacking abuses in the Church—this he considered to be admissible—and not attacking the Church itself. Mauriac went on, in insulting terms, to deny Cocteau all originality as a writer, and called him a man who spent his time "à attraper des courants d'air". Such a letter does Mauriac no credit as a literary critic.

To take up Mauriac's point about Cocteau's lack of originality, it is the converse that is true. Immediately after the First World War Cocteau set out consciously to break with the theatre of "the Banquet Years" and opened up numerous avenues for others to explore by his own continual experimentation in every theatrical field. Furthermore, to quote the testimony of François-Régis Bastide,[18] it was thanks to Cocteau that young people, of which he himself was one, discovered poetry, music, and painting in the provinces in the years 1940 to 1944. This, at least, is a feather in Cocteau's cap.

Cocteau's contributions to the cinema are as varied as those he made to the theatre. They include *L'éternel Retour* (1944), a modern version of the Tristan and Isolda story, *La Belle et la Bête* (1945), a fairy-story, *Ruy Blas* (1947), the remarkable film *Les Enfants terribles* (1950), based on his novel of the same title, and finally the not very successful *Le Testament d'Orphée* (1960), which follows on from the film *Orphée*, and presents a defence of Cocteau before the tribunal of the underworld. In this film Cocteau is surrounded by the characters he had created in his previous works, and they are played by the actors who originally took the parts. Every venture of Cocteau's, in films or in the theatre, is an attempt to modify and enrich these art forms. Cocteau is not a dilettante, as he is often regarded; the variety of his expression is not a dissipation of his talents; he is essentially an *avant-garde* artist.

Dullin (*left*), Copeau (*wearing hat*), and Jouvet (*third from right*) at Limon, 1913

Coll. Rondel, Biblio. de l'Arsenal

4

Copeau as Scapin (*Les Fourberies de Scapin*), Vieux-Colombier, 1920

Coll. Rondel, Biblio. de l'Arsenal

Les Cenci. Producer: Artaud

Photos: Lipnitzki

La Terre est ronde. Producer: Dullin

In spite of his limited output, the Belgian writer FERNAND CROM-MELYNCK was one of the best dramatists writing in French during the inter-war years. Unlike so many of the plays of that time which are now only museum pieces, Crommelynck's plays have continued to be staged in Paris and to provoke reactions as keen as at their first performance.

It was in 1920, with Le Cocu magnifique (Œuvre, December 18th), that Crommelynck made his name. This was the second of his plays to reach the Paris stage, the first, Le Sculpteur de masques, performed at the Gymnase as early as 1911, and actually written in 1905, having passed almost unnoticed. The praises of this one-act verse play are sung in an enthusiastic letter-preface by Emile Verhaeren, but, considered in retrospect, Le Sculpteur de masques has the main merit of presenting, by its very title, a description of Crommelynck as a creator of dramatic masks, outsize and highly coloured, rather than of normal dramatic characters. Real masks were used in this first play and were to appear again in some of Crommelynck's later plays.

Le Cocu magnifique is Crommelynck's best work and has been repeatedly revived. The most important of these revivals took place on December 31st, 1945, at the Théâtre Hébertot,[19] when Georges Marchal offered a new interpretation of the part of the cuckold. Crommelynck intended Le Cocu magnifique as a play on jealousy in the classical manner, and did not consider Shakespeare's Othello to be such a play because the hero's jealousy was the work of another, the villain Iago. One might, of course, argue that Iago merely awakened jealousy that was latent, but Crommelynck maintains that Othello was trusting, his jealousy was not innate, whereas his own hero, Bruno, was jealous by nature, just as Molière's Harpagon was a miser born. But as Robert Kemp wrote after the 1945 revival: "Crommelynck has put his Iago very close to his hero. Shakespeare put him outside Othello and made of him an astounding devil. M. Crommelynck lets him speak in Bruno's soul and gesticulate with Estrugo's arms and make grimaces only with Estrugo's mask-like face."[20] Estrugo, according to the stage directions, is Bruno's double. He is an almost mute confidant, created only to throw into relief, by his gestures, Bruno's illusions of the moment and to help to show how ridiculous is jealousy of the imagination. In the 1945 revival, which was directed by Crommelynck himself, Estrugo, curiously enough, was presented as a separate individual and not as Bruno's double. As for Bruno, he is such a complex character that the play admits of a number of different interpretations. It could be a farce; it could be a study of madness or a dispassionate analysis of jealousy. As played by Lugné-Poë in 1920, Bruno, no longer a young man (Lugné-Poë was fifty-one), was fearful of possible infidelity on the part of his very young wife, and was the natural victim of spontaneous and unjustified jealousy, a Sganarelle in the manner of Molière. Georges Marchal, on the contrary, played Bruno as a poetic and imaginative young man, reminding one of King Candaules, whose delight it was to communicate to others the joys he experienced himself, and in the opening scenes showed him as sound in mind and body. In his performance the audience was able to see the actual infecting of a healthy spirit by jealousy, and not merely watch the progress of a cancerous growth which had taken root before the play began.

The text is open to both interpretations. All it tells us is that Bruno actually does vaunt the perfections of his wife's body, and that he thereby awakens the concupiscence of others. Whether he does this unwittingly, in the fullness of his joy, or deliberately, through some strange caprice of conjugal exhibitionism, only the author could say. Perhaps thinking no evil Bruno sees none, but once he has caught in the eyes of his cousin the glint of a desire that he himself has kindled, he sees evil everywhere. After all, it is Bruno who insists that Pétrus should admire the grace of Stella's leg and the beauty of her breast. Seeing that Stella can awaken men's desires, Bruno becomes convinced that she must yield to them. So he locks her up in the house, clothing her in a long black gown to hide her charms, and giving her a mask to cover the beauty of her face. Still he has his doubts, and only the certainty of her unfaithfulness can cure the distress this doubt causes. He therefore forces Pétrus to accept Stella, and stands by, miserably waiting while the adultery which alone can satisfy him is perpetrated under his own roof. He presents a pitiful yet comic figure, as he calls on them to come out of the room, even though previously he has bidden them take no notice if he should protest. "I want to be a cuckold but not such a cuckold as that. Come on out."

When at last Stella is really guilty he is obsessed with the notion that she is hiding her real lover, and that only by inviting all the villagers to come and share her bed can he discover who the lover is, since the true lover will obviously not come. In his merciless

quest for certainty Bruno even climbs up, disguised, to his wife's
room. As Stella does not refuse him he wonders whether she really
has sunk so low or whether she has recognized him and made fun
of him in this way. In the end the women of the village rise in a
body against the harlot who seems likely to steal all their husbands
and try to drown her, but she is saved by the herdsman who really
loves her. As he alone has not pressed his suit she reciprocates his
love. Bruno recognizes in him the elusive "lover" and tries to kill
him. Stella hesitates no longer, and, happy to be loved by one who
expects fidelity in love, leaves her monster of a husband. Yet even
then Bruno is unconvinced and thinks that her departure is only
another of her tricks to protect the man whom she is still cleverly
hiding. Brushing aside all the self-confessed lovers from Pétrus onward, he continues his relentless search for the hidden lover. There
is no cure for such madness.

This odious, grotesque, despairing husband, who drives his wife
into the arms of every man in the village just to rid himself of an
intolerable uncertainty, was one of the most remarkable creations
the theatre had seen for some time, though the wife is too innocent
and too submissive to the caprices of her jealous husband for it to be
possible to believe completely in her and appreciate her scruples.
Stella's dissimulation is symbolized by a *commedia-dell'arte*-like
mask which Bruno forces her to wear. It is significant that when
Stella takes off the mask Bruno is no longer jealous; he is conscious
only of his love for her when he sees her tearful face—"It is the
mask which makes me angry." The situation is based on correct
psychological observation, although the treatment given to it is
whimsical and sentimental. Indeed, Bruno's own words supply the
key to the play and seem to justify Marchal's interpretation rather
than Lugné-Poë's; "All this is an invention of my tortured brain! I
shall end up by letting the tricks of my imagination get the upper
hand . . . It is true that at times I can no longer disentangle the
knotted threads of imagination and reality." This mental instability becomes more and more accentuated and ends up in a madness
which is self-induced and not the result of justifiable fears in a
man whose wife is young and beautiful; there seems therefore no
point in making him middle-aged in order to explain his jealousy by
a difference of years. But is Bruno grotesque or is he tragic? The
jealousy of a middle-aged man tends to be comical, not so that of a
handsome young husband, and it was the difference in the age of

the actors taking the part of Bruno that caused the question to be raised. The answer is that both productions were successful and so both interpretations are valid, but the young Bruno (Marchal), rather than the middle-aged Bruno (Lugné-Poë), seems to correspond better with the author's intentions as expressed in the text. The play reads like a burlesque, but the tragic undertones are unmistakable.

Three months later, on March 15th, Firmin Gémier produced at the Comédie-Montaigne *Les Amants puérils*,[21] another tragic farce, which Crommelynck wrote in 1913, when he was only twenty-five. It is as full-blooded as *Le Cocu magnifique* and has as its theme love in ugly old age, and the immature love of two children of fourteen. The one drama is superimposed on the other. Elisabeth de Groulingen, the mysterious veiled "stranger", who never takes off her gloves, is in reality an old woman, but art and artifice help her to appear young. She is pursued from town to town by a young man who is passionately in love with her. In the curiously oppressive boarding-house where the action takes place the young man sees the decrepit and degenerate Baron Cazou, Elisabeth's former lover. Many years before, the two had formed a magnificent pair, and the story of their love had been on everybody's lips, but at the time of the action of the play Elisabeth and, particularly, Cazou present the unpardonable mental and physical degeneracy of old age, the isolation of the old—Cazou's sole companion is his shadow, and once the romantic young man has seen Elisabeth as she really is, without the mask of youth which he had forced her to wear, he slips away with a gesture of pity, leaving her absolutely alone. The two innocent children, after watching this tragedy of old age, decide to escape from the ugliness of the world by committing suicide, and drown themselves. Meanwhile a chorus of servants, each a peasant type but with individualized features, comments on the happenings in the house. This group provides a strong contrast with the other characters, who belong to a dream world. Crommelynck has a special talent for creating an atmosphere. This play is a poetic nightmare; it is couched in language which is striking and unreal, and phrases like the following abound: "L'air est serré comme du sable", "Je ne vois pas tes yeux, mais je les sens sur moi comme une pluie chaude!", "Ce désir est en moi comme les os dans ma chair".

Poetry and fantasy are to be found in Crommelynck's remaining plays, but the plays themselves are less moving. This is particularly clear when one compares *Tripes d'or* (Comédie des Champs-Elysées, May 4th, 1925) with *Le Cocu magnifique*. Like *Le Cocu magnifique*, it is a farce in which the progress of a mental disease is carefully followed up, but not even Jouvet could save what was, in fact, the long monologue of a miser who eats his gold so as to have it with him always, and dies on a "chaise percée", dressed-up like Louis XIV.

Carine ou la jeune fille folle de son corps, staged at the Œuvre on December 20th, 1929, and revived there on September 9th, 1949, is a more graceful play, which tells of the sudden disillusionment of the mystical Carine. During a masked fête at her wedding she is brought face to face with ugliness in life, and learns that even her beloved Frédéric had had a mistress. Carine dies, perhaps by her own hand, and Frédéric almost rejoices that she can no longer be hurt by life. The play ends with the suggestion that he will follow her.

The disparity between romantic dreams and physical realities reappears as a theme in *Une Femme qu'a le cœur trop petit* (Œuvre, January 17th, 1934, and February 15th, 1942). A secondary theme is the freedom from restraint offered by make-believe: "I escaped into myself", one of the characters who had been kept more or less a prisoner finally confesses.

Chaud et froid (Comédie des Champs-Elysées, November 21st, 1934),[22] in which the characters blow hot and cold by turns, takes up the theme of cuckoldry again. This time it is real and not imagined: Léona's lovers are legion. One day, as M. Dom lies dying in his room, an unknown woman crosses the stage weeping, in front of the wife's lovers, who are arguing, and goes to Dom's bedside. The maid listens at the door and repeats what she hears. When the door opens again and the woman, Félie, Dom's unsuspected mistress for ten years, comes out, Léona smilingly goes up to her saying: "We shall remember together." This first act is masterly. Realizing that the real infidelity was Dom's, not hers, Léona sets out to snatch back from her rival, as it were posthumously, the husband who had been so different from what she had thought, by remaining more faithful to his memory than his mistress. Not satisfied with this one theme, Crommelynck adds several others and exploits them to the full. For example, starting from the words: "I have an idea . . . I have an idea . . .", attributed by the maid to the dying M. Dom, Crommelynck develops the theme of self-delusion: each and all embroider on the words until, in the eyes of the village notables, the dead M. Dom becomes a great thinker to whom tribute must be paid, and even Léona's former lovers try to atone by serving the memory of the man they had so "misunderstood" and wronged.

This brilliant mixture of buffoonery and the macabre is written in prose full of sensuous imagery, as is usual with Crommelynck. It was the style which provoked spontaneous bursts of applause when the play was performed. "Il me disait", says Félie of Dom, "que mes yeux était longs comme des jours de juin." "La haine", cries Léona, "me nourrit de son lait de panthère!" Meanwhile Dom lies in the bedroom, "horizontal, opaque, étroitment collé à ses os". Finally, in the scene in which Félie surrenders to the kisses of Léona's one-time lover, one reads: "Ce baiser est descendu en elle dur et doux comme un fruit entier." It is language such as this, rather than the dramatic technique, which creates the special world presented by Crommelynck in all his plays.

With *Dardamelle ou le cocu* (Œuvre, April 22nd, 1922)[23] EMILE MAZAUD followed in Crommelynck's footsteps and created another "cocu magnifique". During a very ordinary dispute between a very ordinary couple, the wife, in order to taunt her husband, shrieks at him so often that he is "cocu ... cocu ... cocu ...", that he finishes by believing her, but he turns the tables on her by putting up a notice on the door, "Cocu de 1re classe", as though it were a diploma, has it printed on his visiting-cards, and even arranges a dinner in honour of the event. By the third act the whole town has been drawn into Dardamelle's personal tragedy. The Prefect of the *département* sends him a telegram asking him to stop being "the man with the unfaithful wife" because of the repercussions of the scandal in Parliament. Dardamelle magnanimously consents. The subject is interesting, but the play lacks the truculence of Crommelynck's masterpiece.

The short, simple little play *La folle Journée*, on the other hand, is a masterpiece of its kind. With it Mazaud made his debut in the theatre. It was staged by Copeau at the Vieux-Colombier on July 1st, 1920, and is now in the repertory of the Comédie-Française. The play ends with the parting guest sadly leaving behind him a letter of thanks, which, in his joy at receiving the invitation, he had written before leaving Paris. In it he thanks his more opulent friend and host for a pleasant stay, for the fresh milk, the early morning walk, for everything which, for one reason or another, he had not had, but which represented for him the delights of country life. Behind the comedy of this crazy day lies the touching sincerity of a humble man.

RENE BENJAMIN offers farce of another kind, with characters who are never real human beings. In a programme note to Les Plaisirs du hasard, played at Copeau's Vieux-Colombier on April 21st, 1922, Benjamin defined his own talent when he wrote: "I like the technique of journalists and reporters: I am fond of memoirs and portraits . . . very nearly everything I write provokes a scandal. I state that 50 per cent. of lawyers are mountebanks, and I have the Bar on my track (just as if everyone did not know it already!). I claim that 50 per cent. of university graduates are pedants. They organize a dinner by way of protest (just as if everyone had not known it since the time of Rabelais)." In two cynical diatribes, La Farce de la Sorbonne (1911) and Les Justices de paix ou les vingt façons de juger dans Paris (1913), of which the foreword ends as follows: "I am afraid I may not have plumbed the full depths of man's stupidity", he gave a hint of the content and tone of the plays yet to come.

With sarcasm and caricature as his weapons, Benjamin set out in Les Plaisirs du hasard to make merry at the expense of those who stick by social conventions. He attacks the actual precepts less than those who preach them, and he makes no attempt to discredit one convention rather than another. He seems convinced of the sinister absurdity of the whole of society—for example, in answer to the question: "What is your view of society?" put to him by a professor during an oral examination in which he becomes accidentally involved, Benjamin's hero says: "It is potty, delightfully potty." The eccentricity of the hero, however, prevents society from appearing completely in the wrong, and, in view of the author's evident intentions of satirizing society, this is a weakness in the play.

Benjamin gives even freer rein to his satirical bent in Il faut que chacun soit à sa place, also played at Copeau's Vieux-Colombier, on February 14th, 1924. It is a good piece of dramatic writing, but was killed by the Press, which resented Benjamin's attitude to society. The chief character is Bourdeducq, a "captain of industry", and, as such, a strong political force. Despite the vague rumours that he is to be arrested for forgery, Bourdeducq is full of confidence: "Arrest Bourdeducq! a fine mess they would all be in! . . . I have a dozen contracts given me by the State which only I can fulfil. Without me there would be another thousand millions on the budget!" The Minister for War has him arrested, but, being a past master in the art of blackmail, he gets himself discharged and reappears on the scene more insolent than ever. The final scene of the play is very funny but breaks the dramatic continuity. Three worthy citizens, disgusted by the antics of Bourdeducq and his like, decide to make fools of them. They present themselves at the castle which Bourdeducq has bought from a penniless aristocrat, and in the name of the revolution which, they declare, has just taken place in Paris, judge the inmates, putting "each in his place". Because Bourdeducq is brutal with those weaker than himself, and servile towards those in authority, they decide he would make an admirable policeman.

Benjamin has written a number of short, satirical sketches. Another full-length play, *Girouette* (Variétés, April 3rd, 1935), consists of a series of almost unconnected satirical sketches, including one on the parliamentary system. Once a play passes the compass of a single act, the deficiencies in Benjamin's dramatic technique become obvious. His talent lies in caricature. This brought him many enemies, as did his wartime attachment to Marshal Pétain.

It was Copeau, once more, who produced *Bastos le hardi* (Vieux-Colombier, May 20th, 1923), by two young authors LEON REGIS and FRANÇOIS DE VEYNES. This play, unlike those of Benjamin, is extremely well constructed, and would have held its own in the Paris theatre of the 1860's in competition with the *pièces bien faites* of Scribe and Sardou. It is a satire on democratic government and corruption in politics. The authors claim to show what happens behind the scenes in an election even for the highest places. In their play the Prime Minister chooses the country's figurehead, a King, and the people "approve". Bastos, a harmless, retired businessman, accepts the royal office partly through pique at the surprised exclamation of his portly wife, Agathe: "But you would be ridiculous, you are not at all like a king", and partly because of the charms of the Countess Upsala. He shows a rare inaptitude for the office but accidentally sets the tottering monarchy upon its feet again by thinking only of the countess and his own pleasures:

here, at last, is a King who dares to defy his Ministers and take the government into his own hands! The irony is discreet and the comedy results from the naturalness of the situations and the dialogue, as, for example, when Bastos says to his wife: "Now, come Agathe, do listen to me! You know what the constitution of our country is", and she replies: "No, what is it?" or when the Prime Minister threatens to lay down his "portfolio", and Bastos replies: "Very well, put it on the table."

Bastos was a success outside France as well as in Paris; nevertheless, after Copeau's retirement, the playwrights could find no theatre to take their next play *La grande Pénitence*, and had to stage it themselves at the Atelier (October 16th, 1926), which was lent to them by Dullin. The judge has torn his robe and cannot afford to buy another. Since a judge is not a judge without a robe, nor a State a State without a judge, he calls upon the State to provide him with another robe. The Treasury's calculations run into astronomical figures, but when it is called on to provide three thousand real francs for the robe the financial expert exclaims: "You want money? ... That's a very different matter." The farce concludes with the judge appearing resplendent in a new robe which he declares he has stolen; the honour of Justice is saved, and the financial expert stutters a few incoherent words which are understood by a foreign ambassador to be a profound explanation of the situation. Thereupon the expert lets himself go in a fine peroration: "Budget. Equilibrium. Stabilization. Devaluation. Inflation. Confidence. Parity. Gold ... Circulation. Scale ..."

The work of Mazaud, Benjamin, Régis and Veynes may be looked upon as the effect of Copeau's teaching and influence, and it is not surprising that most of the plays were performed at the Vieux-Colombier. Although Mazaud's *Dardamelle ou le cocu* was first produced by Lugné-Poë at the Œuvre, the fact that Copeau revived it twelve months later at the Vieux-Colombier showed that he considered it to be in the tradition of his theatre. What that tradition was is clearly indicated by the title, with its obvious reference to Molière's *Sganarelle ou le cocu imaginaire*, which Copeau, in fact, staged three months before he put *Dardamelle* on. To the extent to which the writers of farce in the twenties modelled their work on Molière's farces, they were disciples of Copeau.

As far as the theatre is concerned JULES ROMAINS (by name Louis Farigoule) will doubtless continue to remain known as the author of *Knock ou le triomphe de la médecine*, one of the most continuously successful and most widely performed of *avant-garde* plays since its creation by Louis Jouvet in 1923 (Comédie des Champs-Elysées, December 15th). Yet it was not as a writer of satirical farce that Jules Romains began his dramatic career. His first play, *L'Armée dans la ville*, was nearer to tragedy than to anything else. It dates from 1911, and was so unlike the general run of plays of the so-called *belle époque* that without André Antoine and his experimental matinées at the Odéon, where it was performed on March 4th, it would doubtless have remained unstaged. The preface to the text makes it clear that Romains's plays were to espouse the same cause as his earlier writings, the "unanimist" cause (the word is his). "Every dramatic work brings groups to life", he wrote, but the human couple was the only group which had been successfully represented on the stage. Other wider, more important groups, or "unanimes", awaited its attention. Romains's play presents two such "unanimes", an army of occupation and a humiliated town. The town hopes to destroy the army by isolating the soldiers and killing each one separately.

> Vous avez délayé l'armée
> Soigneusement, homme par homme . . .
> Elle était dans la ville, comme la dynamite dans le sable.
> Prenez garde . . . elle se ramasse.

These words of the dying General, who has been shot by the Mayor, testify to the vitality of the group, for, though dispersed and leaderless, the army reconstitutes itself and takes revenge on the town.

Within the corporate being of the town or of the army are smaller "unanimes": the "group of foot soldiers", the "group of horse soldiers", the "men in the café". On the stage these groups are seen coming into "existence"—that is to say, reaching a collective consciousness—then as suddenly losing it again and being "destroyed". The play follows on clearly from the poems published by Romains under the title *La Vie unanime* (1908), which evoke a number of collective beings, a barracks, a theatre audience, a congregation in church. In a short novel, *Mort de quelqu'un*, published the same year as *L'Armée dans la ville*, a block of flats having normally no "total" existence comes, for a few days, into being as a unit, following the death of one of the inmates. The death brings the tenants together and gives them, for a time, a common interest, or, as Romains put it, a "common soul". Two years later in *Les Copains* Romains describes the "creation" (in the "unanimist" sense) of the small town of Ambert and the "destruction" of Issoire, undertaken as a practical joke, played by seven youthful friends, who take their cue from Romains's *Le Manuel de déification*, in which he advocates the creation by individual action of groups so fully conscious of their identity as total beings that they become "gods"—that is to say, deified corporate beings. It is not possible here to examine the Fascist implications of Romains's theory;[24] the repercussions of the theory on the dramatic works are what matters to the playgoer. The denial of a metaphysical god and the deification of a mountain village are clearly illustrated in *Cromedeyre-le-vieil*, written between 1911 and 1918, and staged at the Vieux-Colombier on May 26th, 1920, by Copeau, in whose opinion the play was the only one that had offered anything new by way of serious drama for a full decade. In its conception and technique the play is indeed unusual. In the form of a myth, Romains offers his ideal picture of a united group. He sets this ideal group on one of the rocky peaks of the Velay region, where he was born, and materializes, in the form of houses crowded together and intercommunicating so as to form a single house along a single street, the unity of the inhabitants of Cromedeyre. Cromedeyre is one body, the people and buildings forming, as it were, one flesh, the flesh of Cromedeyre, and into the flesh of this rude body are assimilated the women who were carried off from the village of the plain. This rapt, along with Cromedeyre's break-away from all the recognized churches, forms the action of the play. After the rapt the nuptial rites are celebrated joyously in the new church, which is at the centre of the town, a church which is the church of Cromedeyre alone. The "group-god", envisaged by Romains as the ultimate good, has been brought into being.

The play manages to create a sort of religious atmosphere which is sustained by verse, full, as is all "unanimist" verse, of fleshy, material imagery. *L'Armée dans la ville* and *Cromedeyre* came nearer than any other had done to recreating verse drama, which had been dead since the time of the Romantics. Without rhyme, but making use of assonance and a very marked rhythm, the verse has a kind of rough, incantatory quality, quite suited to such simple emotional scenes as the Army's entry into the town, and the rude civic assemblies. It may also have been destined to play a part in the creation of the group spirit in the audience.[25] The following lines pronounced by the Mayoress in a moment of distress, when her feelings as an individual are, like those of Sabine in Corneille's *Horace*, at variance with her feelings as part of the group, are typical:

> Si la ville était là! Mais je suis seule!
> La ville est partout, sauf entre ces murs;
> Elle est dans la rue; elle est dans la foule
>   Qui marche et murmure.
>
> Elle rampe au loin sur l'ancienne route;
> Elle est dans les champs, foulant les épis;
> Elle empoignera tout à coup le camp
>   Comme une bête au gîte.

The Mayoress, the moving spirit and "creator" of the town, the General, and the Priest Emmanuel, the born leader, the man with a mission, offer the first schematic outline of a character of whom a more detailed portrait is painted in *Le Dictateur*. A first version of *Le Dictateur* was composed in 1910–11, in verse. It was abandoned, partly because as Antoine had left the Odéon there was little likelihood of a play in verse finding a producer, and partly because Romains realized that verse was ill suited to a play so modern, so topical, even, in theme; it had been inspired by Briand's action against the railway-strikers in 1910. Rewritten in 1925, the play was no less topical, though the grounds for its topicality had shifted, and a possible analogy between Romains's dictator and Mussolini caused the play to be turned down by the Comédie-Française despite the approval of the play by Daladier, the Minister for Education. Thirteen years later, as it happened, Daladier was to find himself in a position similar to that of Le Dictateur, being elected by a Left majority and governing with dictatorial powers voted by the Right in the teeth of Left opposition. Romains's main concern was with the growing awareness by his "unanimist" hero of his responsibility as Prime Minister to the various "sections of the community". He comes to feel himself the vital centre of the country, with thousands of lives dependent upon him. It was up to him to assure the continuance of social activities: to quote Denis's statement in "unanimist" style to his friend Féréol: "On sent que des milliers d'accrochages, de jonctions se font soudain sur votre corps, qu'une immense chose fourmillante va converger sur vous, se servir avidement de vous." Féréol, the revolutionary, fails to understand, and the long-standing friendship of the two men comes to an end with Féréol's inevitable arrest by Denis. Denis remains alone, hated by his former friends and with unlimited powers in his hands. The political questions: will Denis become a dictator? will he know where to stop? are left unanswered. The play was performed by Jouvet at the Comédie des Champs-Elysées on October 5th, 1926, three years after the march on Rome. It met with a lukewarm reception but was successful in Berlin and Vienna. From the dramatic point of view the play is weak in that the transformation of the revolutionary deputy into a dictator is presented in theoretical discussions and not in action.

Meanwhile Romains was exploiting his "unanimist" theme in a parallel series of farcical comedies, the Trouhadec plays, all of which are devoted to the burlesque adventure of a professor of geography. The story begins in the form of a film scenario, *Donogoo-Tonka ou les miracles de la science, conte cinématographique*, which was written in 1920, and continues with *M. Le Trouhadec saisi par la débauche* and *Le Mariage de M. Le Trouhadec*. The scenario was then written up as a play for the new ultra-modern Pigalle Theatre, which, with its four lift-like stages permitting rapid changes of scene, was ideal for an action requiring multiple settings. *Donogoo*, as the play is called, was performed there on October 25th, 1930, and on November 5th, 1951, became part of the repertory of the Comédie-Française. At the time when the scenario was published the name of Romains's hero, Le Trouhadec, was generally recognized as being an arrangement of the Breton name Gallouedec, the name of an inspector of secondary schools, the author of manuals of geography. No other similarity was implied. Le Trouhadec is really a dolt, but his image as a great scientist is imposed on a gullible public as a result of what is now known as a "public-relations campaign" of frightening efficiency. The three comedies follow on from *Les Copains*. Lamedin, one of the seven *copains*, saves M. Le Trouhadec's tottering reputation, in *Donogoo*, by creating the town of Donogoo-Tonka, which, though non-existent, was described in error but in detail in the geographer's latest book. Lamedin's publicity for "improving" this imaginary city brings the city into existence, and none is more surprised than Lamedin, when he lands in the country, to find a thriving new city named Donogoo-Tonka. He establishes himself there as Governor, with the backing of his investors' millions, and erects two statues, one immortalizing the "Father of the City", Le Trouhadec, who has just been elected Member of the Institute in Paris on the strength of geographical discoveries, the other to Scientific Truth, known among the initiates as Scientific Error. From then onward these two, by Lamedin's decree, were to be the country's "gods".

The next Le Trouhadec play, performed by Jouvet at the Comédie des Champs-Elysées on March 14th, 1923, and revived at the Comédie-Française on January 14th, 1953, is much more an amusing satire of modern society than it is a "unanimist" play, though it does, unobtrusively, show how the action of society can transform an individual as well as push him into the foreground. The one-time serious-minded geographer is here to be seen at Monte Carlo, whither a sudden and, for him, very novel passion for a young actress has lured him. Favoured by chance at the gambling tables and consequently by the actress, he is protected from the consequences of his follies, which include a newly developed taste for expensive living, by a modern Scapin named Bénin, one of Romains's *copains*.

The man, M. Le Trouhadec, whom Bénin describes as not very brave in battle but bold enough in victory, is seen in the final stage of his development in the strongly "unanimist" farce *Le Mariage de M. Le Trouhadec* (Comédie des Champs-Elysées-Jouvet, February 9th, 1925). Here he accepts the chairmanship of "Le Comité des Honnêtes Gens" and the marriage that this chairmanship entails, with a view to the repopulation of the country. The Comité des Honnêtes Gens, which Bénin daily exercises in word and gesture to make it "le comité le plus comité" the world has ever seen, offers a satirical picture of the modern political "unanime". It learns how to "talk non-stop, since that is the principle behind all political discussion", and ends up by thinking and acting as one man, and becoming an independent, frighteningly uncontrollable machine.

In *Knock ou le triomphe de la médecine* (Comédie des Champs-Elysées-Jouvet, December 15th, 1923) the frightening element is not the group but the individual, the urbane Dr Knock himself. A medical man by profession, he is a dictator by vocation. He is to be seen indoctrinating every single inhabitant of Saint-Maurice, imposing on them all a way of life of his own choosing, a medical way of life, though probably Romains's choice of medicine was simply fidelity to an old stage tradition. What Romains was concerned

with was the "method", and Knock's method was as easily applicable in other domains, politics, finance, the Church. A dictator who
will tolerate no competition, whether in the shape of a superstition,
religious sect, or even a healthy human being, Knock is also
confessedly a "creator", for out of a practice that was as "dissemin-
ated" as the village at the foot of Cromedeyre, he created a
medically conscious "unanime". "You handed over to me a canton
of a few thousand vague and indeterminate beings", said Knock to
his predecessor three months after he took over the practice.
"What I have done is to give them being, to bring them to life
medically speaking." Thanks to the cult of medicine, Saint-Maurice
had become as a single being, with all its nerves reacting to the
same stimuli. This fact finds lyrical expression in Knock's well-
known monologue, as he looks over the mountain town and thinks
of the two hundred and fifty thermometers raised by the "patients"
on the stroke of ten in the morning to take their own temperature,
and of the two hundred and fifty lights burning at night in the
rooms of these two hundred and fifty "sick people", forming a sort
of firmament of which he is the "continual creator". Knock's
approach to the situation, which had at the outset been purely realistic, has become almost that of a mystic, a high priest of medicine.
Closely interwoven into the theme of "unanimist" creation is that
of the gullibility of the masses, and in showing Knock as being on
the point of falling a victim to his own propaganda, Romains's
comedy gives food for thought.

Besides bringing out the evolution in Knock's character, the
monologue pinpoints the fact that the mountain site cannot be
regarded simply as a picturesque setting for a dramatic action, but
that it forms an integral part of the action, as it does in *Cromedeyre*.
The same is true of the shoe-cleaner's saloon and the cycle-shop in
the one-act plays *Amédée et les messieurs en rang*[26] and *La
Scintillante*, which were performed by Jouvet at the Comédie des
Champs-Elysées on December 14th, 1923, and October 7th, 1924,
respectively. In the latter play it is the "woman in her cycle-shop"
and not the woman as a woman that attracts the young viscount's
attentions. In the more worthwhile *Amédée* it is the interruption
of the professional gestures of the shoe-cleaner that draws the
individual customers together and makes them discover their
mutual taste for ritual shoe-cleaning carried out at leisure.

The relation between the individual and the group is given a new twist in *Amédée* and is further developed in *Jean le Maufranc* (Théâtre des Arts-Pitoëff, December 1st, 1926). The group in *Amédée* is founded on the revelation of Amédée's humiliating secret, and so, as long as he works for the group, Amédée will continue to be its victim. Similarly Jean is shown to be a victim, though not the victim of an "unanime". "Society is not the unanime", Romains had written in *Le Manuel de déification*. Jean is the victim of the State, a twentieth-century Democracy, with its hypocritical pretence of freedom. Seeking a means of escape from its never-ending inroads into the life of the citizen, Jean appeals to the "International League for the Protection of Modern Man", only to find that further onslaughts on the shreds of independence still enjoyed by man are contemplated in the name of religion and morals or for the sake of private and public interests. Since dissimulation and hypocrisy offer the sole means of defence, Jean becomes *le maufranc*, a practising hypocrite, but he finds the practice of hypocrisy stifling, so he confesses his imposture to a bishop, under the seal of confession. He refuses the consolation of religion offered by the bishop and demands a new religion—by implication Romains's "unanimist" religion.

The defence of individual privacy is new in Romains's dramatic works, though the problem of the relationship between individualism and "unanimism" had been broached by him the previous year in a lecture entitled "Petite Introduction à l'Unanimisme". Earlier *Le Manuel* had counselled revolt against society, should society become oppressive. In the second version of this play, entitled *Jean Musse ou l'école de l'hypocrisie* (Atelier, November 21st, 1930), Romains, discarding dissimulation and hypocrisy as being no longer an effective means of defence for the citizen, directly incites the audience to open revolt against the growing interference of the State and its agents, such as the League, all of whom work to enslave man. The play is simpler than *Jean le Maufranc*, but the insistence on the thesis is such that there is no real dialogue, no real conflict, no real characters.

With *Boën* (Odéon, December 4th, 1930), Romains tackled directly, and with little concern for its relation to "unanimist" theory, another social theme, that created by "the possession of wealth"—to quote the subtitle: on the one hand charity or generosity, depending on the point of view; on the other the just distribution of wealth. The discussion is not purely theoretical, as Romains studies the effect produced on an individual by the possession of wealth as also that produced by the complete lack of resources. One of the characters newly returned from Russia speaks of an incredible spirit of fraternity which she had experienced there at the time of the revolution, when people were completely destitute.

Grâce encore pour la terre!, written in 1939 in the shadow of the war and reflecting the hopes of "men of good will" that the impending catastrophe might be averted, ended with God's promising a period of respite to the Martin family, very ordinary representatives of humanity whom He had consulted about the unsatisfactory state of affairs on earth before deciding whether to proceed to the Last Judgment, in order to prevent mankind from destroying itself by its own hand, thereby playing the devil's game. The outbreak of the Second World War necessitated the addition of an Epilogue, in which God declares Himself to be on the side of all the Martins and promises them victory. The play was in rehearsal at the Comédie-Française when France was invaded; it was not performed. The solution Romains proposes is an unmistakable "unanimist" solution: the creation of a "world-unanime", to be achieved by the world-wide dissemination of noble, peaceful ideals; for the first time in his plays Romains was preaching internationalism. The evil nature of certain unanimes—by implication the Nazi State— is recognized, and dictatorship joins patriotism in the odium into which the latter had already fallen in *Jean le Maufranc* and *Musse*. After Dr Knock it was Martin's turn to inculcate a certain idea into the masses and become a "unanimist" hero, a creator, though, with the cancellation of God's promised "respite", he had to shoulder arms instead. The play is interesting for the way in which it draws together the various threads used by Romains in his earlier plays, and for the different treatment given to some of them, but an action which shifts from heaven to earth and back to heaven and engages in colloquy characters as diverse as God (who is not very conversant with human affairs), His Minister for Foreign Affairs, His Chief of Police, Saint Patrick dressed up as a Scottish lord, a talkative statue of the Mother Country, and ordinary human beings, can have little more than an intellectual appeal.

In his last play *L'An mil* (Sarah-Bernhardt, March 13th, 1947), which is not specially "unanimist", Romains continued his musings on the possible end of the world, but caricature and coldly calculated gaiety, which give *Knock* and the Trouhadec series their relish, ill-befits a representation of humanity confronted with annihilation, and even Dullin, with all his skill, could not make the play a success.

Romains's other dramatic writings are *Le Roi masqué* (Pigalle, December 19th, 1931), a fanciful story of the potentate of some vague Illyria who goes to Paris for a fling *incognito*, two one-act farces, *Démétrios* (1926) and *Le Déjeuner marocain* (1928), and *Volpone*, adapted from Ben Jonson in collaboration with Stefan Zweig. This adaptation proved to be one of Dullin's most lasting successes. The long run enjoyed by the play in 1928–29, which forced Dullin to defer the production of Armand Salacrou's *Patchouli*, annoyed Dullin intensely; the elegant audiences which crowded his theatre were not the special public which had supported him in his difficult first years at the Atelier, and, as he rightly guessed, they would desert him when he went back to experimentation.

The cerebral nature of Romains's comedies prevents them from having much emotional appeal, though moments charged with emotion do arise from time to time, as when Knock stands and surveys the firmament of "stars" he has created. There is a good deal of photographic realism but little serious character study; even Dr Knock, who for a whole generation meant Louis Jouvet, can hardly be counted as a real human being.

Ever since his experience, one October evening in 1903, in the rue d'Amsterdam, when he had the "revelation" of the street as a collective being, endowed almost with a collective conscience, the group had become the centre of Romains's interest. His concern, in the first place, was with the relationship between groups. Only later did the individual interest him seriously, and then not as an individual or in his relationship with other individuals, but only in his relationship with the group. This insistence on the group as against the individual offered the theatre a new line of approach, and one might have expected it to be taken up by other playwrights. But Romains had no disciple. Something on these lines had been tried by Emile Verhaeren in *Les Aubes*, in 1899, but had reached only the limited audience of the irregular theatre the Œuvre, whereas many of Romains's plays have had a long "international career". Fundamental disbelief, however, comes from Romains's accrediting the group, which after all is composed of separate autonomous members, with a conscience and the power to know itself and reflect on its action. This explains why there is something laboured and artificial in his dramatic writings, despite the amusing satire. The intellectual trick is too apparent for any audience to swallow nowadays. Nevertheless, Dr Knock has continued to lead an active charlatan's existence in the world, though in his appearance in Paris, in 1960, even his patter showed unmistakable signs of wear.

The production by Jean Anouilh of ROGER VITRAC's *Victor ou les enfants au pouvoir* on October 3rd, 1962, introduced the general theatregoing public to one of the precursors of the recent *avant-garde* movement referred to as the Theatre of the Absurd. Since this production it has become evident that the movement represented by Ionesco has a long line of precursors, Alfred Jarry, whose *Ubu-Roi* (1896) is now a classic, Guillaume Apollinaire, and the Surrealists and Antonin Artaud.

Victor[27] was the fourth and last production of the Alfred Jarry Theatre Company, founded by both Artaud and Vitrac, and its first performance took place on December 24th, 1928. Against the three performances given by the company at the Comédie des Champs-Elysées, can now be set a whole season's triumphal run, at first at the old-fashioned Boulevard theatre, the Ambigu, and then at the fashionable Athénée in 1962–63. The success, in the interim, of Ionesco, Beckett, and the early plays of Arthur Adamov, had prepared the public of 1962 for the shock tactics employed in *Victor*, and the production itself, which underlined the farcical element, reminiscent of Feydeau, at the expense of the Ubuesque element, certainly broadened the play's appeal. Nevertheless, it was clear (at least at *one* performance) that certain elements of the audience, attracted by the promised gaiety of the show, were ill at ease listening to this "bourgeois drama, lyrical, ironical, straightforward by turns, having as its special characteristics, adultery, incest, scatology, rage, surrealistic poetry, patriotism, madness, disgrace and death", to quote Artaud's definition of the play.

The play is a dramatic transcription of the surrealist revolt against bourgeois morality, and takes the form of a violently but amusingly satirical burlesque of a "drama". The action takes place between 8 P.M. and midnight, on September 12th, 1909—that is to say, in Vitrac's words, in the society of the Banquet Years, a stinking, bellicose society, which had not yet managed to stomach the defeat of 1870. It is Victor's birthday, he will be nine at 11.30

P.M. In those three to four hours Victor, so far a model child, who is nearly six feet tall and as intelligent as he is tall, suddenly sees how ugly and hypocritical is the world around him. He rebels against its ugliness, smashing everything he can, from the family's precious Sèvres vase to his father's sordid idyll with the lady next door—and with the maid. His death at the end of the play is his final refusal to accept life on the terms agreed to by the others. Every word, every gesture of his, on that ill-fated evening brings embarrassment and consternation to his parents and their guests, particularly the grotesque bit of play-acting with the little girl next door that makes further dissimulation impossible and drives the cuckold husband, an unbalanced ex-soldier of the 1870 war, to hang himself. This he does from a flagstaff on the balcony, wearing his red and blue uniform under his nightshirt, so as to look like the flag he believes himself to be, and he does it to the strains of a military march, *Sambre et Meuse*, played on a gramophone.

The army comes in for its share of satire in the person of the general, who, having given his "word of a soldier" to do whatever Victor asks, allows himself to be mounted like a horse and ridden across the stage, despite the pained protests of the gathered company.

Since his close association with Artaud in the management of the Théâtre Alfred Jarry, Vitrac had drifted away from the Surrealists. In *Victor*, however, the inspiration is still strongly surrealistic, though by no means as completely so as in *Les Mystères de l'amour*, which formed part of the programme of the Théâtre Alfred Jarry on June 2nd, 1927. Among the surrealistic elements used by Vitrac in *Victor* can be counted the dream which is told uncritically by Victor in all its details; the materialization on the stage of Victor's father's thoughts as he reads his wife a salacious page from a cheap novelette; the striking entry of a woman of ethereal beauty, Ida Mortemart, who is the victim of an unmentionable sulphurous affliction. During this scene, at the original performance, rude noises were made in the wings and stink bombs were thrown into the auditorium. Artaud, however, denied all responsibility for these and declared himself to be the victim of practical jokers. In Anouilh's production the lady's entry was made to the opening notes of Beethoven's Fifth Symphony, played on a bass trombone which continued its blasts at appropriate moments.

To the uninitiated the language is no less surprising than the action, though, even at the first performance, it did not create the pandemonium there was after Ubu pronounced his first word "Merdre", in 1896, a pandemonium that was only calmed by the twenty minutes' improvised jig which the actor Gémier danced until he fell exhausted to the floor. To readers familiar with Ionesco texts, Vitrac's language presents no difficulty, though Ionesco's initial approach to language is that of the philologist who considers it in behaviourist terms, whereas Vitrac, following Artaud's teaching, often ignores the utilitarian function of language and concentrates on its sound value alone. Victor's father's infuriated reference to the strange lady visitor is an example: "Ida Mortemart, croupissant comme la mer Morte. Ah! les bulles ... et ça crève! Ida, dada, Ida, dada, Morte? Mortemart? J'en ai marre, marre, marre." The "Friselis, friselis, friselis", "Réso, réso, réso", of the children's mimicry of their elders' love-making is particularly interesting because of the part it plays in the action. There are examples, too, of surrealist automatic writing, like Victor's strange outburst about women imprisoned in blood-stained lace, houses on the march, etc., which he then calmly refers to as "merely the unordered elements of his next French composition".

Les Mystères de l'amour, which was published in the first number of La Révolution surréaliste, gives the impression of being, for the most part, a product of automatic writing, but when Vitrac was no longer in direct contact with the Surrealists, who had expelled him from their number over the alleged commercialization of a programme at the Théâtre Alfred Jarry, nor with Artaud himself, his language became more straightforward, and there was a less deliberate effort on his part to prove to the audience that it had not understood, just when it believed that it was on the point of doing so.

Le Coup de Trafalgar, which was to have been put on in June 1930 by the Théâtre Alfred Jarry but was staged only in 1934 (Atelier, June 8th) by the Rideau de Paris, with Barrault in the cast, still follows the earlier pattern. The play is a further satire on middle-class manners, the army, patriotism, war—the fourth tableau takes place in 1918, in a cellar during a bombardment, when a deserter explains that seeing no justifiable reason for the 1914 war he had preferred to save his life to fight in the "nineteen hundred and later war", which would be bloodless, and would decide everything—a real war? or the surrealist revolution? As usual a certain number of events are never explained, as, for example, the reason why one of the main characters shaves half her head on July 14th, 1914, though the question is frequently put during the rest of the play. At the end, with a single gesture, the hero knocks all the characters over like ninepins. Vitrac seems to be emphasizing the fact that they are all marionettes. In *Victor* the stage was similarly cleared by the characters all committing murder or suicide.

Vitrac's aggressively anti-realistic and bitingly satirical *Le Camelot* traces the career of an educated and enterprising hawker during the years 1919 to 1929; his hero's talent for specious argument enables him to become a Deputy and very nearly a Cabinet Minister before he falls from grace. It was this play that Charles Dullin chose for his experiment in music-hall farce in 1936 (October 12th), as part of his attempt to arrive at a more comprehensive conception of the theatre than was then current. But Georgius, the *café-concert* star, whom he entrusted with the part of the hawker, was not in his element when dealing with a literary text.

In *Les Demoiselles du large* (Œuvre, April 20th, 1938), his one serious play, Vitrac abandoned his opposition to psychological drama which he shared with Artaud, and concerned himself with the development of the characters and their feelings. He studied, as in *Les Mystères de l'amour*, but in a "preciser and less humoristic fashion", the various emotions which love gives rise to. As he did not achieve the desired success with this attempt at tragedy, he returned in the riotous play, *Le Loup garou* (Noctambules, February 27th, 1940), to humoristic farce. The play describes the havoc wrought in a mental home for smart people by the arrival of a patient, André, who declares himself to be a lascivious goat, and it ends with a sort of fox hunt, or goat hunt, to blasts from a huntsman's horn and a gramophone playing hunting music on the stage, with the disappointed women patients forming the pack. André escapes over the garden wall, taking with him the doctor's mistress.

Vitrac's last play to be performed is *Le Sabre de mon père* (Théâtre de Paris, February 17th, 1951). It is a sort of prologue to *Le Coup de Trafalgar*, and takes the action back to 1910. As an attempt to combine conventional drama with Surrealism it is not really successful.

Until recently Vitrac was known only to specialists of the theatre. It was Jean Anouilh's production of *Victor* in 1962 which brought him before the general public's eye, and not only in Paris; the Royal Shakespeare Company staged the play at the Aldwych less than two years later, under the title *Victor or The Children take over.* It is clear that Vitrac has an important place in the history of the French theatre since the First World War; he provides a link between Alfred Jarry's *Ubu-Roi* and the plays of writers like Ionesco, Jean Vauthier, and Jean Tardieu. Since the 1962 production third and fourth volumes of plays by Vitrac have been published. Vitrac also wrote the dialogue for a number of films, but this was quite apart from his work as a surrealist dramatist.

There are some fifty dadaist and surrealist plays altogether; Lugné-Poë put on one or two at the Œuvre, but the rest did not get into the theatre proper. RAYMOND ROUSSEL'S compositions had short runs on the Boulevard, but these were financed by the millionaire playwright himself. First came *Impressions d'Afrique*, which was staged at the Théâtre Femina on September 9th, 1911, and the following year, on May 11th, at the Théâtre Antoine. The play was adapted from his novel. It is a Jarryesque parody of a Boulevard play, the kind seen at the Châtelet; an earth-worm plays a zither, a one-legged man plays a flute made from the tibia of his lost leg, and curious tortures and executions are invented. *Locus solus*, staged at the Théâtre Antoine on December 7th, 1922, was also adapted from a novel, and is equally Jarryesque; so too are the plays *L'Etoile au front* (Vaudeville, May 5th, 1924) and *La Poussière de soleils*, which had three matinée performances at the Porte-Saint-Martin beginning on February 2nd, 1926, and was revived in 1927 (January 12th) at the Renaissance. All consist of strange stories with no real dramatic development. Roussel's audiences proved recalcitrant, as well they might; knives were even drawn at one performance, while the critics wondered whether the dramatist was thumbing his nose at them. Recently, however, there has been an attempt to focus interest on the plays of the surrealist writers because of the theatrical success of Ionesco and Beckett. On January 17th, 1964, the Club du Théâtre Neuf staged GEORGES RIBEMONT-DESSAIGNES'S *Le Bourreau du Pérou* at an evening devoted to the "Hommage et Redécouverte du Théâtre Dada-Surrealiste". The play was first staged in 1926 by Art et Action, and three years later was put on in Prague. The characters do things which one might dream of doing but which ordinary, civilized behaviour excludes, and the possibility of further such actions by the characters produced, as it was intended it should, an uneasy fear in the audience. *L'Empereur de Chine*[28] was likewise too unusual, even for the regular *avant-garde* theatres of the Cartel, and it was left for Art et Action to undertake the production (1925); two years later it was played in Rome. IVAN GOLL's satirical burlesque, reminiscent of *Ubu-Roi, Mathusalem*, about a shoe king— roi du Box-Calf!—who thinks only of business and pleasure and who has all the fears of a king whose life is really in danger from assassins, was put on by Le Loup Blanc in 1927. Mathusalem's tough businessman son wore a mica mask like a certain type of business envelope. He had a gramophone horn for a mouth and shouted "Allô! Allô!" every few words. On his head was a metal telephone, which rang every so often, and a blinking green-and-red light. He had a fountain-pen for a hand. Other characters were dressed like coffee-pots and various kitchen utensils. Film sequences prepared by Jean Painlevé, with Artaud taking several parts, including those of an artillery officer and a bishop, interrupted the action from time to time. The second act, with three different actors representing three different aspects of the same character and all paying court, as I, Thou, and He, respectively to the same girl, gives a curious preview of Jean-Victor Pellerin's *Têtes de rechange*. *Mathusalem* was written in 1919. ROBERT DESNOS, on the other hand, with *La Place de l'Etoile* (1927), which he subtitled "anti-poem", hints at the modern "anti-play", even punning in the title, which refers to starfish, in a manner which was later to be characteristic of Ionesco's dialogue.

There were, of course, many points of contact between the work of the Surrealists and that of other writers of the twenties and thirties. One has only to look at Jean Cocteau's dramatic experiments, his whimsical satire of middle-class manners in *Les Mariés de la Tour Eiffel*, the unorthodox technique of some of his early plays, and the dream sequences in his films. Armand Salacrou was strongly influenced by the group when writing for the theatre in the early twenties. Jean Anouilh has never made a secret of what he owed to his friend Roger Vitrac, and staged *Victor* to "repay his debt".

NOTES

1. The suggestion came from Diaghilev.
2. Revived without an outcry at the Théâtre des Champs-Elysées, December 21st, 1920.
3. Revived, Comédie des Champs-Elysées, in 1946 by Hubert Gignoux and Henri Cordreaux, with marionettes.
4. As an opera, with music by Honegger, Opéra, January 26th, 1943.
5. Music by Poulenc; choreography by Bronislava Nijinska; Théâtre de Monte Carlo, January 6th and 9th, 1924.
6. Music by D. Milhaud; choreography by Nijinska; Diaghilev Ballet, Théâtre des Champs-Elysées, June 20th, 1924.
7. Music by Milhaud, Opéra-Comique, December 16th, 1927.
8. Organized by Comte Étienne de Beaumont at the Théâtre de la Cigale.
9. Revived, Théâtre des Champs-Elysées, May 19th, 1952; Sadler's Wells, January 15th, 1960.
10. Performed in English in 1937 as *Orphée*.
11. Revived, Bouffes-Parisiens, September 22nd, 1954. Performed in English in 1940 as *The Infernal Machine*.
12. Performed in English in 1954 as *The Knights of the Round Table*.
13. Performed in English in 1938 as *The Human Voice*.
14. Performed in English as *Intimate Relations*, 1951; as a "musical tragedy" with music by Poulenc, Opéra-Comique, 1959.
15. Revived, Ambassadeurs, September 1966; performed in English in 1952.
16. Revived at the Comédie-Française-Luxembourg, March 22nd, 1956.
17. Performed in English as *The Eagle has Two Heads*, 1946. Cocteau criticized the English version as bearing little relation to his play. It was too literary, he said, and the title was inexact.
18. *Arts*, June 20th–26th, 1962.
19. Here it alternated with Albert Camus's *Caligula*. In 1921 Meyerhold startled Moscow with his production of *Le Cocu magnifique*. In 1947 a film was made of it by G. de Meyst and another in 1964 by Antonio Pietrangeli.
20. *Le Monde*, January 22nd, 1946.
21. Revived at the Noctambules, March 13th, 1956.
22. In the version bearing the new title *Léona*, which was performed at the Ambassadeurs on February 2nd, 1944, Léona moved in the foreground and M. Dom passed into the background.
23. Comédie-Française-Luxembourg, 1953; Paris Radio, 1951.
24. See P. J. Norrish, *Drama of the Group. A Study of Unanimism in the Plays of Jules Romains*, 1959, p. 125 *et sqq.*
25. Romains had already described such a group in his poem *Le Théâtre*, in the volume entitled *La Vie unanime*, 1908.
26. Comédie-Française-Luxembourg, October 24th, 1956.
27. Théâtre Agnes-Capri, November 12th, 1946.
28. Club de l'Epée de Bois, February 9th, 1967.

III

Studio Theatre: Drama of Subconscious Motivation

Henri-René Lenormand—Simon Gantillon—François Mauriac—Roger Martin du Gard—René Bruyez.

HENRI-RENE LENORMAND was an outstanding figure in the Studio-theatre movement between the two wars. He was also a playwright of international repute and saw his plays staged in Berlin, Vienna, Prague, Athens, Madrid, Amsterdam, Rome, Copenhagen. His work introduced a completely new trend in psychological drama. By 1922, when Pirandello was first performed on a Paris stage, Lenormand had already written a number of plays showing the effect of subconscious motivation on human conduct. "I wanted", he wrote in 1945, "to have done with the classical conception of man ... I submitted the Cartesian hero, whose motives are entirely lucid, to the dissolving influences which emanate from his subconscious mind."[1] Lenormand's insistence on subconscious motivation persists throughout the whole of his dramatic output. It is fundamental to his approach to the theatre.

Another new element is to be found in Lenormand's attempt, in the great majority of his plays, to integrate human beings into the material world, the natural order. "I made him the sport of natural forces; I subjected him to the extremes of climate ... I tried to widen the scope of the theatre, which cannot be limited to individual human beings, and must extend to the whole of creation." Lenormand found a natural champion in Gaston Baty, who staged four of his plays, but whereas Baty's conception of man and man's place in nature is that of the medieval schoolmen, disciples of Aristotle, Lenormand has no such affinity, though the naturalistic philosophy underlying his dramatic theory is not unrelated to their

thought and that of the Renaissance philosophers. Classical literature had gone to the limit in separating man from his historical,
material, and social environment. Baty and Lenormand, on the
other hand, sought to reintegrate man in nature. Both tried to make
out that no attempt had ever been made before their time to reverse
the essential process of classical art. They ignored the fact that
Romantic drama had already reintegrated man into history and
the Théâtre Libre into his social and material environment. They
continued the Romantic trend. What they had to say that was
original was that man cannot be separated from the nature of the
scientists and the geographers. Their ideas had considerable literary
and poetic potentialities. Playwright and producer alike exploited
them, though when theorizing both tended to over-simplify their
attitude by merely opposing their synthesizing psychology to the
analytical techniques of the classical stage.

Lenormand had said much the same thing in 1933 as in 1945
when discussing Claudel, Maeterlinck, Saint-Georges de Bouhélier,
and the young playwrights grouped around Baty. He included the
supernatural, which neither science nor the machine age had
driven from man's consciousness; natural forces included occult
forces, guiding his dramatic hero towards an enigmatic fate. Occult
forces, like the mysteries of time and space, were perceptible realities, just as jealousy, avarice, and lust were perceptible realities for
classical psychology.

These ideas were present from the first in Lenormand's writings
for the stage, some of which were put on at the Grand Guignol and
the Théâtre des Arts from 1905 onward. Into his first play, La
Folie blanche, which contains the germ of the full-length play La
Dent rouge, Lenormand works what he called his "discovery of the
mountain". Four of his early sketches, Le Réveil de l'instinct
(1908), Les Possédés (1909), Terres chaudes (1913), Poussière
(1914), were the original canvasses on which he later embroidered
the important plays Le Simoun, Une Vie secrète, A l'Ombre du
mal, and Le Temps est un songe.

His first success to count in the theatre was with Les Ratés,
which Georges Pitoëff performed in Geneva on January 16th, 1920,
and then in Paris at the Théâtre des Arts on May 22nd. It was
written in 1915. This play is not in line with the rest of his work.
It has its origin in the indifferent fate of his earlier productions, and
reflects his doubts about himself. In a programme note, at the

revival of the play by Baty in 1937, Lenormand wrote: "We want to know what the creature we are afraid of becoming is like, what he would think and what would be the limits of his powers of endurance ... A writer invents for himself the ghosts of his future, and in this way communicates to the spectator very real and acute distress." In his *Confessions* he declares that the artist overcomes his distress by bringing into full consciousness the worst that can happen to him. He claimed for the writing of *Le Lâche* and *Le Crépuscule du théâtre* the same therapeutic effect.

The two main characters of *Les Ratés* are a mediocre actress and her talentless writer husband. Straight away Lenormand uses the multiple tableau form which was to be characteristic of his work. Each tableau conveys a particular state of mind of the characters: the couple's gradual loss of faith in themselves, the collapse of their ambitions, the weakening of their spiritual aspirations, the end of their love for each other, and, finally, the murder and suicide in a sordid hotel bedroom. The pessimistic colouring is a reflection of Lenormand's temperament, though it is given a generalized form in the husband's belief that people always kill the things they love or are killed by them.

All Lenormand's plays are closely bound up with his own life and temperament, particularly with his gloomy meditations on those forces in man which drag him down. His *Confessions* provide an enlightening commentary on his work. They also give the source of many of his plays and name the models of his characters. They show Lenormand turning over in his mind, often over a long period of years, a number of themes, not always consciously discriminating between them. This explains the unity of his dramatic output. A theme which is treated in one play may be fully developed in a subsequent work; one play can form the complement to another: *Mixture*, the drama of the mother, is, for example, the counterpart of *Le Mangeur de rêves*, the drama of the daughter. The date of production is thus no guide to the order of composition.

Le Temps est un songe, written between 1913 and 1918, is Lenormand's first significant play. The combination of personal experience with metaphysical meditation, and Lenormand's flair for exploiting the public's interest in certain scientific or pseudoscientific theories, secured for it an undisputed triumph when it was first performed by Pitoëff in 1919. The public's interest seems to have been successfully revived during the Occupation (Odéon,

June 18th, 1942), but by 1957 the changed intellectual atmosphere dated the play sadly, and its revival at the Théâtre Franklin was a failure. Lenormand states in the *Confessions* that the starting-point of his play was a chance meeting with a woman who claimed to see the future as though it were the present, and he rejected any suggestion that he was interested in theories of time or of relativity as a scientific subject. He accepted, however, to be looked upon as a psychologist interested in whether the impression of being able to see into the future is merely a mental aberration or a true intuition. In the play Romée foretells the death of her fiancé, Nico. Is this a real vision of the future? If so nothing can save Nico. His fate can, however, also be explained by the influence of his surroundings on his mentality. Certain experiences in the East Indies and certain contacts, particularly his contact with an aged priest in Madras who could induce in himself visions of the past and the future, and who maintained that the future is hidden from ordinary men by a veil, had brought Nico round to this way of thinking and had even led him to doubt his own existence. To these influences must be added the effect, on one used to the sun-drenched lands of the East, of the mists which hang over the family's estates in the province of Utrecht. They precipitate the mental and moral disintegration of the hero, who commits suicide—in the place and manner foreseen by his fiancée. Romée had inadvertently mentioned the lake when Nico talked of his early attempt at suicide— by hanging—so a strong element of auto-suggestion could very well have entered into Nico's second and successful attempt. Where the discrepancy lies, if the play is to be considered as a play on subconscious motivation, is in Lenormand's insistence on two different descriptions of the place. He makes Romée *see* it as it *was going to be* at the time of the suicide, and not as it was at the time of the vision. The action can thus only be explained in terms of the occult, and the other elements, climatic, psychological, merely overlay the occult. This defect is eradicated by Lenormand in his subsequent works: where there are apparently occult phenomena, there are also naturalistic explanations. All the elements of Lenormand's *dramaturgie* are here: the personal influence of temperament, the integration of psychology into environmental influences, and the questioning metaphysical speculations. It is the perfect recipe for modern intellectual drama, though the execution itself is not perfect.

In *La Dent rouge*, on which Lenormand was working at the same time, though it was produced only in 1922 (October 10th) by Gémier at the Odéon, there is a subconscious desire by the wife for the death of her husband, and instead of the Utrecht mists of *Le Temps est un songe*, with the optical illusions they can create, or the stagnant waters, which are mysterious and full enough of promise to lure Nico to their depths, there are the dizzy snow-covered heights of an Alpine mountain, equally alluring. Of these provocative heights, as tempting to the chamois hunter as were the stagnant waters to Nico, Lenormand makes truly living creatures. His animism, which is best exemplified in these two plays, was, according to the *Confessions* (vol. I, p. 159), neither a philosophical attitude nor a conscious literary process. It resulted from what he calls his inability to separate outside nature from the human mind.

In *La Dent rouge*, to the effect of nature and climate, Lenormand adds that of the historical moment. The action takes place in 1860. The clash is between the narrow community, for the members of which the existence of mountain demons is still an article of faith, and an American-born girl, who comes of this same stock, and who returns to marry into this superstition-ridden community. After her husband's death on the mountainside the villagers accuse her of witchcraft, and she herself, falling a prey to their superstitions, comes to believe herself responsible for his death. Primitive beliefs and instincts lie just below the surface of the civilized mind. Unlike the Greek fates, which are exteriorized, those against which Lenormand's characters wage an unequal struggle are lodged within themselves.

Lenormand's best play is *Le Simoun*, and it is by this play that he is remembered. It was first produced by Gaston Baty for Firmin Gémier, at the Comédie-Montaigne, in 1920 (December 21st), and, after revivals at the Odéon and the Théâtre Pigalle by Gémier, again with Baty, took its place in the repertory of the Comédie-Française in 1937, in Baty's *mise en scène*. It was withdrawn, however, after a mere thirty performances, as a result of ministerial pressure; an article by Pierre Miller in the *Temps* was responsible. Miller alleged that it was dangerous to put on a play at a national theatre showing colonial settlers in a bad light. The Sahara desert, which is the scene of the action, is an active element in the psychological development of the characters; it is not merely an exotic setting. The disintegrating influence of the hot African sun on the conduct and standards of the white man is Lenormand's main theme. The other important theme, that of incest, is to be found in the original sketch *Le Réveil de l'instinct*, performed by Le Nouveau Théâtre d'Art, in 1908, to the cheers and boos of spectators fighting in the stalls, but the setting and secondary characters of the final version, *Le Simoun*, came out of Lenormand's trip to Ghardaia, in 1913.

The multiple tableau form of *Le Simoun* is not, as was alleged at the time, the misapplication of the novelist's technique to drama. It is ideally suited to the portrayal of a steadily growing, but barely conscious, incestuous love of a father for his daughter, who closely resembles the wife from whom he is estranged. The daughter has come to join her father on the fringe of the desert, and the hot, enervating simoon exacerbates his passion. The crisis is slow to develop but it is tense. In support of the tableau form, which Lenormand also used in *L'Homme et ses fantômes*, Gémier, who performed it, quoted the example of Shakespeare, Calderón, and Lope de Vega, to show that a moral psychological problem does not lose its interest on the stage when it is developed in time and space.[2] It is to be expected that all the examples Gémier quotes are of what the French call "drame"—that is to say, non-classical theatre. Lenormand's work, in form as well as in content, is anti-classical. All the same, the classical device of conflict is used in *Le Simoun*. True, the father offers no resistance to the situation, the African sun has destroyed his willpower, but opposition comes from the other characters, the daughter who has fallen in love with a young Arab chieftain, and from a jealous half-caste rival, who kills the daughter after having encouraged the father's incestuous love, in the hope of shattering the girl's romance with the Arab. The last scene, in which the father, tragically freed from temptation, gazes on his daughter's body, hints at a theme which reappears in other plays and which suggested the title of a play he was to write in 1926, *Mixture*, namely, the ambivalence of human feelings and the instability of the moral conscience: the grieving father actually feels relief.

In *À l'Ombre du mal* (Studio des Champs-Elysées-Baty, October 16th, 1924), of which the original was *Terres chaudes*, Lenormand portrays the effect of a tropical climate on the mind and body of a European. The petty injustices suffered during his early years in a lonely all-black community turn the main character, Rougé, into a sadist and immoralist, bent on taking it out of other people. He orders a Negro he knows to be innocent to be flogged, and knowingly lets a guilty Negro escape unpunished. In a discussion between Rougé and his former superior he argues in a cynical manner, even declaring that one protects oneself from evil by evildoing. Meanwhile the shadow of evil lengthens, and the wronged Negro deliberately kills a white woman who goes to his aid. Her death is attributed to the evil demon Goré-Goré; the district officer wonders if it is not the "soul of the Black", or else the very desert itself, which is at the bottom of their evil conduct, and indeed the atmosphere of Equatorial Africa is very successfully created by Lenormand, with its hot, oppressive sun and its tom-toms, portending an imminent outburst of elemental forces. The creation of this atmosphere is the purpose of the play.

The title of *Une Vie secrète* (Studio des Champs-Elysées, 1929), a play published in 1924 but written between 1912 and 1918, aptly defines the main theme running throughout the whole of Lenormand's dramatic production—it is the enigma of the motivation, the mystery that man is to himself. Freudian themes served his purpose in this respect. He attempts in *Une Vie secrète*, as he says in his *Confessions*, "to show that sexual desire and the instinct of artistic creation are one and the same thing". His many amorous liaisons and the artistic benefit he derived from them are carefully examined in the *Confessions*; the element of prostitution in this way of paying for literary inspiration is not forgotten. The musician hero of *Une Vie secrète*, like the dramatic hero of *Les Trois chambres* (Théâtre Edouard VII, 1931), is shown as trying to renew his artistic inspiration through his sexual experiences. The musician becomes artistically sterile when he is dictated to by his conscience, which Lenormand, who was intensely anti-religious, considered to be the scourge inflicted on humanity by Christianity.

By the time these plays were performed Freud's name and theories were beginning to appear in general conversation, and Lenormand's treatment of the subconscious was, inevitably, ascribed to his influence. It appears that Lenormand had no direct knowledge of Freud when these plays, with the exception of *Les Trois chambres*, which is a much later play and dates from 1924, were written. He had been guided in his study of subconscious motivation by writers like Maurice Maeterlinck and Edgar Allan

Poe. It was in the summer of 1918, when he was convalescing in Davos, that he read Freud's works in W. Brill's translation, but the really effective contact he had with Freud's ideas was made through his mistress, Rose Vallerest, who was suddenly taken away from Davos to Küssnacht, for treatment by a psycho-analyst. It is clear from the *Confessions* that many of the details of his play *Le Mangeur de rêves*, which Pitoëff performed in Geneva in 1922 and then on February 1st in Paris at the Comédie des Champs-Elysées, are taken directly from this episode, and, furthermore, that he began to look at it in the light of his reading of Freud. He makes of his main character, Luc de Bronte, the psycho-analyst, "an eater of dreams whose special function is to devour bad dreams and so exorcize the dreamer". During the course of the action he applies the psycho-analyst's method to Jeannine, a former inmate of a mental home—Rose Vallerest is obviously Lenormand's model. His personal antagonism to psycho-analysts, which he makes clear in his *Confessions*, comes out in the character of de Bronte, who is said by the two women who have been subjected to his treatment to be as unbalanced as they themselves were. This and Lenormand's preoccupation with *la vie secrète* adds piquancy to Freud's comment on the play, when he read it some years later. "Hum . . . very witty." Freud may well have been amused, too, by the ambivalence of Lenormand's attitude. The facts de Bronte brings to the surface of Jeannine's mind do not rid her of her anxieties; they kill her; and the catastrophe is precipitated by Fearon, who is a living example of the harm that can be done by such dangerous probing. Fearon, a respectable young Englishwoman, becomes an international crook after de Bronte has revealed the criminal propensities in her, and by the end of the play she is indirectly a murderess, since she gives Jeannine a revolver, knowing full well that Jeannine will use it to kill herself. The psycho-analyst has unleashed elements too powerful for him to control. It is left to Fearon, in discussing de Bronte's desire to destroy as well as help the women he treats, to point to another important theme of Lenormand's, the "mixture" of feelings in the individual and the difficulty of attempting an analysis.

In *L'Homme et ses fantômes*, which Gémier put on at the Odéon on June 11th, 1924, Lenormand offers a new interpretation, both psychological and physiological, of the Don Juan type, here called l'Homme. An abandoned mistress, in a mental home, mistakes l'Homme for a woman. Later the psycho-analyst, Luc de Bronte (who reappears in this play), tells l'Homme that he is a homosexual, a fact which explains his attachment to his father and his hatred of his mother. De Bronte also warns him that he will be inescapably drawn towards mysticism. In a programme note Lenormand stated that at the age of about fifty the libertine turns to the world of "spirits", that the loss of virility and the consequent progressive separation from the real world make him perceive, as signs from beyond the veil, the memories and remorse which trouble his subconscious. In the play itself de Bronte says to his patient: "Believe me, the ... phantoms which your subconscious conjures up will prey on you as much as your mistresses do." After attending spiritualistic seances and throwing down a challenge to what he believes to be the vengeful spirit of a former mistress, Lenormand's Don Juan dies surrounded by the hostile phantoms of his mind, which are materialized on the stage. When he cries out to his friend Patrice to come to his aid one of the phantoms taunts him saying: "You never loved any but him." This was the answer to the riddle of his own nature, which he had sought in vain in each of his amorous adventures.

Lenormand protested several times against the commonly held belief that he had dramatized Freud's theories. To his producer, Gémier,[3] he pointed out that the argument which appears in L'Homme et ses fantômes is not to be found in Freud; Freud never examined the case of the seducer who feels the physical need of love but who at the same time hates the female sex. Nor did Lenormand believe that Freud had examined the relations between the sexual life of Don Juan and occultism. He even asked Raymond Cognat's help,[4] to destroy the legend that he was a disciple of Freud. He did not deny the part psycho-analysis had played in infusing new life into modern psychological methods, nor did he deny that he had been influenced to some extent by Freud's ideas: to Freud he owed his belief in the symbolic value of dreams and the importance which a child's feelings can play in the subsequent development of his emotional life, but these ideas merely coloured his conception of certain characters. His statement is easy to accept as true.

The occult reappears in L'Amour magicien, staged by Baty on November 24th, 1926. The play puts the question of the problematic existence of an after-life and of the possibility of the spirits of the departed speaking through the mouths of the living. The title suggests that the magician working the oracle is love, which directs the working of the subconscious mind. The spectator is left free to choose between the occult and rational explanations. It was precisely the rational explanation of the "possession" which, in Lenormand's opinion, had prevented the play from being a success. As is fitting for a play of this kind, the action takes place on a mist-covered island off the Brittany coast, Ouessant Island, where fog-horns sound continuously and the beam from the lighthouse sweeps the water, and where the people believe in demons of the sea. His "medium" is an impressionable Irish girl in love with her employer, an unstable character and a dabbler in the esoteric.

Le Lâche (Théâtre des Arts, December 1st, 1925), outlined in 1914 and finished in 1918, is, like Les Ratés, a personal work and an attempt to exorcize his own demons. It recreates the atmosphere of a Swiss mountain resort full of invalids, mock invalids, deserters, and spies, which Lenormand, who was in a Swiss sanatorium during the 1914–18 war, and his producer Pitoëff, who was then working in Geneva, were well acquainted with. Paris audiences did not like the play, with its pictures of fear and cowardice, and it had to be taken off after only eight performances. In Berlin and Vienna, on the other hand, its success was undisputed. Le Lâche could have been written as a pure melodrama of espionage and counter-espionage. It is actually an almost clinical study of the origin and development of a neurosis. The play originates in Lenormand's indignant "No" to the war of 1914–18, and his later condemnation of the "artist's No", as nothing more than a sordid concern for his own physical safety.[5] The story is that of a painter who feigns illness to escape military service and is blackmailed into counter-espionage. By feigning illness this hypersensitive artist turns into a neurotic, and his neurosis takes the form of self-accusation, persecution mania, and a real satisfaction in feeling himself despised as a deserter.

In complete contrast to these subjective works, Mixture (Mathurins-Pitoëff, November 3rd, 1927) provides an objective exposition of Lenormand's belief in the conflicting dualism of men's feelings, yet, despite its objectivity, the play is based on personal experience. It is a theatrical transposition of a mother-daughter relationship of two members of a Cumberland family, acquaintances of Lenormand's. As a result of Lenormand's invitation to see the production, the mother, to quote her daughter's words, became

identified with Lenormand's character—that is to say, that the
ambiguous feelings of the mother towards her daughter, suggested
in the play, became a fact in reality. Lenormand recalls another
example of a play of his influencing human behaviour. The young
Argentine actor who took the part of Nico, in *Le Temps est un
songe*, when the play was staged in Argentina, ended his life, three
weeks after the last performance, in the same way as Nico. In
Mixture Lenormand studies mother-love; the mother is self-sacrifi-
cing in the extreme, and at the same time seeks to harm her child,
so as to have a further reason for loving her. This primary
"mixture" of feelings is further complicated by the mother's craving for an exciting life, a craving which she satisfies by becoming a
thief and worse, using the need to secure her child's welfare as a
pretext. Fearon, who reappears in the play as the mother's accom-
plice in numerous crimes, points out the ambiguity of her feelings
towards her child, but the mother does not admit the validity of the
analysis until it is reiterated by the daughter, whose own feelings
also constitute a "mixture".

A visit to Athens to see performances of two of his plays *Les
Ratés* and *Le Simoun*, and to a performance of Aeschylus in the
theatre at Delphi, prompted Lenormand to renew his inspiration
by means of the old myths. On his return to Paris he wrote *Asie*
(Théâtre Antoine, December 16th, 1931), a modernization of the
Medea legend. Another of his mistresses, a Greek woman, was the
model for his Medea. The play was intended to be the third panel
of a triptych which would comprise also *Le Simoun* and *A l'Ombre
du mal*. Racial conflict and the conflict between different civilizations are elements added to the myth by Lenormand. The incompatibility of temperament of a European man and his Indo-Chinese
wife, which causes the break-up of the marriage, and the martyrdom of children of mixed blood, are the two main themes of the
play. The personal conflict is set within the confines of a broader
conflict between two different civilizations. The hero foresees the
rejection of colonialism by the coloured people, and his wife, whom
he has repudiated, prophesies that the exploited peoples will in-
flict a bloody retaliation on the Europeans, using means supplied by
the exploiters themselves. *Pacifique* (Ambassadeurs, October 13th,
1937) covers much the same ground as *Asie* but cannot compare
with Lenormand's modernization of the ancient myth. Like *Asie*,
however, it gives a foretaste of *Terre de Satan*, which, though not

published until 1942, appears to have been written about the same time, and was certainly finished by 1939.

The superficiality of the Christianity of primitive tribes who still listen to the spirits of the jungle is the main theme of *Terre de Satan*. Whipped to a frenzy by the drumming of the tom-toms and the incantations of the sorcerers, they renounce the god of the Whites, the "corpse-god transfixed with nails", for Goré-Goré, the monkey demon of injustice, torture, and all evil. The question is put whether Goré-Goré is not, after all, a more suitable religious ideal than Christ for most of the black people, and whether the Africans were not happier and less depraved before the arrival of the white man, who, along with his civilization, brought the exploitation of the Blacks. The prophecy made in *Asie* becomes fact in *Terre de Satan*, and a fanatical act by one of the converted Negroes is the signal for the general massacre of all Christians, white and black. There are also moral repercussions on the Whites; on the Catholic priest, who comes to believe in the reincarnation of the devil; on Fearon, who reappears in this play to realize her propensities to the full, revelling in the resurgence of barbarism, which she prophesies, renouncing Christ for Goré-Goré, then, seeing the idol burn, dying at the hands of the Blacks, believing in nothing; on the governor of this dangerous outpost in the Gaboon, Le Cormier, whose wife had fallen victim to the Blacks in *A l'Ombre du mal*, leaving him, so to speak, a walking corpse. In *Terre de Satan* he is, as it were, brought back to life by the love of Sister Marguerite, but she chooses martyrdom at the hands of the Blacks, so as not to lose her soul. In addition to the reappearance of two of his characters, there is, in this play, a real orchestration of all Lenormand's favourite dramatic themes.

La Maison des remparts paints a picture of degenerate middle-class life and manners as dark as the picture of the barbarism of the Blacks in *Terre de Satan*. Immediately on its completion in 1936 it was accepted for production by Gaston Baty, who then, suddenly, rejected it, just as rehearsals were about to begin; there was a threat of excommunication not only for Baty but also for his public, and Baty was a practising Catholic. The Church could not accept the prostitute's vision of God. Lenormand, it seems, was not learned in the matter of converted prostitutes and had not provided the right vision! Later, in 1940, the play was billed along with *Mixture* by the director of the Odéon, René Rocher, for the forthcoming season, but, to quote from the *Confessions* (vol. II, p. 97): "If the Church with a Popular Front Government in power, threatens to take offensive action with out-of-date bodies like the Vigilance Committee [which is subsidiary to the Index Committee] it is to be feared that under a reactionary Government it will throw aside all restraint." Indeed, the Beaux-Arts stepped in to prevent the production of *La Maison des remparts*, and Carcopino, the Minister of Education, stopped that of *Mixture*. Much the same thing had happened in 1924 when Lenormand had submitted *A l'Ombre du mal* to the Comédie-Française. On that occasion it was the Minister for the Colonies who had objected. In England it was the Lord Chamberlain[6] who prevented the public performance of Lenormand's works, and this was all the more galling to him as, in many other countries, his plays were considered good enough to put on in the leading theatres, including national theatres. In his *Confessions* he expresses his indignation at being stigmatized in England, along with other serious French playwrights, as an immoral writer, and also at being refused an interview by the Earl of Cromer to discuss the bans.

In *La Maison des remparts* the moribund Channel town, with its silted-up port and confining ramparts, the disintegrating family estate, the mist-enveloped swamps, the seminary which had become a school for sexual perversion, and the "house on the ramparts", a brothel whose inmates are sickened not so much by men's animal instincts as by the sentimentality which makes the men imagine they are more than mere customers for the woman, all combine to create a setting more oppressive than any Lenormand had hitherto conjured up. This merciless picture of middle-class life is, however, lifted out of the realistic plane by Lolita, a Mexican prostitute who is almost a saintly visionary, and by the curious figure of the judge, who, sickened in turn by the drunken, depraved, sadistic men with whom he has to deal, collects twisted roots as symbols of human viciousness, and for contrast marionettes, "naïve, innocent souls", with which he lovingly converses. "Say what you like," observes one of the characters, "a judge who plays with dolls is somewhat disturbing."

Since circumstances prevented him from producing this play, Baty decided to stage the version of *Arden of Feversham*, which Lenormand had prepared at his request in 1929. Baty's preoccupation with what he called *le drame intégral*, was the reason for his interest in Elizabethan drama. Lenormand's interest, so he himself says in his article "Le Théâtre d'aujourd'hui et les Élizabéthains",[7] derives from the fact of Elizabethan playwrights being intent, like modern ones, on sounding hearts divided against themselves. Arden's wife has sworn an oath to kill her husband and feels bound by her oath; yet is horrified by the crime which she has sworn to commit. Such a character is in keeping with Lenormand's own dramatic characters, but at the Théâtre Montparnasse the production created the impression, particularly in the final scene of recriminations between the wife and her lover, Mosbie, chained to each side of the stage, of being a melodrama inferior to those seen at the Ambigu or the Porte-Saint-Martin. The fault lay with Baty, not with Lenormand, nor with the original text, which is that of a domestic tragedy fully integrated into the social life of the period.

Two plays which are rather outside the general line taken by Lenormand are Le Crépuscule du théâtre, staged in 1934 at the Théâtre des Arts, and La Folle du ciel. The idea for La Folle du ciel grew out of an incident with one of Lenormand's mistresses, and the play certainly existed in some form or other before Le Crépuscule du théâtre was thought of. The main theme of this last work is the necessary survival of the theatre, but the action turns on the production of a play within the play entitled "la Mouette", the story of which corresponds to that of La Folle du ciel. This seeming fairy-story, La Folle du ciel, about a heartless troll, a seagull which turns into a woman then back into a gull, in fury at her human husband's failure to keep his promise not to shoot gulls for food, and finally the reunion of the hunter and his bird-wife in death, which takes the form of an ecstatic illusion of escape to happiness—this seeming fairy-story is the tragedy of the married couple who can neither attain the fullness of love nor escape from it. It is also the drama of the human predicament, of our aspirations, of our desperate need to escape from ourselves, to reach out beyond ourselves. This play is much more poetic than Lenormand's other works for the stage. The action is played out in a dream-world, and tableaux fade into one another like dream sequences in a film. The rôle of the creature both bird and woman, torn between conflicting instincts, needs a delicate touch and was convincingly played by Ludmilla Pitoëff, particularly when, a bird once more, she watches her husband with understanding, imploring eyes, and when, bent over a bowl of goldfish, she fights against the unwomanly instinct to snap one up. It was a part made to measure for Ludmilla Pitoëff.

The starting-point of *Le Crépuscule du théâtre* was the complete failure of Lenormand's *Elisabeth d'Angleterre*, in Berlin in 1930, due to what might be termed "theatre politics", to anti-French feeling, and also to the unjustifiable liberties taken with the text by the producer, in accordance with the then current practice in Berlin. This practice is discussed by Lenormand in his *Confessions*, and he refers critically to the methods of Piscator and other German producers. In the second act of his play he satirizes these excesses in the person of his "producer", Professor Putsch, who changes the Author's seagulls and penguins into apes and replaces much of the text with animal cries and gymnastics; he also talks of staging *Phèdre* in three tableaux and with a jazz band. In the third act the Author is back in Paris, where the star's egoistic handling of "la Mouette" had killed the play. Lenormand is criticizing here those Boulevard stars for whom a play is merely a means for showing themselves off. The Author then refers to misrepresentations of "la Mouette" in other countries, and, in a passage which does not appear in the English version, staged at the Mercury in 1938 under the title *In Theatre Street*, expressed Lenormand's bitterness about the fate of his plays in England. On the London stage, says his Author, his seagull play had become "a kind of pantomime with clowns dressed up like white bears turning somersaults on a carpet of snow . . . The Censor was much troubled by the love scenes . . . I had a discussion with a priceless Official; he wanted to know 'what exactly happened between the man and the gull'! My explanations were considered unsatisfactory and the scenes were replaced by ballets." Lenormand gives dramatic representation to every element which militated against the theatre's continued existence, the cinema, the public's preference for sporting events, stars who cut plays to their own measure, but at the end, in complete contrast to the general tone of his whole dramatic output, which offers only a picture of decadence in every domain, individual, social, moral, artistic, Lenormand sounds a note of optimism. His Author pushes aside the final curtain to come out and proclaim to the audience his faith and Lenormand's in the theatre and in its future.

Lenormand's dramatic work, with its probing of the subconscious elements in human conduct, opened up new horizons in drama. Just how new they were is shown by various critics' references, while discussing them, to Freud and Einstein, though it comes as a surprise to see the name of Einstein linked with literature. In any case, there is no didactic intent in Lenormand's plays. They have a marked intellectual content, but they are essentially poetic creations, arising out of his musing on people and on atmospheres, the product of a countryside and its climate. Where Lenormand presents the clash of civilizations, or of contrasting modes of life within a single civilization, the point at issue is not social criticism but psychology, the difference already drawn by Bergson, between the *moi superficiel* and the *moi profond*. Lenormand shows how lightly the one overlays the other.

In the early post-war years Lenormand's dramatic technique was as new as his subject-matter. Like his subject-matter, it bore traces of the influence of Expressionism, and it was doubtless his Expressionism which explains the particular success of his plays in Germany. His first attempts at writing for the Grand Guignol had taught Lenormand the need for developing a theme in action and not just in dialogue, and he had become a good craftsman, but he did not accept the theatrical conventions of the time, the Aristotelian hero, the belief in the carefully built-up coherent structure. The tableau form which he favoured did not, however, arise out of any preconceived notion of renewing dramatic structure by dividing up time and space, but was dictated by the very method of the analysis of the "secret life" which was the subject of his plays. Its purpose was to follow the different stages in the development of a feeling or complex, or to throw light from different angles upon a character and so reveal the *deep self*. His apparently arbitrary selection of unrelated scenes was, in fact, respect for the irrational and chaotic movement of life. There is no question of an "action" with a beginning, middle, and end in the traditional sense. The unity of a Lenormand play is to be found in a theme, a character, a psychological problem, an idea, which the loosely linked scenes portray. It is not to be found in an action. *L'Homme et ses fantômes* offers a very good example of this. The construction of *La Folle du ciel* is unusual in a different way; it has a peculiar, filmic fluidity, similar to that used by some of the post-Ionesco and post-Beckett playwrights nowadays, but whereas the film was a conscious influence for many of these, it was not so for Lenormand. When Lenormand was evolving his own theatrical technique the film was not sufficiently developed as an art form to be able to influence the theatre in any way. Lenormand actually made a number of excursions into the domain of the film and also that of radio, but the pundits who had at first speculated on his name were dismayed by the exceptional and very sombre nature of his themes. In the field of ballet Lenormand was more successful; here his feeling for music served him well.

Because of the scope and quality of his work, Lenormand is by far the most important of the playwrights to concern himself with subconscious motivation, yet none of his plays met with the persistent success enjoyed by SIMON GANTILLON's *Maya*. After an inauspicious start at the Studio des Champs-Elysées on May 2nd, 1924, it drew good audiences for Baty right up to his last revival of the play at the Théâtre Montparnasse in 1948. *Maya* has been translated into some eighteen languages and has been widely performed outside France, though in England it suffered the same fate as Lenormand's plays, and for the same reasons.[8] The action takes place in a licensed prostitute's room in a Marseille brothel. Gantillon is not concerned with the study of the prostitute herself nor does he aim at presenting a series of realistic "slices of life" (this was not the age of the Goncourts' *La Fille Elisa*), though each scene, apart from the atmosphere, which is undeniably poetic, is, on the surface at least, realistic enough. The "slices of life" would better be described as expressionistic. Gantillon is concerned with what each of the men subconsciously hopes to find in the prostitute and, in a programme note, stated that the prostitute is "the plastic matter of man's desire: the caterpillar whose future wings are coloured by every man with the hues of his desire". For the title of his play, he chooses the name under which the Buddhists have deified Illusion, "Maya". The reference is made clear in the last act by a Hindu, a barman from a transatlantic liner, whose hands move unceasingly as they prepare invisible cocktails, and an over-elegant café guitarist, whose fingers idly pick out a tune from the strings. They are waiting for Bella in her room, but when she returns the Hindu closes the door to her and the reality she represents. "No-one has ever found her in this life . . . to see her is to kill her." The final curtain falls on Bella, the docile prostitute, the woman with the thousand faces, patiently knitting by her window, "having fallen suddenly back into the common run of ordinary life", to quote the programme note.

In *Maya* not only the plot but even all action is suppressed.

Gantillon also departs as far as he can from the classical idea of concentration and adopts a formula of apparent dispersal as daring as Lenormand's in *L'Homme et ses fantômes*, which it preceded on the stage by just a month. The function of the eight separate scenes, linked only by the figure of Bella, is to build up a composite picture of humanity straining after an illusion.

Maya remains a classic example of the "escapist" play which was to become so popular in the *avant-garde* theatres in the ten years following the First World War, particularly in the theatre of Gaston Baty. Baty had already staged, the preceding year, Gantillon's first play *Cyclone*, which bears a certain resemblance to Maurice Maeterlinck's early plays, particularly *Intérieur*: it contains little material which can be called dramatic, yet there is considerable dramatic tension in the whole work. A number of clearly individualized sailors are to be seen in the hold of a ship just before and just after a terrible tornado. A man has fallen overboard and been eaten by the sharks, the rest fall a prey to hallucinations which bring out their individuality in a marked fashion: the ship's Negro cook reverts to cannibal instincts at the sight of a golden tress of hair and does the scalp dance, while another sees in the tress a siren which lures him to his death in the sea. In these expressionistic "slices of life" Gantillon had clearly set out to delve into the subconscious in each of his characters.

Two other plays produced by Baty in 1928 and 1932 respectively have not the interest of *Cyclone* and *Maya* but follow the same pattern. A programme note to *Départs*, which repeats what the characters themselves say, states: "It is torture for man to be imprisoned in his body, he tries to escape from it, fails and tries again ... Life must be voluntarily and deliberately transfigured; no-one can do without an alibi." The alibi is, of course, illusion, so, after the make-believe games of their childhood, brother and sister become a sailor and an actress in the vain pursuit of the "divine illusion" that takes us out of ourselves. This attempt to generalize the theme of *Maya* is not a happy one. *Bifur*, which the dramatist and critic, Alfred Mortier, described as "an excellent piece of *avant-garde* drama of 1896"—that is, of symbolist drama—is reminiscent of Lenormand's *L'Amour magicien*. The problem raised in the play is whether there is a life after death, with a possible transmigration of souls, or whether all that happens is caused by the working of the subconscious mind. In speaking of these two plays in his *Confessions* Lenormand said that, like him, Gantillon had learned to his cost the lesson of not applying the yardstick of rationalism to a character supposed to be "possessed". By means of the *mise en scène* Baty, as might have been expected of him, had brought out the element of the occult at the expense of the rational one, materializing the "transmigration of souls" by making two identical figures approach each other from the two sides of the stage and merge into one as they met in the centre in the half-light.

There is nothing experimental about FRANÇOIS MAURIAC's dramas even though his fourth stage-play, *Feu sur la terre*, was produced in a Studio theatre, the Théâtre Hébertot, on November 7th, 1950. The first two, *Asmodée* and *Les Mal Aimés*, went straight into the Comédie-Française in 1937 (November 22nd) and 1945 (February 28th) respectively, doubtless because of his standing as a novelist. The third play, *Le Passage du Malin*, was performed on the elegant Boulevard, at the Théâtre de la Madeleine (December 10th, 1947). All Mauriac's plays adhere to the classical pattern of a crisis, with the whole action consisting of tension between the characters' feelings, in the manner of Racine. Mauriac alluded to the influence of *Phèdre* on him, and declared that he had no difficulty in creating a dominant figure on whose passion the whole plot turned. Freud is another influence, and Mauriac's characters, with their repressed passions, internal contradictions, and very ambivalent feelings, are modern characters. Lenormand's word, a "mixture", aptly describes them. Mauriac's plays offer the same study of secretive souls as his novels; they have the same peculiarly unhealthy "Maurician" atmosphere, and, like many of the novels, are set in the Landes country, with its stifling pine forests, its large, isolated estates, pictured by Mauriac as owned by morally unsound upper-class families.

Mauriac came to the theatre through the Administrator of the Comédie-Française, Edouard Bourdet, himself a dramatist. He persuaded Mauriac to put into a play the figure of the modern Tartuffe which he had then in mind, and to study from the inside, since Mauriac was an ardent Catholic, religious hypocrisy. This Tartuffe, Blaise Couture, an ex-seminarist, is the real Asmodeus of the play,[9] the evil genius of impure love, though it is to the English youth, Harry Fanning, who is intent on getting to know, intimately, a French family in the provinces, that Mauriac gives the name. The play turns on Couture, the sensuous, proud, possessive, hypocritical, frustrated priest. Couture is even more hypocritical with himself than with others, and his professed mission of mounting guard over the purity of Madame de Barthas, a rich widow who employs him as tutor to her children, veils only thinly his desire for the complete spiritual possession of this otherwise unattainable woman. This spiritual possession is more voluptuous and more exclusive than downright physical possession; Couture even dares to talk to Madame de Barthas of the "perfect union of their two souls", and skilfully contrives to condemn her to an eternal and equivocal *tête-à-tête* with him alone. Madame de Barthas's own feelings are no less equivocal, and it is Couture who hints darkly to her and to her daughter at the real nature of her feeling for Harry, and her real reason for trying to promote her daughter's religious vocation and so end her romance with Harry.

Les Mal Aimés, which was written in 1938 and in which the setting counts for less than it did in *Asmodée*, presents, in the apt words of André Rousseaux, a conflict of caged egoists: two sisters, one of them thirty years of age, in love with a colourless young man, and their egoistic father, whose feelings for his elder daughter have something vaguely incestous about them. None finds satisfaction in love or affection because none really knows how to love. The play has no real end because each, neither really loving nor loved, will continue to torture the other indefinitely.

Mauriac's two post-war plays are less interesting. They offer similar pictures of a love which is vitiated at the roots by pride and is no more than the desire for domination, spiritual or physical, of another human being. In *Feu sur la terre ou le pays sans chemin*, in which the vast forests of the Landes country, with their devastating fires, is clearly evoked, a sister seeks, whatever the cost to others, to obtain exclusive possession of her brother. For long enough she believes that what she seeks is purely spiritual possession. She is finally forced to admit the terrible truth to herself. Her brother and her other victims are unnaturally lucid; they all understand the situation perfectly, yet, strangely enough, make little or no attempt to get out of the hell they have created for themselves. Here, as in the preceding plays, the compression necessary to drama serves Mauriac's subjects ill; he is a better novelist than dramatist. Furthermore, psychological drama in which the action is determined by the development of the characters is no longer in tune with the times, and the type of society in which Mauriac sets his

action is fast disappearing. When compared with present-day productions Mauriac's plays appear as museum pieces, belonging to
another age.

Another novelist, ROGER MARTIN DU GARD, approached the
theatre in much the same spirit as Mauriac. The study in his main
play, *Un Taciturne* (Comédie des Champs-Elysées-Jouvet, 1931),
of the relationship between abnormal people, who may not be
aware of their abnormality, and a society which treats them as
pariahs, belongs to the post-war stage; not so the technique, which
is that of psychological drama on traditional lines, traditional even
to the point of recalling, with the final suicide, the early plays of
Henry Bernstein, one of the most successful writers for the commercial stage. The hero, Thierry, like Lenormand's Don Juan, is
unaware of his abnormality, which becomes progressively obvious
to other characters in the play, but when, in an admirably
developed scene, he is made aware of his "aberration", he shoots
himself: rather death than failure to live up to the moral standard
he has set himself. Another character, Wanda, on the contrary,
accepts herself for what she is—a Lesbian. The play implies criticism of an intolerant society but, by committing suicide, Thierry
allows society to triumph, and this in turn implies criticism of the
character.

The subconscious has interested many playwrights to a greater
or less extent, from Jean Cocteau to RENE BRUYEZ. In a number
of plays like *Le Conditionnel passé* (1927) or *La Puissance des mots*
(1928), dealing with an obsession resulting from subconscious
memory, which were performed by small theatre groups such as the
Escholiers, Bruyez was drawn, despite his professed intention, to
delve into the deep self and to attempt to give scenic expression to
what at times is barely explicable in man and the way his mind
works. In later plays he was more concerned with problems of conscience. He finally broke away from these to write a Mystery play,
taking the subject not from the Scriptures but from the life of
Joan of Arc, *Jeanne et la vie des autres*, which was performed at
the Théâtre Municipal at Orleans, in 1938.

The dramatic characters we have mentioned are far removed
from the crystal-clear characters of the old stage, so understandable,
so true to themselves at all times and in all circumstances. The difference is to be ascribed to the direct influence of modern psychology on dramatic technique. Pirandello, whose *Sei personaggi in*

cerca d'autore was performed by Pitoëff, in a translation by Benjamin Crémieux, in 1923, helped to direct and develop existing tendencies, making the current repertory, including Henry Bataille and even Henry Bernstein, seem as much out of date as Augier and Dumas, or Scribe and Sardou. His influence followed that of Bergson, Freud, Proust, and Einstein, who all played their part in the discrediting of accepted norms. The classical principle which, as far as dramatic technique was concerned, proclaimed that once a miser, patriot, or villain, always a miser, patriot, or villain, was no longer acceptable. Characters became fluid, and often a single character was presented as being capable of extremes, extremes of good and evil, for example, and whole plays were built up on the idea of duality and even plurality of self. If in the philosophical domain the old idealism was content to state that the world is what I think it to be, is my conception of it, the new asked which conception of which me, and, as a result, dramatic characters became impenetrable not only to others but even to themselves. The *deep self*, which was the dominating theme of a writer like Lenormand, also interested writers like Jean-Jacques Bernard, whose plays deal with the failure of men's most secret aspirations, and Jean-Victor Pellerin, who constructs his plays on the dissociation, or rather the dispersion, of personality. These last writers are usually referred to as *des dramaturges de l'inconscient* as distinct from the *subconscient*, whether it be that of Freud or of Maeterlinck. They also form what has been called *l'école intimiste* or *l'école du silence*, and will be studied in the next chapter.

NOTES

1. Preface to *Les Confessions d'un auteur dramatique*, 1949, p. 12.
2. P. Gsell, *Gémier, le Théâtre*, 1925, p. 227.
3. Ibid., p. 229.
4. *Comœdia*, June 15th, 1923.
5. *Confessions*, vol. I, pp. 234–236.
6. See also Dorothy Knowles, *The Censor, the Drama and the Film*, 1934, pp. 157–160.
7. In *Cahiers du Sud*, June–July, 1933; a special number entitled *La Scène Elizabéthain*.
8. See Dorothy Knowles, *The Censor, the Drama and the Film*, pp. 144–146.
9. *Asmodée*, performed in English in 1939 as *The Intruder*.

IV

Studio Theatre: The Unspoken

*Jean-Jacques Bernard—Denys Amiel—Charles Vildrac
—Jean-Victor Pellerin.*

"INTIMIST drama" forms part of a current of non-religious mysticism which can be traced back to Maurice Maeterlinck more directly than the drama which professedly deals with the subconscious. The "intimists" aimed at revealing the reasons and motives to which their characters fail to give verbal expression. To do this they invented a technique which led to their being known as the "school of silence".

As far as technique was concerned, their attempt was not without precedent; Maeterlinck's plays had been performed since 1891, and by 1896 he had formulated his conception of "static drama" in the essay "Le Tragique quotidien".[1] Such drama avoided the presentation of material or moral conflicts and so dispensed with the analytical language needed to put over any such conflict. Maeterlinck's aim was to dramatize the very mystery of living, and to do this he exploited the potential expressiveness of the apparently pointless remarks men make, and of silence itself. We only talk, he maintained, when we are not living, and words never express the special relationship existing between two human beings. In 1893 Lugné-Poë, impressed by the dramatic effect to be obtained by the silences in Maeterlinck's work and in the productions at the Théâtre Libre, to say nothing of the mimed plays of the Théâtre Funambulesque, attempted to interest his friends in the idea of a Theatre of Silence, beginning with the production of Maeterlinck's *Pelléas et Mélisande*, which had been turned down by the Escholiers, with whom he was then working. A misconception seems to have obscured what was original in the technique and had been noticed by Lugné-Poë: Emile Faguet wrote to him: "We are back here at Diderot's dramatic theories."[2] But Diderot's conception of action and grouping on the stage, without dialogue, was not the same. Diderot was concerned with the expressive value of acting, or of a "tableau", not with the expressive value of silence itself, and still less with the "unexpressed", the real thought or feeling underlying a remark which seems to have no connection with it. Diderot wanted to express emotions by action without words. The object of the new "school" was to express, or at least suggest, whether by immobility or silence or by casual conversation, the existence of the unexpressed, perhaps of the inexpressible, the "ineffable", to use Gaston Baty's term.

Henry Bataille, as early as 1907, talked of an "indirect language" which would, in fact, be the most usual language of everyday life, but Maeterlinck had already formulated, in his essay "Le Silence",[3] the theory of indirect language, though he had not supplied the terminology. In the essay he actually quotes from Carlyle's *Sartor Resartus* and *Heroes and Hero-worship*, where he found the germ of the idea. The device was not new in drama even then; one has only to read Musset—for example, Marianne's speech to Octave on his choice of wine, in *Les Caprices de Marianne*—to find a perfect example of "indirect language". The novelists, too, Balzac particularly—for example, in *Le Curé de Tours*—had used it.

Shortly after the First World War Les Compagnons de la Chimère, the group which had formed round Baty, systematized the attempt made by Maeterlinck and Bataille to render the unexpressed by indirect language. Other writers, such as Edmond Fleg and Fernand Crommelynck (*Le Sculpteur de masques*, 1908), had also avoided giving direct expression to their characters' thoughts or feelings, though they had not theorized on the matter. The new group considered that too much talking went on on the stage, and that writers should exploit the theatre as the special domain of the "unexpressed". It was not a question of intercalating *silences* between speeches, but of not voicing feelings directly, of letting them be revealed indirectly and involuntarily through dialogue of which the apparent import is very different.

At the head of the group was JEAN-JACQUES BERNARD, though he disclaimed all right to the title of "dramatist of the theory of silence", which was given to him after he made known his views in the fifth number of the *Bulletin de la Chimère* in May 1922.[4] These views were, in fact, an after-thought, written up at Baty's request for the programme, when the play *Martine* was staged at the Mathurins (May 9th).[5] They resulted from Bernard's reflections on his play and did not precede its composition. While he would admit to no theory, Bernard created a new type of play, and the principle behind it was explained again by him later, in 1931, in two articles in *Les Nouvelles littéraires* of April 25th and May 3rd, entitled "De la Valeur du silence dans les arts du spectacle".[6] Silence, he defines, as everything that the characters cannot or will not say, everything that is outside the scope of the words used, which are a very imperfect instrument for the expression of feelings. "Words never say exactly what they say", Bernard declares, but he criticizes the systematic use of allusive language in Maeterlinck's plays. He refused to consider the unexpressed as an aim in itself; nevertheless, he, and the writers grouped round him, did rely greatly on the unexpressed in their work. The dialogue in *Martine* is perfectly lucid up to the point where words are no longer able to render the full force of the feelings behind them. No attempt is made to give the deepest feelings direct verbal expression; they make themselves felt in the interplay of statement and reply. A wordless dialogue runs parallel with the spoken dialogue. Bernard considers "literature" as drama's worst enemy; a feeling which becomes the subject of comment loses its force, and because drama admits only of those feelings which arise out of the circumstances depicted, there is no need to seek to formulate them in words. Psychological analysis does not enter into Bernard's plays; they tend rather to be plays of intuition: it is clear that understanding, for Bernard, becomes synonymous with feeling. Very often, too, the dialogue is not dialogue in the ordinary sense of the word, since the characters follow their own train of thought, answering themselves instead of the other characters, whose remarks act only as stimulants to individual meditation.

Martine is the most typical product of the school of silence. Its scope is narrow and its subject simple. Its value lies in its depth and not in its breadth. There is very little action, only the birth of a hopeless love in the heart of a peasant girl, her silent misery in the presence of the young man and his bride, and her complete moral solitude in her own marriage with a well-meaning but obtuse peasant lad. Martine is well aware of what her feelings are, and so are the other characters in the play, though Martine never finds the words to express them, and on one occasion flees from the room, having tried in vain to speak to the young couple. Her emotions find expression only in her actions. Here, as in the earlier play, *Le Feu qui reprend mal*, and later in *Le Printemps des autres* and *L'Invitation au voyage*, the heroine sadly resigns herself, once the moment of drama is over, to the monotony of a humdrum existence.

After a few attempts to get away from the technique of *Martine* Bernard returned to it in 1935, with *Nationale 6* (Œuvre, October 18th), a play on a similar subject: a great happiness built up by a girl's eager imagination, a rude awakening and melancholy resignation. The same placid atmosphere of provincial life permeates this play as it does the other, but the young country-woman, who learns the meaning of love on meeting a handsome youth, gives place here to an imaginative girl, whose fancy flies after the cars that pass her house on the N.6, the Lyon road, and beyond to Switzerland, Italy, and the Mediterranean. This is not a particularly good play but it has been widely performed outside France. *Martine* has been performed even more widely, and was finally admitted to the repertory of the Comédie-Française on July 2nd, 1947, though its production there could not be compared with Baty's, in 1922. The setting, particularly in Baty's production, emphasized the theme admirably: Martine's meeting with Julien took place under an apple-tree in full bloom, whereas the blossom had all gone from the tree when Martine met Julien's fiancée. In the final scene the monotonous ticking of the clock brought home, almost physically, to the spectator the deadly monotony of Martine's life with her dull-witted husband.

Another variation on the same theme is to be found in *L'Invitation au voyage* (Odéon, February 15th, 1924).[7] The action takes place in a small town in the Vosges, where a rich manufacturer's romantic wife builds dreams round the figure of a very ordinary young man who had gone out to the Argentine. When he returns to France she goes to meet him with the self-induced conviction that he has come to take her away. The dream comes to an end as he talks business to her, just as her husband always did; only the regret of the dream remains.

The theme of *Le Printemps des autres* (Théâtre Femina, March 19th, 1924),[8] the subconscious jealousy of a widow of forty with regard to her happily married daughter, bears a certain analogy with Lenormand's themes. Bernard's dramatic technique is, however, entirely different from Lenormand's. Whereas in Lenormand's *Mixture* the daughter realizes the motives which lie behind her mother's conduct and explains them to her, in Bernard's play nothing is said by either of the two women; any explanation would be unnecessary. Instead there is the following stage direction: "The women gaze for some time at each other in silence and with understanding. Then they embrace and they separate brusquely. Gilberte goes out with Maurice. Clarisse stands motionless . . ." The play finishes on a significant silence. Each act comes to an end similarly, with a moment of silence. The play shows the same economy of movement as *Martine*, the drama being enacted within the characters themselves. The dialogue has the usual casual air, and not one word is said stating the real subject of the play.

This same technique is to be found in the plays which precede *Martine* and the manifesto. In *Le Feu qui reprend mal*,[9] inferior only to *Martine* among Bernard's plays, the dramatist takes as his theme the unmotivated jealousy of a French soldier who learns on his return from four years of prison-camp that an American officer has been billeted in his house. He doubts his wife's fidelity, and his jealousy and suspicion end by killing the love his wife had never ceased to have for him, forcing her at last to turn to the man who, till then, had meant little to her, though he, for his part, had been moved to sympathy, and then love, by the wife's fears for her soldier husband. Another playwright might have ended on a dramatic scene between husband and wife, followed by her departure to join the man she had grown to love. This scene is, in fact, outlined, but Bernard's plays do not end with such fireworks. As Blanche prepares to join the American her aged father-in-law recalls the endless lonely nights of waiting by the fire for her husband's return. "How do you expect me to go now?" she asks, thinking of her husband vainly waiting her return.

Bernard's other war-play, *La Maison épargnée* (Théâtre Antoine, November 5th, 1919), ends in a rather more dramatic fashion. A Frenchman whose house had been spared by the retreating Germans sets fire himself to the house because he senses the attitude of the villagers whose homes have not been spared, "that is the house of a man who put up a Boche officer—Ah! that's the man who . . . Exactly!" Soon it will be "the house of the spy".

From the justifiable and expressive use of silence the author later proceeds to less justifiable extremes. His characters finish up by saying nothing at all. In *L'Ame en peine*,[10] which Pitoëff performed at the Théâtre des Arts on March 18th, 1926, two months after doing it at Monte Carlo, the characters not only do not succeed in expressing their feelings and emotions but are not really conscious of them. Two strangers, represented as being twin souls, never meet because they do not belong to the same social class, but when they come near to each other in some public place they each experience a momentary calm and a fleeting sense of fulfilment; a renewed period of distress begins for each of them as their ways part again. Such a play, in which the hero and heroine never address a single word to each other and only come face to face as one of them breathes his last, offers a dangerous systematization of the principle of silence.

To some subjects, however, the "system" of silence is admirably suited. In *Les Sœurs Quédonec* (Studio des Champs-Elysées, November 20th, 1931) Bernard depicts the emptiness of the lives of two old maids who have looked after three noisy orphans during their vacation. Nothing is said, but the spectator is fully aware of the feelings of these childless women.

Denise Marette (Vieux-Colombier-Jeunes Auteurs, November 20th, 1925), which obtained the Paul Hervieu prize in 1926, represents the first departure by Bernard from his usual formula, and even the stylized realism, typical of the earlier plays, is abandoned for a more straightforwardly realistic presentation. In addition, one scene uses a technical device favoured by many young writers at the time—namely, the materialization, on the stage, of a dream; it is the heroine's dream about her dead father. The play has a certain affinity with Lenormand's work. *Le Roi de Malousie*, which was staged at the Odéon on May 27th, 1928, takes no account at all of the unexpressed, but licentious comedy and satire are not in Bernard's line. *Jeanne de Pantin* (November 26th, 1933), an excursion into the ideological field, with Jeanne as a modern Joan of Arc, as in Brecht's *Joan of the Stockyards*, did not succeed at the Odéon either. Bernard gained nothing by departing from the stylized realism and the "intimism" characteristic of his earlier plays.

Another of Bernard's experiments which, nevertheless, forms part of his "intimist drama", is *A la recherche des cœurs*, first performed in Geneva in 1931, and then in Paris in 1934. Instead of dramatizing the emotional conflict between two people Bernard sets out to put on to the stage a conflict between a man and a crowd, an employer and his employees. After a *volte-face* the employer sides with the workmen against the other employers, and even against himself. He is misunderstood by the workmen, and his devotion to their cause ultimately costs him his life. Yet, despite the theme, the play was not intended by Bernard as a social play in the usual sense of the term, but as a play about feelings. Bernard is less interested in the ideas at stake than in the individuals concerned. The employer's change of heart over the threatened strike is brought about by silent telepathic communication with the workmen's delegate, a Communist, and a former comrade in arms. It is an obvious weakness in a play which presents a social problem that social, political, and economic considerations should be left completely aside. A further weakness is in the presentation of the crowd, which is inconsistent in its attitude, and far too uniform in its reactions. The use of the technique of the unexpressed is clearly inapplicable to a subject like this; direct telepathic communication cannot be established between an employer and his men on what are, in fact, technical problems. A technique which disregards all the instruments for analysis which the literary language has to offer naturally remains on a superficial level, where moral, social, and psychological questions of real importance are concerned, but the skill with which Bernard uses his limited device sustains a certain placid interest.

In *Le Jardinier d'Ispahan* (Œuvre, April 12th, 1939), though he still makes use of significant silences, Bernard causes his characters to utter loud threats and unhesitatingly voice their distress. For the first time there is no deliberate avoidance of dramatic showmanship. The symbolic title indicates that the problem of destiny is the subject of the play; it is taken from an old Persian tale which tells of a gardener who galloped all night, thinking that he was escaping from death, whereas he was actually galloping towards it. In like manner Bernard's heroine, Madeleine, strives to overcome an unfortunate heredity on her mother's side, but succeeds only in bringing about the catastrophe she has sought to avoid. In a season during which sexual frenzy was the subject of many plays in the Paris theatre (there were Peyret-Chappuis's *Frénésie* and Paul Demasy's *L'Homme de nuit*, as well as Lenormand's adaptation of *Arden of Feversham* and a revival of *La Fille Elisa*), *Le Jardinier d'Ispahan* seemed to be pandering to public taste, but the play is

actually taken from Bernard's own novel *Madeleine Landier*, published in 1933. The English version of the play bears the title
Madeleine (1944).

Another exponent of the technique of silence is Guillaume
Roche, known as DENYS AMIEL. He was at one time secretary to
Henry Bataille, and his first plays clearly reflect Bataille's influence.
The text of *Le Voyageur* was offered by Bataille to the director of
the Comédie-Française, Jules Claretie, but the play had to wait for
the inauguration of La Baraque de la Chimère, on May 2nd, 1923,
to be staged. At La Baraque it appeared as a sort of manifesto of the
group. Amiel confessed to having wanted to make of *Le Voyageur*
a systematic demonstration of his ideas; the three characters in the
play talk ostensibly of their work, of a journey to America, but in
reality refer to the situation in which the three of them are
involved. One of them says: "The most insignificant minutes are
perhaps pregnant with emotional stresses . . . People sit calmly talking; their gestures are those of polite, sociable people, and perhaps
deep within them whirl and eddy covetousness, hatred and all the
passions of the ancestral beast." In a letter to the Press Amiel also
stated that "to be silent" did not mean that men did not speak. Men
can be garrulous, and yet maintain an agonizing silence on the very
things which preoccupy their minds. The critics who said that
Amiel's work hid silence under words were right.

In the preface to *Le Voyageur* Amiel quotes approvingly from an
article by Henri Bidou in *Les Débats*. The new developments in the
French theatre brought about by the spread of Freudianism are contrasted by Bidou with nineteenth-century dramas, in which the
characters are as transparent as glass and always express in words
every thought they had. The text of such plays is self-sufficing;
no feeling, no thought exists beyond what is explicitly stated. To
this Amiel adds: "We have progressed beyond the explanatory
drama in which the author suddenly brushes the actor aside, slips
on his costume and comes to the front of the stage to comment
upon the psychology of the characters. Let the characters speak for
themselves, their inconsistencies and illogicalities express their
essential humanity. We have no better claim than anyone else to be
able to explain them."

There is no external action in *Le Voyageur*, only the changing
emotional relationships between a woman and two men. Despite
herself the woman falls again under the spell of her first lover, and

the second, sensing what is happening, slips away unnoticed, leaving the two together. In the meantime the friendship of the two men has come to an end; their bitter hostility makes itself felt through the casual conversation.

Before this long one-act play was actually performed Amiel had written *La Souriante Madame Beudet*, in collaboration with André Obey. No theatre would take the play, which was eventually put on by the Canard Sauvage on April 16th, 1921. Now the play is quite a classic. It was awarded the Paul Hervieu prize in 1922. In 1923 it was staged at the Odéon, and since March 18th, 1935, has been in the repertory of the Comédie-Française. Madame Beudet, a cultured woman, is unhappily married to a goodhearted but insensitive and small-minded businessman. One day she loads the gun with which he has frequently made the joking gesture of blowing out his brains. After a violent scene between the two the bullet is fired, but contrary to her and our expectation he has turned the gun against her, fortunately without fatal results. Only then does her husband understand how much unhappiness her unfailing smile has disguised, and in his generous but uncomprehending way he concludes that she was unhappy enough with him to wish to kill herself. On this last misunderstanding the authors ironically base the couple's future happiness. Underneath and through the trivial conversation unexpressed emotions make themselves felt with remarkable persistency. It is when Madame Beudet is silent and smiles her sad smile that she is the most eloquent.

Le Couple followed in 1923, at the Théâtre Michel, and *M. et Mme Un Tel* in 1927, at the Potinière. These two titles, particularly the second, indicate clearly that Amiel's interest was centred on ordinary middle-class life. The plays are realistic, and the realism is heightened by the use of the technique of the unexpressed, which is, at bottom, a realistic device: though the characters make no attempt to explain themselves, they reveal their feelings in numerous involuntary ways.

In an interesting one-act play, *Café-Tabac* (Montparnasse-Baty, November 8th, 1932), Amiel pushes his technique to the extreme limit. The play presents a realistic picture of a small café in Paris, where groups of customers are to be seen chatting about their own private interests, not one after another, as is usual in a play, but all together if need be. Amiel's purpose, as he stated in the preface to *Le Voyageur*, was to show how men's personal interests isolate them, how wholly absorbed in them they are, and how their horizon is blocked by their professional outlook, even though they may appear to participate in the "simultaneity" of life.

Several other plays by Amiel were performed at the smaller theatres, such as the Théâtre Femina and the Théâtre Saint-Georges. They include *L'Homme d'un soir* (1925) and *L'Image* (1927), a subtle study of the memory's tendency to embellish the emotions experienced in one's youth, a fashionable theme in the theatre at the time. *Décalage* (1931) and *Trois et une* (1932) followed, both providing very light entertainment. Then came *L'Homme* (1934), a more convincing psychological study, and *La Femme en fleur* (1935), which was written for the actress Valentine Tessier, and depicts the unconscious rivalry in love of a woman of forty and her very modern daughter of twenty and the moment of "recognition" of the situation. Amiel said of this play that it conformed to the dramatic formula outlined in the preface of *Le Voyageur*, and he recalled the comparison he then made between a dramatic text and a fish-pond, between human sentiments and the fish that can be seen moving about in the depths of the water and rising now and again to the surface. The epilogue of *La Maison Monestier* (1939) is pure drama of the unexpressed. Here a local gossip visits the Monestiers' home in order to find out the cause of the recent domestic tragedy; the real feelings of the characters, their egoism, hypocrisy, and animosity, are only thinly veiled by the politeness of the drawing-room conversation. The rest of the play offers the twofold study of a woman in love and a middle-class family in which material interests take precedence over personal happiness. Amiel's later plays include *1939* (1940), *Mon Ami* (1943), in which the technique of the unexpressed is used, and *Le Mouton noir* (1946).

Amiel's themes follow in the tradition of the *Théâtre d'amour* of Georges de Porto-Riche and also of Henry Bataille. *L'Age de fer*, which was performed at the Comédie-Française on October 8th, 1932, is an exception, and treats the craze for mechanization and the consequent spoiling of the peace and pleasures of country life. But Amiel is not deeply concerned with ideas, as he stated to the Press at the time of the performance of *La Carcasse* (1926), which he wrote in collaboration with André Obey. His preference was for simple, commonplace subjects—"The more hackneyed a subject is the more it attracts me." It was possibly this preference which drew Amiel towards drama in which thoughts and feelings are not given verbal expression, but are sensed under the very casual conversation. Most of Amiel's plays belong to the commercial theatre by their tone and technique, the "unexpressed" being their sole link with the *avant-garde* movement. The most *avant-garde, La Souriante Madame Beudet*, which also bears André Obey's signature, is also the best. Amiel's theoretical writings also are of interest.

CHARLES VILDRAC took no part in the discussions on dramatic theories, but some of his plays illustrate admirably the technique of the unexpressed. All of them, like the poems and prose essays with which he began his career as a writer, are imbued with the humanitarian ideals of L'Abbaye de Créteil, which Vildrac helped to found in 1906, with Georges Duhamel, René Arcos, Henri Martin, and Albert Gleizes.

His first full-length play, *Le Paquebot Tenacity* (Vieux-Colombier-Copeau, March 20th, 1920), is a minor masterpiece, and can take its place alongside Bernard's *Martine* as a classic of the drama of the unexpressed. As in *Martine* there is no question of the working of the subconscious. All the characters have a clear understanding of themselves and of the situation, but they do not put their thoughts and feelings into words. They frequently lapse into silence, taking stock of the situation, or coming to some silent decision. Bastien and Ségard, two Paris workmen, are dissatisfied with conditions in post-war Paris and decide to emigrate to Canada. The idea is Bastien's. The *Tenacity*, on which they are to sail, is held up a couple of weeks in port, and during this time both of them fall in love with the pretty servant in the little hotel in which they are staying. Ségard, who confesses to living always in the present, draws a picture of the humble happiness of life in a cottage with Thérèse, and in this roundabout way half confesses his feelings. Bastien, who is more enterprising, makes unambiguous advances to Thérèse, but, as she is unwilling to go to Canada, he runs off with her just before the boat sails, leaving Ségard, the timid dreamer, to set out alone for an adventure that fills him with misgivings. Silences and simple gestures give eloquent expression to the feelings of the three characters, and particularly to those of Thérèse, who feels drawn to Ségard even while she is accepting Bastien's advances. The story is quite simple; there is little external action and no attempt at theatrical effect, yet the play is intensely dramatic. It is a touching little work, and there is a refreshing breath of poetry in it. There is also an element of fatalism, which is not to be found in Vildrac's other plays, where the unexpressed plays a less important part. Ségard confesses to Thérèse, when they are discussing the matter of free choice, that it is never he who has decided to go to the place where he happens to find himself. Hidoux, the drunken philosopher, declares when talking with Bastien that to make a decision is merely to follow the course of events, though he admits that one *can* choose if one *dares*, otherwise the course of events chooses for us.

In *Madame Béliard*, which was staged by Jouvet at the Comédie des Champs-Elysées on October 9th, 1925, and then incorporated into the repertory of the Comédie-Française on January 7th, 1936, Vildrac aimed, as in *Le Paquebot Tenacity*, at creating a conflict of feelings with the minimum use of external events and material factors. The action is set in an industrial milieu but, as Vildrac stated to the Press: "The factory in this play is a mere backcloth and the play is not meant as a realistic study of factory life." Vildrac's intention had merely been to point out that in modern times "Passion can rarely be entirely engrossed in itself." The characters' social status is of little importance, since the drama is enacted within them and not around them. The story is that of a factory manager's passionate love for the woman owner, who is incapable of such love, and the sudden recognition by the two of the incompatibility of their temperaments. This occurs when the woman, learning of her niece's love for the manager, clearly considers that she should make way for the niece. Madame Béliard's lover is revolted by her "monstrous kindliness"—in other words, her inability to feel anything deeply—which brings misery to all. The characters' reactions to the recognition of the situation are expressed, not in what they actually say, but indirectly through their silences, their gestures, and even the way they go about their daily life. "It's the mail. . . . He asked me to have a look at it", the niece says to her aunt, getting silently down to work on it after the manager's resignation and departure.

In *La Brouille*, which was staged straightway at the Comédie-Française on December 1st, 1930, the technique employed is not altogether that of *Madame Béliard* and *Le Paquebot Tenacity* because the complicated, psychological situation which is at the root of two friends' quarrel, their subconscious hostility, the repressed

jealousy of one of them, the pride of the other, is gradually eluci-
dated by the other characters in the play in their efforts to reconcile the two. Though motives are brought to the surface in this
play, the characters themselves make statements which refer to the
rôle of the unexpressed in daily life. One of the two friends says:
"In our families and in society, we only reveal the small part of
ourselves which suits all of them together and is directed to none in
particular; that is why we can only appreciate our friends when we
meet them separately." The wife of one of the two maintains that
we only distort certain complex feelings when we attempt to put
them into words, and that they are well able to make themselves
felt on their own.

Previously, on May 14th, 1926, the Comédie-Française had staged
Le Pèlerin, a one-act play in which the unexpressed is important.
The play depicts the last visit to the old family home of a middle-
aged man who is about to emigrate, and the effect on one of his
nieces of his zest for life, which he inherited from his mother, and
the reminiscing of the man and his sister about the past. The effect
makes itself felt in the niece's silent meditation and in the question
she puts about her cousin in Paris. The first of Vildrac's one-act
plays, L'Indigent, written in 1912, was broadcast by the Comédie-
Française in 1952. It is a dramatic transposition of a poem, Visite,
which uses the technique of the unexpressed more effectively than
the play does. Of the visitor to the humble pair, Vildrac writes in
his poem:

> Il s'aperçut qu'on lui ménageait
> Ces silences qui interrogent.

Poucette, written in 1924 and performed twelve years later by
Pitoëff, turns on a secret silently shared by two persons. The play,
of which the theme is regeneration by love, is one of a series which
reflect the Tolstoyan philosophy of the Abbaye to which Vildrac
belonged. Three other plays apply similar techniques to similar
themes—namely, Michel Auclair (Vieux-Colombier, December
19th, 1922), L'Air du temps (Vieux-Colombier-René Rocher, February 22nd, 1938), and Trois mois de prison (Théâtre Monceau,
February 23rd, 1942), an escapist play. All these plays are critical
of contemporary society; in Trois mois de prison a young couple
escape from life in an ugly environment towards a better life on a
barge on the Seine.

Vildrac concentrated his attention on the humbler classes of society because of the opportunity they offered of studying the workings of men's minds and hearts untrammelled by intellectual subtleties. This precluded the choice of exceptional characters and limited the scope of the action in the plays to very ordinary conflicts, unpretentious enough to be hardly dramatic. As a result, his plays give the impression of pictures painted in various shades of grey.

In addition to these plays Vildrac has made a number of adaptations of Shakespeare, Scribe, and others, and has written a humorous political satire, Le Jardinier de Samos (1932), which he took from a tale by P.-E. Lemountey. The best of Vildrac's dramatic work remains, however, Le Paquebot Tenacity.

Deliberate simplicity and realistic observation which are characteristic of the work of Vildrac, Amiel, and Bernard, stem from their desire to recreate a classical art. But a classical art is a natural product of circumstances and conditions, and when these do not obtain a will to recreate classicism can only develop into formalism. The inherent defect of the "school of silence" is precisely this, and the group's lack of contact with a wide threatregoing public in the early years was responsible for the formalistic use of techniques which might otherwise have developed more freely as instruments of dramatic creation.

A special application of the idea of the unexpressed is to be found in the work of JEAN-VICTOR PELLERIN. The second of Pellerin's half-dozen plays, Têtes de rechange, caused considerable excitement at the time it was performed. Its producer, Baty,[11] recalls that the play was referred to as "The Marriage of Figaro of our time", and the performance as the "advance-guard's Battle of Hernani", but, seen in retrospect, Têtes de rechange is clearly not of the calibre to open up a new dramatic era. Like Pellerin's other plays, Têtes de rechange presents the man and the mask, or rather masks, the moi profond and the moi superficiel, and was, at the time, an interesting theatrical experiment, though it pushed the purely cerebral nature of the action to the very limit of what dramatic art allows, and probably beyond. The technique employed here was first used by Pellerin in the one-act play Intimité, which was staged by Baty on April 24th, 1925, at the Studio des Champs-Elysées. It consisted of the materialization on the stage of the thoughts and even subconscious thoughts of a middle-class couple as they sit, the one reading, the other knitting, after dinner. The text consists of the words which the couple address to each other and those which they speak in their minds to the persons of whom they are thinking. These reply with silent gesticulation. As the two retire to bed the husband is accompanied by the "thought" of the maid in scanty attire, and the wife by the "thought" of a muscular boxer she had seen in a match. During the play the thoughts "fade in" and "fade out" in a manner reminiscent of the cinema. In *Têtes de rechange*, which is a curious adaptation of Pirandellism, the multiple personalities of a single individual, all materialized on the stage, provide most of the *dramatis personae* and nearly all the action of the play. Jacques Audiberti used the same technique with success in *L'Effet Glapion*, in 1959. Pellerin's aim is to dramatize the complete disintegration of the personality. Everything, even to the advertisements in the street, is a pretext for his main character, M. Ixe (X), to project himself into the different individuals who are called to his mind, including a policeman and a sandwich-man, and in the last act, to the great astonishment of the waiter, all these phantoms of M. Ixe's mind arrive at the restaurant, where M. Ixe is to dine with his uncle, and seat themselves at table. As his uncle orders a very ordinary menu the nephew conjures up in his mind strange dishes from far-off lands. The mutual incomprehension of two generations is insisted on in this play, just as the complete isolation of the individual is brought out in *Intimité*. The two generations do not think the same way, nor do they speak the same language. The generation of yesterday is represented by the talkative uncle from the provinces: he gets no further than external realities. The younger generation, represented by the nephew, is lost in introspection. Frequently while the uncle, M. Opéku (O.P.Q.), is talking, his nephew's mind flies off at a tangent, directed by a chance word. The word "hatter", for example, calls up the vision of a hatshop, in which M. Ixe, in imagination, attempts to seduce one of the employees, bewilders the hatter with his talk, and then, to the hatter's great concern and his own equally great satisfaction, buys a ridiculous little hat. The triteness of the "spare heads" is a serious defect in the play, turning it into a purely intellectual game.

From Baty's point of view the expressionistic *Têtes de rechange* was the most interesting play which had come his way so far, because the staging forms an integral part of the work, one might even say of the text. Baty even set out to materialize the hero's re-action to the varying situation by means of the setting. In the first act, which takes place in an office, he placed a huge pointer behind the younger man's desk, and, according as Ixe was answering telephones or talking rationally to Opéku or day-dreaming, the pointer marked *Travail, Point mort, Loisir*. The uncle's "slow-motion" speech, as his nephew ceased to listen to what he was saying, was intended to demonstrate that time was not the same for the two characters on the stage.

In *Terrain vague*, which is an attempt to explore the subconscious and give material representation to the findings, the chief character does not sway between various stages of mind, but passes, with one bound, from soulless work to highly irresponsible leisure. Once he is freed from the burden of work and social engagements, the hero's mind, and hence the stage which represents his mind, becomes a *terrain vague*, to be cultivated as he wishes. With such plays Pellerin becomes one of the chief exponents of "escapist" drama and also expressionistic drama. The play was staged by Baty at the Montparnasse theatre on February 4th, 1931. Previously, on May 10th, 1928, at the Avenue, he had staged *Cris des cœurs*. Today the play makes trite reading, but at the time when it was produced it passed for being extremely original. It demonstrates, even more conclusively than the plays already mentioned, Pellerin's complete inability to handle normal dramatic form. It consists of three unrelated parts, first, *Monsieur pense*, which shows the workings of a mind by materializing the thoughts (this was suppressed when Baty revived the play in 1935), second, *La Cage aux hommes*, presenting completely separately, in a house in vertical section, two unmarried students, a newly married couple, a middle-aged couple, a prostitute and her client, all of whom would dearly like to fall in love with someone or other, and are distressed because they cannot do so, all complain of their solitude, and third *Plein Air*, in which the remedy for man's dilemma is offered by the artist. The vision of paradise on which the play ends is in the tradition of the old "Mystery" plays. Pellerin considered *Cris des cœurs* as the counterpart of *Têtes de rechange*. "Each man", he stated in the programme, "may have several heads but he has only one heart. More often than not, if the heads have a good deal to say, the hearts are silent. This time I have tried to make men's hearts speak, but when they break the silence they do not speak, they scream." The characters in the play are not, however, very convincing. Pellerin is using these so-called characters coldly, to put forward an argument. The conception behind *Têtes de rechange* is more interesting, and there is some pungent satire in it, such as the recital, inspired in Ixe's mind by the "Bourgeois Party's" election placard, of the "bourgeois catechism" of a boy of eight. The play dates; it has gone the way of expressionistic drama. The 1964 revival in the Boulevard theatre of the Bouffes-Parisiens made this very clear, despite the ingenious, fluid *mise en scène* designed to quicken the interest. This production provided a complete contrast to Baty's original, static, pictorial production.

NOTES

1. In *Le Trésor des humbles*, 1896, pp. 159–180.
2. Lugné-Poë, *Le Sot du tremplin*, ed. 1931, pp. 223–224, letter from E. Faguet to Lugné-Poë.
3. In *Le Trésor des humbles*, pp. 7–25.
4. Reprinted in *La Revue théâtrale*, 1947, No. VI, p. 278.
5. Performed in English in 1929.
6. Reprinted in *Masques*, 1933, vol. xxv, pp. 20–34. In 1962 Bernard said that he would have been better advised to use the term "the unexpressed" rather than the word "silence".
7. Performed in English in 1937 as *Invitation to a Voyage*.
8. Performed in English in 1926 as *The Springtime of Others*.
9. Théâtre Antoine, by the Escholiers, June 9th, 1921; Comédie-Française, October 18th, 1929; performed in English as *The Sulky Fire*, 1934.
10. Performed in English as *The Unquiet Spirit*, 1928.
11. 1er Cahier, collection *Masques*, 1926, pp. 23–24.

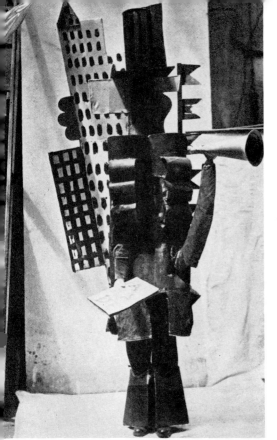

Picasso's costume for Le Manager de New York in *Parade*

By courtesy of Boris Kochno

128

Le Viol de Lucrèce, by La Compagnie des Quinze

Coll. Rondel, Biblio. de l'Arsenal

La Machine infernale
Producer: Jouvet

Photos: Lipnitzki

V

Studio Theatre: The School for Cynicism

*Bernard Zimmer—Stève Passeur—Jacques Natanson
—Armand Salacrou—Paul Vialar—André-Paul
Antoine—André Lang.*

A FILLIP was given to the Paris stage by a group of play-wrights indulging in intellectual cynicism. This cynicism seems to have been a reaction to the confusion, hardship, and insecurity of the years following a war, which Armand Salacrou, one of the group, denounced, on more than one occasion, as "absurd" and "monstrous". The reaction was a spirited one but was not very long-lived, being confined mainly to the twenties. The hard core of the group was formed by Bernard Zimmer, Jacques Natanson, Paul Vialar, and Stève Passeur, together with Salacrou. Passeur and Salacrou have continued to write for the theatre, and the spirit of their work has remained fundamentally unchanged.

The cynicism of BERNARD ZIMMER, the oldest of these writers, is founded on the hostility felt towards contemporary society by a lucid and intelligent mind which, to judge from his plays, found no hope for the future in any political programme. The form which this hostility takes is raillery. In *Les Oiseaux*, for example, which he adapted from Aristophanes, Zimmer's Neptune sorrowfully declares: "I foresee the day when all men will vote ... And then the world, which does not get on too well as it is, will become the defenceless prey of eloquent rascals and shameful promise-mongers." The play was staged by Dullin at the Atelier on January 25th, 1928. Dullin also staged Zimmer's first play, *Le Veau gras* (March 14th, 1924), which was incorporated into the repertory of the Comédie-Française-Luxembourg twenty-seven years later. This series of spirited scenes, showing little concern for logic or verisimilitude, in the manner of Alfred Jarry's *Ubu-Roi*, is eminently theatrical, and assures the play's success today, but when it was first performed its appeal lay in the sarcasm of the social attack, its amoralism, and anti-clericalism. Gaston, the son of a staid, self-righteous village chemist, becomes the gigolo-secretary of a rich, middle-aged duchess who fancies herself as a writer, and has a taste for young males. As he is without news of him and believes him to have got into debt, the chemist sends for his son and prepares to reprimand him. "It is unbelievable that the father of a family should have no redress against an unnatural son who brings dishonour and ruin on him. Look up your books on law and see if some penalty, which we have kept from Roman times, a lengthy term of imprisonment or deportation, cannot be imposed on him." He suffers a complete change of heart, however, when the prodigal turns out to be well-off, and, with an eye to the profit to be derived from the unexpected turn of events, defends the boy against his law-abiding elder son. The local *curé* is also prepared to receive money which, he has every reason to believe, is the reward of vice. The most brutal moment in the play occurs when a postal official, commenting on the fact that the father has fewer clients than of old, says: "You have two sons and neither was killed or even wounded in the war. What can you expect?" To this the father replies that he would rather one of them had been killed: "The Prefect himself would have come to see us ... we should have been held in high esteem ... I would have been on the Town Council. What a pension we should have got from the Government! Colle's son was blown to smithereens at Verdun and just look what a lot of customers Colle has got as a result, and he's only a second-class chemist!" Zimmer similarly attacks the Ministers of Justice, none of whom dared to accept a charge of blackmail against a certain Grussgott, because Grussgott knew the special skeleton that each had in his cupboard. The arrival of the duchess, with wreaths for a funeral, adds gusto to the movement of the play, as does her departure, when she learns that her young "secretary" is carrying on with another woman. With her goes the young man's rosy future.

Les Zouaves (January 26th, 1925) exploits the same vein and was also staged by Dullin at the Atelier, but it is not the clergy, the magistrature, or "la patrie", the usual "legitimate" targets for satire, that bear the brunt of the attack; it is the war profiteers and racketeers of every kind, and such a theme proved to be unpopular. One of the main characters, the president of a patriotic society called Remembrance, has taken care of the soldiers' health during the war by dealing in tin hats, of their comfort by dealing in mess tins, and of their morale by dealing in military crosses. The police come in for their share of the satire. When the profiteer exclaims: "What! An illegal arrest?" a gendarme replies: "This is a Republic. To make illegal arrests and use your truncheon on May Day are the first principles of the profession." Into this picture of insolent and ruthless bluffers and rogues is woven the story of a war hero, an invalid, who is mercilessly trampled on by these *zouaves*, as he calls them when they have finally driven him insane.

In both these comedies Zimmer shows considerable acumen in his observations of society and makes skilful use of caricature. In *Bava l'Africain* (Comédie des Champs-Elysées, May 3rd, 1926) the caricature is less marked, and Zimmer's humour, though still caustic, is less aggressively so. The play presents a good picture of provincial manners, and into the picture is woven a philosophical theme favoured by many of the younger dramatists—namely, the superiority of the imagination over reality. In addition, the play has a distinctly Pirandellian flavour. Bava, who reminds one of Tartarin, is a lawyer's clerk, and is so soaked in books on the Brazzaville expedition that he finally convinces not only others, but also himself, that he is the hero who said to Stanley and his men at Zanzibar: "Foutez-moi le camp." The villagers, who listen to his tales of the expedition in the café, are united in something like an "unanimist" collective being, but the spell is broken by the arrival of a man who really had been in the expedition. This man's authentic but uninspiring account soon bores the villagers, and they regret the fascinating fabrications of Bava. A travelling journalist who "discovers" the "forgotten explorer", and makes a name for himself by the "discovery", provides the cynical touch usual in a play by Zimmer. The doctor, who appears in the second act, provides another. He states that Bava is a mythomaniac, and adds: "If you wish, I can officially declare him to be a madman tomorrow, and without examination." As performed, the play ended with Bava renouncing the award of a journey to the Congo, which he had won in a colonial competition, and settling down in the village to married life with Madame Soin. The written text has a less commonplace ending; Bava falls ill, and before he can be arrested as an impostor he dies, convinced he is the true Bava, and asking Madame Soin to "share his glory". "This is the first time I have died in my bed", he says. Following the line taken by many of the younger playwrights, Zimmer seeks in this play to get away from the crystal-clear characters of the older stage and to create a character who is a riddle to his fellows and to himself. The part was admirably played by Jouvet, who had specialized in acting eccentric dotards since his success as Filliâtre-Desmelin in Georges Duhamel's L'Œuvre des athlètes (1920).

Jouvet went on to stage, on March 28th, 1928, Zimmer's Le Coup du 2 décembre, a cruel caricature of the provincial middle-classes, particularly the representatives of the Law, the University, the Army, and the Medical profession, together with their ladies. The action of the play, which begins as a rumbustious farce, turns on the mistaken belief that a boy of seventeen is the father of the family maid's child. The play ends with the horrified boy sobbing over lost romantic illusions, as the result of the advances to which he had been subjected by all the women who were ostensibly attempting to "save" him. This change of tone spoils the play: Zimmer was trying to kill two birds with one stone.

With Pauvre Napoléon, which was produced at the Comédie-Française on April 15th, 1929, and which recounts an episode during Napoleon's captivity in Saint Helena, Zimmer completely abandoned his caustic style to deal gently with a great man who has become an object of pity, but Le Beau Danube rouge, which Baty staged on April 22nd, 1931, during his first season at the Théâtre Montparnasse, marks a return to the sarcasm of Zimmer's earlier works. The play was inspired by a film-producer's advertisement in Paris for Russian officers, in uniform, and seems to echo deliberately Lenin's belief that the cinema was the most important of the arts for moulding the destiny of a people. Zimmer's hero terms the film "the art of the future . . . a formidable weapon in the hands of future democracies". In the play a number of former Hungarian officers, then in straitened circumstances, are to be seen acting a film of revolutionary propaganda. Their reactions to the criticism directed in the film against the old regime provide the dramatic action. Zimmer himself castigates both regimes. He exactly balances revolutionary and reactionary tirades, and closes the play with the comment by one of the characters on the flight of the hero, Bela Kun, after his brief spell of power: "He has hopped it just like a king."

Zimmer's work for the theatre includes an adaptation of The

Merry Wives of Windsor, but in 1932 he deserted the theatre for
the cinema. He cannot be considered to be among the best dramatists of his time, but his work is historically interesting for the
forceful expression which it gave to the dismay felt by many at
certain aspects of the post-war era. The dramatic form which was
used was broad farce and outsize caricature, highly reminiscent of
Alfred Jarry.

The most impenitent of all the cynics is STEVE PASSEUR. His is
also one of the most important names in the theatre of the inter-
war years, though he never wrote the masterpiece that his first
plays seemed to promise. His dramatic work is based, much like
that of Georges de Porto-Riche, on the cynical observation of men's
egoism in their search for individual happiness, and might well bear
the same collective title as Porto-Riche gave to his plays, *Le Théâtre
d'amour*, but the closest link seems to be between Passeur and
Henry Bernstein, with whom he has been frequently compared.
As in Bernstein's early plays, the situations and characters
imagined by Passeur are pushed to their extreme limit, and one is
confronted with a series of frenzied perverts of one kind or another,
demoniacal characters, with a genius for doing ill and causing
suffering to all around them. But whereas the brutality of Bernstein's heroes stems from their rejection of civilized conduct in
favour of instinctive behaviour, that of Passeur's characters has an
intellectual basis and results from careful thought about the best
means of bringing pressure to bear on one's intended victims.
Passeur has, in fact, achieved what the producer Lugné-Poë, and
also the surrealist poet and actor Antonin Artaud, had had in mind
—namely, *un théâtre de la cruauté*, though Artaud's conception of cruelty is far removed from the devilish refinement to be
seen in Passeur's plays.

The title of the play which Pitoëff staged on June 4th, 1935, at
the Mathurins, *Je vivrai un grand amour*, sums up the theme
which runs through Passeur's dramatic work and is stated in almost
identical terms in many of the plays. At the beginning of this particular play the heroine Claude declares: "I shall live a great love
or I shall not live at all", and towards the end her fiancé Camille,
who had deserted her to marry a woman who could serve his interests better, says to Claude: "Now that I have made you realize that
I shall never stop loving you, I feel that I have come to life again."
Life and love are equated in Passeur's plays, usually by the heroines.

One of the first to equate them is Fanny, the prostitute heroine of *Pas encore* (Atelier, February 3rd, 1927), who is forty-four years old; she begs her former protector, Remantil, a powerful business-man, not to wreck her lover's career, but to allow her to live out this last love with him to its natural conclusion. "I know now", Fanny says, "what is the real value of love. It is the only thing that matters . . ." In *Les Tricheurs* (Atelier, January 30th, 1932) it is an ill-favoured Jew from Smyrna, called Luckmann, who decides to "live a great love" with a woman to whom he knows he means nothing. For this "great adventure" he has two hours at most, the two vital hours of sheer happiness which men and women attempt in vain to prolong through the years. It is enough for Luckmann that, while he himself trembles with desire before the woman he loves, she should be brought to believe in the sincerity of this love. Physical possession is rigorously excluded by him as certain to des-troy the illusion he believes love to be. He even tells Agathe that she herself plays no part in his marvellous experience; she is only a "mirror; it is to oneself that one really says 'I love you'".

In *L'Acheteuse* (Œuvre, April 7th, 1930),[1] Passeur's first play of importance, and the one by which he may well be the most readily remembered, love is already equated with life. When speaking of the man she had loved, Elizabeth, an undistinguished spinster who lives quietly in a country house, says: "I thought that in his eyes I really existed. Yes, that's it, it was that more than anything, I was in fact a real person." Love is also equated by Passeur with hatred. Within an hour of the marriage she has made for love, Elizabeth becomes a Roxane. Her love is turned to hate by her husband's attempted departure with his mistress, and by the humiliating taunts he throws in her face. She had dreamed of a perfect union in which her husband would be her "master"; when disillusioned she sets to work to tame the recalcitrant husband, whom she has "bought", by paying his debts for him. She makes him into a slave and, worse, a marionette that will dance as long as she pulls the strings. But Gilbert has his own method of enslaving his wife and taking his revenge. When circumstances finally release him from his wife's power she takes her own life; with love and hatred both gone, she finds no point in living.

L'Acheteuse is the perfect example of the "cruelty play"; it combines both Sadism and Masochism. Gilbert has grown fond of his debasement and Elizabeth knows it, whereas Gilbert knows that

Elizabeth is the first to suffer from her cruelty to him, and that her cruelty is, in fact, directed against herself. When he is freed he makes no attempt to leave her. He taunts Elizabeth, saying: "I have stayed to make you suffer", to which she replies: "No, you stayed to suffer a little more." He has to be dragged away by his father. Suffering, torture, cruelty, are words which come readily to the mouth of Passeur's characters; they speak of their own suffering or cruelty, or of that of other characters. Elizabeth discovers in herself a fund of cruelty which time would not easily exhaust, and she owes this discovery to Gilbert. She also owes him her discovery of the meaning of power. "Never perhaps in our time has a woman had such absolute power over a man", she exultingly tells him, and this discovery is not to be regretted, whatever the price, in suffering, that has to be paid for it.

In one significant scene in *L'Acheteuse*, after she has declared that she will have Gilbert shot if he attempts to escape, Elizabeth falls weeping into her father's arms, wondering whether she is indeed a worthless pervert, *une vilaine fille*. This scene makes the character of Elizabeth more theatrically acceptable; it also underlines one of Passeur's favourite themes. Fanny, in *Pas Encore*, had already referred to herself as *une vilaine femme*. She is blatantly unfaithful to her protector, declares a merciless war on her young niece when she discovers a rival in her, and, in fact, plays the tune for all the other characters to dance to. When Passeur wrote the final version of this play he entitled it *Une vilaine Femme* (Œuvre, December 12th, 1932), giving a generic name to the type of woman who figures so largely in his plays. Fanny was followed by Suzanne (*Suzanne*, Comédie des Champs-Elysées-Jouvet, January 31st, 1929), a man-tamer like Passeur's next heroine Elizabeth, but with a special taste for brutal, oversexed men, by Armance (*La Chaîne*, Théâtre Antoine, April 17th, 1931), a Cinderella who becomes a ferociously sensual egoist overnight, and a number of others.

Passeur's characters are always in the position of adversaries. They seek to dominate each other, and openly "declare war" on each other. Agathe, in *Les Tricheurs*, attempts to force Luckmann to capitulate, and to aspire to be her lover in the full sense of the term, by herself becoming a servant or slave to him, while she watches for the slightest sign of weakening in him. In *Je vivrai un grand amour* two women, Claude and Dominique, engage in a deadly duel over Camille; when Camille marries Dominique they become as bitter adversaries as Dominique and Claude had been. Two out of the three acts of *Le Château de cartes* (Athénée-Jouvet, January 8th, 1937) offer a long "verbal boxing-match" between Milouette and her former husband, a brutal captain of industry, who declares that so far he has merely wanted to *make* his ex-wife suffer, but that what now delights him is to *see* her suffer. For her part Milouette confesses to him that she has loved him because he is a scoundrel whom she has to conquer fifty times a day. Remantil, Fanny's protector in *Une vilaine Femme*, is a similar brutal type, and is most brutal, not when he uses physical violence on Fanny, but when he tells her that her love life is obviously at an end, since she has been reduced to "paying" her last lover. He, too, is happy to make Fanny suffer. In *107 Minutes* (Montparnasse-Jamois, September 29th, 1948, the title of which is taken from the familiar expression "107 ans", the two adversaries are sisters, one becomes the wife and the other remains the mistress of the same man. This man is a typical Passeurian hero, a will-less creature, who allows himself to be tossed backward and forward between the two women, just as Gilbert had been between Elizabeth and his mistress, or Camille between Claude and Dominique. Such male characters seem to take pleasure in their suffering and in their abasement. They are Masochists, whereas Passeur's women characters are chiefly Sadists. As a result, there is often no real conflict in Passeur's plays. There is a situation, and the characters react to it according to their different temperaments. *L'Acheteuse* illustrates this admirably. Such conflict as there is takes place between those who torture and those who suffer, or rather, the torturer or group of torturers, as in *N'importe quoi pour elle*, is opposed to the victim or victims. There is no inner conflict within the character to give rise to his cruelty. If Elizabeth reveals herself to be a Sadist it is directly after the discovery that, so far as Gilbert is concerned, she simply does not exist. To find a real conflict one must look to *Je vivrai un grand amour*, where the two women engage in a merciless duel for the possession of Camille.

The action of *N'importe quoi pour elle* (Théâtre Gramont, March 19th, 1954) consists of a whole series of verbal jousts between the torturers and their victims, and also between the victims themselves. Passeur, however, introduces a new kind of torture into this play, physical torture, though the torture does

not take place on the stage nor is it actually applied to one
of the characters in the play. The play, like *Je vivrai un grand
amour* and *La Traîtresse* (Ambigu, March 9th, 1946), has a historical setting. In *N'importe quoi pour elle* the struggle between
the supporters of Condé on the one hand and Mazarin and the
young Louis XIV on the other provides the background of
the action and explains how it is that in a final attempt to make the
heroine, who is rightly suspected of having assassinated Gaston de
Chatelinaud, confess to the murder, she is forced, by Gaston's
brother, to watch the beheading of a woman spy off-stage. Such a
procedure belongs to the domain of melodrama, but it gives rise to
the best scene in the play; the heroine, who, so far, has been self-
possessed and even arrogant in the face of the danger, breaks down
and declares wildly that she can no longer answer for what she
will do to escape a like fate, and that fine sentiments and fine
phrases are nothing beside life and love. Passeur may well have had
Kleist's *Prinz Friedrich von Homburg* or Sartre's *Morts sans sépul-
tures* in mind, and comparisons with these plays have been made,
though only in general terms, with reference to the main character's moment of passing weakness and the introduction of physical
torture. But comparisons must be more precise to be of any interest.
One could point to the heroine's lover, Daniel, who maintains, in
true Sartrian fashion, that once a course of action is decided upon,
the consequences of that choice must be accepted in full, or to the
heroine herself, who in this scene illustrates the point which is
fundamental in Sartre's play—namely, the problematic existence
of free choice in the face of torture. The question which Sartre declared he was debating in *Morts sans sepulture*, which was not intended by him as a play on the Resistance movement as such, was
how would a man who has acted like a hero have acted under torture? This is not Passeur's main theme, which is the living of a
great love, but his momentary posing of the question gives a good
twist to the plot and adds to the humanity of the heroine. In the
last act she finds, in her knowledge that she will be dying in the
king's cause, the strength to face her own execution with dignity.

There is a distinctly Cornelian grandeur in the sentiments of the
hero and heroine and in those of the heroine's rival, Faustine, just
as there is in the sentiments of Passeur's earlier heroine Claude, in
Je vivrai un grand amour, when she surmounts her own desire to
keep the fiancé who has returned to her, and sends him away, so as

to ensure that her great love, unsatisfied though it is, shall never
come to an end. It is in the same spirit that Luckmann, in *Les
Tricheurs*, refuses Agathe when she finally offers herself to him. In
N'importe quoi pour elle the love of the hero and heroine is a satisfied love, but a similar element of renunciation enters into it; it is
because they will certainly both be condemned to death that Daniel
"decides" to fall in love with the heroine. As time is short their
love will remain beautiful to the end. These characters and others,
even such as Elizabeth in *L'Acheteuse*, are certainly heroic, but
their heroism is directed towards themselves and not towards any
higher good. They are classical in their lucidity, which shows in
their discussions with each other and in their analysis of their own
motives. Passeur's women characters, particularly, are clear-headed,
intelligent; their "marvellous intelligence" or their "lucidity" are
often commented on by the other characters. They are also strong-
willed. Luckmann and Daniel, who resemble them, are exceptional
figures in Passeur's gallery of male portraits. Passeur's whole
approach to his characters is nearer to that of the seventeenth-
century dramatists than it is to that of his contemporaries, with
their concern for social status and social background. Passeur's
characters are timeless, and so the girl and her aspirations, an old
maid and her disillusionment, a woman on the decline frantically
repeating "Not yet", or who remains obstinately attached to a man
she knows to be unworthy of her, may be placed equally well in a
modern or a historical setting. Besides being true to life in this
timeless way, Passeur's main characters are also exceptional characters, though sometimes to the point of being almost pathological;
this detracts from their permanent validity.

Passeur's insistence on the lucidity of his characters and on
their determination to suffer or make others suffer tends to detract
from their humanity and to make of many of them purely theatrical entities. The impression of cruelty which they appear to wish to
give is too deliberate, and their verbal fencing-matches too clever
for there to be room for real feeling behind it all. The cynical
amorality of so very many of the characters, such as the coldly
deliberate liaison of a divorced couple who come together again
with no thought for the feelings of their partners in their new mar-
riages (*Le Château de cartes*), or the equally deliberate liaison of a
man and his wife's sister (*107 Minutes*), strains the credulity of the
most hardened theatregoer. The strongly theatrical element in

Passeur's plays makes of them a superior type of Boulevard play, and Passeur's acknowledgment of his debt to Marcel Pagnol, who alone, in his opinion, knew how to write a play, indicates how near Passeur came to being a Boulevard dramatist. It was Pagnol, so Passeur said, who taught him that attention must not be divided among four or five characters, but concentrated on one of them, and that everything in the others which does not help to throw the main characters into relief must be sacrificed. Passeur admits to lengthy reflection on the mechanics of play-writing. The cut-and-thrust of his dialogue is purely theatrical, and so, too, are the situations in which the characters find themselves. Many of the means used are flagrantly melodramatic, such as the revolver which prevents Gilbert from running away. The revolver, moreover, is in the hands of Elizabeth's faithful retainer, whom she had formerly saved from prison. Passeur's first acts are extremely forceful and are usually outstanding technically. His working out of the initial situation rarely attains the level reached by the first act: in *Une vilaine Femme*, for example, the violent and gripping conflict of the first act gives place, in the succeeding acts, to a slow analysis of a woman's feelings, and, as always in Passeur, many arbitrary twists are given to the action and even to the character development. In this same play a nice young man of twenty-eight suddenly declares his love for a woman in her forties who has led a notorious life, and in *L'Acheteuse* it is difficult to reconcile Gilbert's warm words of welcome to Elizabeth in the first act with the hatred he spits in her face after he has seen his former mistress. This frequent use of arbitrary developments probably results from Passeur's conception of a good play as being one in which something happens every five minutes. Passeur recently declared that chronicles and detective novels are now his favourite reading matter, and that he prefers Agatha Christie to Paul Claudel, who bores him, and whom he finds incomprehensible. His own unconcern for style adversely affects many of his plays, though *Je vivrai un grand amour* is an example of the precise, forceful writing of which he is capable.

Passeur has been writing for the theatre since 1924, and twenty of his plays have been put into production. Some, like *Défense d'afficher* (1930) and *L'Amour gai* (1933), are too cynical to attain credibility. *Le Témoin* (Œuvre, December 20th, 1935) is much more palatable, despite the number of suicides in it. It differs somewhat from Passeur's usual type of play by raising a general question—

that of the responsibility of a witness who subconsciously wishes the events to take the tragic course which they actually take. Similarly, *Le Marché noir* (Édouard VII, April 29th, 1941), which touches with cutting irony on a topical theme—the black market during the German occupation. The play, nevertheless, preserves the general line of Passeur's plays; his dramatic "formula" has not changed with the years. His characters' sole preoccupation continues to be love, and their one concern is to overcome any obstacles to it. The conflict which his plays present is thus a purely personal conflict, and it takes place strictly in private. Such plays are not in tune with the second post-war era, when other passions and other problems have taken the stage, but Passeur's penetrating psychological analysis and skill in dramatic handling have given lasting interest to *Une vilaine Femme, Les Tricheurs, L'Acheteuse,* and *Je vivrai un grand amour.* The two last have established themselves as minor classics: *L'Acheteuse* went into the repertory of the Odéon in 1933,[2] and *Je vivrai un grand amour,* after a difficult start, has been the most continuously successful, having had seven revivals up to 1947. It avoids the defects of the earlier plays, and, by its entire reliance on the psychological development of its characters for its action, is much more classical in line. This seems to me to be Passeur's best play, though many give first place to *Les Tricheurs.* Antonin Artaud considered *Les Tricheurs* to be a model of its kind. The theme of this play is worked out fully in the first two acts, which are good, but as the situation at the end of the third act is the one already reached at the end of the second, the third act is, in fact, superfluous. *L'Acheteuse* is a gripping play, but is not free from blemishes, such as the arbitrary elements in the character of Gilbert, his surprising *volte-face,* and also the melodramatic touch given by the revolver in the hands of the faithful retainer. With all his plays Passeur offers the public strong meat, but it is not tainted meat, despite the frank cynicism of so many of the characters. Keen intelligence, pointed retorts, and dry humour are characteristic of his work and have caused French critics to compare it with G. B. Shaw's, though it is doubtful whether these critics would ever have invoked the name of Shaw had Passeur not been Irish on his mother's side. His father was French, and Passeur, whose real name was Morin, was born in France, at Sedan, in 1899.

JACQUES NATANSON was born in 1901. He belongs to the generation whose adolescence coincided with the troubled years of the war, and it is to this generation that he refers specifically in his early plays, which depict the disillusioned precocity of many of their number, their affected callousness, and their utter unscrupulousness in their dealings with the opposite sex. Natanson's main theme is love, and his analyses show considerable perspicacity, despite his obstinately cynical approach. The distress caused by inexperience in sexual relationships is the subject of his first play, L'Age heureux (Œuvre, January 22nd, 1922). The desire to hurt because one has been hurt is a secondary theme, and Natanson develops this theme more fully in L'Enfant truqué, which followed in the same theatre on October 10th. This strange title refers to a boy whom an embittered father attempts to turn into a hardened cynic, so as to protect him against the disappointments he has himself suffered in love. The experiment fails; the boy's true nature asserts itself, and he loves and suffers in turn, as his father had done.

Such slight concern with the social status of the characters as Natanson had shown in L'Age heureux disappears in L'Enfant truqué, and the principle is carried still further in Les Amants saugrenus (Théâtre Femina, October 3rd, 1923), in which he strips his characters even of their names. The two "preposterous" lovers who figure in this play are convinced by their former experiences that physical possession kills love, and that love can only exist between two lovers intelligent enough not to become "lovers". The action of the play consists of their attempt to live up to their conviction and their failure to do so. This attempt is accompanied by considerable discussion of their feelings and of the nature of love itself, and ends with their acceptance of the intimacy against which they had at first rebelled.

As a stage play Le Greluchon délicat (Théâtre Michel, January 23rd, 1925), which was successfully revived in 1953, is by far the best Natanson has written. It is more solidly constructed than the preceding plays and belongs rather to the Boulevard than to the experimental theatre. There are certain similarities between the play and Courteline's Boubouroche, but Natanson complicates the plot by making the woman's elderly lover take to the cupboard, in his turn, to make way for his young rival. He prefers to do this rather than be rejected altogether. For her part, the young woman mistrusts the "love in a cottage" proposed by her youthful admirer, who had been prepared to deceive the older man, but whose "delicate" susceptibilities will not allow him to agree to the older man's suggestion that they should share the lady's affections. This is an old-fashioned type of plot, but it is well worked out and the characterization is good. The characters are only given christian names, but their social status is indicated, and even their financial position. When first seen they are brilliantly gay, but later, and rather surprisingly, reveal themselves to be capable of deep feelings.

The dialogue of *Le Greluchon délicat* is very different from that of Natanson's earlier plays, in which the repartees are clipped and short, and many of the scenes are nearly devoid of real conversation, the characters' utterances being reduced to a series of inarticulate exclamations. In *L'Enfant truqué* no speech exceeds six lines; in *Les Amants saugrenus* the idea of indirect dialogue, developed by Jean-Jacques Bernard, is worked to death, and the laconic incoherence of the characters becomes wearisome. This short-windedness, and the constant darting from one subject to another, is, of course, not peculiar to Natanson. In the post-war era of "bright young things" a certain inarticulateness was as fashionable in France as it was in England. When he came to write *Le Greluchon délicat*, however, Natanson more or less abandoned the use of monosyllabic replies and indirect language and made his characters speak more naturally and at greater length. Yet the repartees lost none of their brilliant sparkle, and the witticisms came just as readily from Natanson's pen.

This series of strangely titled plays, each with an unusual adjective qualifying the noun in the title, to indicate the unusual stand taken by the hero or the hero and heroine, comes to an end with *L'Infidèle éperdu*. The play was performed at the Michodière ten months after *Le Greluchon délicat* was staged and marks Natanson's unmistakable translation to the Boulevard. It tells the strange story of a husband who wrongly suspects his wife of being unfaithful, and who sets out to make conquests himself, once he is reassured about his wife's fidelity. The following plays are similar in theme and treatment, and make good simple entertainment, devoid of the irony of Natanson's earlier and more interesting plays.

It was not until 1934 that Natanson produced anything further of interest. With *L'Eté*, performed at the opening of the Nouvelle Comédie on October 2nd, Natanson widened the scope of his work by linking the fortune of his characters to the country's economic fortunes from the time of their engagement on Armistice Day, when the hero, like Natanson himself, was eighteen years old. The repercussions of fifteen years of economic instability on the couple's personal relationship is the subject of the play, which ends arbitrarily, with harmony being established between the husband and wife by the threat of a world war. Here, as in his first plays, the restlessness of the post-war generation is well portrayed, and also the difficulty experienced by the older generation in adapting itself to the complex modes of existence of modern times. His plays had shown that Natanson was a clever writer of dialogue, and in the middle-thirties he stopped writing plays and began to write dialogue for films. He also wrote a number of radio plays, but it is for his first portrayal of the *greluchons délicats* of the twenties that Natanson can best claim to be remembered.

ARMAND SALACROU's use of language offers a complete contrast to Natanson's. The use in the theatre of the language of everyday conversation, the "bafouillage sténographique avec points de suspension", as he called it, was sharply criticized by Salacrou. This, together with his approval of Jean Giraudoux's manifesto in favour of the imperfect subjunctive, which he termed the "only *préface de Cromwell* in the last twenty years", reveals his own conception of dramatic language. All his plays use the literary language, his early plays are blatantly "literary", the later ones more subtly so.

Immediately after the production, by Lugné-Poë in 1925, of *Tour à terre* (Œuvre, December 20th), the first of Salacrou's plays to reach the stage, Salacrou saw himself classed as a "cynic", but his cynicism has a very different ring from that of a Natanson or a Passeur, despite certain resemblances between some of his works and theirs. Salacrou's cynicism is the form taken by his pessimism, which is radical. In his autobiographical essays, as well as repeatedly in his plays, he expresses his dismay at the "absurdity" of the human predicament. He used the word before Camus did so. At its best, his work was, he declared, a metaphysical protest against man's comfortable acceptance of the human predicament, and a prayer that life should be lived in the least unworthy manner possible, but it contains a clear rejection of the affirmation of human freedom, which is the basis of an existentialist moral code. From his early youth, Salacrou was obsessed by the problem of evil, of the unjustified and unjustifiable suffering of the innocent, and he could find no way of reconciling this evil with the notion of a just God. "I want a good God or no God at all", says the Young Man in

Le Casseur d'assiettes (1923), Salacrou's unplayed and unplayable first play; he repudiates a God who juggles with the spheres like a juggler with his plates and breaks them out of "professional necessity". A creation that is godless and purposeless is less absurd than the existence of an all-perfect God who creates man imperfect and condemns him to eternal damnation for sins he cannot help committing. Is life absurd? And what meaning can be given to it? What meaning to death? Salacrou puts these questions unceasingly throughout his work. Life is a brief moment of suffering, a coffin closed at one end by birth and at the other by death. Death is the "black hole" in which everything ends, a notion which Salacrou claims to have accepted by the age of ten. In his self-portrait, in the preface to his second full-length play, *Le Pont de l'Europe*, he makes it clear that, like one of the characters in *Les Fiancés du Havre*, he was "right in the middle of a metaphysical drama". In this preface Salacrou insists on the subjectivity of his characters, terming them the "image of his own metaphysical distress". If he expresses this distress in dramatic form it is in the hope that he may find, in the clash of contradictory explanations, "a means of coming unobserved upon the deity". Of the Young Man in *Le Casseur d'assiettes* he says: "He is waiting for a miracle [to prove the existence of God]—a hopeless occupation." Taken together, Salacrou's thirty or more plays present the drama of an unwilling unbeliever, Salacrou himself, seeking, despairingly, for reasons for believing, yet always remaining convinced that the quest leads nowhere. His plays are not a pure art form but an experiment undertaken time and again, in an attempt to solve the riddle of the human predicament, and to awaken God (if He exists) from His sleep of the Sabbath. "God had to sleep for evil to come into the world. Do you hear? God is asleep . . . Let God be awakened." But there is no answer to the clamour raised to awaken God.

Le Casseur d'assiettes, which ends in this way, outlines most of the themes that are developed in Salacrou's subsequent plays. Like them, it bears testimony to the spirit of revolt and to the perfect good faith which Salacrou claims to be the keynotes of his theatrical work. Like them, it succeeds in rendering the "restless disquiet of his generation", and this was Salacrou's avowed aim. It is also the first of several excursions into the domain of the Surrealists, though Salacrou never adhered, officially, to the group. He would even seem to pass an adverse judgment on the surrealist adventure in the last act of *Tour à terre*, when his hero walks out of the sailors' café, after his surrealist revolt, with his hands firmly manacled. A deliberate atmosphere of unreality pervades these early plays. In the first of them human existence is symbolized by the feverish agitation, confusion, and uproar of the music-hall backstage, of the fairground, the dance-hall. Throughout Salacrou's writings life is frequently linked with the word "nightmare", and is presented openly in this guise in *L'Inconnue d'Arras*. This play is a return to something approaching Salacrou's first manner, after the more realistic *Atlas-Hôtel* (Atelier, April 15th, 1931), and *Les Frénétiques* (Daunou, December 5th, 1934), which he had written at Jouvet's invitation. He had attempted to get away from himself and look closely at society, but had decided that there was no future for him in realistic drama.[3]

Salacrou began as a Pirandellian, and in the first three of his plays to be staged (*Tour à terre*, *Le Pont de l'Europe* by the Théâtre des Jeunes Auteurs, at the Odéon on November 30th, 1927, and *Patchouli* by Dullin, at the Atelier on January 2nd, 1930) the main characters, all seeking to arrive at an understanding of their true selves, complain of the lack of continuity in their personality. In answer to the policeman who comes to arrest him, Pierre (*Tour à terre*) draws a distinction between the criminal he was at the moment he offered a railway signal, red with the "blood" of those killed in the subsequent crash, to Isabelle as a bouquet, and the innocent dishwasher he then was. The idea re-occurs in other plays, but is stated the most clearly in *Les Invités du bon Dieu* (1953), where François declares that life is a procession which moves forward continually and never doubles back on its tracks; every instant we die and are reborn, hence to judge a man is to judge the criminal he *was*, and not to judge the man he *is*, reborn to innocence. In 1960 Salacrou was still meditating on this theme. It is this theme which determines the constant use of the imagery of "drifting" and attempting to "reach anchor" in his dialogue. Salacrou's plays are a constant philosophical meditation, and were so different from current productions that they baffled their audiences and had short runs. Yet they were firmly backed by such knowledgeable theatre people as Lugné-Poë, Dullin, Jouvet, the actor Pierre Renoir, and the actress Valentine Tessier, who all continued to believe in him. The effect of his resounding failures was, however, to cause Salacrou to abandon his *théâtre en liberté*, with the unreality of its atmosphere, the purely verbal development of the situations and characters, all in their various ways an expression of himself.

In *Atlas-Hôtel* and *Les Frénétiques*, both tailored to fit Jouvet's actors, particularly Pierre Renoir, Salacrou turned his attention to characterization, creating Auguste, a modern Don Quixote, the architect, builder, and proprietor of a pseudo-palace, roofless and windowless, on a lonely road in the Sahara, near the foothills of the Atlas mountains, and the film magnate Lourdalec, a cynical, domineering brute. Both characters had living models, and fear of legal repercussions with regard to the film magnate caused Jouvet to turn down *Les Frénétiques*. Some years later Raymond Rouleau produced the play without incident. Dullin took the part of Lourdalec, as he had already done that of Auguste in his own production of *Atlas-Hôtel*, about which Jouvet had also had his doubts. The inspiration for Auguste and his hotel came from a fleeting visit by Salacrou, two years before, to a hotel run by such a man at the foot of the Atlas mountains. Were it not for the importance given to the character of Auguste, the inveterate dreamer whose imagination, working always on a grand scale, conjured up a casino, gambling-rooms, an aerodrome, a cinema studio blazing with lights, the production of water-power he had yet to harness, and were it not for the remarkable figure of his wife Augustine, for the love of whom Auguste had attempted to surpass himself, *Atlas-Hôtel* would have been a typical Boulevard play, relating the struggle of two men, husband and ex-husband, for a woman.

By the harshness of the characterization and the type of action, consisting of the progressive tightening of the vice in which one of the characters holds another, *Les Frénétiques* takes its place beside the "cruelty plays" of Stève Passeur. It is interesting technically, since it offers the first of Salacrou's experiments with stage time —if one is to discount *Le Pont de l'Europe*, with its play within a play. Events which happened ten years before are portrayed in a flash-back with the fade-in and fade-out, as used in the cinema. Salacrou was among the very first to use the flash-back, and it was perhaps no coincidence that he situated the action of the play in the frenzied world of the cinema, which he knew well, for having worked in it from 1925 to 1928.

Salacrou was still feeling his way when he wrote *Les Frénétiques*, and Jouvet's refusal of the play, which prevented him from following a line that was not truly his, was a blessing in disguise. Nevertheless, these experiments in realistic drama proved an admirable discipline, and the four plays, *Une Femme libre*, *L'Inconnue d'Arras*, *Un Homme comme les autres*, and *La Terre est ronde*, in which Salacrou returns to the themes outlined in his early unsuccessful plays, show a sureness of touch in dramatic structure, characterization, and language which these had lacked. *Une Femme libre* and *Un Homme comme les autres*, both of which were performed at the Œuvre on October 2nd, 1934, and November 24th, 1936, respectively, continue in the realistic vein. The story of Lucie, *la femme libre*, who runs away from her conventional fiancé and his family, with its fixed ideas, habits, and morality, and into which she would have been integrated had she stayed, and then runs away from Jacques, whom she never ceases to love, but who, in turn, offers her the closed horizon of marriage, is a philosophical play like the others. This was underlined by Salacrou when he changed the title from *Lucie Blondel* to *Une Femme libre*. Lucie's flights indicate her refusal to accept any limitation of the future. She stands in complete contrast to Aunt Adrienne, who remains throughout her life a prisoner of her upbringing and of the memories of her past, a fossilized member of the *bourgeoisie*, like all the Miremont family, with the exception of Jacques. Nevertheless, Lucie's two flights do not appear as free acts. They are prompted by Jacques's arguments in the first instance, and those of the immoralist Cher Ami in the second. They are also prompted by Lucie's own nature, which is that of a gambler, living in hopes of the daily "miracle". According to Jacques, man is not given the choice of his fate nor even of his words and gestures; they are imposed on him, for such is the "absurd" world in which he lives. Jacques's belief in a mechanistic determination directing every human gesture, as it does the movement of the planets, is stated dramatically in the opening moments of the play, when he is seen hanging up on the sitting-room ceiling the planet Saturn, as the necessary consequence of having hung up in his own room the earth and the moon in their respective positions. Jacques is a true "son" of Salacrou, who writes in *Certitudes et incertitudes*: "In order to bear with my own existence, I took refuge from a very early age ... in complete mechanistic determination."[4] The only character who is free is the monstrous Cher Ami. He has voluntarily dispossessed himself of everything, family ties, civic status, "even of his own thought", but this fetish of freedom has led to the destruction of himself as a human being; he is *cher ami* and nothing else. It is in reaction to his scorn for the "nice little prejudices which assure society's happiness and men's unhappiness" that Jacques, drawing the moral of the play, wonders whether, in the disorganized world of today, one is free to be free, free to rid oneself of these prejudices, which are not merely empty, outmoded conventions, but "the remains of great things destroyed and never replaced", and he concludes: "If men have overturned the barriers before knowing how to set others up, they still have a heart . . . it needs very solid convictions to remain indifferent to a man's tears."

Cher Ami's convictions are solid enough for him to live in the chill climate of a world emptied of all human feeling. Not so Lucie's, and she returns to beg a humble place in Jacques's life. Strangely enough, this "emancipated" woman of twenty, instead of living with her arms "stretched out towards life", as she claims she does, and as Salacrou obviously intends that she should be doing, has simply fled from life, terrified by the portrait of "Madame Miremont at fifty", painted for her by Jacques at their first meeting. Similarly, Jacques is paradoxical, for he is, at one and the same time, a rebel in society and a believer in a mechanistic determination; he later shows himself to be as full of middle-class prejudices as his brother. These inconsistencies adversely affect the argument of the play.

Une Femme libre was Salacrou's first real success in the theatre, preceding by two months *Les Frénétiques*, which had waited five years to be staged. It was because of his need for such a success that he consented to reduce to three acts the four acts of the original version, which he had not yet published. It was performed 175 times and was revived on February 5th, 1949, at the Théâtre Saint-Georges.

This preoccupation with free will was not new in Salacrou's plays. Already in *Le Pont de l'Europe* life is shown as being *imposed* on his hero, made king by chance alone. The railway-lines, which all pass under the Pont de l'Europe at the Gare Saint-Lazare and go ineluctably on their separate ways, would seem to symbolize the relationship between free choice and necessity. The traveller can choose his train, but, once the choice is made, there is no going back on the decision. The question of man's freedom of action crops up here and there throughout Salacrou's work and does not always provoke the same response. It is discussed at length in *Dieu le savait* (Théâtre Saint-Georges, December 2nd, 1950), in a scene which is vital to Salacrou's intention of defining the relationship between God and men, but which is barely integrated into the action, and reads rather like a lecture. "To live", says Daniel, "is to discover one's destiny. It is fascinating to learn what God already knows and what fate He has chosen for you." Using a phrase which now has a familiar ring in literature, he concludes: "Les jeux sont faits." The fact that men cannot be held responsible for their actions does not dispense with the need for a moral code. Daniel's is the wish not to be ashamed of his destiny, and in the presentation of this character Salacrou achieves his aim of "showing the peace that a determinist can find in his belief".[5] One of the subsidiary themes is contained in a comment by the Resistance worker, Bonnet, on his fellow-fighters who died with a smile on their lips, not because of any belief in a life after death, but "because they had fought to the bitter end for the happiness of those yet to be born". This theme is fully orchestrated in *Les Nuits de la colère* (Marigny-Barrault, December 12th, 1946), a "documentary of the Occupation", as Salacrou calls it, and the first of his dramas to place the hope of man's salvation in a new humanism. His characters in previous plays had sought vainly to give a meaning to their lives; here, in *Les Nuits*, situated, like *Dieu le savait*, "in 1944, in France", they find it in heroic and unselfish sacrifice for the sake of others. The play is a plain statement of Salacrou's concern with contemporary problems; no artist, he declared, could shut himself up in an ivory tower in the early forties, when the realities among which he lived were the war and the Occupation. The difficulty was to raise realities above the purely anecdotic or the purely documentary, without having recourse to "allegory or historical costume", as Sartre had done in *Les Mouches*, in 1943. In his search for the appropriate dramatic technique Salacrou's earlier experiments with stage time stood him in good stead. In *La Vie en rose*, a one-act play written for Michel Saint-Denis in 1931, the characters live twenty-four hours in the twenty-five minutes of the performance, and in these twenty-four hours events covering twenty-five years of French national history are referred to as being current events. In *L'Inconnue d'Arras* the whole action is a flashback. Here, in *Les Nuits de la colère*, Salacrou, freeing his characters from the contingencies of time and place, brings face to face on the stage, in one coherent and continuous sequence of events, the living, irrespective of the space which separated them, and also the living and the dead. The play begins with the "liquidation", by men of the Resistance, of a couple of collaborators, for their part in the denunciation and capture of their leader; after this the action moves backward and forward in time; at a certain moment in Act Two, incidents of April 1944—the arrival of the hunted leader at his friend's house, his betrayal by the friend, his wife's despair, his torture by the Gestapo before his execution—are successively superimposed upon a happier visit made in 1938.

In the years immediately following the war the play had for its audience the degree of topicality without which, Salacrou maintained, an author could not obtain a "rendezvous" with the public, but it still remains to be seen whether, beyond the "necessary, ephemeral topicality", this play can pretend to the "universal topicality" of the Classics, and so outlive the generations which experienced at first hand the war and the Occupation. It offers a curious contrast to Sartre's play *Morts sans sépulture*, performed a month earlier, which gives a straightforward representation of a typical incident of the Resistance movement, but, not being intended as a play on the Resistance movement itself, could equally well have been situated in the Middle Ages. Whereas Sartre was concerned with whether a man subjected to torture is really free to choose his conduct, Salacrou was concerned with the different attitudes taken up by Frenchmen towards the Occupation; these are symbolized in the various characters, who, despite their representative rôles, lose neither their humanity nor their individuality. Though the playwright's attention is engaged by contemporary events, the usual Salacrian themes recur, among them the theme of responsibility: "You are responsible for the Occupation since you are alive and you accept it", says the Resistance leader to the representative of "a quiet life at all costs".

L'Inconnue d'Arras,[6] less topical, less readily understandable in the theatre, never had the appeal of *Les Nuits*, neither when it was first staged by Lugné-Poë on November 22nd, 1935, nor at its revival at the Comédie-Française-Luxembourg, on January 11th, 1949, in a production by Gaston Baty, when it gave the impression of being outmoded *avant-garde*. The play, at one time entitled *La Mort est le rendez-vous des vivants*, begins and ends with the same pistol shot, and the entire action, consisting of conversations between the living, the dead, and the dying, takes place within the mind of the suicide during the brief second before the bullet enters his brain. Ulysse's suicide was prompted by his distress after reading a letter which revealed his wife's unfaithfulness, and the subsequent action develops at length the theme touched on by Aunt Adrienne in *Une Femme libre*: the hell of death which is the perpetuation of life as we have lived it. "Shall I remain for ever in this hell with this letter and this rotten woman eternally before my eyes?" Ulysse cries. "Les jeux sont faits pour l'éternité", as Nicolas, his manservant turned "chorus", put it. All the perspectives of the future being closed by death, it is "in the perspective of death" that a man's life takes on its meaning. Ulysse, searching for a justification of his existence among his memories, which are materialized on the stage, finds it in his charitable acts, symbolized mainly by his solicitude for the unhappy "unknown woman" whom he had befriended on the battlefield of Arras. Ulysse realizes, as he relives the incident in his dying moments, that life has had its rewards, and he regrets his suicide, but in vain. Not even God can stop the bullet; responsibility for his actions is man's alone. The encounter between Ulysse and the ghost of his grandfather, who had been killed in action at twenty, is moving. This hero of the battlefield had unheroically married for money and had not lived to enjoy the money; he comes down from his picture-frame to argue that life is worth living. Another interesting encounter is between Ulysse and the double ghost of Maxime—Maxime at thirty-seven, a traitor to his friend Ulysse and a traitor to himself, and the idealistic Maxime of twenty, who stands in judgment over his older, cheapened self.

La Terre est ronde, continuing the series of "experiments" in dramatic form begun with *Le Casseur d'assiettes*, provides Salacrou with an answer, though not the one for which he had hoped. Like Salacrou's first hero, the people of Florence await a miracle, the triumph in a trial by fire of Savonarole, the man of God, over a "false prophet". But Savonarole refuses to take up the challenge, declaring that "a man has no right to challenge God", and his refusal brings his fall from grace in the eyes of the Florentines. Alone and broken in body by torture, he makes a supreme appeal from his dungeon prison to the divinity: "Where have I gone wrong, oh God? Answer me . . . Jesus thou remainest silent . . . How terrible is the silence!" Then comes his final conclusion: life is a mere comedy; before life there is nothing, and after life there will be nothing. It was for nothing that Savonarole had purged Florence of its debauchery; it was for nothing that Silvio had renounced his love for Lucciana and sacrificed his life. If God existed He could not have refused the miracle which would have proved His existence.

The play met with considerable success when it was performed by Dullin in 1938 (November 7th) at the Atelier, and again in 1946 (October 11th) at the Sarah-Bernhardt, but its success came from the public's misinterpretation of Salacrou's intentions.[7] In 1938 it saw the play as a criticism of the totalitarian states and as a reply to Italian demands for Nice, Savoy, and Corsica. In 1946 it appeared to celebrate the death of the Duce and the end of Hitlerism; "dictatorships", Manente had prophesied, "are never more than an eclipse [of man's eternal love of freedom]". The responsibility for the misinterpretation did not lie entirely with the public. Manente's prophecy, children in uniform denouncing and beating "subversive citizens", the salute with the cry "Christ is King", the burning of the Jew (suppressed in the later edition), all called for the comparisons which the public made. It was, however, with the Nietzschean conception of the cyclic nature of events—la terre est ronde—that Salacrou was really concerned. His play was written in 1937 but was ready, in essence, in 1920, at the end of his three months' stay in Florence. Its composition was held back till 1937 by the technical problem of incorporating an historical figure into an imaginary action. The theme of the play is the reform of Florence on lines laid down by Savonarola, and of the final repercussions on the dictatorial monk of the narrow conception of life which he offered to the Florentines, "debauchery or the monastery", and this in the full flush of the Renaissance. In the play Savonarole does not appear with the other characters; he is seen four times in a cell, each time alone, except for a final encounter with his executioner, and there he pronounces four monologues. The last of these, which brings together a number of the themes of the play, was replaced at Dullin's request by the more "theatrical" execution of Savonarole. During the course of the play Savonarole expresses his disgust of men while affirming his love of God, whereas human love leads Silvio to the love of God. When the scandalous Faustine brings news from Rome of discoveries which would seem to present a challenge to the Christian faith, Silvio, in despair at the threat to this faith to which he has sacrificed everything, attempts to wrest from

God the proof of its validity. The violent denunciation of Christianity as bankrupt, voiced in this play, is accompanied by an equally violent denunciation of all other creeds, from humanism, in the person of Manente, to amoralism, in that of Faustine, the mistress of a Cardinal.

La Terre est ronde was preceded by *Un Homme comme les autres* (Œuvre-Paulette Pax, November 24th, 1936) and followed by *Histoire de rire* (Marigny, December 2nd, 1939). Both plays seem to be aimed at the Boulevard public, particularly *Histoire de rire*, which shows technical mastery not unworthy of Georges Feydeau, and which has been continuously successful in the theatre since it was first produced. *Un Homme comme les autres*, a melodrama which might almost be signed by Henry Bernstein instead of Salacrou, was incorporated, after a couple of revivals on the Boulevard, in the repertory of the Comédie-Française-Luxembourg in 1959, in place—unfortunately—of *La Terre est ronde*. The metaphysician and, more especially, the moralist in Salacrou are still to be heard in these two plays, despite their affinity with the Boulevard play, but the voice is muted. *Histoire de rire* is a veritable "ballet" (the term is used by one of the characters) of two adulterous wives who dance off with their lovers and, when the "interlude" is over, dance back to their husbands. This double picture of the adulterous wife completes that of the adulterous husband presented in *Un Homme comme les autres*. This latter play broaches the problem of the advisability in marriage of a confession of unfaithfulness. The question is broached again twenty years later in *Le Miroir* (Ambassadeurs, September 22nd, 1956). In *Le Miroir* the confession is withheld (by the wife), whereas in *Un Homme comme les autres* it is made (by the husband), with unhappy results in both cases. The confession is induced in *Un Homme comme les autres* by the crisis provoked by the monstrously amoral Madame Berthe, Salacrou's most striking character creation; the rest of the characterization in the play is conventional. Madame Berthe, once a happy faithful wife, had been morally infected by her corrupt husband. The victim of an attempted assassination, Madame Berthe had suddenly grasped the full significance of death, and in the light of this repudiates as meaningless the moral code which forbids her to taste certain joys in the years still remaining to her; she repudiates any accusation of sin. God, she declares, is no longer in His church, let God return or let the moral code be changed. The problem of a moral code which has no religious basis is also posed in *Histoire de rire*, and the same regret at living in an age of confusion and uncertain moral values is expressed. In this play comedy turns to drama and ends on the distressing realization by the lovers of the pitiable figures they cut in their adulterous adventure, which is no more than an *histoire de rire*.

Purity, fidelity are basic themes in *Le Soldat et la sorcière* (Sarah-Bernhardt-Dullin, December 5th, 1945), which gives a typical Salacrian twist to the story of Maurice de Saxe and Justine Favart, the opera-singer "Mademoiselle de Chantilly". "Debauchery or the convent", this is the choice with which Salacrou's Justine, like his Florentines in *La Terre est ronde*, is faced. Justine finally submits to the physical servitude to save herself from the convent and her husband from the galleys, though for the Marshal she is nothing but a "living corpse"; only in the final scene does Salacrou, somewhat gratuitously, dim the radiance of his heroine. This play, which was written in 1943 to take his mind off the German occupation of his country, and was conceived as a *divertissement historique*, is a good piece of dramatic writing and has a resonance which surprised its author: not until he saw the rehearsal did Salacrou realize "that the problem it debates is that of death and freedom".

The preceding year Salacrou's sombre and mercilessly satirical melodrama *Les Fiancés du Havre*, written in 1942, was put on by the Comédie-Française (December 10th). It was the first modern play to be staged there after the Liberation; after three years it was transferred to the Salle-Luxembourg. Salacrou's usual satire of the middle-classes is extended here to the lower classes.

L'Archipel Lenoir is much more interesting and can be ranked with *La Terre est ronde* and *Les Nuits de la colère*; all three are excellent plays. The present first act was published by Salacrou in 1945 as a one-act play. He later added a second act, and the extended play was staged by Dullin at the Théâtre Montparnasse on November 8th, 1947, with himself in the rôle of the grandfather whose scandalous misdemeanour threatened the prosperity of the family business, the Lenoir liqueur. The family sitting in council, no longer a corporate body but become, under the shock of the scandal and the consequent threat to their private interests, a number of supremely egoistic individuals (an archipelago in a liqueur sea), orders the old man to take his own life for the benefit of the family and the Lenoir liqueur. A few rejoinders in the play define its main theme and would seem to provide the final conclusion to the quest pursued by Salacrou throughout the preceding plays. "I accuse my mother of my death, for if I had not lived, I should not have known the horror of death"—six years later, in *Certitudes et incertitudes*, Salacrou directs the same accusation against himself as the father of a family. "I am a living being, I might very well not have existed at all, and some time I shall die." What is the point of living if I have to die? "When I am dead I shall be very, very dead", but should the earth be, after all, a marshalling-yard for the "eternal journey", why has God made it so dismal? Why is the journey through the yard such a nightmare? These questions are debated in a joyously satirical comedy with striking dramatic qualities. A question of a different nature is raised at the end of the first act when a pistol shot rings out: who has been shot, the grandfather or his son who has handed him the pistol? The play is a sort of marionette show, but with these marionettes, caricatures all of them, Salacrou probes external appearances, to reach the fringe of the conscious; this is best seen in the granddaughter, in whom a flood of unsuspected sensuality is let loose by the revelation of the grandfather's misdemeanour. Salacrou here shows a depth not to be found in his other plays. The dialogue is brilliant; it is completely and deliberately unrealistic when taken as a whole, though each single response rings true. This adds to the comic element already present in the situation. The comic vein is strong in Salacrou's plays; it goes back as far as *Atlas-Hôtel* and even appears in the sombre drama *La Terre est ronde*, in the scenes with the French soldier, Cognac.

Salacrou's remaining plays, *Les Invités du bon Dieu* (Brussels, Théâtre du Parc, September 11th; Paris, Théâtre Saint-Georges, September 23rd, 1953), an abortive attempt to write a vaudeville in the style of Georges Feydeau, *Le Miroir, Une Femme trop honnête* (Edouard VII, December 1st, 1956), and a few short ones are, like *Dieu le savait, Le Soldat et la sorcière*, and particularly *Histoire de rire*, much closer to the tradition of the Boulevard theatre. Of *Le Miroir* Salacrou himself said that it was a deliberate return, after his earlier experiments with technique, to the tradition of the "well-made play", though not, however, to the "falsely well-made play", with its purely mechanical arrangement of the action. His starting-point was to be a story, and he relied on the moral or social significance inherent in the story to make itself clear, unaided by the author. The suppression at the performance of the prologue, where the questions of death, man's destiny, and the existence of the divinity are broached—as always in Salacrou—strengthened the unfortunate impression of a melodrama in the Bernstein manner which the play produced.

Boulevard Durand is of a very different calibre. It is an exciting play and mirrors an incident in the Le Havre dock strike of 1910 which repeated, so to speak, the injustice of the Dreyfus Case. Salacrou had seen the misery the strikers and their families were reduced to when he was only eleven years old, and he had seen the man whom everybody around him knew to be innocent taken into the prison opposite the Salacrou family's chemist-shop. He had never forgotten the incident and says so in *Certitudes et incertitudes*. His play is not, however, a mere page of working-class history; it achieves permanent topicality, and it was clearly for this reason that André Malraux, the Minister of Culture, stopped its production by Jean-Louis Barrault at the State-subsidized Théâtre de France in January 1961, almost at the last moment. When the play had appeared in print the previous year it had been generally expected that Jean Vilar would stage it at the Théâtre National Populaire, as it was obviously written "*for* a popular audience and dealt with matters near to the heart of such an audience", which is how Vilar defined the ideal play for a Popular Theatre. Furthermore, the play was exactly what Vilar said he was looking for in 1961[8]—namely, a play about "class warfare, not a political play but a play which is both satirical and instructive". Nevertheless, he declared his intention of *not* staging *Boulevard Durand*, adding "Armand knows why". Perhaps he anticipated Malraux's later repressive action. The play's cause was, however, taken up outside Paris by one of the several *centres dramatiques* which have been set up in France with Government support since 1947. The *Centre dramatique du Nord*, from Tourcoing, near Lille, put the play on in Le Havre, and the first performance took place in a cinema hall before an audience which included Juliette Durand, Durand's daughter, who is mentioned in the play, ex-President René Coty, Durand's barrister, and representatives of the steamship company which had had Jules Durand framed so as to have this "troublesome" strike-leader locked up for a few years, but had inadvertently made a martyr of him instead by getting him sentenced to the guil-

lotine for "incitement to murder". The sentence was commuted to
solitary imprisonment for life, and when Coty finally managed to
establish his innocence Durand was only fit to be transferred to a
lunatic asylum. Subsequent performances were given before audiences of dockers and ex-dockers in their seventies, many of whom
had been authentic actors in the drama of 1910, in the trade-union
hall which had been the scene of Durand's activities. There was no
mistaking the degree of audience participation resulting from the
way in which the dramatist had expressed their feelings in dramatic
form. Such a relationship between author and spectator, Salacrou
had said already in 1945, was essential in the drama of today.
Speaking in the theatre after some of the performances, he underlined the topicality of the themes in this story of an ancient wrong,
adding that the play was his contribution to the struggle against
future injustice. There were moments in one's life when one could
not but intervene, and another such moment had been marked by
Les Nuits de la colère—his pro-Resistance, or rather anti-anti-
Resistance, play of 1946. Boulevard Durand's success in Le Havre
secured it a month's hearing in Paris, in a commercial theatre, the
Théâtre Sarah-Bernhardt, where it was difficult to get a seat because of heavy bookings by trade unions. There were lively reactions in that theatre also. Then, for two years, the play was
performed by the same company up and down the country, and if
audiences always came in crowds to see it, it was not because they
were reliving their past, as had been the case in Le Havre, but because, to repeat a Press report, when three hundred disappointed
spectators were turned away from a performance at Poitiers at an
"Experimental Festival" in 1963, "the public found itself, with
this play, on familiar ground". In fact, this was working-class
drama, situated in the hic et nunc, existential and real. The story
of the play is told in fourteen rapid scenes which follow on from
each other, as though in a film. The technique in the trial scenes
is particularly original: only significant statements by witnesses,
Prosecution and Defence, are included, and these are literally high-
lighted, in accordance with Salacrou's stage-directions, by projectors.

After Boulevard Durand, a play which opens out so wide on to
the outside world, Comme des chardons (Comédie-Française, October 18th, 1964) is disappointing. In a world once again severely
circumscribed it examines a personal psychological problem. In a
series of flash-backs, a technique which Salacrou reminded the

critics he had perhaps been the very first to use, a woman of fifty goes back over her past after receiving a visit from her former lover's son. Salacrou's usual reflections on the absurdity of existence and the sadistic cruelty of the deity appear again in the play.

Metaphysical speculations, expressed in this manner, are to be found everywhere in Salacrou's works, in his "Boulevard" plays, and naturally in *Les Invités du bon Dieu*, where one of the characters cries out: "They have lost their heads Up There [in the heavens]", and: "God cannot surely have put us on earth to torture us." This appeal to the intellect makes Salacrou's dramatic works rewarding to the reader even more than to the theatregoer, though they are perfectly valid as stage plays, with the exception of his very early attempts, where he was not yet master of his medium. As far as technique is concerned he may be criticized for not always highlighting his main theme, as, for example, in *Une Femme libre*, and for overdoing symbolism in much of his characterization. Such shortcomings lessen the impact of his plays on the stage and may well adversely affect the durability of his theatrical work, despite the high seriousness and permanent topicality of his themes. Even so, Armand Salacrou is one of the outstanding playwrights of his generation.

Among other young writers to show a cynical turn of mind, PAUL VIALAR may be singled out. A novelist as well as a playwright, Vialar, who was born in 1898, was over five years younger than Zimmer, a year older than Passeur and Salacrou, and three years older than Natanson; he was just old enough to serve in the latter part of the First World War, during which he was wounded. His was not the reasoned cynicism of the older Zimmer, joyously lashing out at the faults and failings of his time, but seems to be the expression of disappointment and disillusionment. The war and its aftermath form the theme of one of two significant plays of his, *Les Hommes* (Théâtre des Arts-Pitoëff, January 16th, 1931), while the other, *Nous ne sommes pas si forts* (Théâtre Femina, November 20th, 1925), originally entitled *Comme les autres*, is concerned with post-war youth. Here Vialar's heroine of twenty-seven, in a society where the lack of a dowry was a frequent obstacle to marriage, decides dispassionately to take a lover. The two admit no obligation on either side. They later fall in love but, through fear of losing each other, keep up the pose of cynical indifference which is a torture to them both. The dialogue is typical of

much of the dramatic writing of the time and consists of an unend-
ing fire of short, clipped phrases and incisive, brutal retorts.
Vialar's war-play, *Les Hommes*, was written at a time when the
war had gone out of fashion as a dramatic subject but had come
into its own in the cinema. In a large fresco, which one might have
expected of the cinema rather than the theatre, Vialar aimed at
depicting every aspect of the war from the day of mobilization,
when volunteers went to the front confident of a triumphal return
within a couple of months, to two or three years after the
Armistice. He evokes the weeks of anguished retreat before an
invisible enemy, the haphazard news of the victory on the Marne,
the long, despairing wait before peace, the trenches under fire, a
pub behind the lines, a house of ill-fame, the seamy as well as the
heroic side of a world war. The sting comes in the last scenes,
where the illusion of an undying comradeship born of the danger
shared in war is seen to founder on the reality of insurmountable
social barriers.

These writers did not have the monopoly of cynicism in the
theatre. There was a strong vein of cynicism in Marcel Achard's
Malborough s'en va-t-en guerre (1924) and Jules Romains's *Knock*
(1923), but cynicism is not the dominant aspect of the work of these
two writers, nor of Marcel Pagnol, whose war-play *Les Marchands
de gloire* (1925) and *Topaze* (1928) are nevertheless as cynical as
anything Stève Passeur ever wrote. One cruelly cynical play,
L'Énnemie by ANDRE-PAUL ANTOINE, son of André Antoine, founder
of the Théâtre Libre, takes love as its theme, and shows a woman,
at three different stages of her life, sending a romantic fiancé, a
staid, middle-class husband, and a Don Juan of a lover, one after
another to an early grave, by her indifference, her unfaithfulness,
or sexual excesses. The action takes place in a cemetery, and the
ghosts of the woman's victims, looking just as they did in their lifetime, rise out of their graves to describe, in a series of flash-backs,
how they died.[9] The dear lady is quite convinced that she is blameless, as we learn when she visits the cemetery with her daughter, a
career girl, with ultra-modern views on love and marriage. Misogyny
so openly stated caused a great outcry from the feminine part of the
audience when the play was first performed at the Théâtre Antoine
on April 5th, 1929. When it was revived on February 25th, 1949,
at the Studio des Champs-Elysées, the word *tendre* was introduced
into the title in an attempt to soften the blow.

When Antoine wrote the play the wave of cynicism had almost spent itself. ANDRE LANG, for example, who had painted cynical pictures of love in his early plays, as in *Le Plaisir d'être méchant* (1923), where a man undresses a married woman who loves him and then declares: "The comedy is over", or in *La Fantaisie amoureuse* (1927), where Cupid, in the guise of a decrepit old man singing to the accompaniment of a concertina, leads hopeful couples into a strange wood where disillusionment and despair await them, turned, in 1930, in *Les Trois Henry*, to a straighforward reconstitution of historical events, and with it gained entry to the Comédie-Française (March 19th). By 1937 he was preoccupied with the threat of a European war, and in *La Paix est pour demain* (Odéon, July 2nd), which has a distinctly Wellsian flavour, his scientist averts the war by bombing, simultaneously, the capitals of France, England, Germany, and Italy, deliberately provoking an attack by the "Asiatics", so as to consolidate the European union. After 1928 the only hardened cynic left in the field was Stève Passeur; he never deviated from his orginal formula of the "cruelty play", not even in his writings for the theatre after the Second World War.

NOTES

1. Revived, Œuvre, 1943; Comédie des Champs-Elysées, 1964, without the final suicide; this made the play more conventional. Passeur was pleased to find that the play appealed to the young generation of playgoers, even though they were not accustomed to strongly constructed plays.
2. Performed in English in 1951 as *No Fury*.
3. Author's note to *Les Frénétiques*.
4. *Théâtre*, vol. VI, 1954, p. 211.
5. *Théâtre*, vol. VI, p. 220.
6. Performed in English in 1948 as *The Unknown Woman of Arras*.
7. The play was incorporated in the repertory of the Comédie-Française on February 4th, 1956.
8. *Arts*, April 12th–18th.
9. This is probably the first use of the flash-back to be made in the theatre. *Les Frénétiques*, by Salacrou, was written afterwards.

Ondine
Producer: Jouvet
Photo: Lipnitzki

Intermezzo
Producer: Jouvet
Photos: Lipnitzki

VI

Studio Theatre: The New Romantics

Jean Sarment—Jean Anouilh.

IF THE war and the difficulties and disappointments of the years
that followed had stung writers like Bernard Zimmer and Stève
Passeur into sarcasm and cynicism, others losing faith in the
value of human activities had recourse to the deliberate, if somewhat sceptical, creation of an illusion that would make existence
acceptable. Commenting in 1929 on what he called the "new
romanticism", Henri Bidou described it as a disillusioned art,
afflicted with "an idea of failure which is like a running sore in
the souls of these young men who have taken part in the war or
who have studied its effects".[1] This general comment could be used
to describe the work of JEAN SARMENT. Many found it easier to take
refuge in the imagination, to keep their childhood dreams, and to
refuse to grow up. Sarment and Jean Anouilh analysed this state
of mind in their plays; one cannot decide, from their works,
whether they advise us to grow up or not; their attitude is the
ambivalent attitude of Musset's Fantasio.

Besides his plays, Sarment also published between 1922 and 1932
three novels and two volumes of poems. The first volume of
poems, which bears the title *Le Cœur d'enfance* (1922), points to
the theme which is to be found in many of his works, whatever the
literary form used; it is the disparity between childhood aspirations,
particularly a very young man's ideal of love, and reality as
known by the grown man. This theme is stated clearly in Sarment's
first play, *Facilité*, written at the age of nineteen. When travelling
to the United States in 1917, as a member of the company of the
Vieux-Colombier, Sarment read the play to Copeau, and while he
was in America with him he wrote *La Couronne de carton*, but
Copeau never staged any of Sarment's works; they were not in line

with the type of play he produced in his theatre. It was left to
Lugné-Poë to put on *La Couronne de carton* at the Œuvre, on
February 4th, 1920, and because Copeau refused to allow Sarment
to go to the Œuvre to play the main part, Lugné-Poë took Sarment
on as a permanent actor in his company. *Le Pêcheur d'ombres* followed on April 15th, 1921, again with Sarment in the main part.
Both productions were given an enthusiastic reception. Sarment
was the first of the new generation of playwrights to establish a
reputation at an early age. The fact that Sarment was expressing a
state of mind common to many at the time must certainly have
contributed to his success.

In his first play, *Facilité*, the hero, Courges, confesses to a friend,
who sees him living with a mistress, that at the age of ten he
dreamed of a love which was tender, pure, irreproachable, then he
adds: "I was more exacting then than I am today." The friend
declares that love is a lottery, and both realize that in hoping for
a Beatrice or an Héloïse they are merely trying to forget that they
are not a Dante or an Abélard. "We complain about not finding
Juliet, but we are not Romeos." This idea is summed up succinctly
by Sarment in the title of one of his best plays, *Je suis trop grand
pour moi*, which was staged at the Comédie-Française on March
26th, 1924. But Sarment had not finished with *Facilité* and added
a third act, changing the title to *As-tu du cœur?* (Renaissance,
October 3rd, 1926), a phrase which occurs several times in the
original text. The purely negative conclusion of *Facilité*, with
Courges putting off, for a day or two, the decision to take another
mistress, gives place in *As-tu du cœur?* to a more positive conclusion: the characters' whole lives are shown to be dominated by
their defeated idealism. These heroes of Sarment's are in the
romantic tradition, but, unlike their illustrious predecessors, they
have a wry smile on their faces as they take stock of themselves.

Several times in *Facilité* the idea is expressed that what we love
in a person is not the person himself but an ideal which we try to
believe is incarnated in that person. *La Couronne de carton*[2] goes
on from there to ask why one should be sincere when that which
others love in us is not ourselves but only the image which they
create of us for themselves. This theme is incorporated in the
romantic story of a prince in love with an actress in a travelling
company. He follows the company *incognito*. Later, as king, he
summons the actress to his Court, but as he wins her love only by

caricaturing himself and his estate in a theatrical cloak and card-board crown, it is a hollow victory.

Le Pêcheur d'ombres,[3] which followed this strange and inter-esting play, is, artistically, the most successful of Sarment's works for the theatre. It tells of a young man, Jean, who loses his reason through thwarted love, and who spends his days fishing light-heartedly for the omble chevalier, or ombre, an elusive type of trout. His reason is restored through the care of the girl whose indifference had been the cause of his madness. His brother, who also loves Nelly, does not believe that Jean is cured, nor that Nelly now loves Jean, and he tells Jean that she is not the girl he origin-ally loved. This is enough to upset the balance of Jean's mind again, and as often as Nelly tells him that she does love him Jean repeats: "The real Nelly did not love me." In one scene there is an interesting conversation between a bishop and a woman whom the bishop had formerly loved. This apparent dialogue is, as often in Sarment, really a monologue in which the character, here the bishop, analyses his own feelings and motives: if he had entered the Church it was because the Church alone could make him rise to the heights from which to "dominate" the woman, but his desire had been blunted by the time the heights had been gained. Sarment makes a similar point in his novels Jean-Jacques de Nantes and Lord Arthur Morrow Cowley.

A misunderstanding over the performing rights of Le Pêcheur d'ombres caused a rift between Sarment and Lugné-Poë, and Sar-ment's next play, Le Mariage d'Hamlet, went to the Odéon, where it was staged on November 10th, 1922, six months after its first performance at Mainz. The play is a caricature of Shakespeare's Hamlet, and ostensibly its purpose is to show that man cannot change his nature. Sarment's Hamlet, Ophelia, and Polonius, who are sent back to earth to take up their lives where they had left off, more or less re-enact the past, even though they know what had happened in their former lives, and though there was no need for them to relive the tragedy. Nevertheless, Sarment's main theme here, as in his other plays, is the disproportion between one's dreams and reality. Hamlet finds living incognito in a country man-sion irksome. He cannot forget he is a king's son and dreams of a heroic life befitting a king's son. When he learns that he is really the queen's illegitimate son by a stable groom he momentarily accepts the painful fact that he was an important person only in his own imagination. But illusion is essential to life, so Hamlet, who is indeed a megalomaniac, seizes on every trifling incident to convince himself and the kitchen-maid that his "noble" reactions to the situation can only be those of a king's son. He is stoned to death by the villagers for strangling Polonius, and dies "nobly", egoistically insisting that the kitchen-maid, who shares his fate, salute him as "my Lord" with her dying breath. The play is interesting, though disconcerting. It begins well with God and Abraham discussing the affairs of Hamlet, Ophélie, and Polonius, who have been awaiting judgment for seventeen years in the next world, but with each successive act it tails off more and more. The flippant tone makes it difficult for any of the characters and their aspirations to be taken seriously. Sarment continually pokes fun at the romantic theme which forms the basis of the play.

The disparity between one's ideal and what one makes of life is better illustrated by *Je suis trop grand pour moi*, telling of the adventures of Tiburce de Mortecroix, his father the duke, and his one-time tutor Virgile. Tiburce has lived with his childhood dream of a perfect love always in his mind, but finds none to measure up to his ideal, not even himself. In his turn, the duke discovers that all he has done during the seventeen years that he has spent writing his memoirs, after his wife's presumed death, is to "embroider on a cobweb", and the cobweb has collapsed under the weight of the embroidery. But, instead of indulging in romantic despair, he finds another cause to which to devote his remaining years. Virgile, Sarment's most striking character creation, is a moral philosopher; he has lived an exemplary life, and says to Tiburce: "Just think, I am the man for whom I have the highest esteem." He is full of his plans for reforming mankind—that is to say, men as men and not society—but has lacked the opportunity to perfect them. When the path is smoothed before him by Tiburce his will to work wavers, and he succumbs to the temptation of a pleasant and easy life. He attempts to delude himself into thinking that he is still working on the task he has set himself, but has finally to confess that he does not measure up to it. The curtain falls as he directs his steps towards the chicken-run. In the earlier scene, where Tiburce's illusions are shattered, Sarment likewise pricks the romantic bubble; Tiburce takes his head in his hands as if he were going to weep; a minute later he lights a cigarette, saying: "There is no point in trying to weep when one does not feel like it." Sarment's heroes see through the deception they practise on themselves. Moute, the facile heroine of *Facilité*, reappears in this play but is transfigured by her sincere love for Tiburce, though Tiburce fails to realize it. She is prepared to act to safeguard her love, whereas Tiburce, the duke, and Virgile, following the lead given by Sarment's earlier heroes, fill their empty lives with dreams. When Sarment's characters take a lover or a mistress it is usually to "fill a void", and never do they have the slightest romantic illusion about their action. The subject of the play is interesting, but Sarment fails to solve the technical problem of linking together the three different stories which constitute the action, and, as in *Le Mariage d'Hamlet*, the best part of the play is at the beginning.

As a professional playwright, Sarment had perforce to take into account the taste of Boulevard audiences. The highly subjective plays, which had won him success at the Œuvre and in the two State theatres, were not suitable for such audiences. *Madelon*, which he wrote with the Boulevard audiences in view, and which was staged at the Porte-Saint-Martin on March 17th, 1925, is more objective, more straightforward, and contains a good deal of external action. The chief character this time is a woman, Madeleine. She is another Moute (*Je suis trop grand pour moi*), but a Moute who has grown in stature, and who is highly individualized. Gay, of easy virtue, the victim of her generous nature, she is often referred to by the other characters as Madelon, the "Madelon" of a rousing military air, which is actually sung in the play. She sacrifices everything to the career of a musician, Marc-Adolphe, whom she nurses to fame. But unlike Sarment's former heroes, who have for such women an affectionate tolerance, Marc treats Madeleine with sheer disdain, even while being ready to use her for his own advancement, just as he uses his youthful dream of a pure love, though he does not even believe in this dream. From benevolent criticism of his romantic hero, Sarment passes in this play to explicit condemnation, and shows him as cruel, egoistic, and unashamedly cynical. In his own performance of the part Sarment insisted on his egoism and cynicism.

Madelon was followed by a number of quite poetic plays: *Les plus beaux Yeux du monde* (Porte-Saint-Martin, March 17th, 1925), *Sur mon beau navire* (Michodière, November 30th, 1928), *Le Plancher des vaches* (Théâtre Antoine, February 10th, 1931), and several others, in which much of the dialogue is reminiscent of

Marivaux, and the poetry is tinged with scepticism and irony. *Léopold le bien-aimé* was refused by the Comédie-Française but tempted Jouvet, who performed it at the Comédie des Champs-Elysées on October 12th, 1927.[4] The action and also the development of the character of the hero, Léopold, turn on the indiscretions of a post-office employee working in the dead-letter office. His muddling-up of the contents of two letters gave Léopold the opportunity of posing as a sort of Don Juan instead of being the lover who had been turned down. He came to believe in his story himself, and was happy until the hard facts of reality destroyed the illusion. The action is well handled, but Sarment seems less concerned with making his characters really live than he was in his earlier plays. Because of Jouvet's careful rendering of the main character, and his skilful juxtaposition of the real and imaginary existences, this had not been apparent, but when Sarment performed the play himself in 1948 he forced the note of sheer comedy, giving a marionette-like character to the *dramatis personae*.

The illusion of happiness, which persists only so long as one is pursuing it, and the disappointment at finding that reality is no more worthy of the illusion than one is worthy of one's own ideal picture of oneself—such is the subject-matter of *Bobard* (Théâtre Antoine, April 9th, 1930), which is not only the best of Sarment's plays technically but is particularly interesting because of the strong personal element it contains. The same ideas are expressed in some of Sarment's poems, which are the most deeply sincere of all his writings. One is in the presence of the disillusionment of a dedicated actor-author in the difficult business world of the theatre, but, as Sarment writes in one of his poems in prose: "A tame butterfly does not fly through a half-open window."

To everyday life, which his play depicts as pointless, commonplace, and empty, Sarment proposes two possible attitudes, the resolute building of castles in Spain or revolt which hides under external conformism. The first attitude is proposed in *Peau d'Espagne* (Athénée-Jouvet, March 23rd, 1933), based on his novel *Lord Arthur Morris Cowley* (1931). It is the story of a bourgeois from Lyon who, during three months of "self-realization", poses as a haughty aristocrat. The second attitude is to be found in *Le Discours des prix* (Théâtre Saint-Georges, September 27th, 1934). The revolt is preached not by a hero but by a school-teacher, who, finding he has lost the final pages of his speech at a school prize-giving, suddenly throws discretion to the winds and, speaking from his heart, advises the pupils to "live for themselves", to play a part in the life of the family, society, and the nation, but to play it *knowingly*, like good actors, while safeguarding their own private inner life, and, finally, to beware of the word "discipline", because what is required of us in the name of "discipline" is servility.

The satirical comedy in this play comes unexpectedly. Another departure from Sarment's usual formula is to be found in *Madame Quinze*, first performed at the Comédie-Française on February 26th, 1933, and revived in the Salle-Luxembourg on April 25th, 1950. Though history forms the background of the action, what interested Sarment was "the much-maligned, well-beloved, timorous, shameless and lonely Louis XV", and his relations with Madame de Pompadour. The Comédie-Française's choice of *Le Pavillon des enfants*, which it staged on May 24th, 1955, is surprising. It is a depressing play and not particularly interesting. It continues the series, begun by *Madame Quinze*, of plays which are less personal, less poetic, and less meaningful than Sarment's early ones. It is by his very first plays that Sarment will be remembered. His work for the theatre includes adaptations of *Much Ado about Nothing* (1936), *Othello* (1937), and Schiller's *Don Carlos* (1942). He has also written the dialogue for a number of films, including two scenes of Duvivier's *Le Carnet de bal*, and in 1944, for a short time, he held the post of Administrator of the Comédie-Française.

Born in 1910 and making his debut in the theatre in 1932, JEAN ANOUILH might be regarded as the last of the generation of dramatists who had carried through the post-war revolution in the theatre and whose classics were duly enshrined in the Comédie-Française, or as the first of a second generation which was later to include Albert Camus and Jean-Paul Sartre. The second appears to be the more accurate assessment of his place in the history of the theatre. Anouilh had the example of Passeur, Salacrou, Pirandello, Lenormand, and Giraudoux before him, and echoes of their work are to be heard in his plays. On the other hand, several of the basic ideas of the plays that Sartre was yet to write are to be found in Anouilh's work from the very beginning. In Anouilh they are the unconscious expression of the dramatist's outlook on life; they are not the illustration of an abstract philosophy, existing independently of its creator.

L'Hermine (Œuvre, April 27th, 1932) was the first of Anouilh's plays to be performed.[5] Its title is significant; it indicated from the outset the colour of the background on which Anouilh was subsequently to paint his pictures of life, whether in the collections entitled *Pièces noires* or *Pièces roses*. *L'Hermine* is also the first of Anouilh's tragedies of the hopeless quest for absolute purity. The central character, Frantz, is essentially a romantic figure, even though his attitude of revolt is not spontaneous and has been forced upon him by his impecuniosity: he has made a virtue of necessity. Nor does he believe in love, eternal and proof against all contingencies, as did his prototype of 1830. "My love", he says, "is too pure a thing to do without money . . . My love is so beautiful, I expect too much of it to risk having it spoilt by poverty. I want to surround it with a wall of wealth." He is less logical when he arrogates to himself the right to kill in order to preserve, spotless, the "white ermine" of his love; he does not see that love cannot survive a crime—the murder of the rich aunt of the girl he loves. Yet he does not commit the murder for the money itself, but because the money is "the exact price" of his "purity". For him the murder is an act of liberation because it will procure for him the happiness that society refuses the poor and lowly. It is also an act of pride: true freedom and true courage consist, for him, in rising above the law, whether human or divine, which forbids man to kill. Stendhal's Julien Sorel and Dostoievsky's Raskolnikov do not seem to be far from Anouilh's mind; he lays down the condition "all or nothing".

After *L'Hermine* came the pointless production at the Athénée, on January 16th, 1933, of an earlier play, *Mandarine*, written when Anouilh was nineteen. It shows the same amoralism and intellectual anarchism as *L'Hermine*, but there is less depth and less technical skill in it. It was followed by *Y'avait un prisonnier* (Ambassadeurs, March 21st, 1935), in which romantic anarchy and amorality are combined with a sardonic sang-froid more typical of the 1920's than of the time when it was written. The play presents the picture of a superficially respectable family greeting, more in embarrassment than in joy, one of its members, Ludovic, a former international financier, on his return after fifteen years of solitary confinement in a prison cell in Italy. Into this picture Anouilh packs all the egoism, hypocrisy, brutality, stupidity, and futility that he had attributed to society in his preceding plays. Sickened by this first contact, as it were, with society, Anouilh's recluse at first contemplates suicide, but then makes off with another liberated gaol-bird, a deaf mute, whom he recognizes as the one kindred soul in this social desert. The pair set out in search of the freedom which possibly does not exist at all. In one pathetic and particularly significant scene Anouilh touches on a theme to which he was subsequently to give more ample development. He shows his reformed ex-convict's dismay at the futile character and futile existence of his former friend, and his own refusal to contemplate for himself any fall from his newly-found state of grace. Technically, this bitter comedy shows a considerable advance on Anouilh's earlier works, but the exhaustive treatment given to the theme in the brilliant first act leaves little material for the rest of the play. Mistakenly staged as a light comedy, the play was not much of a success.

Le Voyageur sans bagage (Mathurins-Pitoëff, February 16th, 1937) was much more successful.[6] Like Y'avait un prisonnier, it is an escapist play, but it states the problems more clearly. It is also enhanced by an element of poetry which is not to be found in the earlier play. The initial situation is very much that of Jean Giraudoux's Siegfried (1928), to which it has often been wrongly likened. The subject is, however, entirely different. Whereas Giraudoux studies the problem of Franco-German relations, Anouilh is concerned only with the progressive revelation of a human personality. His hero, having lost his memory on the battlefield, is in the unique position of being able to begin life completely afresh. The play, as a result, takes on something of the character of a laboratory experiment. The ex-soldier's family is traced, and the attempts made by each member of his family to awaken some chord of memory in him are shown. It is not, however, the development of the material situation which interests Anouilh; it is the development of what might be termed the mental situation. Anouilh is here following in Pirandello's footsteps, and, as in Pirandello, the dramatic, even tragic moment of "recognition" occurs when the character realizes that what he has taken for the situation is not in fact the situation. It is his family's reconstruction of his past that reveals to Anouilh's apparently gentle hero, Gaston, what a brute and a cad he had been. He is appalled by the discovery and says to his brother's wife, his mistress in former days: "Yes, I repudiate my past and all the people who came into it including myself. You may be my family, my love affairs, the real story of my life, but I don't like you and I'll have none of you." Happier than the rest of men, happier than Oedipus, to whom French critics likened him because they saw in him the same growing anguish and the same struggle of a man against a past which takes him in its grip and overwhelms him, Gaston is in a position to repudiate his past and his family. Anouilh makes a further point: if Gaston were to return to his family he would become the prisoner of his former self, because, for his family, he would still be the brute and cad he once had been. According to Anouilh, a man is the prisoner of the idea that others have of him. Inès, in Sartre's play Huis clos, can almost be heard already saying to her companion in Hell: "You are a coward because I say so."

"If I remember one thing in my past I shall remember every-thing . . . There is no retailing one's past . . ." Gaston declares, and, indeed, when he is confronted by the various members of his family his attitude, in moments of stress, becomes very similar to the atti-tude he had adopted towards them in his youth. This idea is developed further in Eurydice, where Anouilh's heroine anxiously questions whether all the ugly things one has seen remain with one for ever, whether hands retain every gesture they have made, and lips every word they have spoken. Anouilh seems to believe that unless a man happens to be in Gaston's place he remains irrevocably chained to himself. But should a person exist who has known none of the world's ugliness, whose every memory is beautiful, may that person not hope for happiness? Anouilh's Antigone, in the play of that name, replies: "No."

In addition to stating many of the ideas that were to become so familiar in his later plays, Le Voyageur sans bagage offers a good dose of social satire by means of the secondary characters. In the chief character there is an admirable analysis of the development of a state of mind: from calm and ironical indifference Gaston passes to anxious questioning, then to revolt and disgust at what he learns, and, finally, to joyful relief at escaping from the nightmare. These different states of mind and the transition from one to the other, were convincingly brought out by Georges Pitoëff, who gave one of the best performances of his career in this part.

Pitoëff next staged La Sauvage (Mathurins, January 10th, 1938),[7] which had been written two years before Le Voyageur sans bagage, and in its rebellious, despairing heroine Ludmilla Pitoëff found a part which was ideally suited to her. Indeed, it was these two plays which attracted the general public to the Pitoëffs, though it was not until its revival at the Comédie des Champs-Elysées on March 17th, 1945, that *La Sauvage* became a commercial success.

Thérèse is a girl brought up to poverty who tries to adapt herself to the world of riches and fails. For Anouilh, the poor are afflicted by a crippling sensitivity which makes it impossible for them to be helped from their poverty even by those who love them. They cling to it as desperately as the rich cling to their wealth. Between the two worlds of riches and poverty there is an insurmountable barrier. "You don't know", says Thérèse, "what it means to sink into the mire, to wallow in it ... You don't know what real life is, Florent." This complete isolation of the individual, and his inability to communicate with his fellows, remains one of the key notions of Anouilh's drama. Eurydice, in the play of that name, expresses the same idea when she cries out how unbearable it is to be shut up alone in the hermetically sealed sack of one's own skin, able to communicate with each other only by a sort of morse code which we call speech, and she evokes the telling image of two prisoners eternally confined to their own cells, tapping messages on the wall. Thérèse and Florent have no real points of contact. The barrier of Florent's wealth is also the concrete manifestation of a barrier of a different kind, the permanent barrier between one human being and another; it does not imply any attempt on Anouilh's part at social drama. Anouilh's aim is to comment on human nature and the human predicament; he avoids social "commitment".

In *La Sauvage* Anouilh combines the theme of the inescapable bondage of a man's past with that of his solitude, but Thérèse, less happy than the *voyageur*, has to carry the weight of her "luggage" for all time. She finds she cannot repudiate her past, since to do so she would have to repudiate herself, so she returns to the poor, who represent her past, and rejects the happiness proffered by Florent, just as Eurydice, unable to stifle the memories of a sullied past, and doubting the love which has been debased by her experiences, rejects Orphée. Antigone, who is purity itself, goes further, and rejects life because she has been taught that to live is to accept inevitable degradation. In Anouilh's play, if Antigone defies Créon's decree it is not in order to rest her brother's spirit, as in the Greek original, but to escape from a world of endless, sullying compromise which, as the liberated gaol-bird in *Y'avait un prisonnier* had discovered before her, was not "the beautiful world of one's youthful belief". Flight is the great temptation for all Anouilh's heroes, even if flight means death. Antigone, Eurydice, Jeannette (*Roméo et Jeannette*),[8] Gaston, Ludovic, Frantz, Marc (*Jézabel*), all take to flight in some form or other, and they are all the same figure as *la sauvage*, thirsting for an impossible purity. Antigone is prepared to die for this purity, and so is Jeannette, Gaston steels himself to "kill" his other self for the sake of it, to "kill" Jacques Renaud so that "Gaston" may live, but this is an act of self-betrayal that neither Thérèse nor Eurydice can bring themselves to commit.

Side by side with these searchers after the absolute there are the "unworthy", like Créon and Florent. What distinguishes these two "races", as they are called by M. Henri in *Eurydice*, is the unequal intellectual and spiritual awareness to which they attain. People like M. Henri, or the chorus in *Antigone*, who are lucidity incarnate, belong to a third category and can only act as witnesses or commentators in the play. The real, live characters in the plays, and hence the real actors, are the "searchers", and the action of the play consists in their reaching a greater awareness of themselves and of the situation. Anouilh's characters are not in essence creatures governed by their temperament nor by the dictates of their social position. Such psychological or social traits as they may have are pointed, so as to throw into relief the degree of spiritual and intellectual awareness which is theirs. Between the "searchers" after the absolute and the "unworthy" there is no contact; they do not speak the same language; the scene where Thérèse breaks with Florent, or where Antigone and Créon come face to face after Antigone's defiance of Créon's orders, illustrates this clearly.

Not content with the repudiation of a vile society, a vile family, and even of a vile self, Anouilh makes the hero of the *pièce rose*, *Le Rendez-vous de Senlis*, "invent" for himself the ideal family of which he had always dreamed. But though the picture is intentionally rose-coloured, Anouilh is unable to obliterate entirely the black outline of his sketch. The salvation of his hero Georges, who has left his wife and family for the pure maiden of his dreams, is of doubtful duration, moreover it is achieved at the expense of others.

The first of the *Pièces roses* belongs to the inter-war years; it is *Le Bal des voleurs*.[9] Though it was written in 1932, just after *L'Hermine*, the play was not performed until 1938 (September 16th to November 1st), when it was put on at the Théâtre des Arts by the Compagnie des Quatre Saisons. Anouilh had intended to write a play which would rival the Boulevard productions of Louis Verneuil or Yves Mirande, but instead he composed a comedy-ballet in which everything dances, from the characters to the acting and the words themselves. Molière, Musset, and the *commedia dell'arte* all contributed to the spectacle, which was produced by André Barsacq, a brilliant graduate from Dullin's school.

Le Bal des voleurs was accompanied by Darius Milhaud's music, played by an ubiquitous musician whose clarinet underlines the characters' changes of mood and the vicissitudes of the action with a running musical "commentary". Milhaud provided, as it were, an ultra-modern Greek chorus, using music instead of words. The play tells the story of three thieves who pillage the town of Vichy with impunity, thanks to the numerous disguises they assume. At times they do not recognize each other's disguises and are robbed by one another. The situation is further complicated by the activities of two other "respectable" thieves, two financiers, but everything works out as it should in the end, and a carnival atmosphere persists throughout. The theme, for there is one, is the same as that of *La Sauvage*, since the lovers, marionettes though they be—the word is used by one of the characters to describe the others—find themselves separated by their different social environments and prisoners of their pasts, but, as Anouilh had deliberately dipped his pen in rose-coloured ink, his heroine is prepared to marry a thief and even become a thief with him because she believes in love and, alone among Anouilh's characters, dares to declare: "No, I am not ashamed."

When Barsacq succeeded Dullin at the Atelier in 1940 he opened with this play, and between that date and 1953 he produced seven more of Anouilh's plays, the most outstanding production being, of course, that of *Antigone*,[10] which ran for 476 performances in 1944 to 1945, and was revived by him in September 1947, January 1948, and September 1950. *Le Bal des voleurs* was followed at the Atelier by the second *pièce rose*, *Le rendez-vous de Senlis*,[11] on January 29th, 1941, and by *Eurydice* on December 18th. Though *Eurydice*[12] is classed as a *pièce noire*, the world which Anouilh creates in it is as unreal as the world of Musset. The third of the *Pièces roses*, *Léocadia*,[13] which was produced at the Michodière on November 30th, 1940, is a strange fantasy presenting a hero and a heroine who come to consider the humble joys of everyday life more precious than the illusory joys of the imagination. Quizzically,

Anouilh casts doubts upon the authenticity of the grand passion the hero would feign experience.

Play followed play from Anouilh's pen. The first of the *Pièces brillantes, L'Invitation au château* (Atelier-Barsacq, November 4th, 1947),[14] is on much the same lines as *Le Bal des voleurs*, and has had a success second only to that of *Antigone*, though there is little in it besides a complicated plot and entrances and exits arranged with the precision of a ballet. The list continues with two *pièces grinçantes, Ardèle ou la Marguerite*[15] and *La Valse des toréadors*,[16] both centred on the General Saint-Pé and his wife, and both staged at the Comédie des Champs-Elysées, the first on November 4th, 1948, and the second on January 8th, 1952; with *La Répétition ou l'amour puni*,[17] into which are woven scenes from Marivaux's *La double Inconstance* and elements of Molière's *L'Impromptu de Versailles*, performed by Barrault at the Marigny on October 26th, 1951, and *Colombe*[18] and *Médée* (written in 1946),[19] both staged by Barsacq at the Atelier on February 11th, 1951, and March 25th, 1953, respectively. In all of them Anouilh remained his own prisoner, pacing round and round within the confining walls of his themes, chained to them even as his characters Gaston, Thérèse, Eurydice, Jeannette, or even the ludicrous General Saint-Pé, were chained to their pasts with the heavy fetters of memory.

A rebellious spirit, an anarchist, but not a revolutionary, Anouilh has rarely got away from the recurrent theme of joyless childhood, nor from his preoccupation with poverty and degradation—moral as well as physical—seen in sharp contrast with heedless wealth. In his early years he struck a resounding note in the theatre with his heroes' revolt against the corrupting power of money, against the ugliness and stupidity of much of life, but his inability to get outside himself condemned him to the reiteration of one note, each repetition becoming less convincing. In *Antigone* he seemed to be momentarily assailed with doubts and, despite his evident intention to extol Antigone's refusal to accept life debased from the ideal, he makes her death appear not as a heroic sacrifice but as a pitiable suicide, and he betrays a grudging sympathy for Créon and those who, saying "yes" to life, take hold of the helm and steer the ship. The force of Créon's arguments at first led the public to think that this was a play in favour of collaboration with the Germans, but Antigone's unyielding opposition to Créon's order, her cry that she was not there to understand but to say "No" to Créon, gripped an ever-increasing public, which came to identify its own attitude to the German occupying authorities with Antigone's defiance of Créon. With the Liberation the play lost its particular urgency, but its continued success in France, and subsequently in other countries, has proved its intrinsic worth. In an action which is highly dramatic Antigone now stands as the symbol of youth's resistance to the compromises and concessions which older people, with their experience of life, are willing to make, but she was not the first of Anouilh's characters to rebel against the terms of life, nor was she born of the war and the Occupation. The earlier plays show that already before the war Anouilh had delighted in despair; already he was convinced of the vanity, futility, and absurdity of the world. Can there be any justification for living? Is it possible to live? These are the questions he has asked from the outset. His *Pièces noires* reply in the negative. One must lie or die, and death, the same grotesque adventure as life itself, is not the gateway to another life but the final curtain to existence. In his *Pièces roses*, however, Anouilh condones a certain type of lie and even envisages a love so sincere that it can lead to life. This is all the more curious, as in his darker mood he makes a mockery of love, first in *Roméo et Jeannette*, then in the devastating *Ardèle*, in which the only love that is not a horrible comedy—and here Anouilh's cynicism and pessimism are unbounded—is that of two unlovely and unlovable hunchbacks, who seek to join each other in death, since they cannot do so in life. In this play love no longer appears as the victim of social contingencies, as in *L'Hermine* or *Eurydice*. It is a mere animal instinct—such is the lesson of *Ardèle*. Despite the deceptive comedy of the situations and characters, the play marks the depths of Anouilh's pessimism. Perhaps these had also been reached in *Roméo et Jeannette*, where Anouilh defined his vision of the deity as a species of sleeping monster that could not be roused with impunity, but was inevitably awakened by the "odour of love", which its keen sense of smell found particularly offensive. Once awake, it would nose into men's business and things would "get cracking as in the army". Such a picture is reminiscent of Giraudoux's vision of a sleeping deity, but it has an earthiness not to be found in Giraudoux.

Anouilh's drama offers an indictment, savage and at first sincere, of an absurd world, where impurity, hypocrisy, injustice are the order of the day. It puts in a claim for the right to be poor without suffering humiliation, the right to repudiate family, society, life itself, should it be rotten, the right to refuse to acquiesce in whatever we judge to be degrading; but it does not tell us in what name this claim is made. It is not made in the name of religious faith. Nor is it made in the hope of a better, purer future, to be achieved by man's own efforts—never for one moment do Anouilh's characters think along these lines. Faced with the impossibility of recapturing the purity of childhood, Anouilh's early heroes and heroines react by taking to flight. The first to accept life, and to accept to perform as well as possible the tasks which life brings with it, is Créon, and Anouilh makes him argue convincingly. This attitude is new in Anouilh's work. It is maintained by Frédéric, in *Roméo et Jeannette*, who tentatively suggests that one should grow up and live one's life, absurd though life may be. Jeannette, however, confuses the issue by pointing out that to accept to grow up is to accept to fall from grace—"I do not wish to say 'yes'. Everything is too ugly." Jason, in *Médée*, goes a step further than Frédéric; he accepts outright to "be a man"—that is, to try to effect a compromise between youthful intransigence and life with its shortcomings. At the age of thirty-five Anouilh was clearly moving away from the position he had taken up in his twenties.

A new note is struck in *La Valse des toréadors*. Its hero, the ridiculous and despicable General Saint-Pé, is the first to discover that despite everything he has kept a soul capable of remorse and pity. Jeanne, in *L'Alouette* (Montparnasse-Jamois, October 14th, 1953),[20] is the first to be proud of her human achievements and to love humankind in spite of, or even because of, its imperfections; nevertheless, like Antigone, she refuses to accept for herself a life of compromise and debased ideals. But Anouilh did not follow up the lead he had given himself in these two plays, as *Ornifle ou le courant d'air* (Comédie des Champs-Elysées, November 3rd, 1955), the third of the *Pièces grinçantes*, was to prove only too clearly, and this lack of any constructive element is surprising in the work of one who, from the outset, had shown such a strong preoccupation with the absolute. The particular quality of Anouilh's drama lies in the striking expression it gives to the anxiety of a generation haunted by doubts, poverty, and insecurity, yet in which the best are urged on by some inner ideal to make a protest. Anouilh seemed to have something to say, but no message was ever given, and his later plays have made it clear that none was intended. From the *Pièces noires* and *Pièces roses* and the *Nouvelles pièces noires* Anouilh had progressed to the *Pièces brillantes* and *Pièces grinçantes* in which he mocked the very poverty, purity, and integrity which had seemed so close to his heart in the early years. From *Colombe* and *La Répétition ou l'amour puni*, from *Ardèle* and *La Valse des toréadors*, nearly every trace of white, the chosen background for his earlier plays, has disappeared, and the blemishes are thrown into ugly relief, while in *Ornifle* all purity has been dispensed with, and the stain alone remains: "We priests are humanity's dustbins", says Father Dubaton, who has been called to the bedside of Ornifle, a vulgar, cynical, and sated Don Juan. But audiences continued to throng the theatre, unmindful of the missing figure of *La Sauvage*. The significant playwright of the inter-war years had degenerated into a successful purveyor of entertainment for the Boulevard. Indeed, Anouilh has recently stated that a dramatic author's business is to be a maker, or manufacturer, of plays, so as to supply the needs of the actor, who has to perform each night for a public which comes to the theatre to forget its troubles. So much the better if now and again a masterpiece turns up, but such an occurrence must be incidental.

Pauvre Bitos (Montparnasse-Baty, October 11th, 1956)[21] is the fourth and last of the *Pièces grinçantes*—at least, as far as Anouilh's description of them goes. The attitude which he expressed in this play, and subsequently in *L'Hurluberlu, La Foire d'empoigne*, and even in *Becket* with regard to a number of topical questions such as the Resistance movement and the post-war treatment of collaborators, provoked a good deal of polemical writing, and the dramatist's attitude in these plays can be taken as indicative of the real attitude behind the apparently deliberate ambiguity of *Antigone* of 1943. Under the title *Poor Bitos, Pauvre Bitos* had a very successful run in London (1963–64), where there was no particular reason for concern over Anouilh's caricature of the French Revolution in his grotesque and historically inaccurate portrait of Robespierre, nor over the deliberate parallel which was drawn between the Terror of 1793 and the tribunal of the Liberation in 1945. There were also glib jibes at parliamentary democracy and the "masses" ("mediocre", and later, "imbecile"). According to their political views, people took sides for or against the play.

Gabriel Marcel managed to take sides against the play on purely technical grounds; he confessed to not being worried in the slightest about the "scandal of the purge", but found the play "bitter and boring" and ending in "grimacing confusion". The critic of *Rivarol* (October 18th, 1956), on the other hand, defended this "courageous play" against its adversaries, and even against its "right-wing champions", who all refused to perceive beyond history and politics, beyond Robespierre and the Purge, the excellent comedy of character that the play happened to be. Bitos was not only Robespierre, he was not only a Purger of 1945, he was also an individual, a poor specimen of humanity, for whom Anouilh had shown some compassion.

L'Hurluberlu ou le réactionnaire amoureux (Comédie des Champs-Elysées, February 5th, 1959)[22] is another topical satire, but this time Anouilh resorted to ambivalence of attitude. Its targets are much the same as in *Pauvre Bitos*, though by putting on a play within a play, as he had done in *La Répétition*, he was also able to hit out at the anti-theatre of the fifties, particularly at Samuel Beckett. *L'Hurluberlu* was to have been staged in May 1958 but was held over till the following February because of the political situation in France. Its hero had joined the Forces Françaises Libres in 1940, had been promoted the youngest general in France at the Liberation, and then had been "retired" for conspiring against the regime. When the play opens the general is back in his village, plotting once again, after vainly attempting to write his memoirs, to overthrow the Republic, so as to give back to a "corrupt" France its integrity and its grandeur. Though Anouilh denied that he had had any particular person in mind when writing his play, it was generally assumed that there was a clear reference to General de Gaulle in the original data of the play. From there Anouilh went on to create a "reactionary", or rather a fascist-minded, Alceste, for whom he obviously had a certain amount of sympathy. His sympathies are even clearer in *La Foire d'empoigne* (Comédie des Champs-Elysées, January 11th, 1962), in which he presents a personal view of the Hundred Days, with a buffoon of a Napoleon, concerned only with the effect of his entrances and exits, and a worldly-wise and liberal Louis XVIII playing Box and Cox, and others repeatedly turning their coats. Any resemblance to the real Napoleon or to the real Louis XVIII is quite fortuitous, says the dramatist in a programme note. In this play, also, Anouilh establishes a parallel between the events of 1945 and those of a previous moment in history. This time it is 1815, though with no mention of the White Terror under Louis XVIII. Anouilh shows only one head falling, that of General Ney's, and this through Ney's own fault. In these last plays the anarchist, which Anouilh had shown himself to be in his earlier compositions for the stage, had now revealed himself as an anarchist of the Right, to use the term applied to him by Arthur Adamov in an open debate, published in *Arts* on September 27th, 1961. Keep out of politics, get married, have many children, keep your place, and do your work, is the counsel given by Anouilh's king; it was the pure Vichy doctrine, some critics protested.

La Foire d'empoigne, together with *L'Alouette* and a picture-book play, *Becket ou l'honneur de Dieu* (Montparnasse-Baty, September 30th, 1959),[23] constitute Anouilh's *Pièces costumées*. *Becket* is based on Auguste Thierry's now exploded views of that particular chapter of history, but since Thierry gave Anouilh the "ambiguous Becket that he needed", as he stated in a programme note, that was all that mattered to him. Anouilh's Becket is a Saxon, and so a member of a defeated race whose country is occupied. The modern references are clear enough to give the impression of deliberately playing to the gallery. But how much more dramatic the situation would have been if, of two men, *both* of the race of conquerors, one, the churchman, should have shown more concern for the interests of the conquered race than the other, its king! Anouilh, however, fastens on Becket's supposedly Saxon origin and makes it the mainspring of the action: as a Saxon Becket could never love his Norman master as wholeheartedly as Henry loved him, and, indeed, in the early part of the play Becket seems even to collaborate with Henry the better to defeat him later. *Becket* is not a historical play, in any case Anouilh calls it "costumée" and not "historique". It is the tragedy of a broken friendship into which is woven Anouilh's own preoccupation with absolute values. When questioned by Henry whether, as archbishop, he loved God, Becket could only reply that it was "God's Honour" that he loved, because "God's Honour" imposed on him a certain line of conduct which the love of God might not have prescribed. For the first time in a play by Anouilh the character who is the ideal of purity incarnate is neither unlikeable, ridiculous, nor doomed.

180 FRENCH DRAMA OF THE INTER-WAR YEARS

With the unpleasant "realism" of *L'Orchestre* (sex-talk in an all-women orchestra in a brasserie), a one-act play billed with *La Foire d'empoigne*, and with *La Grotte* (Montparnasse-Baty, October 5th, 1961),[24] the audience is brought back to the modern world. *La Grotte*, in which he juxtaposes, or rather "superimposes" the one upon the other, the drawing-room and the servants' quarters, in order to demonstrate, by the tragic events which ensue, that there should be no contact between the two worlds other than at the press of a bell, harks back to a class society. The play is technically interesting because there are characters in it and a setting, but no subject. One of the characters is a playwright who is trying to write a play, this play, in fact. He does not know what course the action will take, and tries out various versions of a scene in front of the audience, making comments and changes as he goes. The characters ultimately escape from his control and take on a life of their own. The play is in no way Pirandellian, though Pirandello's influence is visible in earlier plays. What one sees is the author at grips with all the problems involved in writing a play, and, as Anouilh says in a programme note, "*La Grotte* is a play which has not been written." If Anouilh really had the whole action in hand from the start, then this is a literary composition after all, but if he did not, in fact, succeed in writing the play he meant to, then *La Grotte* is merely a clever piece of dramatic acrobatics, and the wager, which was a risky one, was lost, as the play did not have a long run.

If one looks back over the whole of Anouilh's dramatic production one finds such a similarity between his themes that one is tempted to say that he has written only one play, but that his one play has been re-written time and time again, and that each successive handling of the play has brought out more clearly the amazing ingenuity of the author. The fundamental elements of Anouilh's thought are to be found in *La Sauvage*, with further developments of the themes in *Le Voyageur sans bagage*, *Eurydice*, and *Antigone*. In later plays they are watered down, or seasoned with topical allusions, to appeal to the numerically more important audiences of the Boulevard.

As a craftsman Anouilh is second to none in the contemporary French theatre. He is equally at home, technically, in serious drama which is almost classical in form, in light comedy with a complicated plot, in pseudo-historical plays in multiple tableau form, or in entertainments to which one might almost give the name of *comédies-ballets*. In all of them Anouilh reveals himself as a literary writer who shuns the ordinary spoken language for the stage and uses a deliberately poetic style.

Anouilh, the playwright, has also extended his activities to the cinema. The films on which he has worked include *Monsieur Vincent*, which received the highest French award for the year 1947. In collaboration with Roland Laudenbach he wrote the scenario and dialogue for *La Petite Molière*. It was not made into a film, but was staged by Barrault just as it was written, first at the Bordeaux Festival in 1959, and then as the second production at the newly constituted Théâtre de France. Anouilh has also shown himself to be a successful producer.

The heroes of the plays of both Sarment and Anouilh live with ideals which they fail to bring into relation with everyday existence; those of Sarment accept their failure more easily than those of Anouilh, who make a determined effort, at least in the early plays, to achieve the ideal of integrity which is the legacy of childhood. Sarment's first plays gave the promise of better to come, but the promise was not fulfilled. Anouilh, from the outset, was obviously a real man of the theatre. Seen from this distance, Sarment's plays seem very pale, whereas those of Anouilh are highly coloured. But Anouilh's colours are crude, and many of his post-war plays are not only *bien faites* but *trop faites*, decidedly high and gamy.

NOTES

1. *Les Débats*, February 18th, 1929.
2. Awarded the Paul Hervieu prize in 1920; revived at the Comédie-Française, March 19th, 1934.
3. After a number of revivals the play entered the repertory of the Odéon, on November 22nd, 1940.
4. Revived, Comédie-Française, September 29th, 1941; Comédie Wagram, March 13th, 1948.
5. Performed in English in 1955 as *The Ermine*.
6. Revived, Michodière, April 1st, 1944; Montparnasse-Jamois, April 6th, 1950. Performed in English as *Traveller without Luggage*, 1959.
7. Revived, Comédie Champs-Elysées, March 17th, 1945. Performed in English in 1957 as *Restless Heart*.
8. Atelier-Barsacq, December 3rd, 1946; performed in English in 1949 as *Fading Mansion*, and in 1965 as *Romeo and Jeannette*.
9. Performed in English in 1952 as *The Thieves' Carnival*; as a ballet by Léonide Massine in 1963.

10. Performed in English in 1949 as *Antigone*.
11. Performed in English in 1957 as *Dinner with the Family*.
12. Performed in English in 1950 as *Point of Departure*.
13. Performed in English in 1954 as *Time Remembered*.
14. Performed in English in 1950 as *Ring round the Moon*.
15. Comédie des Champs-Elysées, May 30th, 1951, and July 8th, 1958. Performed in English in 1950 as *Ardèle*.
16. Performed in English in 1956 as *Waltz of the Toreadors*. Filmed in 1962 by Peter de Sarigny and John Guillermin.
17. Performed in English in 1961 as *The Rehearsal*.
18. Performed in English in 1951 as *Colombe*.
19. Performed in English in 1957 as *Medea*.
20. Performed in English in 1955 as *The Lark*.
21. Performed in English in 1963 as *Poor Bitos*.
22. Performed in English in 1966 as *The Fighting Cock*.
23. Revived, Montparnasse-Baty, October 28th, 1966. Performed in English in 1961 as *Becket*. Filmed in 1964 by Peter Glenville.
24. Performed in English in 1965 as *The Cavern*.

VII

Studio Theatre: Fantasy and Fairy-tale

*Marcel Achard—Régis Gignoux—Alexandre Arnoux
—Émile Roudié—Jean Variot—Jules Supervielle.*

MARCEL ACHARD began his career in the theatre in 1919 as a prompter for Copeau at the Vieux-Colombier, but it was Dullin who, in 1923, staged his first play of importance, *Voulez-vous jouer avec moâ?* The play met with great success then and again in 1943, when it was revived at the Bouffes Parisiens. In 1955 it enjoyed a long run at the newly opened Théâtre en rond, to which it was particularly suited because of the strong circus element in it. Indeed, the *dramatis personae* are circus characters, and the play's title consists of the opening words of a circus performance. When Achard wrote the play he had in mind the three famous French clowns, the Fratellini Brothers, whom he had seen at work in Copeau's dramatic school as well as in the circus arena, and he clearly modelled his Crockson, Rascasse, and Auguste on Albert, François, and Paul respectively. These clowns, in turn, were modelled on characters of the *commedia dell'arte*. Pedrolina, or Pierrot, as he had become in France, specially attracted Achard, and after appearing as Auguste in this play, re-appears as Howard in *Malborough s'en va-t-en guerre*, as Cadet in *Je ne vous aime pas*,[1] Jef in *Jean de la lune*, and in the title-rôle of *Pétrus*. As Auguste he is an amateur clown in a circus, as Howard he is a naïve, romantic page, living in a strangely medieval eighteenth century. As Cadet he is an ironical pierrot in the Jules Laforgue manner, who has stepped out of the world of fantasy into the world of today. As Jef he also belongs to the everyday world but has a new-found sentimental optimism, which persists in the character of the itinerant photographer Pétrus, in Achard's last real "pierrot" play.

Pierrot was not the only character of the *commedia* to attract Achard. Isabelle, the coquette, beloved by the three clowns, is Columbina (but she is more refined and more emancipated than her Italian prototype), while the cowardly braggard Malborough is clearly the *capitano* of the *commedia*, and Bettina, lady-in-waiting to Malborough's wife, is the *soubrette*. Harlequin, too, makes an appearance as the down-and-out Charlemagne (*La vie est belle*), though he looks at times suspiciously like pierrot. The likeable, intelligent adventurer Domino (*Domino*) is an even more complete Harlequin, who skilfully manages the love affairs of others with personal unconcern—at least until the final act of the play, when he, too, falls in love.

If Achard was attracted by the stock characters of the old Italian stage it was because they lent themselves to psychological studies in a Pirandellist vein. The instability and fluidity of the world of the *commedia* is reproduced in Achard's comedies. "Qui êtes-vous?" is the bewildered question put by the heroine of *Jean de la lune* to her husband. "Mettons que je suis un grand type qui t'aime comme un imbécile", is Jef's enigmatic reply, and so persuasive is his faith in her virtue that the fickle coquette is charmed into the rôle of a faithful and loving wife. Achard's treatment of this original theme is poetic and moving, and Achard made his name with the play. It was staged at the Comédie des Champs-Elysées on February 3rd, 1929, by Louis Jouvet, who found the part of the naïve, enigmatic pierrot much to his taste; he later played the pierrot again under the name of Pétrus.

La belle Marinière followed *Jean de la lune* on October 4th, 1929, but it was staged at the Comédie-Française, where the lowliness of the characters and the background, the conversational tone of the dialogue and a suggestion of reality in caricature, made it seem out of place. The subject may be the conflict of love and friendship and the cruel play of fate, in the classical manner, but the scene is a canal barge, the heroes a bargee and his mate, and the heroines the bargee's wife and sister. The wife, who at first resents the undue place the mate holds in her husband's affection, eventually falls in love with him and deliberately causes the two to fall out with each other. The mate has to go, but without him the barge is a dreary place, and he is soon pressed to return. The mate and the wife then decide to go away together, and the play ends on the melancholy parting of the two friends, marked at first by the bargee's complete

failure to understand the situation, and, finally, by his tragic realization of his double loss of wife and friend. There is often a disconcerting disparity between the social situation of the characters
and their poetic musings, although, by its realism, the bargee's
wedding-feast invited comparison with Zola and Maupassant and
also the accusation of *populisme*.

With *Domino* (Comédie des Champs-Elysées-Jouvet, February
2nd, 1932) Achard returned to the tradition of *Jean de la lune*
without attaining its perfection. Domino, a smooth-tongued down-
and-out, is engaged by Lorette and Crémone, her former lover, now
her husband's business associate, to pay court to her, so as to divert
her husband's newly raised suspicions. It is reminiscent of Musset's
Le Chandelier, but the theme is re-thought by a disciple of Pirandello. Domino gradually assimilates, as it were, the part of the man
he pretends to be, and becomes for Lorette the embodiment of the
ideal that Crémone had formerly been. As Crémone watches this
re-staging of his past he falls in love again with Lorette, but he has
lost his past to Domino, just as he has lost Lorette herself to
Domino. Jouvet played the part of this modern harlequin, which
was as much in his line as that of the modern pierrot.

Not content with repeating old successes, Achard adopted, in
La Femme en blanc (Théâtre Michel, March 8th, 1933), a dramatic structure similar to that used on the screen when a character's
past is revealed by a flash-back. Here it provides an interesting
picture of a period some twenty years before. As in a film, the
story which the hero tells is enacted before the spectator's eyes. As
a young officer he had been the lover of Manuela's mother, *la
femme en blanc*, a strange, irrational creature, who had committed
suicide on learning of his infidelity. Back again in 1932 the spectator sees the young Manuela, who had been fascinated by this
man's amorous past and had wanted to marry him, confronted with
this doubly criminal situation. Knowing he was on uncertain
ground with such a theme, Achard deliberately avoided treating it
seriously and adopted a tone of airy mockery. With Gaby Morlay
in the parts of both mother and daughter, success was assured, but
it was not an experiment to be tried a second time, so Achard
looked again to the twentieth-century pierrot for inspiration, and
Pétrus appeared at the Comédie des Champs-Elysées-Jouvet on
December 7th the same year (1933). In the first act there is a flippant gaiety strongly reminiscent of Courteline. The scene is enacted

at night at the police-station, the characters being the fickle lover, his despairing mistress, who has twice fired at him in the street and missed, and the enraged passer-by, Pétrus, the hapless recipient of the bullets. But whereas a playwright like Courteline was always content to remain within the world of reality, Achard adds a touch of fantasy to disguise the commonplace. Pétrus makes heroic but vain efforts to reconcile the lover and the girl, with whom he himself has fallen in love. Finally—and here the action takes an unexpected turn—he is to be seen as a photographer at Luna Park, quietly and happily married to the would-be murderess. The murder, this time effective, of the fickle lover casts a shadow on the happiness of the placid hero, because his wife has been seen at the victim's hotel, but Pétrus's faith in his wife is so great that he confidently affirms her innocence. He is right, for the real murderess is the new mistress, whose aim, unlike the old one's, has proved accurate.

In 1938 Achard returned from Hollywood, where he had gone to work with Lubitsch after the filming of *Jean de la lune*. He brought back with him an idea for a play, *Le Corsaire* (Athénée-Jouvet, March 25th), showing actors and technicians discussing the film they are making, the story of which actually runs parallel with the personal love-story of the actors who are playing in the "film". The subject of Achard's play is the dawn of sublime love in the midst of the hollow artificiality of filmland, but the play seems also to suggest that in order to become perfect lovers one must first *act* the part. The story which is being shot is that of an eighteenth-century pirate, Kid Jackson, who falls in love with his captive, Evangéline. Later, when the pirate is captured and is to be hanged, Evangéline begs him to kill her; on the ship he had promised to do so, should he be unable to protect her in any other way from outrage by his fellow-pirates. This melodramatic story, which is closely interwoven with the story of the actors themselves, presented Louis Jouvet and Madeleine Ozeray with the difficult task of assuming two very different rôles each, and of gradually developing them until the cinema stars became identified with the characters of the film within the play which the two stars were making.

To the play, which is Pirandellian in conception, Achard adds an element of social satire which is not in his true vein. Admittedly, there is satire in *Malborough s'en va-t-en guerre*, Comédie des Champs-Elysées-Jouvet, December 8th, 1924),[3] but it is not serious, and the hero, a general who planned a whole military campaign so as to bring about the death of his wife's page instead of the defeat of the enemy, is a sufficiently ludicrous caricature to escape being taken seriously; indeed, he followed in the tradition of Alfred Jarry's *Ubu-Roi*, without, however, attaining Ubu's sinister proportions. This element of burlesque is absent from *Le Corsaire*.

With *Adam* (1938), which was staged at the Gymnase, begins a long series of almost exclusively Boulevard plays, many of them commercially successful, but none presenting any special interest to the historian of drama. One is confronted with titles such as *Chiche* (1946), *Savez-vous planter les choux?* (1947), *Patate* (1957), and *Machin chouette* (1964). The idea for *Patate*, which ran for seven years, dates, according to Achard, from the time of *Jean de la lune*. After showing that love can work miracles, he planned to treat hatred, which has no such powers, but, as his experience of hatred was limited at the time, the play did not take shape until twenty-five years later. Such is Achard's account of its origin. Its hero, "Patate", a likeable *raté*, can stand beside Jean de la lune and Domino as a dramatic creation, but the clever manipulation of plot and effects stamps the play as a Boulevard comedy. Achard has lost the poetry of his early years when, Musset-like, he presented his Fantasio-like heroes in a setting somewhere between real life and a world of dreams.

With *Le Prof' d'Anglais ou le système Puck* (Comédie des Champs-Elysées-Jouvet, April 30th, 1930), REGIS GIGNOUX entered into competition with Marcel Achard. The hero, Valfine, played by Jouvet, is a poor schoolmaster, a poet, totally removed from reality. He thinks of everything and everybody in terms of Shakespeare's plays, and thus imagines a Romeo-and-Juliet relationship between his pupil and her young friend Pascal, whereas Pascal is really in love with Valfine's wife. When Valfine finds himself accused of condoning his wife's misconduct he is absolutely at a loss, because husbands who act in this way do not exist in Shakespeare—in Shakespeare there is only Othello. In due course the grown-ups sort out their problems, and Valfine comes upon his Romeo and Juliet just as they are exchanging their first kiss; this restores his faith in his god Shakespeare.

Other plays by Gignoux, such as *Le Fruit vert* (1924) and *Le Cheval de cirque* (1928), are more straightforward examples of light comedy, though they also contain a touch of moral and social satire.

ALEXANDRE ARNOUX is a poet who has made occasional excursions into the theatre over a long period of years, the first being in 1909, when a short verse play of his, *La Mort de Pan*, was staged at the Odéon. He returned to the theatre in 1921, when Dullin was on the look-out for new ideas in stage technique, and supplied him with *Moriana et Galvan* (Atelier, March 2nd, 1922). The spoken text, which is barely a page long, is based on a Moorish Romancero, and offers an admirable opportunity for miming. Dullin's actors, who included Antonin Artaud, all wore expressive masks, and masks were also used by the professional mime, Marcel Marceau, when he revived the *mimodrame* in March 1951. *La vida es sueño*, which Arnoux had just adapted from Calderón, followed soon after *Moriana et Galvan*. Then came *Huon de Bordeaux* (March 21st, 1923) and *Petite Lumière et l'ourse* (May 21st, 1923), all at the Atelier. *El médico de su honra* was also adapted from Calderón by Arnoux and was staged by Dullin on February 8th, 1935.

Huon de Bordeaux is a delightful rendering of the story, told by medieval minstrels, of the exploits which Charlemagne required of Huon for having unwittingly killed his son, Karlot. There are no heroes in the play; the style is simple. When Huon is sentenced to death without trial the old duke, Naimes, rises to his feet saying: "God be with you." "Where are you going?" Charlemagne asks. "When the king loses his senses, his counsellors take their leave", replies Naimes. These lines are indicative of the absence of rhetoric, and this is equally true of the frequent passages in verse which occur. The play is loosely constructed in a succession of short tableaux, a fact which presented Dullin with technical as well as financial difficulties. The Théâtre Pigalle, with its modern machinery, was better equipped to stage a play of this kind, and Douking's sensitive production there on December 20th, 1946, did justice to the undeniable qualities of this popular epic.

Whereas in *Huon de Bordeaux* Arnoux had the legend to draw upon, for *Petite Lumière et l'ourse* he was dependent on his own imagination. In it he recounts a dream, set in a modern world, where electricity and trade unionism are two great forces. The second act materialized a dream which is dreamed by two children, and is an imaginative translation of what they have heard their elders say in the first act. The passage from reality to the dream and back again is marked by an acrobat who does cart-wheels across the stage in silence. Ellibu, the gardener who plays the flute, becomes, in the dream, a sort of Pied Piper, having at his heels the children's two teddy-bears, who have grown up into live bears. A flash of lightning which zigzags through the darkness is King Potentiel (the metamorphosed electrician) making his attack on the children and their party—"the electrician", Rag, the boy, had said in the first act, "told me that the potentiel was a sort of king, like the kings of ancient times; he passes a fluid through the wire, and when people do not obey him he orders a short-circuit and sets the house on fire". In the dream Princess Tétragone, Potentiel's hated daughter, saves the children from her father. The next day, when the dream is over and the children are setting out for school, the little girl asks: "What is tétragone?" "It is a plant or a princess . . . I am not quite sure which", the boy replies. This is a play for children of all ages, well written by a literary playwright.

Arnoux's remaining works include a further adaptation from Calderón, and radio and stage plays based mainly on folk-lore—for example, the broad outline of *Le Cavalier de fer* and *La Rose de l'Alhambra*, which form the volume entitled *L'Enchantement de Grenade* (1951), are taken from hispano-arab folk-tales preserved in Washington Irving's *The Alhambra*.

Two original plays should be mentioned, *L'Amour des trois oranges* and *Faut-il brûler Jeanne?*

The first of these two, which was performed at the Théâtre Montparnasse on April 22nd, 1947, was the last of Baty's productions in Paris. The play tells of Carlo Gozzi's meeting in a country inn with Sacchi's company of actors and Théodore Ricci, a vivacious girl whom he helped to fame in Venice, where she acted in his plays. The play closes with a striking epilogue, showing the chance meeting of Gozzi at the age of eighty, and Théodore, a needy old woman, at the door of the crumbling theatre. As they mount the dilapidated stage their imagination takes them back twenty-five years to their last triumphs, and the whole theatre seems to come to life again; there, in front of an attentive audience, amid the actors Sacchi-Truffaldino, Brighella, Pantaloon, under the lighted candelabras, all conjured up by his imagination, Gozzi dies. In this play, in which the protagonists are taken from history, Arnoux creates, by his prose style, an atmosphere as deliberately unreal as that of his fairy-tale plays, but it must be admitted that the "literary" quality of the dialogue is unintentionally undramatic.

Faut-il brûler Jeanne offers an unusual treatment of the story of Joan of Arc. Joan is saved from the stake as the result of the intercession of the saints, but God makes the condition that Joan shall no longer hear her Voices. Thus Joan, who is represented as being rescued from prison in Rouen by the soldier La Hire, finds herself absolutely alone, to face the perils of her apparent victory. "Lord, Lord, why hast Thou forsaken me?" she cries. "If I have fulfilled my missions, I am no longer needed . . . and if I am now an obstacle to Thy wishes . . . it would have been better had I been burned at the stake in Rouen." Her prayer is granted, and God wipes from the memories of men and from History the episode which is here enacted. The play is strewn with modern allusions, which give an added piquancy to this imaginary story of Joan of Arc. After being put on by Radiodiffusion française on March 3rd, 1951, the play was staged at a "people's festival" on May 27th in Rouen, with the cathedral as its setting, but it has not yet been seen in a theatre.

Arnoux's most satisfactory stage play is, to date, *Huon de Bordeaux*. Three months before Dullin staged it Firmin Gémier put on another play with the same title for the Théâtre Populaire at the Trocadéro. It was by EMILE ROUDIE. Since folk-lore seemed to offer the theatre something new, Dullin, Copeau, and Baty asked JEAN VARIOT, who was of Alsatian stock and well versed in Alsatian folk-lore, to dramatize some of the tales. Variot published his dramatized versions of Rhineland folk-tales under the collective title *Théâtre du Rhin* (1926); one of these, *La Rose de Rosheim*, a sixteenth-century tale, was performed at the Théâtre des Champs-Elysées on April 4th, 1921. On February 21st, 1922, Baty opened at the Comédie des Champs-Elysées with *La Belle de Haguenau*. Copeau staged it at the Vieux-Colombier on October 23rd, and two years later it was set to music by Maurice Fouret and performed at the Trianon Lyrique. On November 27th, 1923, Dullin staged *Le Chevalier sans nom* (*Théâtre du Rhin*), a thirteenth-century folk-tale, in Paris, after having first performed it in Strasbourg on November 19th. Variot's best play is, however, *La mauvaise Conduite*, a very free adaptation of Plautus's *Menaechmi*, which was staged at the Vieux-Colombier by the Compagnie des Quinze on November 7th, 1931. Variot leaves the choice of period and setting to the producer, but favours a Mediterranean background. There is a single set: a public square, with Ménéchme's house on one side and that of his mistress on the other. There is much com-

ing and going, and innumerable surprises and mistakes arise out of
the arrival of Ménéchme's double. The situations are extremely
daring and the dialogue very outspoken, but the play is not merely
a comedy of action; it contains a strong element of satire, and all the
characters, lawful wives, courtesans, faithful servants and hangers-
on, bourgeois adventurers, sailors, doctors, and the police, feel its
edge.

In 1931, at the age of forty-seven, the poet and novelist JULES
SUPERVIELLE turned his hand to play-writing. With the exception
of *Voleur d'enfants*, which is based on his novel bearing the same
title, and its sequel *Le Survivant*, his plays contain lengthy passages in verse. Indeed, the only type of play which interested him
was the poetic play, because it took him into a world quite different
from the world of everyday life. It was not a question of escape, but
one of transfiguring reality. For his first play, *La Belle au bois
dormant*, Supervielle took from fairy-stories the Sleeping Beauty
and Bluebeard, together with their Fairy Godmothers, and Puss in
Boots, who is in attendance on Beauty. La Belle and Barbe bleue fall
in love, and it is to save La Belle from Barbe bleue, who is un-
reassuringly torn between his higher feelings and his lower instincts, that La Belle's Fairy Godmother plunges her and Le Chat
botté into a deep sleep. Barbe bleue chooses to keep them company. All three are finally awakened by the Prince, but La Belle
refuses to conform to the tale as told by Perrault, and marry the
Prince Charming. She remains true to Barbe bleue. The twentieth
century, in which the Prince has awakened them, and in which
science, medicine, and the "art of killing" in war have been perfected, is not a century in which these three characters can live.
The whole aspect of the world they knew has changed: crowded
dwelling-houses replace the green forests, there are noisy factories
and chimneys pouring out smoke, and people have no time for a
kind thought or for feelings. The play ends with the three characters being gradually changed into pictures illustrating Charles
Perrault's tales. In the third version of the play, published in 1953,
the line between the spiritual and the material is drawn more
clearly than in the earlier version, and the Prince is made to share
the fate of the other three legendary characters. Even though this
is a fairy-story, there is some good psychological observation, particularly in the presentation of Barbe bleue, and Supervielle passes
easily from realistic analysis to the purest fantasy. Where he is

weakest is in dramatic structure; each scene is treated almost as a separate poem. This defect certainly militated against the success of the play when Pitoëff staged it at the Athénée on March 2nd, 1932, after performing it in Brussels on December 24th. The second version of the play was performed by Jouvet in South America in 1940.

In *Shéhérazade*, another fairy-story play, this lack of continuity in the action is still more clearly marked. Supervielle's Barbe bleue reappears as the cruel sultan Shariar, and a subtitle for the play could well be *Le Sultan poli par l'amour*. The play ends rather like *La Belle au bois*, with the characters re-entering the domain of legend, meanwhile the Winged Horse has been called on to save Shéhérazade and the sultan's brother from the torture ordered by the sultan, and the sultan's palace itself has taken to the air. *Shéhérazade* is not the work of a real man of the theatre, but it was well served by the setting of the courtyard of the Palace of the Popes, in Avignon, and the music of Darius Milhaud. Jean Vilar, who staged it there with great success in July 1948, said that the play seemed to have been specially written to be performed in the open air. At the performance in the Palace of the Popes, as the powerful spotlights swept upward, picking out windows and turrets which until then had been in complete darkness, the fairy-tale palace seemed really to take wings and come to rest on a mountain-top. When Vilar put the play on at the Théâtre Edouard VII, on August 28th, he said he found it very difficult to enclose the legend within the limits of an indoor theatre stage.

With *Robinson*, the second version of which was performed at the Œuvre in November 1952, Supervielle rewrites the story of Robinson Crusoe and Man Friday, making of it a story of the triumph of love over death. Robinson runs away to sea, thinking that Fanny loves his brother. When he returns eighteen years later with Fanny's father, who had been shipwrecked on the same island as himself, he finds Fanny's daughter, who is also called Fanny and who seems to be the reincarnation of her mother, waiting for him. There is nothing incongruous in their marriage, as time seems to have passed Robinson by without leaving any trace. A strong element of comedy runs through the play, both in the action and in the language, which is strewn with alliterations, puns, or mutilated words, even in the passages in verse.

By the nature of its subject *Le Voleur d'enfants* (Œuvre, October

L'Ecole des Femmes. Producer: Jouvet

Têtes de rechange. Producer: Baty

Coll. Rondel, Biblio. de l'Arsenal

Madame Bovary. Producer: Baty

Photo: Lipnitzki

16th, 1948) differs greatly from Supervielle's other plays. Its hero is Colonel Bigua, a childless South American, aged forty-five, who creates a family for himself by "adopting" unwanted children. He falls in love with one of them, a girl of sixteen, and suffers the tortures of the damned. He only finds peace, after his attempted suicide, when the girl returns to his house with the baby she has had by another of his "adopted" children. Such a subject is fraught with the perils of bathos, but Supervielle's treatment of it shows a sureness of touch which is conspicuously absent from his other plays. His own sympathy for Bigua, whom we first see in a dressing-gown and soft hat, busy at work at a sewing-machine, making baby clothes for non-existent babies, makes of this eccentric colonel a convincing and pathetic figure. Yet real though the characters of the play are, the atmosphere which Supervielle succeeds in creating is as poetic as that of his fairy-story plays.

Le Voleur d'enfants is a good play and it is Supervielle's best, but it is with Bolivar that he has obtained the most success in the theatre. Bolivar was staged at the Comédie-Française on March 1st, 1936, with incidental music by Darius Milhaud and dances arranged by Serge Lifar, ballet master at the Opéra; then, on May 12th, 1950, Bolivar was put on at the Opéra itself, as an opera by Darius Milhaud. The action of both play and opera covers the years 1802 to 1830, and represents Simon Bolivar's struggle to rid South America of the Spanish army of occupation and establish free republics. Supervielle's main concern is not, however, with the historical events, but with the private life of the Liberator, particularly the sense of irrevocable loss the death of his young wife had brought to him: "I have made war looking for you, as if I had to cut down an infinite number of enemies to reach you, my beloved", Bolivar says, addressing himself to the vision he has of his wife as he lies dying. There is no real dramatic action, merely a series of tableaux linked by the person of Bolivar. Only once is there real drama, and this is in the scene of the monstrous ball given by the Spanish General, Bovès, in which he makes the widows of those who had died fighting for Freedom dance with the victorious enemy soldiers while they wait their turn to be shot. This defective construction may well result from Supervielle's original intention of making the story of Bolivar into a film scenario, but the fact remains that only in Supervielle's last play, Le Voleur d'enfants, is the dramatic structure satisfactory.

In addition to these plays Supervielle has written a rollicking one-act farce, originally entitled *Adam*, and later *La première Famille*. Adam has an eye for the ladies and casts a net, literally, over the girl who has also caught the fancy of his very inventive son. Eve and three talking animals, including a diplodocus, complete the *dramatis personae*. The diplodocus is harnessed to a cart, which is the son's latest invention, and the two young people make off in it. Adam consoles himself by drinking, together with Eve, something of his own invention, wine. The play was performed in 1934 by the Compagnie des Quinze.

A mimed farce, *Les Suites d'une course*, which was admirably performed by Barrault in 1955, an adaptation of *As You Like It*, and another of *A Midsummer Night's Dream*, staged by Jean Vilar in Avignon in 1959, complete Supervielle's work for the theatre. The themes of his plays, his imagery and other devices, are the same as those used in his poetry and in his novels, but the plays themselves take second place in Supervielle's literary works.

The fairy-story plays and works of pure fantasy discussed in this section form part of the attempt begun in the 1920's to break away from the realistic tradition. The direction taken by the reaction was largely determined by social conditions, and just as the return of Alsace-Lorraine to France after the First World War stimulated interest in Alsatian folk-lore, so the difficulties of the early post-war years provoked what contemporary critics were pleased to call "the flight from the real" into the more comforting world of the imagination. Other playwrights had momentary flights of fancy. Cocteau had his talking horse, mirrors as the gateway to the underworld, and a sphinx in a transformation scene. Lenormand momentarily abandoned, in *La Folle du ciel*, his clinical studies to picture a world of talking birds, bird-women, and trolls, and Salacrou, in his early surrealistic plays, presented music-hall clowns, and Mephistopheles disappearing in a blaze of magnesium, but his *fantaisie* is bitterly satirical and has none of the sentimentality of Achard's picture of the circus world.

NOTES

1. Atelier, March 17th, 1926.
2. Théâtre de la Madeleine, May 16th, 1928.
3. Revived at the Atelier-Barsacq, at the Concours des Jeunes Compagnies, June 1949; at the Marigny-Barrault, March 25th, 1950.

VIII

Studio Theatre: The Literary Play

Jean Giraudoux—André Gide—André Obey—Jean Giono—Jean-Richard Bloch—Paul Claudel—Postscript.

MAY 3rd, 1928, marks the date of one of the most striking events in the history of modern French drama, the establishment of the "well-written play" in opposition to the "well-made plays" of the so-called *belle époque*, which were still going strong in the Boulevard theatres. On this day Louis Jouvet produced *Siegfried*, the first dramatic work of JEAN GIRAUDOUX, already known by readers of novels and essays as a writer of outstanding literary talent. Jouvet had not expected to make a penny piece out of the production, but its remarkable success proved him wrong. It was clear that there was a place in the theatre for "fine writing" as against clever handling.

Ever since the failure of Victor Hugo's *Les Burgraves* the divorce between literature and "good theatre" had been practically complete. Scribe and Sardou, the chief exponents of the "well-made play", had given little thought to style, and, since Dumas *fils*, playwrights had been more concerned with imitating the contemporary idiom than with "fine writing". In the newly established experimental theatres of the twenties a certain amount of attention had been paid to literary style, it is true, by Jean Sarment and Marcel Achard, but it was Giraudoux's success with *Siegfried* (to be followed by *Amphitryon 38* the following year) which did most to revive the concept of dramatic literature. In Giraudoux's play the characters took the trouble to round off their sentences and to "have their say". They acquired the right to the monologue and the tirade. *Siegfried* was written according to the definition of drama that Giraudoux was to propose nine years later, in *L'Impromptu de Paris*, a sort of manifesto-performance imitated from Molière's *Impromptu de Versailles*. In this manifesto Giraudoux draws a distinction between what he calls the "spoken" play and the "written" play, and, lambasting the critics for "making a millionaire out of Bataille and a failure of Becque", he, in fact, defines two types of drama on these lines. He also defines the place of style. A play is a "show" (*spectacle*); its task is to appeal to the senses and the imagination, and style is the means by which this may be achieved. Style is the prism which throws upon the mind a myriad rainbow hues which are not to be understood any more than one understands the sparkle of the sun upon the ice. To attempt to understand a play is not to understand the theatre. His producer Louis Jouvet expressed similar views in *Prestiges et Perspectives du théâtre français*. To stress the expressive content of language was certainly to render the theatre a great service at the time; nevertheless, it would be difficult to imagine an audience that did not hope to find some meaning in a play, and in point of fact Giraudoux's own productions were never devoid of intellectual content. It was, indeed, paradoxical of a playwright whose plays are the plays of a moralist, steeped in philosophical lore and packed full of ideas, to affirm, as he does, that a play need not be "understood".

An idea was the starting-point of *Siegfried*. "I wanted", he wrote in *Un Passage*, "to discuss Germany and even a megaphone is not loud enough for this." Such a starting-point was a long way from the purely "expressive" powers of language; it was also a long way from the starting-point of a dramatist of the traditional type, who was, more often than not, content with one or more "characters" and a "situation" and the desire to see what happened. Giraudoux started from a political *theme*, and the theatre seemed to him to be the ideal place for airing the vital problem of Franco-German relations. The problem had already been outlined by him in 1922 in the novel *Siegfried et le Limousin*, and had been used again in *Siegfried von Kleist*, a romantic-type drama which Giraudoux had taken from his novel and then discarded. (His publication, in 1934, under the title of *Fin de Siegfried*, of the fourth act of this discarded play shows his continued preoccupation with the theme.) Ever since he first crossed the Rhine he had been obsessed by the Franco-German "demon": he recalls the fact in *Visite chez le prince* (1932). His sojourn in Germany, undertaken to advance his studies of German language and literature, which he was pursuing under the direction of the well-known germanist Charles Andler, had revealed to him a very different Germany from the Germany of his favourite reading; this was followed by his wartime experiences, related in *Lectures pour une ombre* (1917), *Amica America* (1918), and *Adorable Clio* (1920), which provoked a profound spiritual conflict in him. "It is what the Germans taught me about themselves and their country that I, with my Frenchman's outlook, have tried to put into *Siegfried*."[1]

Siegfried is the French soldier Jacques Forestier; he has lost his memory on the battlefield, and has been re-educated as a German, by a German nurse. He symbolizes the France and Germany which Giraudoux believed had to come to terms with each other somehow, if peace was to reign in the world. With Geneviève, Forestier's French fiancée, who had been brought to Germany by Siegfried's political enemies to identify him, Giraudoux introduced the theme that he was to develop fully in *Amphitryon 38* and *Sodome et Gomorrhe*—namely, that of the human couple as such, a general philosophical theme. Throughout most of the play the French element in the conflict is the rational element, and the German the poetic and irrational. Siegfried, having become an important statesman, is about to present Germany with a model constitution which is highly distasteful to his opponent Zelten, who represents the romantic element in the German mind. Zelten defines Germany approvingly as "a poetic and diabolical conspiracy" and "not a social and human enterprise". In the final scene, at the frontier station, Giraudoux, surprisingly, reverses the distribution of values; the German side of the station is modernized and well organized, whereas the French side is poetically old-fashioned and quaintly uncomfortable. Germany offers Siegfried the honour of ruling a great people; in France only a dog watches for his master's return. In the second act Geneviève, faced by Fontgeloy, a descendant of the French protestant émigrés to Germany, explains the difference between the two countries as being the effect of different cultures working on the one human nature, which is substantially the same everywhere; humanity is constant but has different modalities. This seems to be the formula which Giraudoux proposes, as reconciling all differences, but the spectator is left in doubt as to which is the instinctive and which the rational of the two peoples. Zelten's attempted political revolution, the possible political repercussions

in the country of the revelation of Siegfried's identity, do not interest Giraudoux. The promotion of Franco-German understanding
is his theme, and this is thrown into high relief by the final words
spoken by Geneviève, as Siegfried-Jacques crosses the frontier back
to France: "Siegfried, I love you." Never before had she called him
by that name. The struggle for the possession of Siegfried, between
Geneviève and Eva, "symbols" of France and Germany (to quote
the text), reflects the struggle in the hero's own heart; it also
objectivizes the conflict Giraudoux felt within himself between the
"human" aesthetic and moral ideal of France and the "cosmic"
ideal of German philosophy.

A vital issue in the play is the nature of patriotism. By his
education, or rather his re-education, Siegfried is German, and
that country's history offers him Sedan and Sadowa as victories of
which to be proud, yet when he learns his real identity he in-
stinctively turns to the land of his birth, and so it would have been
whatever countries had been involved in the story, because, according to Giraudoux, the simplest feelings in man are the strongest.

In *Siegfried* Giraudoux, indifferent to dramatic action as such,
offers his audience poetic variations on a theme. The version which
was performed in 1928 owed much to Jouvet's guiding hand; the
version which he staged on April 13th, 1931, threw into higher
relief the drama of the man Siegfried-Jacques. Instead of playing
Fontgeloy, as he had done in 1928, Jouvet played Zelten, bringing
out all the lyricism in the part; Pierre Renoir retained the heavier
rôle of Siegfried. When the play was revived in 1952 the actors had
to face up to the inevitable comparisons with Jouvet's company;
Jouvet himself had died shortly before, in August 1951. They had
to contend, too, with strong anti-German feeling in this second
post-war period. Furthermore, the very deliberate literary style of
the play belonged to a dramatic period which had come to an end.
Nevertheless, the revival proved that there was still a public for
Giraudoux's plays.

In *Amphitryon 38* (Comédie des Champs-Elysées-Jouvet, November 8th, 1929) the theme of the human couple is woven into that
of the relationship between the gods and men. Jupiter wishes to
obtain Alcmène's favours but learns that true married love defies
even the gods. He was no more able to disunite the human couple,
Alcmène-Amphitryon, than God was able, in *Sodome et Gomorrhe*,
to bring together the man and the woman who had each begun to

live for himself. Having become a man, Jupiter has the restricted vision of the universe proper to man, but his jubilant statement, that never has he felt so truly the master of the gods as since he has taken on human form, may be intended as a declaration by the author of man's superiority over the divinity. Pride in the quality of humanity and satisfaction with the human condition, even its very precariousness, run through the whole play. Death is not seen as a limiting factor; Alcmène considers it to be the priceless recompense of life and thinks that to accept immortality is to betray humanity. For the same reason Alcmène refuses any insight into the future, any knowledge of any kind that passes human understanding, and she knowingly and freely accepts the illusions into which the gods have plunged mankind, because, by reason of his ignorance, man has to depend on himself alone; he is under no obligation to the gods. To man alone, in the person of Amphitryon, goes Alcmène's gratitude. Alcmène is the centre of the myth, according to Giraudoux, and she is here portrayed with the qualities of mind of an honest bourgeoise defending her love against the wiles of a god. She cannot trick the gods, as she tries to do by inviting Léda to take her place at the rendezvous, which she mistakenly believes is with Jupiter in the likeness of her husband, but she can teach Jupiter the true meaning of love, fidelity, and friendship. Alcmène's continued happiness is assured, though Giraudoux ironically bases it on ignorance of the true situation, reversing the rôle played by such ignorance in Greek tragedy.

This was the first of Giraudoux's plays to obtain international success, and the success was due to the brilliant intelligence which animates it. It was performed in London in 1938, after a few minor changes required by the Lord Chamberlain. Of recent years, in Paris, the theatre has moved away from the reinterpretation of ancient myths; even so, the play had a good run when it was revived in Paris in April 1957. There was a further revival in 1959.

The same concern with a theme is as evident in Judith as in the two preceding plays. Again it is the relation between the human and the divine, but centred, this time, not on love but on war. War which, in Amphitryon 38, makes a fleeting appearance at the command of Jupiter, who wanted a short, bloodless war to get rid of Amphitryon for a night, enters into the very substance of Judith. Its unheroic face is held up to the light with unexpectedly realistic descriptions of the horrors of the battlefield. The first act presents "the transition from the human being to the heroine", to quote the chief rabbi, the transition from the Judith who refuses to believe that she has been chosen by God to save His people, to the cruel, arrogant Judith, determined to succeed where the army had failed. Throughout the play pride is the keynote of her conduct. This chosen one of God is thrown by pride into the arms of God's self-acclaimed Enemy No. 1, Holopherne, the sceptic, who preaches to the Jewish maiden life and its pleasures, unspoilt by guilt and the shadow of Jehovah. Let others in their pride invent a deity in order to sin against Him, Holopherne wants only to feel himself to be an integral part of the great universe. In love with love but uncommitted to any man, Judith recognizes Holopherne as the great lover of her dreams. The next day she kills him, not to save the Jews, but for love. She loudly proclaims this love. She has loved and she has killed the man who took her. Not for her the rôle of instrument in the hand of God for the liberation of His people. The play ends disconcertingly with a drunken guard taking on, for Judith, at any rate, the appearance of an angel and commanding her to accept the Jews' version of her action. This "visitation" may be interpreted as a miracle or as an hallucination. However that may be, it is obviously meant to signify that the two truths, Judith's and the Jews', are not mutually exclusive. Judith's own adventure is contained within the adventure of the Jewish people, but it is an entirely personal adventure, and is motivated independently. "I killed in the name of another god than our God," she says, "but He has managed to take the credit to Himself, the hypocrite." The god of the Jews is nothing more than the collective voice of the people, the prophets and rabbis, and Judith refuses to conform to the will of this false god. She accepts to do so only when she comes, through the angel, to an appreciation of the Universal Order or Supreme Law, in the name of which, already, Alcmène, a mortal, had rejected Jupiter's offer of immortality and had refused Jupiter the "official night", while silently accepting that she has received his favour unknowingly. For Alcmène the gods were subject to the "supreme law of the world". Arguments like these, on the nature of the divinity, are not easy to follow in the space of a single performance. Giraudoux had overstepped the mark, and *Judith* had only a short run at the Théâtre Pigalle (November 4th, 1931), in spite of all Jouvet's skill.[2] It must be added that the play did not have the advantage of being performed by Jouvet's homogeneous company in the intimate atmosphere of the smaller Comédie des Champs-Elysées, and this may also have contributed to its lack of success, but there is no doubt about its being intellectually overloaded.

After the "tragedy", *Judith*, comes a "comedy", *Intermezzo* (Comédie des Champs-Elysées-Jouvet, February 27th, 1933),[3] which is played out in a fairy-tale atmosphere and tells of a girl of twenty, Isabelle, who falls in love with a ghost, a likeable young ghost in dark attire, serious, talkative, and strangely enamoured of life. By her attachment to this ghost, who symbolizes the appeal of the cosmos, of the "extra-human", to use Giraudoux's term, Isabelle breaks out of what Giraudoux, in *Eglantine*, calls the "terrible convent of humanity", but she is led back to it through the love of an imaginative civil servant, the inspector of weights and measures, who has a gift for savouring life to the full, and who seeks happiness within the limits of the human predicament. He is the antithesis of the narrowly conformist school inspector. In his examination of Isabelle's pupils the school inspector appears as the ridiculous embodiment of the spirit of "rational" primary education, majestic in its obtuseness; elsewhere he seems to have a broader function: that of "inspector of humanity"; he declares humanity to be a "*super*-human enterprise which aims at separating man from the 'vulgar mass' of universal nature". He comes to restore the "normal" order of things in the little provincial town, where ill-treated children run away from home, the poorest, not the richest, inhabitant wins the lottery, death comes to the old, not the young, and, as he puts it, "the middle-class moral code has been turned topsy-turvy", where, in the words of the inspector of weights and measures, "a strange influence, the effects of which I consider to be good, is gradually undermining the principles, incidentally quite false, on which civilized society is based". The school inspector has the ghost "executed", but the ghost arises, phoenix-like, from itself, after it falls under the executioners' bullets, and fixes a rendezvous with Isabelle in her room. This scene caused some speculation as to the true nature of the ghost before his "execution". When the question was put to Giraudoux he replied that he did not know, but the play is clearly a meditation on the link between man and the cosmos, whereas melodrama is the place for a character who dresses up as a ghost. The ghost in Jouvet's production, it must be said, looked solid enough, and was elegantly attired in a black evening cloak. Barrault, in his own production in 1955, was an exceedingly ghostly ghost, clad in grey tights and thin drapery. At the rendezvous fixed by the ghost a verbal duel for the possession of Isabelle is fought between the inspector of weights and measures and the ghost, between the purely human and what is not of this world, between life and death. For the inspector, death holds no terrors, it is inherent in the human condition, and he proposes life conscientiously lived as the only justifiable road to death. Isabelle is moved by his plea; the ghost has lost. His parting prediction to Isabelle, as he gives her up to the inspector of weights and measures, contains a statement of one of Giraudoux's favourite themes: marriage clouds the intuitive vision of the world of the virgin, the creature who is nearest the deity; it spells her "death". Already in the opening scenes of the play the promise of the woman-to-be, that every virgin is, was alluded to when Isabelle's pupils sang La Marseillaise des petites filles, and the song foretold Isabelle's inevitable betrayal of the ghost, which the ghost had not foreseen:

> Le pays des petites filles
> C'est d'avoir plus tard un mari.

After her good-bye kiss to the ghost Isabelle falls into a deathlike trance and reacts only to the words "silk velvet", pronounced amid the numerous sounds of ordinary everyday life which the druggist deliberately "orchestrates" around her to bring her back to consciousness. The interlude is over, the excursion outside the human domain to the land of heart's desire is ended—everything is back to normal, a cripple from the orphanage wins the motor-cycle in the lottery, and a millionaire the largest cash prize. But if the "Isabelle episode is closed", that of Isabelle's pupil, Luce, is still to come, some three or four years hence, so the school inspector predicts. The action takes place on various levels, and the gap separating the levels on which the school inspector and Isabelle move is greater than that separating Isabelle from the ghost. The rôle of the druggist is to prepare the transition from one level to another and even within Isabelle herself, between an Isabelle full of the joy of life and an Isabelle enamoured of the mysteries of the after-life.

In this play there is a variety of characterization unusual in Giraudoux. In addition to his typical virginal heroine, there are two acidulated spinsters, one annoyingly deaf, taken straight from farcical comedy; they are the incarnation of uncharitable village gossip. The two executioners who answer the call for one, made by the modern Pantaloon of a school inspector, savour, like him, of the *commedia dell'arte*. In Jouvet's production they both wore top-hats and white gloves and made identical gestures, but the fact that Giraudoux's main preoccupation was with the theme rather than the characterization is borne out by the transference of whole sections of the dialogue from one person to another in a different posthumous version of the play.[4] The fantasy of the theme was well reflected in Jouvet's extraordinary settings. In the third act the ugliness of Isabelle's provincial bedroom caused the Parisian audience to boo when the play was first performed, but the boos changed to applause as, at the sound of the ghost's voice, the ugly room was transformed by lantern projections, from behind the canvas walls, into an enchanted garden. In the first act a stretch of green grass gradually rose from the footlights to the back of the stage, where screens, with a few massive ferns painted upon them, and an extensive blue horizon, furnished by the cyclorama, created the impression of a spacious meadow, while music by Francis Poulenc caused strange echoes to fill the air. In addition to this music there is the music of the text, which was specially effective in Isabelle's conversations with the ghost, and in the inspector of weights and measures' lyrical musings on life and the prospects of a post in Gap or Bressuire, Belleville or Vaugirard, which life offered. The part of the inspector of weights and measures remained one of Jouvet's favourite parts, and he planned to play it again in the second post-war period. The musical term which serves as a title for the play underlined the intention of this "impressionistic symphonic poem", as it was called by the critics, and conferred still more prestige on the *théâtre littéraire*, which already counted Supervielle's *La Belle au bois dormant* and Gide's *Œdipe*.

Tessa, which followed on November 14th, 1934, at the Athénée, is an adaptation of *The Constant Nymph*, by Margaret Kennedy and Basil Dean, and the amusing one-act play *Supplément au voyage de Cook*, which Jouvet presented as a curtain-raiser, is inspired by Diderot's *Supplément au voyage de Bougainville*; it sets a happy picture of primitive life, lived naturally against a dark picture of life in organized society.

Giraudoux's view of events in Europe in 1934, from his ringside seat as a diplomat, was to determine the subject of the next play of this self-styled "journalist of the theatre". In *Amphitryon 38* Giraudoux had described peace as the interval between two wars; the "second" war was to be the subject of *La Guerre de Troie n'aura pas lieu* (Athénée, November 21st, 1935), rendered into English in 1955 by Christopher Fry as *Tiger at the Gates*. In an effort to combat its seeming inevitability, Giraudoux set out to debunk the so-called heroic adventure of war, convinced that satire was more effective than preaching the horrors of war to those who had never experienced them. Questioning whether the Trojan War could or could not have been avoided, Giraudoux was able to fulminate against the absurdity of all war, show war to be a collective delirium, and preach peace.

The title of the play hints ironically at tragedy, as every spectator knows that the Homeric conflict must, in fact, take place and is inevitable, but Giraudoux's purpose was to reach beyond the sequence of events (the abduction of Helen and the punitive Greek action) proposed by the reason as the cause of the conflict, and to arrive at the ultimate cause of war in general, which he sees as the irresistible appeal that war makes to men's instincts, the baser as well as the finer instincts. No ideological claim is as pressing, no practical reasons as compelling; indeed, if Helen had not existed she would have had to be invented. She is the excuse, according to Giraudoux's Ulysse, for the Greeks' predatory designs on Troy.

Fate must share with man the blame for war, and, to quote Ulysse again, war arises not from a clash of interests but when the qualities of two nations are complementary—in *Siegfried* Giraudoux, more optimistic, had seen these as working for peace. From time to time men must slaughter each other to reassure the gods. An indispensable preamble to the slaughter is the discussion between Heads of State, and such a discussion between Hector and Ulysse forms the culminating point of the play. "On the eve of war", says the more farsighted Ulysse, "it is usual for two representatives of the conflicting nations to meet in some unsuspecting village, on some terrace by a lake, in the corner of a garden. They agree that war is the greatest scourge of the world . . . they part with a brotherly shake of the hands . . . The next day, however, war breaks out." Lines like these brought the names of Briand and Stresemann to the mind of the audience in 1935, despite Giraudoux's contention that the play dealt only with the problem of war and peace and contained no allusion to contemporary events. Ex-combatants both, Hector and Ulysse want no more war, but Ulysse adds that he is less sure of "what war wants". To save the peace, Hector submits to every indignity, yet, ironically enough, it is his own preventive action, his silencing with his spear of a Trojan war-monger, that opens the gates to the war that is already on the march. Ulysse had sensed the imminence of this dreaded yet desired conflict, and feared it might be precipitated by some petty, unfore-seeable incident; it is, in fact, started by a lie, because the dying Trojan deliberately falsely accuses a Greek of his murder. Such is the power of words. Their power is illustrated earlier in the duel of the epithets. "Before hurling their javelins at each other", said the Surveyor, "Greek warriors hurled epithets." Insults are an incen-tive to killing, the poet Demokos explained, they prevent enemy armies from becoming too considerate of each other. Taking up a position ten paces from Paris, he engages in a practice verbal duel with him, but Hécube, with her "tu es un serin", beats them both in the art of provocation.

Another highlight of the play is Hector's address to the Fallen, in which Giraudoux attempts to bring some discrimination into the cult of the Unknown Warrior: "You cannot persuade me, by a mere ceremony, to confound the dead who are to be admired and those who are not . . . War seems to me the most sordid and hypo-critical nostrum for establishing man's equality." This address is also Giraudoux's supreme protest against the monstrous folly; the real victors are those who have come through it alive, the dead are the vanquished. The poets of the home front, ever ready to intone a hymn to war, international lawyers, who can prove that black is white and then that white is black, because "law is the most powerful of the schools of imagination", are also targets for attack.

Giraudoux's Troy is divided into two camps, the returning warriors and the women, all of whom know that war is a hollow fraud, and the bellicists—that is, those who are unfit to fight. The bellicists crystallize their desires round the Sphinx-like Hélène, described by Ulysse as "one of those rare creatures put into circula-tion on earth by fate for its personal use . . . fate's hostage". Hélène is not the witless puppet that she seems pleased to appear. She has her feet firmly on the ground. At the same time she is capable of intuitive, natural divination. She, however, refrains from looking too carefully at her visions or even examining too carefully her own thoughts. For mankind she has neither love nor pity, only indifference. She is not even in love with Paris, but feels only a "magnetization", almost on the level of the minerals. Andromaque, in despair that the lives of Hector and her fellow-men should be staked on such a sham, begs Hélène to love Paris truly, so that the sacrifice may be justified; perhaps, too, the hand of fate may be restrained by a real love. This single note, struck in this play, was to be fully orchestrated by Giraudoux seven years later in *Sodome et Gomorrhe*.

With Hélène, a discordant element of flippancy enters into this picture of the terrific struggle put up by Hector against a veritable coalition of forces making for war, and in which he was even prepared to pass for a coward should this advance the cause of peace—in 1935 Hector's attitude was adversely criticized as being an open invitation to war. Since 1935 the "Trojan" war *has* taken place, and it is possible that the present peace may be but another interval between two wars. *La Guerre de Troie n'aura pas lieu* is as topical today as when it was written[5] and as a prophecy come true it is disturbing. The performance, in July 1954, in the ancient Roman theatre at Fourvière, near Lyon, where the comic elements paled before the grandeur of the tragic theme, proved it could move an audience, and eight years later Jean Vilar revived it, again with complete success.

After his next play *Electre* (Athénée, May 13th, 1937), which Jouvet staged in much the same style as *La Guerre de Troie n'aura pas lieu* in white and gold settings, Giraudoux made the following statement: "I work with Jouvet; yes, I am his pupil ... Out of a text written for a few readers he makes a *spectacle* for all."[6] How Jouvet tightened up the written text, so that it could come over best in the theatre, can be seen by comparing the written text and the text as performed. Dr Donald Inskip has made this comparison for *La Guerre de Troie n'aura pas lieu* in his book *Jean Giraudoux, the Making of a Dramatist*.

In *Electre* the framework is essentially the same as in Sophocles' play, though the purpose is different. Like Sartre's *Les Mouches* (1943), Giraudoux's *Electre* shows idealistic impulses as continuing to exist in a world which no longer looks to a transcendental God. "By its ability to forget, and by its fear of complication, humanity allows the most heinous crimes to sink into oblivion", said Giraudoux, in speaking of his play. "But in every age arise the pure of heart who refuse to allow these crimes to be overlooked, even should the means they take to prevent it lead to other crimes and new disasters."[7] His Electre is such a person. Absolute values, Truth and Justice take precedence for her over human welfare and human happiness secured by compromise and cowardice. Her clash with Egisthe is the same as that of Anouilh's Antigone with Créon; it is a clash of values, the one abstract, the other practical, and it is Electre who wins: through his contact with her, Egisthe is transformed from a cowardly self-seeking regent into a hero. At first he attempts to tie her hands by marrying her to a gardener, by "killing her", as the Beggar puts it, commenting on the action like the Greek chorus. Then the king in him comes to the fore, he offers to pay with his life for the murder of Agamemnon, but pleads for the opportunity to defend his people against the invader. In her quest for truth and absolute justice Electre is necessarily the enemy of a society intent on preserving its happiness however questionably obtained, and, as its ruler, Egisthe aims at preventing Electre from "making a sign to the gods"—that is to say, from provoking the intervention of fate. Giraudoux here offers a clarification of his conception of fate or the gods. Egisthe declares the gods to be without consciousness at the top of the scale of being, as the atom is without consciousness at the bottom thereof. They respond blindly to the "sign" and in a wholesale manner, striking indiscriminately at the guilty and the innocent. If Electre prods this somnolent destiny it is not for love of the deity, but to save humanity from itself—that is, from egoism, and happiness born of complete abandon. This is stated in the second scene. Electre is the defender of human values, even though she brings death and destruction to Argos. The air is fresher, and dawn breaks over the ruins of the town, of which the well-being had been founded on hypocrisy and lies. The unity of the play is, however, badly strained by Giraudoux's linking together in a single person, Égisthe, the problem of just retribution for crime and the life and death of hundreds of innocent people.

Unlike all earlier Electras, Giraudoux's heroine does not know the truth about her father's death; her hatred for her mother is as unreasoned as it is unrestrained, but on this hatred and her devotion to her father's memory Giraudoux hinges the dramatic action. Her idealization of her father provokes Clytemnestre's passionate avowal, "Yes, I hated him", which seals her fate. The very human reasons which Clytemnestre gives in this fine tirade for her hatred of Agamemnon underline Giraudoux's transformation of her character. Electre, as might be expected of one of Giraudoux's heroines, discovers her true nature after she has been embraced by her brother, yet she is never touched by the humanizing influence of love, and remains throughout a stern seeker after the absolute.

The introduction of the Eumenides, three young children who grow, during the single day the play's action occupies, until they reach Electre's age and take on her shape, so as to harass Oreste to the point where, they predict, he will kill himself cursing his sister, is an interesting innovation of Giraudoux's. Like Sartre's flies in Les Mouches, they represent the sense of guilt and also the existing bad order of things which Electre seeks to sweep away. The characters have not the warmth of those of La Guerre de Troie n'aura pas lieu, and the adulterous little empty head, Agathe, despite the rôle she plays in precipitating the final tragedy, is as strangely out of place in the dark history of the Atrides as are Giraudoux's verbal pirouettes. These weaknesses contributed to the unfavourable reception given to the play when it was revived at the Comédie-Française in October 1959, nevertheless Electre has an important place in the history of modern French drama as a skilful modernization of a classical theme.

Verbal conceits are in their place in the story drawn from folklore which Giraudoux relates in Ondine (Athénée, May 4th, 1939; May 7th, 1949).[8] This is the last of the "spectacles" to result from the close collaboration of the author and his producer Louis Jouvet, and probably the one in which Jouvet's influence was greatest; so obviously does the play depend on stage machinery that Jouvet's influence seems to have affected its very composition. Tchelitchew's settings were very spectacular, and in the first act a poor fisherman's hut suddenly took on the appearance of a grotto under the sea, with undines swimming in it. In the second act the palace court-room, presented in perspective, gave the impression of extending backward indefinitely. Jouvet also had recourse to this seventeenth-century type of setting in Judith and in L'Apollon de Bellac (Athénée, April 19th, 1947), a one-act "fantasy", which is set in the ante-room of the "Office of Inventors, great and small". Here Agnès, who "bears a striking resemblance to Madeleine Ozeray", the actress, according to an indication in the Fragments inédits, is looking for a post. She is advised to tell all men that they are handsome, and when she practises on an ugly chandelier it lights up in response.

Ondine is based on the story, written in 1811, by Friedrich de la Motte-Fouqué. Giraudoux first read it in 1909, when studying for the *agrégation d'allemand*, and in 1939 presented his play as a belated student's "commentary", which should have been done for Professor Charles Andler. The "commentary", however, reverses the values of the German original: instead of being the story of the water-sprite who marries a man to acquire a soul, the play becomes the tragedy of man divorced from nature and stultified by his confinement within the strictly human sphere. This is not the first appearance of an undine in Giraudoux's works. To quote only from the plays, there is a passing reference to undines in the final version of *Intermezzo* and Isabelle is seen in conversation with an undine, in a scene discarded by Giraudoux, and in which are already to be found some of the themes of *Ondine*. Ondine is a force of nature but also love incarnate, and Hans's tragedy is that he is as unequal to such a love as he is to the revelation of nature which Ondine brings. He deserts her for Bertha, who represents the narrowly human, and for this he must die. For his inability to commune with the rest of the universe homo sapiens has only himself to blame: "Man wanted to have his own soul", says Yseult to Ondine, "he has stupidly broken up the general soul into little pieces." If Hans maintains man's right to be free of all that is not man, Ondine, though destined to return to nature with no recollection of the world of men, strives to forge a lasting link with it by training her body to go on repeating a few simple human gestures, even though they can no longer have any meaning. This idea of nature bearing for ever the mark of the passage of man, and regretting man, is one of the most striking in the play. Another idea, that of love surviving even the loss of memory, is expressed at the end of the play: "And who is that handsome young man?" asks Ondine, as, unrecognizing, she looks at Hans's body. "How I should have loved him!"

In the play there are some curious details, particularly in the second act: the lesson in hypocrisy given to Ondine at Court by the Lord High Chamberlain, the effects produced by Ondine's startling frankness and her inability to lie, and specially the acceleration of time by the Illusionist, Ondine's uncle, a speeding-up which, in the space of a few minutes, allows a preview of a series of events and a change of heart which actually cover ten years. After this the action switches back to the real time of the Court scene. The ironic tone of this act comes strangely after the lyricism of the first, but the poetry returns in the closing scenes of the play.

In *Ondine* man is shown to be estranged from nature. In *Sodome et Gomorrhe* the two sexes are estranged. The problem of the human couple, as outlined in *Ondine*, is of secondary importance. Earlier in the one-act play *Le Cantique des cantiques*, which was staged by Jouvet at the Comédie-Française on October 12th, 1938, but which is the least successful of his dramatic writings, Giraudoux concerned himself with the mystery of love: love follows its own laws, and merit has no meaning for it.

Love is the pivot on which all the arguments of *Sodome et Gomorrhe* turn, for there is no real action in the play. Taking from the Bible only the name of the two towns and the fact of their destruction, Giraudoux embroiders on the theme that men and women are eternal strangers to each other. They cannot reconstitute the perfect couple united in love, demanded by God as His condition for sparing the cities. There is no question for Giraudoux of the ten Just Men of the Bible story, nor even of "one Just Man", to quote the words of the "Gardener" in the play. Giraudoux was not interested in justice, nor was the "God" of Giraudoux's play interested in man as an individual but only as one element in the couple. The couple is Giraudoux's version of the platonic myth of the androgynes, and he sees the unity of the couple destroyed by the original sin of pride: his man and woman accuse each other of indifference, of non-participation; each, in turn, assumes superiority over the other. God's creation, as the "Archangel" explains in the Prelude to the play, was compromised by this separatism and this assumption of superiority. Samson and Dalila, who are introduced in the second act, do not constitute the perfect union any more than the heroine, Lia, and her husband, Jean, had done. The sexes meet death and destruction separately, as they had met life. This work is a philosophical poem in prose rather than a play. Dramatic interest is killed almost at the outset because the fate of Sodom depends on Lia, and Lia's character is thoroughly explored by Giraudoux in the first act. The part was taken, at Giraudoux's request, by Edwige Feuillère, and the play was staged at the Théâtre Hébertot (the former Théâtre des Arts) on October 11th, 1943. This was the only occasion on which, during Giraudoux's lifetime, the production was not by Jouvet, and it suffered by not being presented with the special type of static acting referred to in *L'Impromptu de Paris*, which Jouvet had devised for a Giraudoux text, so as to throw it into relief. Jouvet also slowed down the tempo of the actors' speech and invented a type of incantation which, together with an "orchestration" of the voices, underlined the emotive content of Giraudoux's prose.

The fruitful collaboration of the playwright and his producer came to an end with Giraudoux's death in 1944. Jouvet had to work alone to produce *La Folle de Chaillot*,[9] and when Barrault produced *Pour Lucrèce* Jouvet was also dead. These three last plays fall below all that Giraudoux wrote, or rather rewrote, guided by Jouvet's experience.

The date of the first performance of *La Folle de Chaillot* was almost foreseen by Giraudoux. On the manuscript he predicted: "This play was first performed on October 19th, 1945, at the Athénée." The actual date was December 19th. The production was subsidized by the Ministry of Fine Arts. The costumes of the four madwomen, which were to date from the beginning of the century, were obtained by Press appeals to the Paris public, and the performance took on the air almost of a national event. The four madwomen are completely individualized. This was new for Giraudoux, the individuality of his characters had always been somewhat tenuous, his interest lying elsewhere. The Madwoman of Chaillot, magnificently portrayed by Marguerite Moréno, was modelled on Madame Bijou, a woman of some eighty years of age who appeared every evening at seven o'clock precisely, silent and carrying numerous parcels, on the terrace of the café Chez Francis, in the Place de l'Alma, where, in fact, Giraudoux sets the first act of his play. The second act takes place in a cellar, the "palace" of the Madwoman of Chaillot, in a setting by Christian Bérard as striking and unreal as that which he had designed for the café terrace. The play, which was written during the war, represents the hoped-for liberation of Paris, the symbol of civilization, from the racketeers who grow fat at their fellow-citizens' expense. These persons, referred to as *mecs*, are the object of a scintillating tirade by the ragman, a part played by Jouvet in the original production. With nothing more original for his theme than this threat made by speculators and the trusts against freedom and happiness, Giraudoux proceeded to write a satire in fairy-tale form. The Madwoman of Chaillot, who hears the speculators plotting on the café terrace, lures them to her cellar with the pretence that there are untapped oilwells in the sewers leading from it. Before their arrival they are condemned by the four women, after a strange trial in which the ragman pleads, in humoristic fashion, a fatal defence. Once they have gone down into the sewers to prospect, the trap-door is closed on them, and in place of these useless parasites come shades of nature's friends, botanists and zoologists.

At first sight the play would seem to link up with *Pleins Pouvoirs*, particularly the last chapter, which Giraudoux published in 1939, and, indeed, when Georges Wilson revived it at the Théâtre National Populaire in November 1965 he described it as a "denunciation of capitalism" or, to quote from Giraudoux's text, "the reign of the Golden Calf". Furthermore, he saw it as being much more topical in 1965, the age of the "struggle against middlemen", than it was in 1945, the time of the "return to the land". One could question such a favourable interpretation which seeks to attach importance to the theme because, despite the social and political data from which the play sets out, Giraudoux does not, in fact, stray far from his usual preoccupation with the cosmos and man's place in it, even though he does denounce man as "the jockey and not the inhabitant of his globe". Social injustice clearly takes second place to man's offences against trees and animals and even to the theft of the "only ripe melon of the year". Giraudoux does not get down to the subject he has set himself, and the final triumphal ballet of kindly, humble folk, all characters from fairy-tale and not real life, makes this very clear. There is hardly any dramatic action to count, or even any plot; instead, Giraudoux trusts to "fine writing" and to a number of striking speeches. This dates the play, and, since Brecht, so does his refusal to treat the social subject seriously.

In *Pour Lucrèce*,[10] which is a transposition of the story of the rape of Lucretia, here called Lucile, the plot, on the contrary, plays an important part. The action consists of a duel to the death between Lucile, Giraudoux's Lucretia, who judges all men by the single word "purity", and Paola, the embodiment of passion, whose infidelity to her husband Lucile has denounced. By her own standard Lucile finds herself wanting; she had believed Paola's story that she, Lucile, had been violated while she was drugged. The distressing images which torture her mind are therefore of her own creating. This was a fall from grace which Lucile could not accept. She dies, deliberately leaving her husband, a petty prejudice-riddled creature to whom she has confessed her supposed misfortune, in ignorance of the truth. As in *Sodome et Gomorrhe*, Giraudoux here attacks men as being cynical, egoistic creatures, capable only of taking up "attitudes" and not of real feeling, and he ends his play on the same note: the wilful separation of the sexes.

When the play was staged at the Théâtre Marigny on November 4th, 1953, there was much discussion about the complete authenticity of the text. As with the other plays, more than one version exists of certain scenes, and Barrault, like Jouvet before him, for *La Folle de Chaillot*, had to make his choice; it was the same as Jouvet had made in 1951, when he proposed to stage the play with Edwige Feuillère. What might have been the final form of *Pour Lucrèce* or *La Folle de Chaillot* can only be a matter of pure conjecture, since Giraudoux was no longer there to remodel his text in the course of the production. At the same time as he was writing these last plays, Giraudoux made an excursion into the world of the cinema, adapting a short novel by Balzac, *La Duchesse de Langeais*, and writing the dialogue for *Les Anges du péché*, which, for him, is strangely stark, though it is well suited to the imagery in the film.

Though he was the most unorthodox of dramatists, Giraudoux succeeded in imposing himself upon a whole generation, and he can still draw an audience in this very different second post-war theatre. Nevertheless, opinion is sharply divided about him: he is praised by Ionesco, in spite of the fact that Ionesco's conception of dramatic language is totally opposed to Giraudoux's, Jean Vauthier is highly critical of his plays, and Arthur Adamov professes a respectful indifference to them. Giraudoux's plays are the brilliant expression of a sensitive mind and a thinker of keen intelligence. His themes have permanent topicality; but the stamp of the writer's temperament and of his times is so marked that there is a danger that the plays may ultimately appear to belong too exclusively to a past age and become museum pieces. They "date". Too individualistic to form a "school", Giraudoux, by his repeated successes, helped to pave the way for André Obey, and for Cocteau, who, as he said himself, made his *real* debut in the theatre only in 1934, with *La Machine infernale*. For his part, Jean Anouilh appears as a disciple of Giraudoux; his style of writing and type of theme and dramatic treatment, particularly in *Antigone*, bear a strong resemblance to Giraudoux's. Several poets and novelists followed

Giraudoux's lead and turned to play-writing; among them Super-vielle, Mauriac, and Jean Giono, and the line has been continued by Thierry Maulnier, Julien Green, Henri de Montherlant, Albert Camus, and Jean-Paul Sartre.

Long before Giraudoux, ANDRE GIDE, the most interesting moralist of the first half of the twentieth century in France, had turned to play-writing. He used dramatic dialogue for the exploration of moral concepts which are pushed to the extreme limit of their sig-nification. To live at the extreme limit of his possibilities was always Gide's desire, though the direction taken by these possibili-ties was not always the same. Drama provided an ideal medium for the inner dialogue, which was Gide's way of thinking. It resulted from the duality of his nature, attributed by Gide himself to his conflicting heritages, Southern and Huguenot on his father's side, Norman and Catholic on his mother's. The different stages of Gide's moral evolution are clearly reflected in his plays, if one considers the dates at which they were written and not the dates when they were first put on. Saül, written in 1897–98, was performed only in 1922, when Copeau, searching for literary drama, staged it at the Vieux-Colombier on June 16th. Le Roi Candaule, written in 1899, was performed at the Œuvre in 1901. Le Retour de l'enfant prodigue, dating from 1907, was given a reading on February 23rd, 1933, by the Rideau de Paris at the Théâtre de l'Avenue, with curtains as the only setting, and then was staged properly by the company in 1934 and 1939. On October 16th, 1937, at the Comé-die des Champs-Elysées, the company gave a reading of Philoctète, which had been written in 1898. Before that date this "moral treatise", as it was termed by Gide despite its dialogue form, had only been performed privately in 1919, and again in 1921, when it was given by the group Art et Action as part of a series of per-formances entitled "Théâtre de Chambre".

Keeping the dates of composition in mind, one sees that Saül follows on from the essays entitled Les Nourritures terrestres (1897), in which the summum bonum is equated with living fully in the experiences of the senses, though in the 1927 preface to the book Gide attempted to limit its scope by terming it a "manual of deliverance", deliverance from the puritanical moral code under which he had been brought up. The biblical story is used by Gide to depict the slow disintegration of a man who cannot resist the demons of his desires. "Je suis complètement supprimé", Saül exclaims, recognizing the complete effacement of his personality, brought about by the indulgence of an over-exacting temperament. *Saül* is the counterpart of *Les Nourritures terrestres*. The torments and the evil of uncurbed desires reappear in the unstaged *Bethsabé* (1903), whereas in the meantime, in *Philoctète*, self-transcendence had been offered as the highest moral achievement, placed well above the civic virtue of Ulysse, who preaches man's duty to his country and his gods. In *Le Roi Candaule* the king, the most richly endowed of all men, carries the generosity in which he seeks his true nature to the absurd limit of sharing his beautiful wife with his friend, and, like Saül, pays with his life for his aberration.

   Le Retour de l'enfant prodigue was a reply to Claudel's attempt to bring Gide into the fold of the Church. In this work Gide distinguishes sharply between *la Maison*, the Church, with its dogma and its militant clergy, and the Prodigal Son's father, the Creator, whom the Prodigal would have found at the end of his journey had he realized it. Gide was to reaffirm this position in 1916, when he wrote in his *Journal* (p. 533) that God must be sought not at the beginning but at the end of man's evolution. The Prodigal's return to the "house", with its closed ethic, is brought about not through love of the father, although he had felt the father's presence greatly in his destitution, but through sheer lassitude, produced by the task of working out for himself a new moral code, which might not turn out to be very different from that of the Church. When the youngest son, added to the biblical story by Gide, sets off, in turn, away from home, he is encouraged by the Prodigal Son to be strong and never to come back.

   Gide claimed that the writing of these early works had exercised a cathartic effect upon him, enabling him to achieve a certain serenity.[11] *Œdipe*, which he composed in 1930, is the first of his plays to show this serenity. Saül's fears of the sorcerers and David's submission to the prophet Nathan, in *Bethsabé*, have no parallel in the supremely confident Œdipe. Three years earlier, while meditating on the Oedipus story, which he called the triumph of the conventional moral code, Gide referred to the "palace of faith", which he knew so well from the inside because of his early upbringing. "Everything in it is arranged to foster laziness and dispense the mind from effort . . . one goes into it with one's eyes closed, blinded, as Oedipus went in." Gide's Œdipe, following Gide's own example,

refused to enter the palace of faith; he was not prepared, like Gide's
Prodigal Son, to retrace his steps to it. In this play is to be found a
complete reinterpretation of the legend in twentieth-century
terms. The theme, according to Gide, was the very "topical" clash
between the freedom of the mind and submission to religious
authority. It could have been incorporated into a naturalistic
drama, but in the interests of the theme itself Gide, rejecting *episodism*, a term he found preferable to "realism", with its multiple con-
notations, sought in mythological and biblical stories the prestige
of "distance", which Racine defined and justified in his preface to
Bajazet.[12]

The two opposing personalities in the play are the rationalist
Œdipe, a clear-sighted anti-mystic, who rejects the teaching of the
Church and offers a humanistic solution to the essential questions and not only to that posed by the Sphinx, and Tirésias, the
representative of the Church, for whom there was no salvation
outside the Church, and whose power lies in men's fear of God.
Œdipe, presuming himself to be a foundling, sees in such an origin
a call to valour. Having no ties with the past, no-one to live up to
but himself, and everything to create or conquer, family, country,
throne, he is essentially a self-made man, and he glories in it. As
Tirésias puts it, he makes a god of himself. As long as God had
led the way to glory, Œdipe had consented to follow, but when God
had led him into crime—the killing of a man, Laiüs—Œdipe had
turned aside and taken the road to the Sphinx, placing his confidence in man alone. When at the end of the play, as a result of his
own inquiry, he discovers the extent of the crimes into which he
has been led, he accuses God of base treachery; there was no question of repentance in his mind. He then asserts his own free will by
a final act of deliberate, gratuitous self-blinding, which he intends
as a superhuman gesture, to astound all men and the gods. His
voluntary exile is yet another individualistic act; he is determined
to remain master of his destiny. Though vanquished, he is greater
than Tirésias and Créon, who, barricading themselves behind
doctrines and systems, risk nothing and achieve nothing. Convinced of the nobility of Œdipe's conduct, Antigone, renouncing
the Church so as to remain faithful to God in her heart, sets out
with her father. Earlier in the play, Œdipe, a firm believer in
human effort, has chided his sons for thinking that they could take
their ease because their father had conquered the Sphinx. But after

his victory Œdipe himself had become complacent in his happiness, and this he later denounces as being his greatest crime, since through it he had linked up with his past.

While Gide's suffrage clearly goes to the notion of rationalistic individualism, he adopts an objective attitude and allows the different characters, including the chorus, which represents the people of Thèbes, to voice criticism of individualism. For their part, the inhabitants of Thèbes are blatantly self-seeking, clerical rather than religious, and, by their complete subservience in the religious and political fields, offer a painful contrast to Œdipe's Promethean attitude. The picture of the town is very different from that presented by Sophocles and may be intended by Gide as a picture of contemporary society. In any case, Gide's reference to the 1920's is quite clear in the portrait he paints of Œdipe's sons. Both are openly cynical; both are tormented by le mal du siècle, about which Étiocle has written a book with the subtitle Notre Inquiétude. Another contemporary note is to be found in the Freudian references to the two sons' repressed desires concerning their sisters. Gide prolongs, as it were, the father's incest, visiting the sin of the father upon the sons.

The topicality of Gide's theme was underlined by modern colloquial twists in the dialogue, and by the jokes and puns, all of which were criticized when Pitoëff, striking a purely Greek note in his production, staged the play at the Théâtre des Arts on February 18th, 1932. On the other hand, in the production four months later at Darmstadt the actors, wearing what Gide called an outrageous mixture of ancient and modern dress, performed before a set consisting of the columns of a Greek temple and a backcloth on which was projected a picture of Notre Dame de Paris. Gide expressed complete approval: the real interest of his play was not that of ancient tragedy; it lay in the clash of ideas.[13] In Paris the original production was not a success. Pitoëff's voice and accent, together with his inability to wear the peplum with dignity, militated against the play; so did the public's unfamiliarity with reinterpretations of the ancient myths. True, Jouvet had scored a triumph with Giraudoux's Amphitryon 38, but the play had an amusing plot and the production was impeccable. On the other hand, Giraudoux's Judith, like Gide's Œdipe, performed three months after it, was greeted as an admirable piece of writing by a man of letters, non-theatrical, and quite unplayable. With his production on July 21st, 1949, at Avignon, and on April 5th, 1951, at the Théâtre Marigny, in Paris, Jean Vilar proved that though Œdipe was a curious piece of literary writing, limited in scope as a play, it was, in fact, highly scenic, and he furnished a commentary on the play by his stage set, which consisted of a stylized miniature palace and two miniature houses.

Œdipe's claim, as he departs from Thèbes after blinding himself, that he is happy because his suffering may bring happiness to men, announces a new theme in Gide's work. It reappears in his re-interpretation of the Homeric hymn in Perséphone, a short opera written in 1933, in collaboration with Igor Stravinsky at the request of Ida Rubinstein, and performed by her at the Paris Opéra on April 30th, 1934. The production was by Copeau and the choreography by Kurt Jooss. It is not present in the earlier outline, Proserpine, written in 1904.

In 1932 Gide announced his conversion to Communist ideals, and went on to declare his revised belief that social problems should take precedence over moral ones. This was the background against which he began Robert ou l'intérêt général, which deals with the employer-employee relationship in industry. The play was written by August 1935, but straight away Gide blamed himself for his "mistaken" effort in writing a realistic play, and resolved not to repeat the mistake. After his visit to the Soviet Union and his subsequent change in outlook, Gide completely revised the play in an attempt to develop the character study at the expense of the social conflict, which was his original theme. This is the version that has been published. In it the typical Gidian problem of sincerity is posed through the main character, Robert, an unscrupulous, hypocritical industrialist, whose sole concern is to amass a fortune. An anti-clerical note is struck by the close link which Gide forges between this hypocritical representative of capitalism and the Abbé, the representative of the Church. This revised version did not satisfy Gide, and, in fact, it is not easy to believe in these characters who give the impression of a number of masks, each signifying a specific attitude. To counterbalance the inhuman capitalist, for example, Gide creates in Ivan an inhuman Communist.

Another clear attack against Catholicism was delivered by Gide in his humorous curtain-raiser, Le treizième Arbre, which was written for Pitoëff in 1935, but was staged in Paris only on January 13th, 1939, at the Théâtre Charles de Rochefort, by the Rideau

de Paris. The attack is here extended to the aristocracy. The con-
servative and aristocratic inhabitants of the castle, together with
the Curé, are confounded when it is discovered that an obscene
carving on a tree in the castle grounds is the work of the Countess
herself. Victory goes to the "moderns", one of whom is a disciple
of Freud.

Gide's other works for the theatre are adaptations and translations.[14] His adaptation of his own burlesque murder story, Les
Caves du Vatican, the story of a "gratuitous act", was staged at the
Comédie-Française on December 15th, 1950. An adaptation made
by Yvonne Lartigaud had already been performed by Firmin
Gémier's company, Art et Travail, at the Studio des Champs-
Elysées on October 24th, 1933. Gide directed the rehearsals and
refused to allow the suicide with which this version ended. His
own adaptation ends with an intimate scene between Lafcadio and
Geneviève, or, as played first in 1933, at the final meeting between
Lafcadio and Julius, in which Lafcadio confesses to the murder.
Despite the ingenious arrangement of the text, in numerous scenes,
the adaptation is not real drama.

The thorny question of translation was one which Gide admitted
he had meditated upon for a long time, often spending more time
on his translation work than on the writing of his own plays. It was
Gide's stated belief that the written language should not be very
different from the spoken language in its elements; but he polished
the spoken language he took as his material. "The great classical
artist", he wrote, "strives not to have a particular manner; he
strives in the direction of banality. If he reaches this banality without effort it means that he is not a great artist."[15] Effort and discipline are the basic principles behind Gide's literary work, as they
were his receipt for all good creative work. Harmony, serenity,
order were his goal, both as an artist and a moral philosopher.

In the theatre Gide's aristocratic temperament was an obstacle to
his complete success; the need for the dramatist to count with and
on the general public alienated Gide from the stage; truth, for him,
was not on the side of the majority. The sole opportunity for agree-
ing with popular opinion was provided for him by Charles Chaplin.
"It is so good to be able not to despise what the crowd admires", he
wrote after seeing The Gold Rush.[16] Drama, he considered as a duel
in which "disdain for the public"[17] was an element essential for a
triumph; from this duel the public should emerge vanquished but

happy. It was a fundamental error on the part of modern dramatists not to despise their public enough.

But if Gide's own plays did not place him in the forefront of the
dramatists of his day his influence on drama was incontestable:
with his transposition of biblical and classical themes, he set a
precedent to be followed by Giraudoux and many others; with his
critical writings, particularly his lecture, *L'Évolution du théâtre*,
which dates from 1904, he proposed "new forms of heroism and
new heroic figures", together with the "alienation" (distance)
destined to counteract the "episodism" (realism), the fomula then
normally accepted. His ideas penetrated into the theatre itself
through the producer Jacques Copeau, who openly acknowledged
the influence Gide had had on his artistic development. The closest
contact existed between these two men from 1903 right up to the
time of Copeau's conversion. Copeau himself said that never had he
felt so at one with any playwright as when he and Gide were preparing the production of *Saül*. For his part, Gide confessed to being painfully aware of Copeau's perspicacity in discerning his,
Gide's, limitations, an implied condemnation which may well have
adversely affected any vocation he had for the theatre. At the same
time (this was June 1914), he looked to Copeau for a subject for a
comedy, feeling himself capable of developing a subject in dramatic
form, though incapable of finding one for himself. The confession
is significant; it expresses Gide's essential lack of dramatic inspiration. However interesting his plays are, as an expression of his
thinking, they are not the creation of a dramatist.

ANDRÉ OBEY has long been known to theatre audiences in many
countries as the author of *Noé*. The play was first staged on January 7th, 1931, at the Vieux-Colombier by La Compagnie des
Quinze, formed by members of Copeau's group, Les Copiaus,
which had been disbanded in 1929, when Copeau became an unsuccessful candidate for the directorship of the Comédie-Française.
The new company was directed by Copeau's nephew, Michel Saint-
Denis, and included Copeau's daughter, Marie-Hélène Dasté, but
was independent of Copeau himself. It was joined by André Obey
at Ville-d'Avray, where it went to prepare its repertory. There
Obey watched its members drill themselves in a type of theatrical
gymnastics quite independent of any text, and the plays which he
wrote specially for them utilized to the full the plastic virtuosity
of the actors. Indeed, the settings designed according to Copeau's

principles, together with the special style of acting and the studied diction of Les Quinze, formed such an integral part of the performances that for many years in France no other producer would risk performing the plays of Obey. Working almost exclusively on texts by Obey, Michel Saint-Denis concentrated on gesture and diction; gesture was stylized and diction modulated until it bordered on incantation. The sound of the text, independently of the sense of the words, was used to convey the intensity of the feeling to be expressed, and the dialogue became a musical accompaniment to the action, which approached ballet in its formalism. A new convention was obviously being developed, and there was a danger of its becoming rigidly stereotyped. The form the productions took was determined more by the special training of the troupe, and by Saint-Denis's particular methods, than by the texts themselves. The troupe was perfectly homogeneous. Its refusal, following Copeau's lead, to have star actors caused a levelling out of the various dramatic rôles. With the exception of Noé, and later of Don Juan, both played by outsiders, no one character stood out in relief against the others; no one moment in the action fixed the attention more than the others, but every detail of acting, setting, and characterization was equally compelling in its perfection. Despite their tremendous vogue in France and abroad, conditions of the theatre in Paris made existence precarious for Les Quinze, and, following the loss of some of its members in 1934, including Michel Saint-Denis, the troupe decided to retreat to Aix-en-Provence, to begin training again. The last of their productions before separating from Saint-Denis was Obey's *Don Juan* (1934), which they performed in Brussels and London, but not in Paris. The play was completely rewritten by Obey under the title *Le Trompeur de Séville*, and was staged by Copeau at the Porte-Saint-Martin on January 28th, 1937, with an improvised company including Marie-Hélène Dasté and a few members of Les Quinze. The chief part was played by the Boulevard actor, Pierre Blanchar, who followed Copeau to Ville-d'Avray, to rehearse in the premises where Les Quinze had worked before. Obey made a third version of the play under the title *L'Homme de cendres*, which has been in the repertory of the Comédie-Française-Luxembourg since December 21st, 1949. In 1935 Saint-Denis left France for England, and opened the London Theatre Studio at the "Q" Theatre.

Noé,[18] the first of Obey's plays to be performed by Les Quinze, consists of a series of frescoes, some offering very homely comedy, others moments of almost epic grandeur. While Noé busily chats, as on the telephone, with God, whom he only hears with difficulty, fear, then faith, flash across his face: God has replied, and the audience gathers from Noé's remarks that the Ark is to have no helm. Marc Connolly's *Green Pastures* (1930) comes to the mind; Noah requests God's permission to take aboard two "kags of lik-ker", only to find God on the side of prohibition! But Obey's Noé is not the humorist Connolly's is. He is a very ordinary man, with the ordinary man's virtues and vices. His chatter is homely—he even speaks twentieth-century Parisian slang—his intelligence is not too keen, but his patience and faith are boundless. The animals, submissive to the divine will and knowing what men, with their intelligence, do not know, come of their own accord into the Ark. Their anger against Noé's sons, when discontent breaks out among the sons, and their commiseration with Noé, provide a touching moment of understanding between man and beast; Noé speaks to the animals of God, and urges them to a raucous and inarticulate prayer. Yet back on land they turn into wild beasts again. Noé's children are just as cruel: they struggle for a peak of rocky ground, protruding above the water, and when the water subsides selfishly go their way, leaving Noé alone with his wife, whose poor brain has been unhinged by her sufferings. Men are incorrigible; they straightway fall back into the very vices for which the vast majority of them have just been annihilated by God. And as for the Deluge, Noé cries in despair: "Seigneur! Seigneur! Vieux cama-rade . . . C'est loupé! Foutez-nous tous dans le jus! Et qu'on n'en parle plus." Nevertheless, Noé regains his confidence in God and begins to demolish the Ark, so as to rebuild his house. His faith and optimism contrast touchingly with the pessimism of Cham, the rationalist, determined to understand and dominate his surround-ings.

Le Viol de Lucrèce, based on Shakespeare's poem, followed Noé on March 12th, and provided a "spectacle" in which there was greater harmony between conception and execution than in any other performance by Les Quinze. Before writing for Les Quinze Obey had declared that his sole ambition was to take his place in the theatre behind Cocteau and Claudel, both of whom had his deepest admiration,[19] and in this particular work he openly ack-nowledged the influence of Cocteau's ideas on play-writing. *Les*

Mariés de la Tour Eiffel would seem to have provided a model for the play, as Obey repeatedly takes the words out of his characters' mouths and puts them into the mouths of two narrators, stationed, for the most part of the time, in wooden pulpits on either side of the proscenium. At such times the actors are reduced to miming their parts. Obey may also have been influenced by Claudel's enthusiasm for the Japanese Noh play. In any case, Les Quinze were well trained in the technique of the Noh play. As Tarquin approached Lucrèce's bed, which was placed on a raised platform towards the back of an otherwise bare stage, he went up and down invisible stairs, along invisible corridors and through invisible doors, sometimes pressing forward with fevered haste, sometimes hesitating at the thought of the deed. He spoke no words, but a vivid picture of his progress through the house was evoked by the narrators. Such a work was a natural choice for Barrault, who revived it in February 1961, proving that *Le Viol de Lucrèce* can still hold an audience.[20] It can, however, hardly be described as a play. For the most part it is a piece of miming supported by the rhetoric of the two narrators. The style varies from lyrical prose to slang, but the slang grates on the ears in a context like this. Obey's other "Shakespearian" play, the one-act *Vénus et Adonis* (Atelier, December 5th, 1932), which offers a rather neat dramatization of a purely lyrical theme, again shows Obey's taste for ultra-modern, bantering dialogue. There is a similar spirit of inventiveness: the childlike Eros practises shooting arrows, and Death, an elegant lady wearing a half-mask and long white gloves, comes to claim Adonis.

Bataille de la Marne (Vieux-Colombier, December 5th, 1931), which won the Prix Brieux, was even further removed from the dramatic norm than was *Le Viol de Lucrèce*, and might best be defined as a spoken oratorio for chorus and soli. To evoke the events of August and September 1914, Obey uses a visionary messenger, a narrator who comments on the action as in Greek tragedy, an allegorical figure representing France, and two groups of people: the peasants, terrified by the invasion, then happy to get back to their recaptured, though devastated, villages, and the soldiers, disheartened at first by their retreat, then encouraged by Joffre's order to advance. The text, of which the language often has a suggestive quality reminiscent of the writers of the "school of silence", was supported by song, and at the beginning of the play the advance

of the German troops was suggested by means of a Bach chorale
sung more and more loudly in the wings. Six soldiers, turning
about and advancing, represented the miracle of the Marne. Following them came the delighted peasants, the radiant figure of
France, and the messenger who, from a position of vantage on a
wall, described the battle in progress. The fading chorale suggested
the enemy's retreat, and the French soldiers' song, *Auprès de ma
Blonde*, rang out in its stead. The play, or rather poem in dialogue
form, was mimed, almost danced, by Les Quinze. A single taxi-
driver had, apparently, transported the whole of the Paris garrison
to the banks of the Marne, and music, rather than realistic sounds
of battle, evoked the course of events. There is a certain ironical
truth in Obey's own statement that what was most worth retaining
of *Bataille* was the actual production, but that, the production alas,
could not be printed.

Loire (Atelier, April 28th, 1933) is a curious synthesis of themes
from *Bataille de la Marne* and *Noé*. Instead of the struggle of man
against man, which is the theme of *Bataille*, it represents man's conflict with the elements and also the irresistible power of flood
waters. A symbol from beginning to end, the play, with its
choruses, is cast in much the same mould as *Bataille*. The interest
lies in the symphonic treatment of the text and the epic nature of
the subject: the sudden flooding of the valley by the apparently
peaceful river, the resistance of those who live on its bank, and
the abatement of the flood, which devastates the homes of the
sacrilegious creatures who sully the river's waters, and span it with
bridges, but brings a new fertility to the land. Many of the symbols,
like the river, the tributaries (her daughters), and the chorus of
her waters, fail to catch the imagination, but the animals and their
friend, the old oak-tree, provide some delightful moments. The
marooned and hungry fox, infuriated by the lordly mockery of the
owl, threatens him:

> Si tu bées encore du bec, c'est de toi que je déjeûnerai
> ... [*au chêne*] ce boban-là se crayait roi!

THE OWL: Faut pas le dire! Faut pas en parler!
THE FOX: Eh! ben, close le bec.
THE OWL: Cloc. [*bruit du bec qui se ferme*]
  Later:
THE OWL: Je peux t'y parler, Renard?
THE FOX: Allez, décolle ton bec.

Crime et Châtiment
Producer: Baty
Photo: Lipnitzki

Le Temps est un songe, with Georges Pitoëff and Marie Kalff

Le Mangeur de rêves, with Ludmilla and Georges Pitoëff and Marie Kalff

Later, to a Daughter of the Loire:

THE OWL: Demozelle.
THE FOX: Clos donc ton bec, toi!
THE OWL: Cloc.

The play—ballet or allegorical pantomime—was enacted in a stylized setting representing the Loire valley, with a Touraine village in the foreground and some of the valley's Renaissance castles in the background, without regard for perspective, and once again provided a perfectly ordered and fascinating, if somewhat childish, "spectacle".

Copeau, who watched over the work of Les Quinze, considered that Obey was the only French dramatist who had been prepared to adopt the methods of the Vieux-Colombier and its School, and to profit by their experience. Obey declared that as the result of long discussions with Copeau he had sought to develop his own particular dramatic style. Copeau was his teacher, Les Quinze the source of his inspiration. In Copeau's production of *Le Trompeur de Séville* there was a "simultaneous" setting, as in the medieval Mystery plays. Several mansions were grouped around a small square, which the spectators' imagination had to transform into a courtyard, the dining-room in Elvire's house, an ante-chamber in the royal palace. The impression of a dream world was reinforced by music by Darius Milhaud. Much the same type of setting was used at the Comédie-Française for Obey's final version, *L'Homme de cendres*. The interest of the play is mainly of a technical order. Obey makes as free with the element of time as he does with that of place: the prologue links incidents from Don Juan's birth to the age of fifteen, and when Don Juan dies he dies alone in the middle of the stage, even though all around the edge of it stand wife, mother, king, servants.

Symphonic structure and the use of *dramatis personae* who are cyphers rather than characters reappear in *Ultimatum*, which is closely linked with *Bataille de la Marne* by its theme, for it tells the story of the outbreak of the First World War in a set which "represents Europe". The play, of which part only was published in 1945, is contemporary with Giraudoux's *La Guerre de Troie n'aura pas lieu*, and shows Obey's concern with the fate of nations, victims of particular interests and tragic misunderstandings.

Before writing for Les Quinze, Obey had collaborated with Denys Amiel as early as 1921, but the tragi-comedy *Les Amis de la dernière heure* (Canard sauvage, December 22nd, 1923) was by Obey alone; it depicts the reaction of the prison doctor, almoner, and others during an unexpected delay before an execution.

Obey has continued to write for the stage, and whatever its success, each of his plays shows him to be, in the same sense as Jean Cocteau, a man of the theatre. Three are worthy of mention: *Maria* (Comédie des Champs-Elysées, March 22nd, 1946), *Lazare* (Marigny-Barrault, November 21st, 1951), and *Une Fille pour du vent* (Comédie-Française, April 15th, 1953). *Maria* treats the problem of artistic composition, recalling by its theme and structure Pirandello's *Sei personaggi in cerca d'autore*. In it Death "takes the trouble to come in person", in the guise of a bearded man in a black overcoat and top-hat. The play was a very honourable failure.

Lazare is more important. Unlike *Maria*, it is extremely simple in structure, and consists only of a series of conversations between Lazare, the doctor, the grave-digger, Jésus, Judas, and others, immediately after Lazare's return home from the grave. The whole play is a meditation on death and life. The grave-digger takes a professional view, describing the art of grave-digging in detail. Lazare, who seems to have retained some human consciousness in the grave, professes a pantheistic view, talking nostalgically to Jésus of the unutterable joy of feeling oneself dissolve into nature, becoming oneself earth, water, roots. He is resentful at being forcibly brought back to life, "cruelly torn up from the earth", put back in human chains and into the limiting prison of one's own body, just as water to drink is imprisoned in a glass. The miracle of the resuscitation of Lazare, Jésus learns, had been incomplete: Lazare had to be made to "live". Obey, rather strangely, makes of Lazare the prophet of Jésus's death, and Jésus, accepting the prophecy, goes immediately to meet His death. The play aroused considerable controversy, but, disconcerting as it is, it cannot be easily dismissed, and Barrault showed courage in accepting the difficult task of bringing such a theme into the theatre.

Une Fille pour du vent (Comédie-Française, April 15th, 1953), a good play in theme and spirit but cast in the now familiar Greek mould, recalls Giraudoux's dramas on more than one count, particularly *La Guerre de Troie n'aura pas lieu*. This story of the sacrifice of Iphigenia is used by Obey to debunk war. Like Giraudoux, Obey refuses to accept the idea of the existence of "enemy" nations, and points to the coldly calculated self-interest of powerful factions as the cause of war: the country's ruler and his High Priest need an initial success to launch their deep-laid plot, and Iphigénie is sacrificed when it is certain that the required winds will blow, and when they have, in fact, already started blowing. Many of the lines carry an echo of Giraudoux's play in style as well as thought. Like Giraudoux, he thinks that war is sheer folly, and, like Giraudoux, he is afraid that peace is merely an interval between two such moments of folly. Like *La Guerre de Troie n'aura pas lieu*, Obey's play is full of contemporary allusions, from the elevation of Hitler to the inglorious death of Mussolini. Obey's Iphigénie is no resigned dupe: she terms "senseless words" the "honour and glory" of the country for which she is to be pointlessly sacrificed, "lies" Agamemnon's "sacred war", and as she goes to the slaughter, encouraged in her revolt by the ghost of the first soldier to die in the Trojan war, and whom she alone can see, she cries to all around: "*You* are the condemned."

Besides his original work, Obey made an excellent adaptation of *Richard III*, which was performed by Dullin in 1933. He also adapted *The Oresteia*, which Barrault put on at the Bordeaux festival in 1955, and subsequently in Paris at the Marigny Theatre (October 5th).

On March 25th, 1946, André Obey was appointed director of the Comédie-Française; he resigned the post on February 6th the following year, after carrying through the fusion of the Odéon and the Comédie-Française with a view to reserving the Salle Richelieu for the classical repertory, and staging new plays, particularly modern ones, at the Salle-Luxembourg.

The fifth production of Les Quinze was *Les Lanceurs de graines* (Atelier, November 1932), JEAN GIONO's first composition for the theatre. This and Giono's other plays are very like his novels in style and theme, but add nothing to the reputation he has gained as a novelist. His is not essentially a dramatic talent, and Giono announced his intention of writing no more for the theatre. Instead, the cinema claimed his attention and he made a film, *Crésus* (1960), the text of which vividly recalls *La Femme du boulanger*, which first appeared as a film (1938) made by Marcel Pagnol on Giono's short story, *Jean le bleu*, before Giono wrote it up as a play in 1942. It was staged on May 17th, 1944, at the Ambassadeurs. His second play, *Le Bout de la route*, had a very long run at the Théâtre des Noctambules, from May 30th, 1941.

The only action is the arrival of a stranger in the last village on a mountain road, and then his departure. He leaves because, obsessed as he is by the thought of his unfaithful fiancée, he cannot return the love of one of the village girls. The same sort of countryside forms the setting of *Les Lanceurs de graines*, which, like *Le Bout de la route*, is more of a pastoral poem than a play. Here nature itself seems to join forces with those who defend her against the would-be destroyers of her beauty. The language is full of imagery, but lines such as these are not dramatic.

> CATHERINE: Oh! ce temps me pèse aux reins comme un sac.
> or
> CATHERINE: Tu nous a manqué, Aubert, avec ton regard qui léchait les bons endroits comme une douce langue de chien.

Giono is a novelist and himself admits to being a novelist trying his hand at drama. That is true even of *Voyage en calèche*, the most successful of his works for the stage. A cloak-and-dagger story, set in Italy in 1797 during the French occupation, this play, quite understandably, provoked considerable opposition when it was performed at the Vieux-Colombier in 1947 (December 22nd), because it showed French occupation troops in a bad light. In the less charged atmosphere of 1965 a second version, staged at the Théâtre Sarah-Bernhardt under the title of *La Calèche*, tends rather to evoke the shade of Edmond Rostand, and is, to quote the playwright's own description of it, "sheer entertainment on a romantic theme, innocent of any message". It is hard to recognize in this play the hand of the writer whose chief concern had been contemporary life in Provence.

One of the first of the consciously "written" plays of the modern period was *Le Dernier Empereur*, by the novelist JEAN-RICHARD BLOCH. It dates from 1919, and was performed at the Odéon on November 17th, 1926, and then in Geneva and Germany, where it was staged with great crowd movements. Its theme, as in Bloch's later play *Toulon*, is political, and the action moves forward in a series of tableaux, presenting a young idealistic Empereur, who attempts to govern with and for the people, thus uniting against himself all the reactionary forces in the country. He sees the choice before him as lying between the dictator's whip and the prophet's torch, but he cannot choose until, finally, he understands what his real purpose should be, and goes over to the people to lead them "from below". Bloch himself felt that his play did not measure up to the grandeur of the theme, and preferred to it three short plays which he had grouped under the significant title of *Offrande à la musique* (1927). If prose was not to be a mere vehicle for dry intellectual argument inspiration had to be sought—in music, painting, or architecture.

When PAUL CLAUDEL first began using dramatic form in the 1880's Wagner's musical dramas were providing the model for young writers, mainly Symbolists, who aimed at writing poetic drama as far removed from the plays, in alexandrines, of Edmond Rostand or Jean Richepin, as from the conventionally realistic plays of the commercial stage, or the starkly realistic plays of the Théâtre Libre. Joséphin Péladan and Edouard Dujardin, two of the most fervent Wagnerians, attempted, even, to imitate the Wagnerian *leitmotive* by drawing on the resources of language alone. Yet, despite obvious imitations of this kind, it was not until Claudel began to write that Wagner's dramatic technique was seriously applied to French drama. Claudel favoured vast, indeterminate, and timeless settings for general conflicts transcending those of ordinary reality, characters of a pseudo-mythical kind, grandiose symbols, and moments of mystical exaltation.[21] In his early plays his dramatic structure is particularly reminiscent of Wagner's; there are three or four long acts, each presenting a critical moment in the action; the external action is reduced to the minimum, and the speeches are almost monologues, even in debate. They are couched in language which expresses, by its musicality, the feelings of the speakers, in the same way, in theory at least, that Wagner's instrumental music, by its affective content, expresses those of the characters in his musical dramas. Claudel took from Wagner the belief that there is a language of sound, which alone can express such emotions as are not directly perceptible to the intelligence, so that, if a man is to be recreated in his totality on the stage, music, whether it be that of instruments or that of words (and Claudel considered verbal music superior to instrumental music), must be called into play, and with it the art of the dance or gesture. The Wagnerian belief in the necessary synthesis of the arts is basic to Claudel's approach.

Claudel was the first playwright to restore an essential rôle to the sound of words and to diction. For well over a century actors had aimed at natural speech rather than intoned declamation, whereas Claudel applied the principles of symbolistic poetics to theatrical diction. He composed with speech sounds as though they were musical notes. He based his verse on the rhythm of breathing, and used the intonations of speech as a musician uses notes of various pitch. This made him particularly sensitive to the quality of his actors' voices, to their attention to pitch, to the stress accent on consonants, the length of syllables, and he recommended his actors to look for the musical element in the text rather than for the intellectual content. Giraudoux was to take up a similar attitude, and, despite fundamental differences of outlook and technique, he was to make a similar declaration of faith in the phonetic and affective value of language, and no more than Claudel did he accommodate style to character. The musicality of the text was uppermost in Claudel's mind. He considered Le Père humilié to be the most musical of his plays, and in 1912, in his conversation with Lugné-Poë, who was producing L'Annonce faite à Marie, he defined this play as being "for the most part an opera with purely verbal music, particularly the last scene in the fourth act".[22] It was for this reason that he was not satisfied with Lugné-Poë's "thunderous voice" as Anne Vercors, nor with Magnat's "precentor's voice" for his builder of cathedrals, Pierre de Craon. During the rehearsals at the Œuvre his request for the kind of incantation to be found in plainsong at first drew protests from the actors on the ground that it was not "true to life", and they were "stupefied" by his suggestion that every gesture, as well as intonation, should be carefully studied and not left to the inspiration of the moment. Claudel's views about diction never changed, as may be seen from a letter to Gaston Baty in 1920, about the possible production of his translations of Agamemnon and the Choephori at the Comédie-Montaigne. For these plays, as also for his translation of the Eumenides, he envisaged a form of declamation as carefully scored as music, and in which the essential element was not the meaning but the intensity, the mood, the fortes and diminuendos, and the overlapping of spoken parts. He directed that some of the interventions of the chorus in Les Choéphores should be whispered, some sung, some accompanied by percussion instruments, and others by music. For this he sought the aid of Darius Milhaud. He readily acknowledged his debt to music, and on one occasion, in 1948, when he used the device of the inner dialogue (he introduced a "Voice" into "le

Cantique de Mesa", which occurs in the closing moments of *Partage de midi*), he asserted that he had taken it from Beethoven.

With its realistic tradition, the early twentieth-century Paris stage was clearly not the place for plays on the lines upon which Claudel was working. As it was, *L'Annonce faite à Marie*, the first of Claudel's plays to reach the stage, was produced in 1912 only before the limited public of a studio theatre, the Œuvre. The last scene, in which the characters sang at length the praises of the dead Violaine, proved to be an entirely lyrical piece of writing, quite unsuited for the stage. When Charles Dullin agreed to produce the play at the Comédie-Française in 1938 Claudel rewrote the whole act, but in the final version of 1948, when he himself directed its production at the Théâtre Hébertot, he applied the same principles of diction and gesture that he had sought to impose on the actors at the Œuvre in 1912, and which he had described in the programme of that performance.

L'Annonce faite à Marie was followed at the Œuvre in 1914 by *L'Otage*, after an audience had been prepared by enthusiasts like the poet Carlos Larronde, who read selected passages at special meetings. In 1914 *L'Echange* was presented to a similar group of initiates by Copeau, at the Vieux-Colombier. A few sporadic revivals of these plays followed, the main ones being Gémier's production of *L'Otage* at the Odéon in 1928, after that of *L'Annonce faite à Marie* at the Comédie-Montaigne in 1921, and the Comédie-Française production of *L'Otage* in 1934, and later, in 1955, of *L'Annonce faite à Marie*. But with these exceptions—one can hardly include the 1921 production of *Partage de midi* and the 1916 production of *Tête d'Or* before the still more limited and specialized audience of the theatre laboratory Art et Action—Claudel's considerable dramatic output failed, for some fifty years, to reach the stage, at least in France. Now, to quote Jean-Louis Barrault,[23] Claudel's work has been "placed in orbit; it can keep going for ever; the Catholic rocket is no longer needed to project it into space"— the reference is of course to the Catholic revival which took place in France during the years of the German occupation and those immediately following. What Barrault fails to mention in this assessment of the situation is his own part in putting Claudel's play into "orbit". Through his initiative, Claudel's major dramatic work *Le Soulier de satin*, written between 1919 and 1924, was staged in Paris in 1943 (November 27th). The full text would have taken some nine hours to perform, but Barrault, who was then a temporary member of the Comédie-Française, worked over the text together with Claudel and finally produced a version with a playing-time of five hours; their earlier version, which would have covered two performances, each of three hours, having been re-jected by the actors of the Comédie. After Barrault left the Comédie in 1946 to form his own "Théâtre-Français", he set out to do for Claudel what Jouvet had done for Giraudoux. He wished, also, to retrace Claudel's life back in time through his works. Beginning with *Partage de midi*, which he staged at the Marigny in 1948 with Edwige Feuillère in the part of Ysé, he went on, in 1951, to revive *L'Echange*, which had been performed in Paris in 1937 by Georges and Ludmilla Pitoëff and in 1946 by Ludmilla and her son Sacha. In 1953 he staged as a play *Le Livre de Christophe Colomb*, which dates from 1927; in 1958 he produced *Le Soulier de satin* at the Palais Royal with his own company, and in 1959 opened the Théâtre de France, formerly the Odéon, with *Tête d'Or*, Claudel's first play. At the time of its production the play had an uneasy, fascist ring, and, in the scene where Tête d'Or brushes the politicians aside, it had an unexpected topicality. Exis-tentialist thought, however, seems to have made this seventy-year-old meditation on the fact of existence less forbidding; indeed, the existentialist *angoisse* of the hero had a particular interest for the young generation of which Barrault's audiences were almost ex-clusively composed. As early as 1939 Barrault had asked Claudel for the play, along with *Partage de midi* and *Le Soulier de satin*, and Claudel had refused, saying that it was an incomprehensible hotch-potch which would only provoke laughter, and that it had become practically unreadable to him. Yet in 1925 he had listed the play along with *Partage de midi* and *Le Soulier de satin*, as being the most important of his works.[24] Ten years later, when Barrault renewed his request, Claudel set to work to rewrite the play. For it to be understood nowadays, he said, "one would have to recreate the prison-like atmosphere in which we lived at the time of Taine and Renan, to rebuild the materialistic lid under which we stifled. I can only see one way out and that is to have *Tête d'Or* played in a concentration camp, by prisoners, inside the barbed-wire, and during an aerial bombardment. The tubercular prisoner who was taking the part of Cébès would really die", etc. Claudel gave up at the beginning of the second act, telling Barrault to do what he liked with the play after his death.[25] As for *Partage de midi*, Claudel replied in 1939 that he would never allow its performance and that *Le Soulier de satin* was so long that Barrault should produce the fourth part alone, under the title of *Sous le Vent des Iles Baléares*; this part had been written first and was complete in itself. It had originally been intended as the prologue to another play, *Protée*, of which the first version dates from 1913. In the meantime, in 1955, Jean Vilar had produced Claudel's second play, *La Ville*, with the Théâtre National Populaire at Avignon, where earlier, in 1947, he had arranged for the production, by Maurice Cazeneuve, of *L'Histoire de Tobie et de Sara*, "a morality play in which", according to Claudel, "the word is helped by the resources of music, the cinema and mime". *Le Pain dur* and *Le Père humilié*, which continue the story begun in *L'Otage* and date from 1914 and 1916 respectively, were first performed, the one at the Atelier in 1949, the other at the Théâtre des Champs-Elysées in 1946, an attempt to stage the latter in 1941 at the Œuvre having been stopped by the German censorship. The trilogy was presented as a whole for the first time in November 1962 at the Vieux-Colombier, where, just after the First World War, its production had been contemplated by Jacques Copeau. Baty and Gémier had also considered producing it at the Comédie-Montaigne in 1921. The last of Claudel's plays to reach the stage was *Le Repos du septième jour* (Œuvre, October 1st, 1965). It is a static composition and, as B. Poirot-Delpech said in *Le Monde* (September 30th), only the language, its "carnal envelope", gave any consistence or reality to its abstract theological developments.

The revolution attempted by Claudel was not a revolution in poetic style alone. He deliberately set out to create a didactic Catholic drama, in opposition to the purely lay theatre, particularly psychological drama and social comedy. The favourable reception given to the first performance of *L'Otage* was attributed by him to its answering a fundamental need that the non-religious art of the day failed to satisfy. In his opinion not only could the Christian faith be *served by* dramatic art, but Christian faith could *serve* dramatic art; the Fall was the very stuff of drama because of the image it offered of a struggle between good and evil, between the spirit and the flesh. Human actions could be set against the vaster drama of salvation. So far so good. In an age which favoured conventional art the vaster conception of drama was a welcome change. However, Claudel's reiterated claim that one's own well-being in the hereafter is the only aim worth pursuing, and his view of history as progressing necessarily towards the establishment of the Catholic faith everywhere on earth, was too much of a good thing. This was art serving faith with a vengeance.

Claudel's conception of drama stems from his own conversion, and a strongly autobiographical element colours his whole dramatic output from *Tête d'Or*, his "adieu to paganism", onward. *Tête d'Or* bears the stamp of the years of painful adaptation lived by Claudel between his mystical experience on Christmas Day, 1886, when, as he wrote in *Ma Conversion*, his "heart was touched" and he believed, and his official conversion to the Catholic faith in 1890, which followed the completion of the play by a few months. The "poor child" Cébès, who sought of Tête d'Or an assurance that human life had a meaning and received the answer that man had only "the human hour" and "dies for ever", was Claudel himself. So, too, was Tête d'Or, whose aim was the conquest of the universe —by force. At this time Claudel was conscious of a "fermentation of genius" within him and, though anxious to "measure himself against the universe", feared defeat like the "unfortunate Verlaine and Villiers de l'Isle-Adam".[26] He attributed his own moments of deep despair to Lambert and Isidore de Besme in *La Ville*, and all the characters in the play *L'Echange*, as he wrote to Marguerite Moréno in 1900, were himself and reflect the "painful bondage" of his year of service in the diplomatic corps in America. Claudel is also the Emperor in *Le Repos du septième jour*, which was written in China in 1896, when, confirmed in his faith, he was contemplating retreat from the world into monastic life.

Claudel's first attempt to create a character other than himself was Ysé in *Partage de midi*, a drama otherwise directly inspired by an episode in his own life. Claudel (Mesa in the play) met her on the ship during his return to China shortly after having experienced a sense of "rejection by God", when he was in a Benedictine monastery in Ligugé, in 1900. Rodrigue, the hero of *Le Soulier de satin*, meets the same woman as Prouhèze. Prouhèze, like Ysé, is married and out of reach. Bewilderment at the part forbidden love has to play in human life is one of the themes of *Partage de midi*, which portrays the tragic consequences of the love of a man for a woman and a woman for a man when each allows the other to usurp the place due to God alone, and when each is prepared to satisfy love, even at the price of sin. *Le Soulier de satin*, written some twenty

years later, offers Claudel's explanation of the rôle played by such
a love: it was the instrument of man's salvation, and each of the
lovers is shown as holding the "key to the other's soul". Some hint
of such an idea is already to be found in *La Ville*, when Lâla defines
woman as "the promise that cannot be fulfilled", the promise of
Paradise regained.

The progress of Claudel's "evangelization" can be followed from
Tête d'Or to *Le Soulier de satin*. Indeed, in his statement to Frédéric
Lefèvre Claudel referred to *Le Soulier de satin* as *Tête d'Or* in
another form, adding that it epitomized both *Tête d'Or* and *Partage
de midi* and even provided the conclusion to *Partage de midi*. In
Le Soulier de satin Claudel preaches that it is only by repeated
victories over the self that one can pretend to a real conversion, and
shows his characters struggling against their passion, and seconded
by grace. The experience upon which *Partage de midi* was based
had clearly brought home to him the "rôle of sin in the economy
of grace". "Love outside the sacrament of marriage, is it not a
sin?" asks Prouhèze of her Guardian Angel, to which he replies,
"Even sin can serve." "So it was good that he should love me?"
asks Prouhèze. "It was good that you should teach him the meaning of desire," comes the reply.

This scene between the sleeping Prouhèze and the Angel is at
the centre of the dramatic action of the play, because it contains
Prouhèze's consent to death so that she may become the star that
leads Rodrigue to God. It is also at the centre of Claudel's conception of the human predicament. The Angel likens himself to a
fisherman who has caught a fish on his line and is drawing the line
in slowly so that the fish may not struggle and break free. The fish
is also the bait to catch another fish; yet it is not the woman in her
that Prouhèze must offer to Rodrigue if he is to be led to God, but
the "Child of God" that she must first perfect in herself. It is clear
from the start of the play that this "Child of God" is what Rodrigue is looking for, although his desire for her bodily presence and
physical possession obscures his vision. Prouhèze has given her soul
to Rodrigue, but the Angel insists that Rodrigue must freely return
it to her if she is to bring him salvation. Prouhèze must disappear
from Rodrigue's sight, even as Beatrice had disappeared from
Dante's. Her thrice-repeated withdrawal of her presence constitutes
the necessary "betrayal" which creates in Rodrigue an emptiness
which God alone can fill; by seeking to rejoin Prouhèze, Rodrigue

is led to God. Similarly, the salvation of Camille, whom Prouhèze marries under duress at Mogador, after her first husband's death, depends on Prouhèze. It is her renunciation of her human attachment to Rodrigue in answer to Camille's appeal to her charity that brings out the saint in her, and leads Camille to his Maker. In a comment on his play in 1944 Claudel insisted on the close link between the notion of sacrifice and the Christian doctrine of the Communion of Saints. This conception of the sacrifice of immediate joy to gain Eternal Life was, he affirmed, basic to all his dramatic work, and dramatic action itself was, for him, no more than a complicated machine, designed to make his characters respond willingly to their vocation. Since it would seem that only through a love of this kind can one attain Eternal Life, it is as great a sin to reject it as to seek only the pleasure of love, and this is why, in the first scene of *Le Soulier de satin*, the dying Jesuit prays God to afflict his brother Rodrigue with such a love, and in this way lead him back to Him, and away from the conquest of material things, which had become his sole aim. And it is this mystical "deliverance" that is proclaimed in the last line of the play. Rodrigue, the conquistador, is a direct descendant of Tête d'Or, the man who dares to measure himself with the universe. Both he and Tête d'Or find their strength to pursue their aims in the void created by the loss of loved ones, but whereas Tête d'Or directs his efforts solely towards establishing his own domination over men, Rodrigue places his earthly ambitions at the service of God, for once Prouhèze has become a "sword through his heart" he is tempted by nothing in this world.

The personal adventure of each of the characters is closely bound up in events of the fifteenth and sixteenth centuries, which, strangely enough, Claudel thought of as the most glorious period of Catholicism. All the characters play a rôle in the efforts of Spain, the Defender of the Faith, to extend the Catholic faith to all parts of the globe, and each is linked with a particular area. For Rodrigue it is America, where, like a new Cortez, he opens up a route between the Atlantic and the Pacific so as to carry the faith to the peoples of the Far East. He is ready, too, with a plan for England, to which the King of Spain has already despatched the Armada in order to stamp out "the heresy of Cranmer and Knox" and to "nail bloody Elizabeth to her rock". Rodrigue's plan is to associate England with Spain and to open up America to England and all European peoples, thereby uniting them in peace and the Catholic faith. For her part, Prouhèze takes a stand against Islam in Africa, which, in the person of Camille, looks to her for salvation. The Viceroy of Naples deals a blow to Protestantism at the battle of Prague, while (later one gathers, in spite of chronology) the Turks are routed at Lepanto (1571) by his son Don Juan d'Autriche (born, it would appear, in 1620). Don Juan is joined by Marie des Sept-Epées, Prouhèze's daughter by Camille, but miraculously like Prouhèze's soul-mate Rodrigue! The Renaissance, the Discovery, the Counter-Reformation, the campaign of the Cross against the Crescent, all are grist to Claudel's mill, and his disregard for chronology and historical truth is "daring".

The stage of his drama is "the whole world", and a great variety of characters throng his play. All are intimately bound up with each other, and form a vast community of interdependent lives; Rodrigue, to quote his Jesuit brother, can only save himself by saving others—the doctrine of the Communion of Saints is firmly worked into the pattern of the play. On the stage the credibility of the characters is severely taxed by the incredibility of the situations in which they find themselves, and the characters are symbols rather than human beings. There are other still less dramatically credible characters, including the theologically minded Angel and the saints, the symbolical Double Shadow (Rodrigue and Prouhèze in the moment of their single embrace on the ramparts of Mogador), and the Moon. It is the task of the Moon to reply to the Shadow's accusation against Rodrigue and Prouhèze of having been false to the embrace, and also to define the rôle of human love in the divine scheme of things. In a Claudel play strictly human drama is overshadowed, and every element, the seas, the heavens, and the "Beyond" itself, are marshalled in an attempt to integrate it into a cosmic drama in Wagnerian fashion. Little wonder, then, that Le Soulier de satin verges on opera, particularly in the lengthy metaphysico-lyrical developments, while the diction adopted in the Barrault production, together with the ample score by Honegger, served to emphasize the operatic nature of the text. The influence of the Spanish comedias worked in the same direction. One is confronted by an "enormous drama in four journées presenting", as Claudel told Frédéric Lefèvre, "an incongruous mixture of buffoonery, passion and mysticity". It was modelled on Calderón, in deliberate opposition to French classical form, for which Claudel had little affection, despite his use of it in L'Echange. "It is a woof", said Claudel, "made from a blue thread, a red and a green which constantly appear and disappear", meaning the main characters and their lives.

In 1941, when Barrault renewed his request for a play, Claudel proposed *Le Livre de Christophe Colomb*, adding that it would prepare the way for *Le Soulier de satin*, and, indeed, this play, written two years after *Le Soulier de satin* was completed, is on the same model. In defiance of historical truth, Columbus is presented in this play as a mystic who establishes the Christian faith, all over the globe, albeit by means as questionable as slavery and genocide. As with Rodrigue, Colomb's desire, which Claudel overtly presents as symbolical of the desire of *all* men, strains beyond the possession of this earth to that of the "world beyond", and, like Rodrigue, he is guided to it by a woman, the very Catholic Queen Isabella, who, in the final scene, intercedes for him in heaven. The characters have little human quality and little dramatic validity. They are not caught up in any dramatic conflict, nor do they engage in real dialogue. The whole play is reduced to a discussion between Colomb and the chorus, and Claudel attributed the idea for this to Aeschylus's *The Suppliants*. The chorus is assembled on the proscenium to listen to the Explicateur read and explain "Le Livre de la Vie et des voyages de Christophe Colomb qui a découvert l'Amérique, et ce qui est *ultra*." The story of the discoverer's life is told, picture-book fashion, in twenty-seven scenes, and it is witnessed by the dead Colomb, who has left the stage to sit among the chorus, which represents posterity. Colomb II, as he is then called, encourages Colomb I, on the stage, to set sail for the west and fulfil the destiny that has been written into his name: Christophe, Bearer of Christ, and Colomb, the Holy Ghost—pictured on a screen as a radiant dove hovering over the revolving globe, before it is released on stage as a real dove. Were it not for the childish implications which are read into the discoverer's name and presented as the very substance of the play, such a simplified biography of Columbus in picture-form might have provided a colourful spectacle, making good entertainment. But the didactic purpose makes it leaden. Barrault's production of the play, with incidental music by Darius Milhaud, in which, at Claudel's suggestion, he united the cinema with the theatre, was offered by Barrault as an example of "total theatre". Already in *Le Drame et la Musique*, written in 1930, at the time of the production of

Christophe Colomb in Berlin, as an opera, with a full and entirely different score by Milhaud, Claudel had explained his idea of what operatic music should be and do. His idea, he said, was inspired by the use made of music in the Japanese Noh play. He also advocated some form of stage *décor* as fluid as the music, the poetry, and the dramatic action. This fluidity could be achieved by the use of a film screen instead of the usual fixed setting which only detracts from the poetic illusion. On the screen would be shown fleeting phantoms from the past, warning shadows of the future, elusive thoughts which crowd the characters' minds, or surges of feelings so confused as to defy verbal expression. In Barrault's production the screen was provided by the sail of a ship, which formed the central element of the setting. On it was to be seen the dove in its flight, the hand of God moulding the earth, and also the states of mind of the various characters who were acting out their parts on the stage. It was because of this "coincidence of the arts"—to use Baudelaire's phrase—that the term "total theatre", as used by Barrault with regard to *Christophe Colomb*, was generally misunderstood. The "totality" of Claudel's dramas is in the texts and is independent of the use of film strips, instrumental music, mime, lighting, and stage sets, though these "tricks", as Barrault calls them, do help, in a production, to throw the "totality" into relief. Claudel aimed at presenting an image of the cosmos, and he found in Barrault a producer after his own heart. Barrault's conception of acting is that it interprets the whole of nature, from the animal and vegetable world to the elements, in addition to its main task of portraying man. The opportunity was afforded Barrault to use his talents in the swimming scene in *Le Soulier de satin*, and in *Christophe Colomb*, where the hero wades into the waves—mimed by actors—to rescue a drowning sailor. In addition to playing the parts of Colomb and the sailor, the actors had at the same time to convey the idea of the "element of water and the buffeting force of the waves".[27]

With *Jeanne au bûcher* Claudel went still further along the road to the dramatic oratorio, and in so doing returned to the purely lyrical drama of his youth, though in a much simplified form. The performances of the Medieval Studies Group in Paris University, in 1933-34, led to Ida Rubinstein's proposal to stage a vast Mystery play, and this proposal, in turn, inspired in Claudel's mind a vision of Joan of Arc tied to the stake and surrounded by the united

French nation. The work, with music by Honegger, was presented by Ida Rubinstein on May 12th, 1938, in Bâle, and on May 6th, 1939, in Orleans, as an oratorio with the choruses grouped round the leader. In a static production at the Opéra on December 18th, 1951, in which the crowd, or chorus, was ranged on either side of the stake to which Jeanne was tied, Jean Doat gave pride of place to the music. Rossellini, on the other hand, removed the chorus from the stage proper, and laid stress on the visual element by making Jeanne come down from the stake, to take her part in the incidents depicted in the play, and in settings provided by film sequences. His production was seen in London on October 20th, 1954, under the title *Joan of Arc at the Stake*.

Claudel's last work for the stage, *Tobie et Sara*, was also written at Ida Rubinstein's request. Claudel originally intended to write a lyrical drama, with music taking first place, but subsequently decided to subordinate the music to the dramatic element. Even so, this is not a dramatic work. Such plays require a *tour de force* of production to make shows of them. Barrault's prestige and skill obtained a hearing for *Partage de midi*, *Christophe Colomb*, *Tête d'Or*, and *Le Soulier de satin*. This latter play proved it can attract an audience in a provincial *Centre dramatique* like Strasbourg, where Hubert Gignoux produced it in 1965, but of all Claudel's plays only *L'Annonce faite à Marie* has had, or can hope to have, the truly popular appeal Claudel was anxious for in his proselytizing zeal.

The only other play to have popular appeal, despite successes like that of *Les Choéphores* at the Provins Festival in 1967, is *L'Otage*, the first part of a trilogy of which the idea is taken from the *Oresteia*. The action of these three plays covers some fifty years of social and political history, beginning with the abduction of Pope Pius VII to Fontainebleau in 1813. The French colonization of Algeria, the unrest in divided Poland, the gradual industrialization and laicization of Western society, and the "humiliation" of the Pope through the loss of his temporal power, all come into it. The unflattering portrait which he had painted of the Jews in *Le Pain dur* made Claudel, who feared possible repercussions of its performance on his career as a diplomat, refuse Lugné-Poë's offer to stage the play after *L'Annonce* and suggest *L'Otage*. Each of the plays is self-contained, though it is with *L'Otage* that the story of Sygne de Coûfontaine, the old aristocratic spirit incarnate, and

Turelure, the embodiment of the spirit of the French Revolution, begins. Here Sygne accepts the cruel bidding of God, made in the person of his minister Badilon, to sacrifice her love for her cousin Georges and marry Turelure, a former servant of the family, in order to save the Pope, the symbol of Christendom. The story ends in the third play, *Le Père humilié*, in which God's and the Pope's debt to the family is repaid by the Pope's nephew Orian, when Sygne's granddaughter, Pensée, knows she has conceived a child by Orian, who risks damnation by sacrificing his vocation to his love. The whole dramatic action arises out of Sygne's refusal, symbolized by her rejection of her own son, Louis, to come to terms with the new society born of the Revolution and symbolized by Turelure. After changing his opinions and allegiance with each change of regime, Turelure reappears as "Premier" under Louis Philippe in *Le Pain dur*, a realistic play, and the one technically good stage play Claudel has written. In a scene which is as brutal and melodramatic as any Henry Bernstein ever wrote, Louis unwittingly revenges his mother by killing his father for 20,000 francs. He then marries his dead father's mistress, the Jewess Sichel, and of this marriage is born Pensée, who is blind. Before this, Louis sells to his future father-in-law (for four francs a kilo) the immense bronze Christ that Sygne had painfully put together again after the Revolution, but which Turelure had replaced on the wall by a picture of the citizen king. There are other symbols in this realistic play, and they are, according to Claudel, capitalism born of the Revolution (Turelure), colonialism (his son), nationalism and also "the soul in exile" (the Polish girl, Lumîr), feminism (Sichel), economic materialism (her father, Ali Habenichts).

At the same time as he was working on his trilogy, and on his translations of Aeschylus, Claudel wrote a burlesque, *Protée*, inspired by the title of the lost conclusion of Aeschylus's *Oresteia*. In this fantasy Menelaus (Ménélas) is, as one might expect, a comic figure, though not in the way one might expect, seeing that Helen (Hélène) is depicted as being virtuous after all. Burlesque is to be found also in the "farce for a marionette theatre" called *L'Ourse et la lune* (1919). Shortly after, in 1921, Claudel made an incursion into the domain of ballet with *L'Homme et son désir*, which was performed, to Milhaud's music, by the Swedish company of Rolf de La Mare, at the Théâtre des Champs-Elysées. There was nothing untoward in this, as he had always paid attention to the plastic element in the theatre; but his ballet has not become part of any repertory.

Claudel's general theme, as a dramatist, could be summed up in the Portuguese proverb, *Deus escreve direito por linhas tortas*, which serves as an epigraph to *Le Soulier de satin*. But Claudel irritates by brashly crediting himself with a knowledge of the ways of God. Moreover, his God is a senselessly cruel God, who grants salvation to those whom He has predestined to love each other but never to be united, and He requires the complete humiliation of His chosen ones, even in their flesh; Violaine, in *L'Annonce faite à Marie*, becomes a leper, while Rodrigue, in *Le Soulier de satin*, becomes a cripple. In addition to this, Claudel twists history for ideological purposes in a manner that is quite unacceptable. Finally, the text, with its contortions of style, corresponding to contortions of thought, is exasperating.

From the technical point of view, Claudel's enormous dramatic output offers considerable variety and therefore interest. After the first formative influence of Wagner's musical dramas, of Aeschylus, Shakespeare, and the Spanish *comedias*, came that of the Oriental stage, particularly the Noh play. This last influence can be seen in *Le Soulier de satin*. Claudel even tried his hand at a true Noh play, with *La Femme et son ombre*, which was performed in 1923, in Tokyo, at the Imperial Theatre, to music by a Japanese composer. The recitation, *modo plano*, of the text of a Noh play and the strictly controlled and symbolical gestures were in line with the type of acting he had tried to elicit from his actors, in 1912, for the performance of *L'Annonce faite à Marie*, and about which he never changed his mind. With all its shortcomings, Claudel's work, like Brecht's, and despite the gulf that separates the two, constitutes an experimental approach to the theatre. His experiments make it, therefore, of great interest to the playwright and to the historian of the theatre, if not to the theatregoing public itself.

Postscript

A number of playwrights, at present active, who are by no means disciples of Claudel, use a technique which, in many ways, resembles that of Claudel. By means of stage directions incorporated into the text, JEAN VAUTHIER "orchestrates" intonations, gestures, off-stage sounds, and details of *décor*. JACQUES AUDIBERTI claims to have been influenced by opera rather than by drama; he has given the subtitle "opérette philosophique" to *Le Mal court* (1947); he has written a libretto called *Altanima* (1956), and an *Opéra parlé* (1956), now called *La Hobereaute*, and, finally, *L'Opéra du monde* (1965). His first plays were dramatic poems in prose, but in *Altanima* and *Opéra parlé* the composition as a whole is modelled on opera: the use made of voices, lyrical choruses, and strongly rhythmical monologues is intended to remind the audience of an opera. There are scenes with two or three "voices" intended to constitute "duets" and "trios". The same technique is resorted to in plays not referred to as operas or operettas—for example, *Les Patients* (1961), called a "poème à voix". JEAN TARDIEU also works with words used as elements of sound, put together in musical forms. His *Théâtre de chambre*, composed of playlets with titles such as *La Sonate et les trois messieurs ou comment parler musique* (with characters simply named A, B, C) and *Conversation-sinfonietta*, in which a "conductor" and a "choir", with bass, contralto, tenor, and soprano *speaking* voices, go through an "Allegro ma non troppo" and a "Scherzo vivace", with crescendos and diminuendos, claims to be verbal "chamber music". His second volume of *Théâtre* (1960), entitled *Poèmes à jouer*, contains "scores for the stage", "choruses", and solo parts; there is even a play with no visible actor, merely a voice accompanied by modulated stage lighting.

GEORGES SCHEHADE is another writer who takes words for musical elements. He theorizes on the subject in *La Soirée des proverbes* (1954), in which Argengeorge reads from a book about the emancipation of words which "aspire to more consciousness, to the happy life of birds and lions"; in their wake comes "meaning like a dog with a muzzle, even less important than a poodle!" All this is reminiscent of both Claudel and Giraudoux.

NOTES

1. Interview: *L'Intransigeant*, May 8th, 1928.
2. Revived by Barrault at the Théâtre de France, November 22nd, 1961. Performed in English in 1962.
3. Performed in English in 1961 as *The Enchanted*.
4. A similar transference can be observed in the different editions of *Siegfried*.
5. Alice Cocéa intended to stage it in the spring of 1943, but it was immediately banned by the Germans.

6. *Les Nouvelles littéraires*, May 15th, 1937.

7. *Le Figaro*, May 11th, 1937. The play was revived at the Théâtre de l'Avenue, on March 30th, 1943.

8. Performed in English in 1955 and 1961 as *Ondine*.

9. Performed in English in 1963 as *The Madwoman of Chaillot*.

10. Performed in English in 1958 as *Duel of Angels*.

11. Letter to André Rouveyre, November 5th, 1924, in *Divers*, 1931, p. 142.

12. André Gide, "L'Évolution du théâtre", lecture delivered in 1904 and published in his *Nouveaux Prétextes*, 1911.

13. *Journal*, June 1932.

14. *Amal et la lettre du Roi*, translated from *The Post Office* by Rabindranath Tagore, staged in 1928 (May 16th) by La Petite Scène, in 1937 (February 17th), by Pitoëff; *Arden de Feversham*, translated 1933; *Antoine et Cléopâtre*, a truncated version performed by Ida Rubinstein at the Opéra on June 14th, 1920; second version produced on April 27th, 1945, at the Comédie-Française by Barrault; *Hamlet*, Marigny-Barrault, May 4th, 1942; *Le Procès*, adapted from Kafka's novel *The Trial*, using a scenario by Barrault, Marigny-Barrault, October 10th, 1947.

15. "Billets à Angèle", *Œuvres complètes*, vol. XI, 1936, p. 36.

16. *Journal*, April 19th, 1927.

17. *Œuvres complètes*, vol. III, 1933, "Lettres à Angèle", No. VII, p. 200.

18. Revived Comédie-Française, March 31st, 1941. Performed in English in 1933 as *Noah*.

19. *Nouvelles littéraires*, December 8th, 1928.

20. The play was earlier revived at the Théâtre Hébertot in May 1943. It was turned into an opera in 1946 by Ronald Duncan, to music by Benjamin Britten, and performed in Mulhouse in April 1948, and then in Paris at the Théâtre Sarah-Bernhardt in May 1948. Revived Rouen in November 1965.

21. The culminating point of the action of the third act of *L'Annonce faite à Marie* is marked by a miracle. Here, though the source of the exaltation is Claudel's militant Catholicism, and though certain details of the miracle are taken from a German legend, the development of the act recalls the celebration of the rites of the Holy Grail in *Parsifal*.

22. Lugné-Poë, *Dernière Pirouette*, 1946, p. 33.

23. *Le Monde*, September 16th, 1961.

24. *Nouvelles littéraires*. April 18th, interview with Frédéric Lefèvre.

25. Jean-Louis Barrault, *Nouvelles Réflexions sur le théâtre*, 1959, p. 250.

26. *Mémoires improvisés*, 1954, p. 52.

27. Jean-Louis Barrault, *Nouvelles Réflexions sur le théâtre*, 1959, pp. 207 and 270. Recently (1963) Barrault "walked and cycled on air", in Ionesco's *Le Piéton de l'air*.

IX

Studio Theatre: The Play of Ideas

François de Curel—Edouard Schneider—Henry Marx—Gabriel Marcel.

THOUGH by the "Studio theatre movement" is usually meant the movement initiated by Jacques Copeau and continued by the Cartel and Barrault, the term has a wider sense and can be used to embrace the works of philosopher-dramatists such as Gabriel Marcel. Their works rarely appeal to Boulevard audiences, those of Jean-Paul Sartre being the exception that proves the rule. FRANÇOIS DE CUREL, who was still writing in 1927, belongs to an earlier generation than Marcel, having been born in 1854, and after his repeatedly unsuccessful efforts to gain an entry into the Boulevard theatres, might well have ceased to write for the stage, had André Antoine not opened the doors of his studio theatre, the Théâtre Libre, to him in 1892. From there, Curel went on to other theatres, including the Comédie-Française, where *La nouvelle Idole* (1897), which portrays a fanatical devotion to science on the one hand and Christian faith on the other, figured continuously in the repertory from 1921 to 1935. The bulk of Curel's work, written before the First World War, consists of psychological studies such as *L'Envers d'une sainte*, one of his best plays, or plays in which social, moral, and political discussions are combined with a psychological study, as in *Les Fossiles* and *Le Repas du lion*. This latter work, a play about the relationship between employers and employees, also brings into question, as Gabriel Marcel was to do later, the "authenticity" (*i.e.*, genuineness) of the hero's actions. After the war Curel's plays contained studies of physiological factors which explain his characters' conduct, and repeatedly presented sex-desire as the dominant factor. Despite the difference in the type of theme treated by him over the years, his work remains fundamentally the same throughout; the "ideological" substance is constant. The sole exception is *Terre inhumaine* (Théâtre des Arts, December 13th, 1922), and this is the only one of Curel's plays which obtained some measure of popular success. By its setting and the incident it portrays, it is a war play. It also contains a striking study of sex-desire, in which brutal sensuality is associated with a contrasting presence of mind; a French officer, on a mission of espionage, and a German princess lavish caresses upon each other, but each remains keenly alert, steeled with the cold intent to kill so as not to be killed. Such a setting gave Curel an admirable opportunity of developing his favourite moral thesis—namely, the persistence of the animal in civilized man—a thesis which, after the performance of *La Fille sauvage* in 1902 at the Théâtre Antoine, had led critics to talk of "Curelian Darwinism". Curel had a clear awareness of the main currents of thought in his times, and used the theatre as a means of giving concrete expression to his own meditations upon them. Unfortunately, he did not know how to dispense with the "reasoner", a modernized version of the chorus in a Greek play, who fitted badly into the post-1918 drama. In his later plays he failed to build up his characters properly, sacrificing them to his preoccupation with ideas, and this is all the more curious as he himself recognized, and even made one of the characters, a playwright, in *La Comédie du génie* (Théâtre des Arts, March 13th, 1921), state that in the theatre ideas are of value only in so far as they provoke a reaction in the characters; "I value them", he says, "for their inflammatory powers." But, with few exceptions, Curel's characters never took form and substance, and it is by this lack of substance in the characters that his characters fall short of Ibsen's, to whom they were frequently compared by his contemporaries.

Curel's influence is patent in the work of EDOUARD SCHNEIDER, but Schneider was more austere than Curel, and carried his intellectualism further still. In his foreword to his best play, *Exaltation*, which was performed in Geneva in 1926, and the following year in Paris at the Théâtre Antoine, he states his conviction that the play of ideas, which is intended to express the attitudes of the mind and heart when they are at grips with the fundamental problems of life, necessarily ignores the incidental reality of the daily round. This particular play, which was awarded the Eugène Brieux prize, depicts the struggle between human and divine love, and the keen antagonism of mother and daughter, resulting from the clash of two incompatible ideas, a clash which remains too intellectual to make good drama. Like his non-dramatic works, *Les Heures bénédictines* (1910) and *L'Immaculée* (1918), *Exaltation* reflects Schneider's Catholic outlook. An earlier play, *Le Dieu d'argile* (Théâtre Antoine, October 27th, 1921), suffers from the same intellectualism as *Exaltation*. Once again Schneider depicts two irreconcilable forces, pride and love, struggling in the higher regions of thought and conscience; the characterization suffers, and plot is squeezed out.

Despite his inauspicious entry into the theatre—the Vaudeville in 1920—with *L'Enfant maître*, HENRY MARX succeeded in getting his next play, *L'Homme en marche*, performed at the Comédie-Française on June 15th, 1923. His three other plays are all cast in the same mould, that of the Passion play, according to Marx. This particular play is the Passion of the Intelligence and shows *l'homme en marche* in the guise of a saint bearing his cross and crucifying his inner divinity. The action of the play is in terms of a Way of the Cross, at the end of which man is not God but a corpse. Following Curel's example, Marx attempts to incorporate the personal problem of his hero, who is led to question the genuineness of his own life, into a social and political framework. He seems to conclude that the perfectly upright public figure is as much a fiction as the perfectly upright private individual. In all his plays, despite the social framework, the characters are lacking in humanity, and are expressly made by Marx to use a mode of expression which is the language of thought, not that of speech. Such works belong more strictly to the library shelf than to the stage.

This is partly true of the dramatic output of GABRIEL MARCEL, the Christian existentialist philosopher. Marcel was "discovered" as a dramatist in 1949, at the age of sixty, when his play *Un Homme de Dieu*, written in 1925, was performed in Paris at the Théâtre Montparnasse by the *Centre dramatique de l'Est*.[1] This is Marcel's best-known play, and also his most representative. Marcel began, however, to write for the theatre in 1911, and a few of his works were put on in the twenties by small theatre groups such as the Escholiers. Between 1911 and 1951 he published twenty-two plays, several of which are still unperformed. *Le Cœur des autres*, the first of his plays to reach the stage (March 17th, 1921), caused Marcel to be hailed both as a "new Ibsen" and a "new Curel". The play itself contains a discreet reference to Curel, and earlier in his preface to *Le Seuil invisible*,[2] published in 1914, Marcel proposes these two dramatists as models, as against the exponents of the play of violent action, Bernstein and Méré, or Brieux and Hervieu, both masters of the outmoded "thesis play". In his comments on *L'Iconoclaste*, published in 1923, Marcel declared that it would be completely erroneous to see in this play of his the illustration of a theme which had first been formulated in abstract terms; it was based on a situation which had been *felt* and lived in all its aspects at once, a characteristically existentialist claim.[3] Marcel aimed at what he called *le tragique de pensée*; this could not exist in the rarefied atmosphere of philosophical dialogue but only in an atmosphere of emotion, with real flesh and blood creatures, living the same life as us. This conception of drama leads him to criticize playwrights like Claudel, who situate the action of their plays in remote or indeterminate milieux, and who are concerned with the fate of legendary or stylized figures instead of characters who are real living human beings. Marcel, being a teacher of philosophy, might be suspected of turning drama into a metaphysical exercise, but his interest in dramatic form, on the one hand, and the concrete nature of his thinking, on the other, blend drama and dialectics so effectively that the "idea" and the "action" coincide, and the progress of the one is also the progress of the other. Since an existentialist philosopher refuses to consider any but concrete situations, the natural expression of his philosophy is drama. Little wonder, then, that Marcel—and later Jean-Paul Sartre—turned their attention to the theatre. Marcel himself has maintained, and rightly so, that existentialist thought has made it possible for a much closer bond to be formed between the theatre and philosophy than has hitherto existed.[4] The idea of *l'être en situation*, which he was to elaborate later in his philosophical works, at the same time as Karl Jaspers in Germany, was already implicit in *Le Palais de sable*, which he wrote in 1913. All his characters are fully involved in the action in which they are placed; none is a reasoner who looks at the action from outside and comments on it; none is the author's mouthpiece; the characters *are* the action. Neither is there any question with Marcel of drama being put at the service of a philosophical system in order to illustrate or popularize it. On the contrary, it is in his plays that the first glimmer of a number of ideas which he was subsequently to develop in his philosophical writings

is to be seen. Marcel's evolution as a philosopher is from German
Idealism to the more concrete philosophy of Existentialism, and in
the theatre from dramas of thought which are relatively abstract,
La Grâce and Le Palais de sable, to dramas which reflect the impact
of life. It was the attempt to trace soldiers posted as missing, which
he undertook for the Red Cross during the First World War, that
provided the impact, bringing Marcel face to face with the "terrible
reality of human suffering".[5] This led him to re-examine the
relationship between the soul and the body. He states his disagreement with Henri Bergson and his arrival at the conception of the
"self incarnate", of a participation which knows no bounds between
the body and the self (ego). He envisages the same participation between the self incarnate and others, and between the self incarnate
and the universe. It is impossible to estimate what one would have
been like had one not been in contact with such and such a person,
book, etc. These ideas are fundamental to Marcel's dramatic thinking. He sees people as existing for and by others, determining each
other's destiny whether they will or not. He does not see them as
objects in the presence of others. In Le Quatuor en fa dièse, written
in 1916 to 1917, Claire, who has divorced her first husband, a
musician, and married his brother, Roger, is distressed when she
learns of the continued affection of the two brothers for each other,
but is finally brought to a closer understanding with Roger by
the music of her first husband. When Roger protests that it is a
terrible thing not to have been loved for oneself, Claire asks
where does a personality begin and where does it end. These three
characters are not three objects with limits as clear as their
physical contours. In Le Cœur des autres, written in 1920, Marcel
shows the husband as "objectivizing" his wife by using her as
material for his books, and so destroying any possibility of participation. Here Marcel is back at his original theme of solitude, at the
difficult problem of "authentic" communication between human
beings. This problem is posed in his first play La Grâce, written in
1911, and seems to stem from his experience of solitude as an only
child, which he mentions on various occasions. It is at the centre
of Marcel's dramatic work, and also orientated his philosophical
research. L'Iconoclaste, written between 1916 and 1920, and first
entitled Le Porte-glaive, is the expression of the interest Marcel had
taken in psychic research since 1916. In it a psychic experience
brings together two men, a widower and his friend, who have both

loved the dead wife. Jacques, who is on the brink of suicide, invokes the spirit of his dead wife, and lives and marries again at the behest of the spirit, or so he believes. For Abel, who is unaware of Jacques's state of mind, his remarriage is a betrayal of the dead woman. The play poses the problem of the nature of true fidelity, and offers two different examples of mistaken, or false, fidelity; both men make the mistake of "objectivizing" the woman. The nature of true fidelity is another recurrent theme in Marcel's dramatic works, and appeared in his plays before he treated it in his philosophical works.

The problem is faced in *La Chapelle ardente*[6] together with the question of death, which is yet another recurrent theme in Marcel's plays. Like sickness, as in *La Grâce* or *Le Chemin de crête*, death can isolate people or bring them together; indeed, the sick or the dead are Marcel's chief characters. They may inspire men's actions, as in *L'Iconoclaste* or *La Chapelle ardente*, or may even intervene clearly in men's lives, as in *Le Monde cassé* or *La Soif*, where they become a means of reconciliation between the characters. The mistaken fidelity of a mother to her son, who was killed in action, causes her to prevent her son's fiancée from remaking her life with another younger man whom she has grown to love. She brings about, instead, a marriage between the girl and an ailing man, for whom she can feel only pity. Her attitude is similar to that of the two men in *L'Iconoclaste*, and like them she does not visualize the situation frankly. She never consciously tries to prevent the girl from making the marriage she desires; she persuades herself that the girl does not love anyone but her dead son, and does not wish to remake her life. This attitude could be diagnosed as a repression, and there are a number of points here, and in other plays, where Marcel's ideas seem to converge on those of Freud or recall Pirandello and the "school of silence", but actually the woman's attitude is one of "bad faith", or *la mauvaise foi*, as one was later to see it at work in Sartre's plays. Indeed, in one of Marcel's later plays, *L'Emissaire*, a character, Antoine, says: "Sartre is right, we are besieged by bad faith ... It is at the back of our lapses in memory, each time it is in our interest not to remember." "So now you are a follower of Sartre?" says Bertrand. "Truth is truth," Antoine replies, "whoever is the man who discovered it." "And so you accuse yourself of bad faith!" says Sylvie. "I don't know; I shall never know", Antoine replies. In the case of the bereaved mother in *La*

Chapelle ardente her fidelity is nothing but an egoistic form of the love of self, and Marcel declares her to be guilty of a sort of spiritual infanticide, that of her son's fiancée, but insists that her gravest sin is her refusal to face the fact. Most of Marcel's characters are unaware of their motives, and even of what sort of person they themselves are. They are strangers to themselves; Marcel's term for this is *l'ame en exil.*[7] But if uncertainty about oneself cannot constitute the basis of drama, tragedy arises when one's misunderstanding about oneself and about one's behaviour to others spreads distress among them. This is clearly the case with the bereaved mother, and, in *L'Iconoclaste*, also with Abel. The technique of this play is quite different from that used in the earlier ones, and is already the technique which was to be developed by the playwrights of the "school of silence": no direct pressure of any kind is exerted, nothing is plainly stated, the spell woven by the mother over the girl is wordless.

Fidelity which is not real fidelity forms the theme of *Le Mort de demain*, written between 1919 and 1920, in which a woman convinced that her husband will be killed reveres him already as a saint, and fails to make the necessary adjustment to his real presence when he returns home on leave. In this play, as in *La Chapelle ardente*, death is not the liberating force that it is in *L'Iconoclaste*; the characters do not manage to break through the limiting wall of solitude, or, to use the terms of Marcel's *Journal métaphysique*, the *lui* never becomes a *toi*.

The last of these *Trois Pièces*, which all have the First World War as a backcloth, is *Le Regard neuf*. A young soldier returns home, where, contracting out of the family by which he *is*, he looks at the family, as it were, with the eyes of a third person, so bringing to light the real, sordid reason for his parents' marriage, which neither had clearly realized, and which had helped to make each what each had, in fact, become.

The last of Marcel's compositions for the stage before his conversion—in 1929 he was converted from agnosticism to Catholicism through the influence of François Mauriac—was *Un Homme de Dieu*.

The unexpected return, after twenty years, of a married woman's former lover forces her to face up to the question of what had been her real reason for confessing her unfaithfulness to her husband. At the same time it forces her husband, a clergyman, to attempt to elucidate his real reasons behind his forgiveness of his wife's conduct. The confession and forgiveness, both equally ambiguous acts as performed by the hero and heroine of this play, appear, in fact, to be motivated by fear, to be the result of an inability to live "authentically". When the wife's illegitimate daughter learns the truth about her birth, and realizes the emptiness of the functional life of her so-called father, she goes off to join a married man whom she loves, and whose children she has lovingly tended because his wife is in an asylum. She thus rejects, by a conscious choice, the moral alibi to which her mother and the clergyman had resorted. There is, however, no more question of these two characters having had deliberate recourse to "bad faith" than in the case of the bereaved mother in La Chapelle ardente. No more than she were they conscious of the ambiguity of their motives. In his own analysis of Un Homme de Dieu[8] Marcel points to the similarity between his play and Les Mains sales, by Jean-Paul Sartre, or, at least, the final act of Sartre's play; each hero is seen attempting to fathom, after the event, the real reason for his action and failing to do so. Sartre's hero chooses to attribute a political sense to his action, but Marcel's hero inquires in bewilderment: "Who am I?" It is in the existentialist sense that this question must be understood—Marcel himself was careful to point out that Un Homme de Dieu and La Chapelle ardente, which were both written about the same time, were the two first existentialist plays to appear in France—that is to say, plays in which the main characters are called upon to decide what they are. Is his clergyman merely the sum of his functions? Was his forgiveness of his wife purely professional, or was it really "authentic"? He cannot tell. The final cry, "Oh to be known for what one is . . . or to be blotted out", was interpreted on the stage, when the play was first performed, as a cry of despair, indicating the complete collapse of "the man of God". Later the actor Jean Deschamps gave a different interpretation of these words, making of them a cry of hope of a new existence in the beyond.[9] Such an interpretation is in keeping with Marcel's philosophical views. It is a question of being known, not as an "object" possessed of a number of definable qualities, but as the complete unanalysable whole. Such a desire presupposes a demand for the existence of a divine mind, or All Knower. Marcel wrote this play at the time when he was about to be converted, and much of his own experience went into it. From a number of points of view this play may be compared with *Le Chemin de crête*, which Marcel wrote in 1936, but the ambiguity of the character of Ariane, round whom the whole action of the later play turns, is much more radical, and is not removed, even at the end of the play. It is the firm establishment of the ambiguity of her character and motives which, in fact, forms the *dénouement*. Ariane is generally considered by the other characters in the play to be saintly; she, apparently, always attempts to do good, yet does only harm, and seems secretly pleased to do this harm. Being a victim of disease, she has watched others live instead of living herself, and herself admits that this disease has considerably modified her attitude to life, and she persists in treating herself as an invalid, even when there is every reason to believe that she is cured. Because of her illness, Ariane favours her husband's liaison with Violette, and Violette is convinced of Ariane's sincerity in favouring the liaison, yet, as she says, Ariane could not have more successfully destroyed it had her sincerity been a mere blind. A notable difference between Ariane and the "man of God" is that the latter seems strangely detached from his act of forgiveness, whereas Ariane is passionately present in everything she does. The play offers interesting matter for study, but is too dense for the stage, where the very complexity of Ariane's character militates against any possible impression of reality. It was performed at the Vieux-Colombier in November 1953,[10] but did not have the success of the less concentrated *Un Homme de Dieu*. This latter work together with *La Chapelle ardente* are, as stage plays, the best Marcel has written.

Though published only in 1945, *L'Horizon*, first entitled *Le Survol*, follows on after *Un Homme de Dieu*, and was inspired by the experience of a famous medium, Pascal Forthuny. Marcel's medium mistakenly predicts Germain Lestrade's accidental death, whereas it is Germain's friend Bertrand, who was also present at the séance, who is killed. In anticipation of his death, Germain, like the soldier's wife in *Le Mort de demain*, identifies himself with what he possesses, and endeavours to close his hand, as it were, over his possessions, even to orientating his friend towards his own future widow. Bertrand's death is instrumental in bringing to light the authenticity, or lack of authenticity, of the various characters. Germain's wife says: "I was very nearly duped by your solicitude, which was anything but disinterested, and behind which there was only mistrust and egoism. I almost believed that you were generous—as if anything but miserliness could be expected of you. Yes, you are a miser and not about money alone." Here and in some of the preceding plays is indicated a problem which Marcel was to treat in a philosophical work, *Etre et avoir*, in 1933. Two more questions are raised in this play through Valentine, who is in love with Bertrand, and who fears that Bertrand's death may perhaps have been a suicide, which is the most absolute of refusals of any real communion with others. Moved by Valentine's sincere love for Bertrand, Germain assures her that her love had been reciprocated, though he knows this is not so, and it is through this act of charity that Germain and his wife are at last brought together.

After the publication of *Un Homme de Dieu*, Marcel published nothing more until 1933, when the volume containing the play *Le Monde cassé* and the theoretical work *Position et Approches concrètes du mystère ontologique*, appeared. His conversion to Catholicism had taken place in the meantime, and the repercussions are apparent in this volume. For the second time in his plays he depicts the intervention of divine grace, but from the inside, as it were. The first time in *La Grâce*, written when he was an agnostic, his view was purely objective. In *Position et Approches*, Marcel expounds in metaphysical terms, as he himself tells us,[11] what Christiane, the heroine of his play, feels intuitively, and explains by comparing the world to a watch which will not go because the spring is broken. When the man she loves unbeknown to him becomes a monk, Christiane enters on a loveless marriage, in a sort of "spiritual suicide", and seeks to fill the emptiness of her existence by leading a life of distractions not wholly blameless. When the monk dies she learns through his sister that he had had a supernatural intuition of the love she had borne him and of her consequent despair, and had prayed for her. The moment of illumination, or grace, which results from this knowledge, saves Christiane's marriage by putting an end to the solitude of husband and wife. "No one is alone," Christiane tells her husband, "there is a communion of sinners as there is a communion of saints", and Marcel offers this communion of sinners as a contrast to *le monde cassé*, a world of which the heart has stopped beating, a world in which an "authentic" life, based on "authentic" motives and feelings, cannot be lived. By entitling his one-act verse play, which the Comédie-Française staged in 1938, *Le Fanal*, or "beacon-light", Marcel insists on the active rôle that a death can play in the lives of those who remain behind, how, through true fidelity, an absence can become a salutary presence. This theme is already to be found in L'Insondable, an unfinished play dating from 1919.

From Le Monde cassé, in which he depicts the society of the 1930's onward, there is a distinct broadening of horizon in Marcel's plays. The action of Le Dard (Théâtre des Arts, March 2nd, 1937) is set against the background of Hitler's persecution of the Jews and the horror of the concentration camps, but there is no resemblance between this play or any of the following ones, L'Emissaire, Le Signe de la Croix, La Fin du temps, or Rome n'est plus dans Rome, and the social plays of the late nineteenth and early twentieth centuries. Marcel is concerned, not with the social situation as such, but with the fundamental problem confronting the individual who is involved in the situation. Le Dard, or barbed arrow, is the uneasy conscience of a man of the extreme Left and of lowly birth, Eustache, who is married to Béatrice, the daughter of a rich, upper middle-class family. Eustache's friend, Werner, a German singer, has left his country, in a spirit of solidarity, with his Jewish accompanist, who has since died as a result of the treatment he has received. Because of his very success in France, Werner, in turn, becomes a prey to an uneasy conscience. His compatriots in the Nazi extermination camps are ever present in his mind, and he finally decides to return to Germany, even though it means certain arrest. His concern is not for the cause, but for suffering human beings. Before leaving, he commends to Béatrice's care his friend Eustache, whom he calls a "poor in spirit"; the thought of Werner and of his fate will help her in her task. As in Le Fanal, the play ends with a promise of the salutary presence of the dead.

While abandoning none of his usual themes Marcel, in L'Emissaire, which he began to write in 1945, portrays the conflict of collaborators and men of the Resistance movement, and, so as to underline the fundamental ambiguity of human actions, makes one of the characters believe that by collaborating he is helping to prepare a fine future for France. When one reads in Marcel's Postface[12] to the play that the play is addressed to "non-fanatics", it is difficult not to wonder how far the ambiguity goes, particularly when the dramatist adds that his Resistance hero must realize that his actions have borne poisonous fruits. Marcel's next global statement about the "degeneration" of the Resistance movement into a "sinister comedy", as he calls it, makes painful reading.

In *Le Signe de la Croix* Marcel comes near to anti-semitism. The play was written over the period 1938 to 1948, and represents the attitudes of different members of the Jewish community in and to France in 1938, 1942, and 1948. Most of Marcel's characters exhibit feelings not unlike those of a traveller towards the hotel in which he may happen to spend the night. His hero, Simon, who refuses to leave the country despite the threatening danger from the Nazis, passes judgment on his Jewish brethren, accusing them of deliberately forming a "tribe" within the French nation, and of themselves sowing the seeds of racial discrimination by their "provocative" sectarianism. It is significant that Marcel, by leading his hero towards some sort of Christian faith, takes care to detach him from the "tribe", the attitude and activities of which he, the hero, condemns. In the *Postface* Marcel maintains that there *is* a Jewish problem, and that a "frenzied and laicized Judaism is in danger of degenerating into a new nazism as indefensible as the German brand". In both these plays it is the obvious topicality of the theme that arrests the attention, yet Marcel, on his own affirmation, sees the inextricable situations in which the characters find themselves rather as a particular expression of the human predicament in which Faith, not reason, nor feeling, provides the sole guiding-light. He claims for the plays a metaphysical rather than a social or political import.

Rome n'est plus dans Rome (Hébertot, April 18th, 1951), a better-known play, turns on the question of whether, in the face of a third World War, flight to the new world, in order to preserve the traditions and culture of France, would be justifiable. There is an obvious reference here to a number of precipitous departures from France at the time the play was written, and also a reference back to the French exodus to London during the Second World War, which Marcel seems to condemn. The play ends with a radio appeal to the French by the hero, from his hiding-place in Brazil, to remain in France and fight on the spot; it is sheer presumption, he says, to think that one can take one's mother country away with one. Marcel puts the question in view of an imagined threat from the East, and makes his hero change his point of view, rather gratuitously, as the result of a religious experience. True, Marcel thinks always in terms of a final "illumination", but the sudden substitution of religious for political thinking is unjustified; difficulties are brushed aside, not solved.

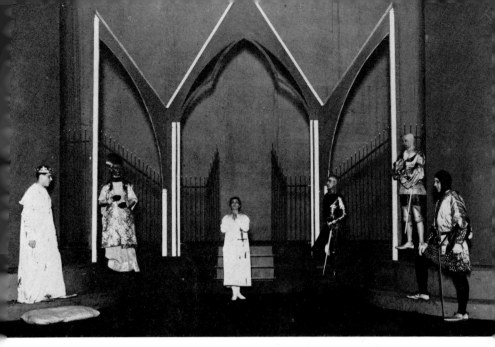

Saint Joan

with Ludmilla Pitoëff

Coll. Rondel, Biblio. de l'Arsenal

Numancia. Producer: Barrault

Photos: Lipnitzki

Le Livre de Christophe Colomb. Producer: Barrault

In *Mon Temps n'est pas le vôtre*, published in 1955, Marcel turns his back on the thorny social and political problems which form the framework and, one would be justified in thinking, the full substance of these plays, and takes up again, after some twenty years, from *Le Monde cassé*. The play presents a middle-aged father of a family and a Catholic priest, both faithful to the traditional values of yesterday, completely nonplussed by the world of today, with its "collapsing values", as Marcel says in the *Postface*. It also contains an element of his own reaction to the new developments in musical composition, with which, as a musician of the old school, he did not feel himself in harmony. There is a strong satirical element in the play, similar to that which distinguishes his *Théâtre comique* published in 1947, and there is also the evident determination of the Christian Existentialist to lead his characters to what he terms *l'autre royaume*. This determination is equally clear in his play *Croissez et multipliez* (1955), which deals with the vexed question of the attitude of the Roman Catholic Church to birth control, not, however, on the level of theological discussion, but in terms of human beings who have to face up to the problem in their relationship with each other.

By writing drama which is not drama of "doing" but drama of "being", and envisaging characters who, in their relations with each other, are not objects for each other but exist for and by those around them, Marcel attempted something new, at least in the early years, but the plays themselves, which make interesting enough reading, particularly when taken in conjunction with Marcel's philosophical works, only come over the footlights with difficulty, and this is specially true of the *dénouements*, so many of which consist of an "illumination". The subject-matter of the plays, often giving a large place to ill-health, is depressing, and the dramatist seems to go out of his way to be sympathetic to such unpleasant attitudes as collaboration with Nazism and anti-semitism.

NOTES

1. Later at the Œuvre on November 19th; Théâtre Charles de Rochefort, April 1st, 1950.
2. Contains Marcel's first two plays, *La Grâce* and *Le Palais de sable*.
3. *La Revue hebdomadaire*, January 27th, 1923, pp. 492–493.

4. "Théâtre et Philosophie", in *Recherches et Débats*, Cahier No. 2, October 1952.
5. Ibid.
6. Written 1919–20, performed on September 25th, 1925, by the Théâtre des Jeunes Auteurs; revived 1950 (Théâtre Charles de Rochefort).
7. *The Drama of the Soul in Exile*, translation by R. Heywood of Marcel's lecture at the Institut Français in 1950.
8. *Les Nouvelles littéraires*, January 20th, 1949.
9. *Opéra*, March 23rd, 1951, "*Un Homme de Dieu* n'est pas une pièce désespéré". R. Guilly.
10. Performed in English in 1958 as *Ariadne*.
11. "Théâtre et Philosophie", in *Recherches et Débats*. No. 2, October 1952, p. 35.
12. In *Vers un autre royaume* (1949), containing *L'Emissaire* and *Le Signe de la Croix*.

X

Boulevard Theatre: The Sex Play and the Play of Manners and Character

*The Boulevard—1. The Sex Play: Henry Bataille—
Henry Bernstein — Paul Géraldy — André Josset —
2. Manners and Character: Edouard Bourdet—Marcel
Pagnol—Maurice Donnay—Edmond Sée—Léopold
Marchand—Henri Clerc—Charles de Peyret-Chap-
puis—Martial Piéchaud—Edmond Fleg—Jacques
Copeau—Pierre Hamp.*

IF ACCOUNT is taken of output alone the Boulevard far out-
weighs the experimental theatres in importance, but the
situation is reversed if the measure applied is quality or originality. The aim of the Boulevard is, above all, to supply entertainment for the greatest number possible, and to be ahead of its times
would be to defeat its purpose. It relies to a large extent on craftsmanship. Alexandre Dumas *fils*, who was one of the most popular
playwrights of his time, even declared that a man with no standing
as a thinker, moralist, philosopher, or writer could very well be a
first-rate dramatic author.

Like the experimental theatres, the Boulevard has its classics,
and Dumas's *La Dame aux camélias* (1852) is one. Marcel Pagnol's
Marius, played on the Boulevard in the inter-war years, may well be
another.

The declaration of war in 1914 brought theatrical activity,
which was already slowing down, in the commercial theatres at
least, to a standstill. Unlike the war years of 1940–44, which saw
the emergence of dramatists such as Jean-Paul Sartre and Albert
Camus, those of 1914–18 were marked by complete stagnation, and
when the war was over, and programmes for soldiers on leave were
no longer needed, all that was attempted in the commercial

theatres was to start again where they had left off in 1914. The same stars, the same five or six playwrights who had guaranteed their pre-war successes, even the same plays, were billed again, but the new public no longer had any use for the "thesis plays" or the ponderous social satire which had pleased their elders. Some of the other dramatic forms continued to exist but were modified to suit the new times; they were also influenced by developments in the experimental theatres. Some playwrights, such as Marcel Achard, who began their careers in the experimental theatres, went over entirely to the Boulevard, to become purveyors of purely commercial productions. Others, like Armand Salacrou, carried over with them something of the experimentalists' spirit when they wrote for the Boulevard. Occasionally, Studio theatre plays have been adopted by the Boulevard and enjoyed runs comparable with those of the successful Boulevard shows. Jean Cocteau's Les Parents terribles is a striking example.

1. The Sex Play

One of the most consistently successful of Boulevard dramatists in the first third of this century was Henry Bernstein. He began his career in 1900, at the same time as his rival Henry Bataille, but whereas Bataille's success was confined to France, Bernstein's plays were performed in commercial theatres in a large number of countries. Both dramatists were specialists in what the French call the "physiological play", a term which one might equate to comedy of humours. Both followed on from Georges de Porto-Riche, whose plays, published in 1898 under the collective title Théâtre d'amour, stressed the purely physiological element previously neglected by dramatists in their analyses of the passion of love. Temperament, not the psyche, was Porto-Riche's starting-point, as it was to be that of Bataille and Bernstein, at least in their early plays, though certain developments can be observed in the subsequent work of both writers. Just as François de Curel, the champion of the play of ideas, came to appreciate the part played by instinct and the senses in men's behaviour, so Bataille, the champion of the instincts, came gradually to consider the part which ideas could play. Bernstein, too, developed a respect for ideas, together with an interest in social problems, though many of his plays are interesting merely because of their excellent craftsmanship. Well acted by artists such as Lucien Guitry and later by Gaby Morlay and Jean Gabin, Bernstein's plays always made for a pleasant evening's entertainment in the theatre. Other exponents of the "physiological play" who drew large Boulevard audiences up to about 1930, were Romain Coolus and Pierre Wolff, who was generally known as the most "Parisian" of French dramatists. In the hands of Paul Géraldy and André Josset the "physiological play" developed exclusively into the sex play in the 1920's.

The first post-war play by HENRY BATAILLE, L'Animateur (1921), marks the final stage of Bataille's evolution as a dramatist. He had begun with plays showing passion running riot, of which the two best are Maman Colibri (1904) and La Femme nue (1910). Then followed plays in which passions came into conflict with ideas or worked along with ideas. Finally, in a social trilogy consisting of L'Amazone (1916), a war play, L'Animateur, and La Chair humaine (1922), Bataille presents ideas which give rise to powerful emotions and even dominate the ordinary impulses of human nature, such as the ties of kinship between father and daughter in L'Animateur. La Chair humaine presents an illegitimate son as a "hero" when at the Front but a shameful liability in peacetime. At the same time as he worked on his social trilogy Bataille wrote L'Homme à la rose (1920), in which a Don Juan, aged forty, is present incognito at his own supposed funeral, where he learns that he counts for nothing when deprived of the support of his reputation, and, indeed, in the last act he is to be seen having to pay in hard cash for the favours of a scullery maid. Bataille continued his analysis of sexual passion in La Tendresse (1921), which the critics extravagantly termed his Bérénice, and in La Possession (1921). Right up to the end he exploited the vein he had opened up with Maman Colibri and La Femme nue, but the successful revivals of these two plays after the war told against the success of his current productions.

During his lifetime Bataille was the object of great adulation and of bitterly hostile criticism. The prefaces to his plays and his Écrits sur le théâtre testify to this. The controversy continued after his death, and in 1937, when L'Enfant de l'amour (1911) was playing to full houses at the Théâtre Antoine, the critics attacked him as a romantic sentimentalist, because of a bed shown on the stage with a bunch of flowers and a birdcage on it, and as a belated devotee of naturalism in the theatre, because of the simplicity of his technique. Lucien Dubech's prophecy, made in 1920, that the success of Bataille's plays would be seen by later generations as one of the great scandals of the time, seemed to be coming true. The attack on Bataille had, however, a wider significance; it was an attack on the whole pre-war conception of theatre, which the Boulevard was seeking to preserve, and which, in respect of characterization, subjects, and style, belonged to an age as remote in feeling as that of *La Dame aux camélias*. The abundant flow of language in which his characters indulged was notably out of tune with the elliptical style favoured by the new post-war playwrights. All the same, as a theorist he influenced writers like Denys Amiel, Paul Géraldy, and Jean Sarment, who openly acknowledged their debt to him. In his *Écrits sur le théâtre* Bataille writes of "exact lyricism"—that is to say, lyricism which must be in keeping with the character because the function of art is to stylize nature without deforming it. It is in the *Écrits* that he writes, too, of an indirect or unexpressed language underlying direct or expressed language, and maintains that it is the language normally used in everyday life, expressing, as it does, one's unspoken thoughts or one's subconscious motivation. This he considers to be the language proper to the theatre. The relation between "inner truths" (secrets which man does not voice intentionally) and the outer truths, the juxtaposition of the inner hidden world and the outer apparent world, is drama in a nutshell. Bataille did not practise what he preached, but his preaching led to the practice of the School of Silence.

Right up to the eve of the First World War HENRY BERNSTEIN indulged in violent drama of action, which he conducted with amazing sureness of hand, pursuing the plot to its logical conclusion and grouping characters as Scribe and Sardou had done before him. Eroticism was the hallmark of his subjects. In 1913, with *Le Secret*, which went into the Comédie-Française's repertoire in 1932, Bernstein ventured on a new dramatic path, aiming at character analysis rather than at plot, and making elements of character responsible for the dramatic crisis. He attempted to explore subconscious motivation and made of his heroine, Gabrielle, something of a Dr Jekyll and Mr Hyde. After the war Bernstein seemed to set out to challenge Pirandello for the public's favour by developing the vein first exploited in *Le Secret*.

Judith (1922), Bernstein's first production after the war, was not, despite the biblical theme, a departure from the "physiological play" so consistently cultivated by him. Indeed, the biblical story served merely as a framework for the personal tragedy of Judith, frigidity incarnate, at grips with primitive desire, Holopherne. Unlike Giraudoux's Judith, who kills for love, Bernstein's kills in despair at finding she is not made for love. Then hearing the slave lament, "She has slain her lover", she is beset with misgivings about her real motive for killing the man who had been her lover for a night.

The theme of La Galerie des glaces (1924) is equally "physiological". The painter hero presents a clinical case of sexual disquiet similar to that of Somerset Maugham's hero in his short story Rain. Though the hero's lack of self-confidence was taken at the time by the critics as symbolic of the anxiety and disquiet typical of the post-war generation, the essentially Freudian inspiration of the play was made plain by Bernstein in the text itself; Freud is referred to by a doctor friend of the heroine who explains that people like her husband, who lack self-confidence, often derive that confidence from the sexual act, thereby, as it were, recreating themselves. Such is the main subject, but Bernstein obscures the issue by hinting at a Pirandellian dissolution of the personality: he details the painter's various reactions to the fleeting images of himself which he sees reflected in the people round him, as in so many mirrors. Like several of his subsequent plays, La Galerie des glaces has no real conclusion; its hero is likely to be besieged by other doubts, just as the hero of Le Venin (1927), dominated by his senses, is likely to relapse into intermittent infidelity to his wife. In these plays there is a change of technique: Bernstein no longer condenses his action into one violent crisis.

In Félix (1926) he experiments with the technique of the School of Silence in one scene: his heroine obtains what she wants of her husband without making a single request or uttering a single reproach; without a word her husband grants what he knows to be her wish. After the play's revival in 1930 Bernstein stated his misgivings about this technique. Such a fluid dramatic form seemed to him to be admirably suited to express the state of people's minds in the early post-war years, but he had begun to feel the need for a partial return to the dramatic form he had favoured earlier. Drama, he argued, demanded precision and strong relief. Le Messager (1933), another variant of the eternal triangle play, combines a violent dramatic action with Bernstein's now extended character analysis. The technique of the unexpressed is used again in Le

Bonheur (1933), in which a wealthy actress and her would-be assassin, an anarchist for whom the actress embodies unjust society, fall in love with each other at his trial without exchanging a single word.

The subjects of *Espoir* (1934), performed in England under the title *Promise*, and *Le Cœur* (1935), had a topical interest because in both plays the pre-war and the post-war generations confront each other. Bernstein, at the age of fifty-eight, placed his hope for the future in the younger generation. The topical card was, however, very obviously played in January 1940, when Bernstein put on at the Ambassadeurs an anti-nazi play, *Elvire*, with the Romanian comedy actress Elvire Popesco playing a tragic part for the first time in her life—that of a refugee.

By his techniques as well as his subjects Bernstein attempted to keep up with the times. In *Mélo* (1929) he constructed his play in twelve tableaux, one of which is silent. He intended that the "cinematographic element" should be strong. The play was later filmed, with Gaby Morlay. Another version with Elisabeth Bergner was entitled *Der Traümende Mund* (*Dreaming Lips*). Whatever the form or subject, there is one fundamental theme which can be traced throughout Bernstein's dramatic productions: it is stated in the closing lines of one of his last plays, *Victor* (1950), where, to voluptuous music from a gramophone, a husband lovingly embraces his wife, who had been tempted to leave him for another man. The husband: "Tu es en forme ... Tu es d'une souplesse." The wife: "Oh! fous-moi la paix." The husband, whispering: "Ma beauté, ma chose." Curtain!

PAUL GERALDY, whose real name is Paul Lefèvre, is the son of a forgotten poet. He made his debut in the theatre on March 17th, 1917, at the Comédie-Française, with *Noces d'argent*, which was championed by Edmond Rostand. Géraldy also came under the influence of Henry Bataille, but the model which he followed the most closely, particularly in his trilogy (his major contribution to the theatre), *Aimer* (December 5th, 1921), *Robert et Marianne* (November 23rd, 1925), and *Christine* (November 11th, 1932), which were played at the Comédie-Française, was that of Porto-Riche's *Théâtre d'amour*. In his other plays as well, even in the four written in collaboration with Robert Spitzer, Géraldy limited himself almost exclusively to the sex play.

When a play is a real sex play the sex relationship is not the beginning or end of the plot, nor is it introduced to add spice to it.

It is studied for itself. Whether the characters marry or divorce is of little consequence. The marriage or liaison is already in existence when the play begins, and what matters is the sex relationship itself, the course which it has followed, and the form under which it will continue to survive if it does survive. Géraldy's master, Porto-Riche, had concentrated on the physical side of the relationship. Géraldy gives greater emphasis to the sentimental aspect. When he wrote *Noces d'argent*, a comedy of family life depicting the painful moment when the young brood forsakes the nest, he was not yet a specialist of the sex play proper, though it was clear that he possessed keen psychological insight. The German push in February 1917 adversely affected the run of the play in Paris, but outside France *Noces d'argent* enjoyed phenomenal success. *Aimer* is a true sex play: its subject is the relationship between a man and a woman after many years of marriage. The dramatic situation is created by the arrival of the tempter, who appears to open up a vista of all kinds of happiness so far closed to the wife. But the husband believes that true happiness is to be found only in complete understanding and absolute confidence, and they must be lasting. The whole action consists of the wife's struggle against the attraction of the unknown. The play ends with her final realization of where true happiness lies.

In *Robert et Marianne* there is no external disruptive influence; the marital relationship founders on its own rocks. It is not a question of whether the husband and wife will separate. What is in question is the basis on which they can continue to live together. As in Porto-Riche's *Amoureuse*, Géraldy's play shows the married couple endangered by the different part played by love in the life of a man and of a woman. Love fills the whole existence of a woman to the point of stifling the full development of her personality, whereas it is never a man's whole life, though it may take first place in his life. Porto-Riche's heroine is very highly sexed, and her physical enslavement of her husband ruins his whole career. Géraldy's heroine's love for her husband makes her possessive, and it is only when she is ready to accept the fact that a man's life is one of outside activity, and when she is ready to love without being loved, that the miracle of married love occurs. Before this, Robert remarks, in a moment of crisis, that what a man asks of a woman is friendship in love, and that is what she cannot give. This is what Marianne ultimately learns to give.

In *Christine* Géraldy comes back to the question of the different natures of the man and the woman, and also develops a theme already present in *Aimer*—namely, that married life is an art, and a difficult one at that. He describes the dawn of love and the mental and physical exaltation which accompanies it, and he shows separation as making each of the lovers aspire to an indestructible union. They believe that they can "re-invent" marriage. But love dies when it ceases to hope and fear; "living together seems to separate us", Christine says sadly. "Women find it so hard to do without happiness", Géraldy had already written, in his *Maximes sur l'amour* (1929), which, along with the trilogy, contains the essence of his meditations on the subject. Jacques, the husband, cannot let love fill his whole life and only realizes that life and love are the same when Christine leaves him. For Géraldy life is love.

In these plays there is no action in the normal sense of the term, there is no story. Any external event is merely the spark that sets off the chain of internal reactions, and what conflict there is, is not between the different characters but between a character and himself; the issue is of little importance because Géraldy believes that the meaning of life is in life itself, and life continues; it is not ended by the drop of the curtain.

Duo, which Géraldy adapted in 1938 from a story by Colette about a married couple, adds a fourth panel to what had been a triptych, and shows the intolerance of the senses as worse than the intolerance of the heart. Another play, *Do, mi, sol* (1934), despite its Géraldian theme, is not far removed from the "very Parisian" Boulevard comedies *Si je voulais* (1924), *Son Mari* (1927), and *L'Homme de joie* (1929), containing a skittish treatment of the Don Juan theme, which Géraldy wrote in collaboration with Robert Spitzer. Two of these plays have been successfully revived since the last war.

The sex play is very differently represented in ANDRE JOSSET's extremely successful first work for the stage, *Elizabeth la femme sans homme*, with which René Rocher reopened the Vieux-Colombier on October 19th, 1935, under the name Théâtre René Rocher. The play was finely acted, with Germaine Dermoz in the title-rôle, and shares with Giraudoux's *La Guerre de Troie n'aura pas lieu* the honours of the season. It stands to Giraudoux's play in the same relation as Dumas's *Henri III et sa cour* stood to Hugo's *Hernani*, the one being good theatre, the other good literature. The two main characters are Elizabeth and Essex, but the play is not an historical drama, nor does it bear any resemblance to the historical tragedies of La Calprenède and Thomas Corneille on the subject of Elizabeth and Essex. Mr Ivor Brown referred to it as a "psycho-physical" play.[1] The term is justified by the Freudian twist given to the play in the last act, when, after the execution of Essex, Elizabeth forces Mary Howard to describe her physical relations with Essex, so as to be able to compare them with her own sexual experience. The strange "liaison" between Elizabeth and Essex, Elizabeth's undoubted love for Essex but her refusal to become his mistress, provides the theme of the play. The political reasons which Josset gives for Elizabeth's refusal are, however, cancelled out by the final explanation, which he clearly prefers— namely, the fact that she was brutally raped at the age of fifteen and had never got over the repulsion she felt for men as a result. The boldness of the theme, which served the play well in 1935, did not help it when it was performed at the Comédie-Française in 1955. There was time then to note that too many aspects of it, and notably the ambitious Essex's supposed passion for a queen thirty-four years older than himself, remained obscure.

René Rocher also staged Josset's Les Borgia, famille étrange (1937), but this play did not have the same impact on the public. There was no "physiology" in this play, as there had been in Elizabeth, Josset declared, only "psychology". The same holds true of Le Bal des Adieux (1955), situated in the reign of Louis XVI; again the theme is a courtier's love for the queen.

2. Manners and Character

Psychological studies and social comedies have always been popular with the ordinary theatregoer, and the number of writers of such plays is legion. The two most important are Edouard Bourdet and Marcel Pagnol. A few plays of this kind by Jacques Copeau, Georges Duhamel, and Pierre Hamp were put on in the Studio theatres and were more literary in their treatment, though less popular in their appeal.

Le Sexe faible, which has been in the repertory of the Comédie-Française since 1957, was one of the Boulevard's biggest successes in the inter-war years. It was first performed in 1929 at the Michodière, where it ran for three years before being replaced by

La Fleur des pois, another of EDOUARD BOURDET's successful satirical comedies of manners. But Bourdet was not, in fact, the mere Boulevard entertainer that he was taken to be by his contemporaries: *Le Sexe faible* bore the same relation to the 1930's as *Le Mariage de Figaro* bore to the late eighteenth century. The society that Bourdet painted is no longer in the public eye, but his plays still hold the stage, and the majority of them have been revived, some of them several times. They owe their survival to Bourdet's mastery of dramatic technique and to his psychological insight. His critics attacked him for failing to make his moral outlook clear in his plays. To this Bourdet replied that the art of the satirical realist is a highly moral art, because it shows the consequences of people's actions. His declared aim was to make his characters act "in character", not to subordinate them to an idea, as did Dumas *fils*, with whom he was often compared. The characters should not exist to illustrate a theme; the theme should be the pretext for the creation of characters, who then become autonomous.

In *Vient de paraître*, which preceded *Le Sexe faible* by two years and was the first of Bourdet's plays to be put on at the Michodière, Bourdet presents various types of people in the literary world, all slightly caricatured, but his satire touches only lightly the commercialism that threatens literary production. He is a more courageous satirist in *Le Sexe faible* and, though he does not pass judgment on any of his characters, he provides a cynical commentator on human foibles in the person of a *maître d'hôtel* who is in everybody's confidence. This character, taken by Victor Boucher, whose brilliant acting played a considerable part in the success of the comedy, is a real *deus ex machina*, and cleverly serves the ends of the moneyed cosmopolitan clientele of a palatial Paris hotel. In this society of "kept" men, created by the recent emancipation of women, the normal marital and extra-marital sex relationships of pre-1914 comedy are completely reversed.

In *La Prisonnière* (1926), his first play of importance, Bourdet had not yet developed his satirical vein; he offered a careful analysis of the states of mind of an unwilling lesbian. The treatment is frank without being brutal. When it was first produced in Paris in 1926 the play was considered as going to the very limit. In London the following year the Lord Chamberlain, who was unofficially present at an Arts Theatre production of the play in English, under the title *The Captive*, declared that there could be no question of licensing it for public performance in this country. By comparison, the treatment of male homosexuality in *La Fleur des pois* is flippant, but the fact that the subject was handled as light comedy meant that the play was not considered scandalous. *La Prisonnière* was revived in 1950, with Pierre Blanchar once again playing the part of the fiancé who becomes a distressed husband. The play, which has become a sort of classic, is unmarred by any wrinkles.

All Bourdet's plays turn on sexual problems of one kind or another, from the very first of them, *Le Rubicon* (1910), to *Père* (1944). In this last play the main theme is the posthumous cult of a great man by one who believes herself to be his daughter; but a secondary theme is the fear of possible incest providing a secret stimulant to passion. Even the history of Marguerite de France becomes, in Bourdet's play *Margot* (1935), the story of the repressed passion of a sister for her brother, Henri III. In his satire of the provincial upper classes, *Les Temps difficiles* (1934; Comédie-Française, 1948), which shows a family of manufacturers attempting to weather an industrial crisis by marrying off one of their number, a girl of eighteen, to a rich man, Bourdet obscures the issue by gratuitously making the man an enterprising degenerate. He abandons his usual themes only in *Fric-Frac* (1936), a gay "documentary" on Paris spivs. As the slang title indicates, his spivs are not averse to a little housebreaking. A good film was made from this comedy in 1939, with Fernandel, Michel Simon, and Arletty.

Bourdet was not only a successful writer of comedy, with a command of traditional dramatic technique equal to that of Georges Feydeau, he was also a successful administrator of the Comédie-Française from 1936 until 1940, when, after a serious accident, he relinquished his post, leaving Jacques Copeau to take his place. Immediately on his appointment Bourdet gave a new lease of life to the Comédie-Française by a number of reforms, which included opening its doors to independent producers like Copeau, Baty, Jouvet, and Dullin.

Topaze, by MARCEL PAGNOL, was staged at the Variétes on October 9th, 1928, with a success comparable to that enjoyed in 1923 by *Les Vignes du seigneur*, by de Flers and Croisset. Pagnol's farcical comedy has its serious side, and is to some extent a social play, illustrating the clash of conventional morality with conditions resulting from the First World War. Its hero was born of Pagnol's own experience—Pagnol himself began his career as a teacher of

English, first in Provence, which furnished him with the material for his widely performed trilogy, *Marius, Fanny, César*, and later in Paris. In *Topaze* a badly paid teacher is contrasted with an unscrupulous business tycoon, whose respectable representative he becomes after he has had to leave the school for refusing to write a good report on an ungifted son of wealthy parents. In due time he becomes more competent than the tycoon, and supplants him both in business and in his mistress's favour. The corruption does not stop there; in the final and most cynical scene of all one of Topaze's former worthy colleagues prepares to follow Topaze's example.

An earlier play by Pagnol and Paul Nivoix, *Les Marchands de gloire*, a cynically gay picture of the exploitation, after the First World War, of the glory of the men who died for their country, is in the same vein as *Topaze* but is not of the same calibre. Both plays differ absolutely in tone from the simple story told in the trilogy of Marius the bartender, torn between his yearning for the sea and his love for Fanny, a lobster girl in the port of Marseille, the worthy Panisse, who accepts to become the father of Fanny's child by Marius, César, the keeper of the café on the quay-side, with its customers who play cards, tell tall stories, and exchange imaginative banter, or adopt sudden, bellicose attitudes of short duration. These characters, taken by Pagnol from a setting he knew so well, have become unforgettable types. Unlike most comedies of manners, bound as they are to the times they depict, the Marius trilogy is evergreen, whether on the stage or on the screen. Pagnol turned his attention to the cinema, despite his success on the stage with *Marius* in 1929 and *Fanny* in 1931, and founded the company called Films Marcel Pagnol. In addition to adapting plays by Courteline, Jean Sarment, and others, he made a number of original films, all of which are set in Provence, though *Merlusse* (1936) recalls the first act of *Topaze* by recreating the atmosphere of an educational establishment. In *Manon des sources* and *Ugolin* the problem posed is the vital problem for the whole of Provence—that of the water supply.

Water, bread, a mother, her child, the commonplace in fact, this, says Pagnol, is always his subject, whatever the artistic medium chosen. Pagnol's films read like plays; he considered the text to be the most important element of a film as it is of a stage play. Indeed, the film, with its photographic reality, close-ups, camera angles, its visual representation of what in the theatre must be couched in words, and the camera's capacity for getting right at the heart of the scene without having to provide for the exits and entrances of the characters, as on the stage, is described by Pagnol as "perfected theatre", which, of course, led to the film he had made from *Fanny* being dubbed "canned theatre" by his critics. Pagnol's conception of the new art of the sound film was diametrically opposed to René Clair's, as Clair applied it in *Le Million*, where dialogue is reduced to a minimum and appears only as part of the general element of sound. Pagnol has not deviated from this theory of cinema, which he put forward in 1933-34, in the short-lived revue *Les Cahiers du film*, and in 1963 he protested against the alleged originality of the Italian neo-realistic school, saying: "As if the 'Films Marcel Pagnol' had not done all this a long time ago."

In *Judas* (Théâtre de Paris, October 6th, 1955) Pagnol sets out, for once, from an idea and not from observed reality. After Paul Raynal, and after Pierre Bost and C.-A. Puget, Pagnol sought to explain the reason for Judas's betrayal of Christ, and found it in the phrase: "Do what thou hast to do." The Scriptures had to be fulfilled, and Judas was the instrument chosen by God. This poses the metaphysical problem of the reconciliation of the necessary and the foreseen with free will in man. The first scenes of the play are striking, but Judas's vain wait for the miracle that would reveal Christ's godhead during the crucifixion, which takes place in the wings, is a debatable ending from every point of view. Pagnol was less well inspired here, and in the cynical Parisian comedy, *Fabien* (Bouffes-Parisiens, September 29th, 1956), than when he was depicting the life of the butcher, the baker, the bartender in Provence.

In general, in the twenties and thirties, comedies of manners and of character were the work of the older generation of playwrights, MAURICE DONNAY, EDMOND SEE, LEOPOLD MARCHAND, and did not change much from what they had been before the war. It was only the manners that had changed. The bridge-playing craze in Paris, together with the agencies that supplied bridge or dancing partners, form the butt of Marchand's amusing comedy *Le Valet maître*, which vividly recalls *Le Sexe faible*, being played nine years afterwards at the same theatre, the Michodière, and by the same actor, Victor Boucher. The final scenes show the valet bridge-player at an international congress of diplomats, defending, cards in hand, the interests of his country in the case of some Turkish oilfields. Newcomers like HENRY CLERC conformed to the accepted pattern; in

Le beau Métier, which is in some measure a "thesis" play, Clerc rehabilitates the Civil Servant, as if in reply to *Topaze*, staged the year before. The still younger CHARLES DE PEYRET-CHAPPUIS was clearly influenced by Jules Renard and Henry Becque, particularly in *Feu Monsieur Pic* (1939). MARTIAL PIÉCHAUD, a novelist as well as a dramatist, was mainly concerned with the ordinary everyday life of people in the provinces; his neat little one-act play, *Le Quatrième*, showing the effect on three old maids of the visit of a childhood friend who had gone to Paris to win fame and fortune was performed at the Comédie-Française in 1928. EDMOND FLEG, himself a Jew, offered some interesting studies of the Jewish temperament and of Jewish ideals. His verse play, *Le Juif du pape* (1925), set in Rome in about 1523, has a permanent politico-religious interest: it tells of a pope (Clement VII) and a Jew who, in a Europe at war, both dream of universal peace and unite in a premature effort to realize this dream.

JACQUES COPEAU, who had done so much as a producer to change the course of dramatic history in France, is disappointing as a playwright. *La Maison natale*, which has been performed in English under the title *The House into which we are born*, is a thoroughly old-fashioned comedy of manners. The play, which was finished only in 1923, was begun in 1905, and in the meantime his work at the Vieux-Colombier had drawn him away from everything that had satisfied him in these earlier years.

A possible line of development for the comedy of manners was indicated by the socialist novelist PIERRE HAMP, whose novels, bearing the collective title of *La Peine des hommes*, constitute a fine series of social and philosophical studies of the different trades and industries. Hamp's play, *La Maison avant tout* (1923), is just such a study, and *Le Déraillement du T.P. 33* (1927), a dramatic counterpart of his novel *Le Rail*, tells of a railway accident for which the company, in defence of its own interests, throws the responsibility on to an innocent employee. More important than the plays themselves is the idea put forward by Hamp in an interview in *Humanité*, before the première of *La Maison avant tout*. He was struck by the complete ignorance shown by French "dramatists" of the working people, and Hamp includes factory owners in the term "working people". Take, for example, *Le Bourgeois gentilhomme*, he says: "However stupid M. Jourdain may be, does Molière appear to have understood that this bourgeois had a business house to run, that he had his bills to meet, his employees' wages to pay, that he had to think in order to buy and then sell at a profit? No! Molière does not." He concedes that work came in as a literary theme with Balzac and Victor Hugo but was inadequately developed. In Zola it was the style that was inadequate. "The whole of our civilization", Hamp concludes, "is based on work. Work is the very essence of modern life; it should therefore be the essential matter of art. There is no such thing as man in the abstract. Man is a function of his profession . . . His trade forms his character." It also creates his interests. Art must therefore be recreated by modern man. The troubles and anxiety of a man who buys and sells a commodity, who has to struggle to exist, and who, having assured his existence, is aiming at something better, is dramatic material, no less rich than the tragedies of great dynasties. *La Maison avant tout* is the drama, the tragedy even, of a commercial passion.

These ideas of Hamp's have a curious topical reference in the French theatre of the 1950's and 1960's, and make one think of *Paolo Paoli* (1957), by Arthur Adamov, or *La Remise* (1962), by Roger Planchon, or the production at Planchon's Théâtre de la Cité at Villeurbanne of Molière's *George Dandin* (1962), in which the producer Jacques Rosner tried precisely to show a man in terms of his trade or profession, and to represent materially the means by which Dandin had made his money; next to Dandin's house he set outhouses with farm instruments and piles of hay. Farmworkers moved the hay and went about their work as the dramatic action indicated by Molière's text proceeded. The extent to which "living", and the means which man must employ in any social organization in order to "live", enters not only into his daily actions, but into the very texture of his being, and must be present in the spectator's mind. In Molière's day the spectators were aware, from their own experience, of the issues involved; the present-day producer must provide the necessary background knowledge as best he can.

NOTE

1. *Observer*, April 24th, 1938. The English adaptation by Yvette Pienne, which retains the French title, was licensed after a number of changes had been made. It was widely performed in other countries. Revived, Renaissance, September 9th, 1945.

XI

Boulevard Theatre: Comedy and Melodrama

1. Comedy: *Georges Feydeau—Robert de Flers and Francis de Croisset—Tristan Bernard—Sacha Guitry —Louis Verneuil and Georges Berr—René Fauchois —Alfred Savoir—Jacques Deval—André Birabeau— Claude-André Puget—*2. Melodrama: *Henri Kistemaeckers — Pierre Frondaie — Charles Méré — the Grand Guignol.*

1. Comedy

LIGHT comedy is one of the mainstays of the Boulevard; the comedies of GEORGES FEYDEAU, who died in 1921, have been consistently successful right up to the present time. *L'Hôtel du libre échange* (1894), performed in English under the title *Hotel Paradiso* (1956), and *La Dame de Chez Maxim's* (1899), have been constant favourites on the Boulevard. In addition, from the time of the Second World War, and particularly since 1950, the Comédie-Française and Jean-Louis Barrault have taken him up, and their revivals of *Feu la Mère de Madame, Le Dindon, Un Fil à la patte, On purge bébé, Mais n'te promène donc pas toute nue, Occupe-toi d'Amélie,* and *La Puce à l'oreille* have made Feydeau a classic. The last two have been performed in English under the titles *Look after Lulu* (1958) and *A Flea in her Ear* (1966). The sheer gaiety of the situations, and the speed of the plots, which function like clockwork, make these plays permanently acceptable as light entertainment.

ROBERT DE FLERS and FRANCIS DE CROISSET also continue the tradition of the Banquet years ("la belle époque"), but they tackled contemporary themes in *Les Vignes du seigneur* (1923), an outstanding success of long duration, and in *Les Nouveaux Messieurs* (1925). The first of these two plays mirrors a class of society that had emerged towards the end of the war, the newly rich, and shows it hovering hopefully on the fringe of the upper middle-class. Despite its topical slant, the play is first and foremost a piece of light entertainment; it presents amusing situations, as in the scene in which a very drunk young man confides in his best friend that he is that friend's wife's lover. The scene remained linked with the name of the actor Victor Boucher, at least until the play was revived in 1949, with Pierre Dux. There are also witty passes, as when a Frenchwoman indignantly remarks on hearing a hungry Englishman request a big meal: "What else does he want? A colony?" The development of the trade-union movement inspired the satirical comedy *Les Nouveaux Messieurs*, but, like *Les Vignes du seigneur*, the play remains resolutely on the surface of the problem. The craftsmanship in both is excellent.

The amiable TRISTAN BERNARD, a contemporary of Georges Feydeau, continued to hold his own on the post-1918 Boulevard stage, and in 1931, in the Théâtre Albert Iᵉʳ, which he renamed the Théâtre Tristan Bernard, he prepared the atmosphere for the performance of his plays by improvised chats, interlarded with amusing stories, which he delivered personally in front of the curtain. His early play *L'Anglais tel qu'on le parle* (1897) has remained one of the Boulevard's evergreen successes.

The work of SACHA GUITRY, whether in light or more serious mood, stands apart from that of other Boulevard writers and, by comparison with the prose of the normal Boulevard play, seems almost poetic, possibly because it is so intensely personal. Guitry's plays were all "made to measure"; the first five or six were written with one eye on his father, the actor Lucien Guitry, although, at the time, father and son were estranged from each other, because of Guitry's thoughtlessness in one of his father's productions, in 1904. They remained estranged for thirteen years. Later, several plays were written specially by Guitry for his father to perform, but very early on he began to write for another star actor, himself. It was not so much that he created suitable parts for himself as that he put himself on the stage just as he was, even when it was in the guise of well-known figures, such as Franz Hals or Talleyrand. The impression given was always that of Guitry parading in costume. Yet his career as an actor did not open auspiciously. An incident at Saint-Valéry-en-Caux, following that with his father the previous year, had caused him to turn instead to writing and to sketching, for which he had quite a talent. It was only towards the end of 1906, when he had suddenly to take over the lead in his own play *Chez les Zoaques*, at the Théâtre Antoine, that Guitry became, for good and all, an actor as well as a playwright. Both his acting and his writing show the influence of his early years, when his father's profession had brought him into contact with many of the best-known actors and playwrights; indeed, for ten years, as Guitry himself tells us, he and his brother went every Sunday to "kiss Madame Sarah" as others went to Mass—piously; "Madame Sarah played a great part in our lives." In 1900, at the age of fifteen, he watched Sarah Bernhardt rehearse Edmond Rostand's new play *L'Aiglon*.

Guitry wrote some hundred and thirty works for the stage. They range from revues, operettas, satirical or sentimental comedies, to dramatic biographies, and there is a good deal of chaff among the grain. The subject-matter of many of them can be summarized in the title of one play, *Le Mari, la femme et l'amant* (1919), and, indeed, in the earlier *Faisons un rêve* (1916) Guitry had named his characters le Mari, Elle, and Lui. His favourite play, *La Jalousie*, which has been in the Comédie-Française repertory since 1932, contains a good study of jealousy in love, as well as providing amusing situations like that of the husband who has been unfaithful to his wife and does not know what interpretation to put on the reason his wife gives for her late return, because it is the very reason he had thought up to excuse his own late return. Guitry's aged professor hero, in what might be termed his version of Courteline's *Boubouroche*, *Le Veilleur de nuit* (1911), on the contrary, feels no jealousy, and even finds peace of mind in the knowledge that his mistress has a young lover. "Two men are not too many to give a woman all the love she needs", he says. Guitry's infectious gaiety veils the amorality of the situation here, as it does in many other plays of his.

The series of dramatic biographies are among the more interesting of Guitry's writings for the stage, though not for any detailed portrait of their subject, be it Deburau, the pierrot who attracted the whole of Paris to the Funambules in 1840, La Fontaine, Mozart, or Pasteur—Guitry, on the contrary, favoured rapid sketches, or what he called portraits in pastel shades. They are interesting for the light they shed on Guitry himself, particularly his cult of greatness. "We should bless the name of these men of genius," he writes in *Franz Hals*, "we should love them and serve their name ... I watch over all the great men I admire." The full title of this play, *Franz Hals ou l'admiration*, defines its main theme. Adrien Van Ostade, who is much admired as a painter, in turn admires Franz Hals. Hals is overwhelmed by Rembrandt's genius; he also admires and is admired by Van Dyck. A sentimental episode introduces dramatic action into what would have been only the expression of the mutual admiration of these great men. There are no sentimental complications in *Pasteur* (1919), which was written for Lucien Guitry and was acted by him; this is unusual. The play is very loosely constructed, and there is only the merest hint of progression in the action. The play consists, in fact, of a series of tableaux, showing Pasteur in various episodes of his life. At one moment he is to be seen addressing members of the Academy of Medicine on his discoveries, and at the next facing the first human being, a child, whose life depends on the accuracy of the conclusion he has drawn from his experiments in the laboratory. *Mozart* (1925) was written for Guitry's wife, Yvonne Printemps, to allow her, in the title-rôle, to show off her talents as actress, singer, and dancer.

Where Guitry is the most interesting is in a play like *Le Comédien* (1921), in which he is concerned with acting, or in *Un Sujet de roman* (1923), which is, so to speak, the sequel to *Le Comédien*, because it treats the task of the writer as against that of the actor. Both plays show the artist to be a slave to creative work and point to the sacrifices that it requires of him. While *Le Comédien* contains an expression of Guitry's almost fanatical love for the theatre, together with an outline of his conception of the dramatic art, the latter play insists on the solitude of the writer of genius, and the necessity for the writer to aim at truth in whatever he writes. In *Monsieur Prudhomme a-t-il vécu?* (1931), written round Henri Monnier, Guitry states this categorically: "Take as models people you have watched as they lived ... caricature them if you cannot paint a proper portrait ... but for heaven's sake make them true to life." Guitry's *comédien* expresses the actor's joy in bringing to life and giving a definite form, in one creative moment, to the character which has only slowly come into being in the writer's mind. In this creative moment the audience is seen as a precious collaborator of the actor, but the actor who does not care a rap for his audience, or who merely panders to it, is denounced as being unworthy of his profession. *Quand jouons-nous la comédie?* (1935)

contains a further expression of Guitry's ideas on the art of the actor and the playwright, and in *On ne joue pas pour s'amuser* (1925), or what might be termed "the art of being a good actor", Lucien Guitry, in the part of the elder actor, attempts to inculcate into the young actor the theory of the essential interpretation and not imitation of nature. These plays concerning actors are the best of Guitry.

Guitry's somewhat facile optimism is expressed in the substance of his plays and also by direct statements, perhaps the most clearly in *Mon Père avait raison* (1931): his determination to accept only the joys of life and shut the door on troubles and grief, his belief in man and in the goodness of man, and his conviction that love is the most precious thing in the world.

Guitry's virtuosity expressed itself in his use of dramatic structure. One might have taken him for an *avant-garde* dramatist in two or three of his plays, had his ingenuity been the expression of a dramatic theory. In 1916, in *Faisons un rêve*, he used the stage-business of a telephone conversation throughout a whole act; Jean Cocteau was later to use this device in *La Voix humaine* and exploit its dramatic possibilities to the full. *Je t'aime* (1920) is a plotless comedy of uneventful love, whereas *Talleyrand* (1947), taken from Guitry's banned film *Le Diable boiteux*, goes to the other extreme and presents a rapid series of completely unconnected scenes of historical events with Talleyrand as master of ceremonies, ushering on to and off the stage Napoleon, Louis XIII, Charles X, and Louis-Philippe. Several comedies feature the old and sure device of a play within a play, and often the audience is made use of in one way or other. Sometimes actors are placed in the auditorium; in this way, in the third act of *Pasteur*, the audience was transformed into the Academy of Medicine, listening to Pasteur's address, made from the stage in Pasteur's own words. In the first act of *Mariette* (1928) the actors perform the inner play, an opera, with their backs to the real audience. They face an imaginary audience at the back of the stage, on the other side of the "footlights". On the stage, in an "orchestra pit" beyond these "footlights", the orchestra, which has just played the "opera's overture" from its usual place in the house, plays for the "opera" singers.

The cinema, which Guitry at first saw as a danger to the live theatre, finally claimed his attention. He made some twenty-five films and proved himself a virtuoso in this domain as well, particu-

larly in *Le Roman d'un tricheur*, where, for the first time, a commentator was used in a film. His films include excellent film
comedies and historical frescoes (*Remontons les Champs-Elysées*
and *Les Perles de la couronne*), constructed on the same lines as his
play *Histoires de France*. His history is not meant to be taken
seriously; it was just another aspect of his showmanship. He offers
one of the few examples of the complete man of show business, and
the theatre to which he belongs is the theatre of sheer entertainment; the plays he wrote, like the films he made, were the means
for putting on Guitry the entertainer.

Like Sacha Guitry, but ten years younger, LOUIS VERNEUIL
(Louis Collin du Bocage, husband of Sarah Bernhardt's granddaughter) was an actor as well as a writer of light comedy, but he
cannot compare with Guitry in either capacity. Like Guitry, he
produced films as well as plays. He successively directed ten theatres
in Paris; in two plays specially written for her, *Daniel* (1920) and
Régine Armand (1924), he brought Sarah Bernhardt back to the
stage after the loss of her leg; for twelve years he formed a combination, like that formed by Guitry with Yvonne Printemps, with
the Romanian actress Elvire Popesco. Popesco's strong accent limited
the type of part she could take, and in the series of plays which
Verneuil wrote for her she was always cast as a passionate and
turbulent sentimentalist, and, of course, a foreigner. She was typi-
fied by Verneuil in *Ma Cousine de Varsovie* (1923), which had an
astounding international success. Popesco revived it in 1955, three
years after Verneuil's death. These plays were put on mostly at
the Théâtre de Paris, though *Vive le roi* was staged at the Odéon
in 1925, and *Pile ou face* went on to the Odéon in 1934, ten years
after its first production at the Théâtre Antoine.

In another series Verneuil had as a collaborator GEORGES BERR,
a Comédie-Française actor and teacher at the conservatoire.
Their command of dramatic technique caused them to be known
as *vaudevillistes boulevardiers*, though after 1918 the term lost
some of its point through the disappearance of vaudeville, with its
rhymed couplets. The themes chosen by the joint authors often had
a topical slant, but the social satire takes second place, and interest
is concentrated on the unusual situations, and the unexpected
turns taken by the action. Tax-evasion is the subject of *L'Ecole
des contribuables* (1934). Fromental, a Treasury official, finds
himself faced with a school for the teaching of tax-evasion founded

by his son-in-law. This family link brings about his dismissal from his post, thus forcing him into the opposition camp. With as much zeal as he had formerly used to bring tax-evaders to book, he trains his clients, including an ex-Minister of Finance, how to evade the tax laws. Earlier, in *La Banque Nemo*, Verneuil, as sole author, wrote a gay satire on another aspect of the financial world. It was first performed by Victor Boucher at the Michodière in 1931. The legal world came in for gay attack from the two authors in *Maître Bolbec et son mari* (1926), inspired by the rapid increase in the number of women barristers. Maître Bolbec's husband has to take over the running of the house, and, in order to see his wife at all, has to seek an interview with her on the same footing as her clients. In *Mon Crime* (1934), a sort of parody of Eugène Brieux's serious study *La Robe rouge* (1909), the authors satirize a jury's deliberation, and show an innocent person confessing to the crime for which she has been charged because of the benefits which accrue from the confession; a subsequent confession, for similar reasons, by the real criminal after the acquittal, and the concern of all in preventing the exposure of the judicial error, complete the story. Despite the apparent topical slant, such plays clearly do not reflect the preoccupations of the time in any serious manner.

With these and many other gay "Parisian" comedies, Verneuil and Berr, separately or together, prolonged the tradition of de Flers and Caillavet, themselves successors to Meilhac and Halévy. Verneuil's plays were particularly popular in Central Europe between 1920 and 1930, and in Berlin he was considered the most typically Parisian of writers.

Like Verneuil and like Guitry, RENE FAUCHOIS was an actor as well as an author, and had performed, watched by Guitry, alongside Sarah Bernhardt in *L'Aiglon*. This helped to set the pattern for Fauchois's early plays, heroic verse dramas such as *Louis XII* (1902), *Beethoven* (1909), and *Rivoli* (1910), which had met with great success at the Odéon but are now quite unplayable, *Rossini* (1922), written in collaboration with Sacha Guitry, or verse tragedies like *La Fille de Pilate* (1908) and *La Mort de Patrocle* (1926). Fauchois also wrote a number of light comedies, and is mainly remembered for one of them, *Prenez garde à la peinture* (1932), performed in English as *The Late Christopher Bean* (1933). The substance of the play was drawn from the book *Vincent Van Gogh* (1923) by Fauchois's friend Gustave Coquiot. Fauchois's stated intention was to present the picture of a mediocre family which is drawn into the public eye because of its contacts with an obscure painter who becomes famous after his death. There follows a hectic search for masterpieces given to the family by the painter and which had been used to stop the holes in the attic roof and the chicken-run, and the uneasy consent to a plan for making money out of the painter's name. There are several harsh scenes presenting sharks of the art world, but these are incidental. The action takes place in Provence, and the film version of the play presents the countryside as well as the accent of Provence. Mention might be made of two other comedies, *Le Singe qui parle*, performed in 1924, a melodrama set in a circus, and *Mlle Jockey* (1926), presenting life on the race-courses.

Alfred Poszanski, the son of a wealthy Jewish industrialist, was born in Lodz, in Russian Poland, in 1882. He left it at an early age because of the oppression of the Jews in that country, and settled in France, where he took the name of ALFRED SAVOIR. His radical pessimism, engendered by his early experiences, and his disillusioned view of life made Paris producers—except Lugné-Poë, who staged his first play *Le Troisième couvert* (1906), a sombre drama of an illegitimate child driven to suicide by his mother—unwilling to put on a play written by Savoir alone. For fifteen years Savoir collaborated with a number of playwrights, his first being Fernand Nozière, to whom he had been introduced by Lugné-Poë, who staged *Le Baptême* (1907) and *La Sonate à Kreutzer* (1910), written by the two together. Savoir's first individual success came in 1921 at the Potinière, with *La huitième Femme de Barbe-bleue*, which was revived in 1940 at the Théâtre Edouard VII. The play foreshadowed *L'Acheteuse* (1930), by Stève Passeur. Indeed, Savoir's mirth is as bitter as Passeur's. He used farce as a vehicle for his lashing wit and biting sarcasm, and made his characters throw harsh, unpalatable truths in his spectators' faces, as though in a game. Despite the farcical element, his subjects are fundamentally cruel.

After his difficult beginning Savoir deliberately set out to cater for the French post-war taste for comedy. *Banco* followed in 1922. It is the story of an inveterate gambler who brashly tells his ex-wife, now married to another man, that he intends to spend the night with her, but succumbs to the temptation of a pack of cards on the table; the night is spent at the card-table instead. *La Grande-Duchesse et le garçon d'étage* (1924) was another success. This story of an affair between a Grand Duchess and the Boots—in reality the son of the millionaire hotel proprietor—provides a fund of amusing, risqué situations. The play also presents a curious picture of exiled Russian nobility, coloured by Savoir's philosophical musings on mankind in general.

Savoir's special turn of humour caused him to be generally known as the Bernard Shaw of the Boulevard, particularly after his two irreverent historical plays, *La petite Catherine* (1930), a satirical piece on the budding monster who was to become Catherine the Great of Russia, and *La Margrave* (1932), a satirical picture of the Court of Anspach in the eighteenth century, in which short shrift is given to historical exactitude.

Had he so wished, Savoir could doubtless have taken his place among the *avant-garde* dramatists of his time, and, as if to point out the fact, he published in 1930, under the collective title of *La Fuite en avant, trois comédies d'avant garde*—*Le Figurant de la Gaîté, Le Dompteur ou l'Anglais tel qu'on le mange*, and *Lui*. An earlier play, *La Couturière de Lunéville* (Vaudeville, February 5th, 1923), could also have been included, because in it Savoir leaves the beaten track of psychological analysis and realistic presentation to follow the lead given by Pirandello and young French playwrights like Jean Sarment, and present the *man* and the *mask*, the individual as he really is and as he is in society. Like a cat playing with a mouse, his heroine, a famous actress, plays with a man who seduced and abandoned her sixteen years before and does not even remember her. She appears before him alternately as the modest dressmaker she was then and as the seductive, depraved actress she is now, and the two rôles taken together present the two aspects of the heroine's character, sweet and loving by nature but embittered by circumstances and vengeful. When he tries to kill the heartless "actress", who has ordered him to break with the loving "dressmaker", it is clear that the real woman and not the *mask* has won. *Le Figurant de la Gaîté* (Danou, March 26th, 1926), which was successfully revived on February 19th, 1949, at the Théâtre Montparnasse, has a similar theme. A student, who is a supernumerary at the Gaîté Théâtre, becomes a rajah, then an archbishop, or whatever his costume dictates: the *mask* supplants the *man*, and, tragically, it is the *mask* that wins the love of the princess.

The two other plays in this collection ran into censorship trouble in England,[1] *Le Dompteur* (Théâtre Michel, December

18th, 1925), because it was understood as a caricature of a well-known English peer, *Lui* (Potinière, October 28th, 1929), because of the subject. They were seen only in two private theatres, the former at the Gate in 1930, the latter at J. T. Grein's Cosmopolitan Theatre in 1931. The story of the English lord who follows a travelling circus from place to place in the hope of seeing the brutal lion-tamer eaten by the lions is the story of an idealist who takes the side of the oppressed against the oppressor. The lord is forced to become a lion-tamer in his turn, though he refuses to use the whip, and is only eaten by the lions the day he loses faith in his ideal. But idealism does not die, and the lord's seat at the ringside is taken by his son. *Lui* is a discussion on the deity, whose power and even existence is denied by the members of the Congress of International Free Thought, assembled in a Swiss hotel. The one discordant voice is that of an escaped lunatic, who proclaims himself God and offers to perform miracles. The members are led to take the lunatic seriously by a series of strange happenings in the suddenly avalanche-bound hotel.

Two other plays worth mention are Savior's cynical war-play *Madeleine ou la Pâtissière du village* (1932), and *Marie* (1933), which puts the problem of the nature of true love, and progresses from farce to tragedy as it concludes that true love is necessarily egoistic.

Savoir is more than just a clever dramatic craftsman: had vaudeville, with its rhymed couplets, not disappeared from the Paris stage, the term *vaudevilles idéologiques*, often applied to Savoir's plays, would, in fact, be an apt description. As it is, Savoir provided a link between the Boulevard and the experimental theatres, and helped to familiarize Boulevard audiences with a more literary type of play and with techniques that were new to them, though not so new to *avant-garde* audiences. It is significant that Louis Jouvet produced two of his plays, one of them, *La Margrave*, in his own experimental theatre (November 18th, 1932), the other, *La Pâtissière du village*, in the up-to-date Boulevard theatre, the Théâtre Pigalle (March 8th).

JACQUES DEVAL (Jacques Boularan) is a truer product of the Boulevard than Alfred Savoir, and has written continuously for it from 1923 on into the 1960's. Aiming more at immediate results than at writing works of permanent value, he has deliberately limited himself to the field of facile comedy, though it is obvious from a play like *Prière pour les vivants* (Athenée, September 28th, 1933), which is intended as a dramatic synthesis of the life of a very ordinary individual, beginning in 1873, when he is born into a home devoid of any moral sense, and closing in 1933, when he dies, leaving his son to live in his turn the same cruel, petty, selfish existence, that Deval was capable of more significant works. But the lack of public enthusiasm for this story of man told in bitter and realistic "slices of life" drove Deval back to lighthearted comedies and adaptations of English and American popular successes, his most recent being *Speciale dernière* (1961), from Ben Hecht and MacArthur. *Prière pour les vivants* was accepted at the Comédie-Française in 1964.

In a number of his plays Deval chooses important themes but then seems to turn deliberately aside from them, as if suddenly mindful of the Boulevard audience's aversion for serious-minded plays. Two such themes are outlined in *Etienne* (1930) and *Mademoiselle* (1932);[2] the plays were first staged at the Théâtre Saint-Georges and then went into the repertory of the Comédie-Française in 1954 and 1957 respectively. The unusual hero of *Etienne* is a boy of seventeen who is caught between his father, a pompous, self-righteous windbag, and his long-suffering mother. The play is concerned with the moral and emotional development of the boy as he seeks to better the relationship between his mother and her unfaithful husband, but the punch is taken out of it by Deval's deliberate recourse to caricature, to provide innocuous entertainment for the Boulevard. In *Mademoiselle* the theme is the social catastrophe for one woman and the immense joy for another that the arrival of an illegitimate child represents, but the seriousness of the theme is glossed over, to some extent, by the introduction of farcical elements, such as the drunken, blackmailing butler who is easily parted from his booty. The play is an excellent piece of stagecraft. It consists of two essentially contrasting elements: the picture of a milieu with a portrait inset. The clash between the picture and the portrait is deliberate, and results from the status of the sitter and from her character—Mademoiselle is a person who feels things deeply, whereas the milieu is shallow and frivolous. She is a governess in an upper-middle-class family which is barely a family, so totally is every member of it absorbed in his own affairs and pleasures. Deval studies the development of the maternal feelings in the heart of the dried-up spinster, cleverly avoiding any pathos, and the inconsequential behaviour of the child's real mother as she gets caught up again in the mad social whirl which for her means life.

The most consistently successful of all Deval's plays, since Elvire Popesco first performed it at the Théâtre de Paris on October 13th, 1933, has been *Tovaritch*. Sir Cedric Hardwicke and Eugenie Leontovich acted in the English version in 1935. Vivien Leigh appeared in New York, in 1963, in a musical which was a thinned-out version of the original. The play follows the tradition of Savoir's *La Grande-Duchesse et le garçon d'étage*, and of similar ones by Abel Hermant, J. Kessel, and others. A Russian Prince and his wife, a Grand Duchess and the Tsar's niece, are butler and maid to a French socialist Deputy; such a situation gives scope for a study of manners, characters, and racial peculiarities. At a dinner-party given by the Deputy, a People's Commissar, who is negotiating the sale of rich oil-fields in the Urals, persuades the Prince to hand over the huge sum of money he holds in trust from the late Tsar, for his future successor to secure these resources for the nation, so putting the destiny of Mother Russia before considerations of regime. This sudden confrontation of the Russia of yesterday with the Russia of today, coming after three acts of fantasy and scintillating dialogue, is disconcerting, but Deval's skill as a dramatist carries it through. The play was still fresh in 1948.

In all his plays Deval tells a good story and he tells it well, be it highly amusing, deadly serious, or even tragic. If some, like *Le onzième Commandement* (1932), hide a moral lesson under the sugared exterior, most are intended by Deval as pure entertainment: "If the story has a happy ending", wrote Deval in the programme of *La Manière forte* (1954), a revised version of *Dans sa candeur naïve* (1925), "it is because it would be really too depressing for it to have an unhappy one." So the young man to whom the heroine has entrusted the task of preventing her, by force if need be, from falling into the arms of a local Don Juan, not only wins the fight that necessarily ensues between himself and the girl, but also, finally, wins the girl too. In *Romancero* (1925), of which the original title, *La Corrida*, more aptly describes the course of the action, a similar duel is fought between a prostitute in the Panama of 1920 and a Spanish priest, who dares temptation in the brothel in order to bring back the lost sheep into the fold.

At times Deval meditates lightheartedly on a problem. In *Ce*

Soir à Samarcande (1951) it is the problem of predestination. In *Et l'enfer, Isabelle?* (1963) it is both the powerlessness of the law when the action of murder cannot be proved, even though the intention to murder is irrefutably established, and the limits of human knowledge—can magic kill? But if the law is powerless "what", the public prosecutor asks the accused, as he unwillingly dismisses the case, particularly as there is another potential victim in the offing, "what about hell, Isabelle?" This ingenious theme is presented with the mastery of dramatic technique usual in a play by Deval. At other times Deval writes plays as *noires* as Jean Anouilh's, gloating over the "rottenness" of mankind, and at the same time striking off comedy, like Alfred Savoir, from the excessive cruelty of the action. *Charmante Soirée*, performed by Michel Simon in 1955 and again in 1964, is an excellent example of this.

ANDRE BIRABEAU is a successful playwright who has written purely for after-dinner audiences. He has always seemed even more determined than Jacques Deval to limit himself to light entertainment, and even managed, in *Baisers perdus*, with which he made his entry into the Comédie-Française (April 11th, 1932), to write a lively comedy on the subject of a man who, believing himself not to be the father of his own child, systematically destroys her happiness and his wife's, until he finally discovers his mistake and deplores the wasted years. In *Dame Nature* (1936), in which the chief character, a boy of fourteen who is unhappy at home and has turned for affection to an orphan girl of sixteen, learns with amazement that he is about to become a father, Birabeau seemed to aim merely at scoring an easy success, but the subject is not one for light comedy. Nor is the problem of racial prejudice, over which he skates in *Pamplemousse* (1937). Birabeau finds an easy solution to a family's embarrassment, on discovering the colour of the skin of the husband's illegitimate child, by making a bachelor uncle, a rake, accept the paternity. Birabeau's most interesting play is *Le Chemin des écoliers* (1924), which offers a clever study of holiday-makers in an overcrowded seaside resort who are accommodated in a boarding-school. After some ten, twenty, or thirty years they find themselves back in their childhood setting, with their memories, and with the values they learned at school reversed by life. But it is the setting which plays the principal part in this comedy, and not any one of the characters.

The name of CLAUDE-ANDRE PUGET, the youngest of these playwrights, is mainly associated with Les Jours heureux, a light comedy featuring adolescent love; it dates from 1938. Among the fairy-tale plays and extravagant romantic pieces which followed can be singled out Un nommé Judas, written in collaboration with Pierre Bost in 1954. The subject seemed to be in the air, and this tragedy of Judas, who had convinced himself of his mission to bring out the God in Christ made Man by forcing Him to perform publicly a miracle to save Himself from the Cross, offers an interesting contrast with the spectacular play by Marcel Pagnol, staged the following year.

Much of the work of these authors is mere "after-dinner" comedy, destined for "tired businessmen", but what it may lack in seriousness it makes up for by superb craftsmanship.

2. Melodrama

The pièce bien faite, with its melodramatic plot and passionate love interest, had already lost much public favour when its main exponent for some forty years, Georges Ohnet, died in 1918. His "masterpiece", Le Maître de forges (1884), still reappears on the Boulevard whenever a theatre finds itself in low water. Of those who continued to write in this vein, the three most important have often been referred to disparagingly as the "Méré-Kistemaeckers-Frondaie firm".

HENRI KISTEMAECKERS began to write for the theatre in 1899. There are neither ideas nor analysis of character in his plays, which stand only by their "strong" plot and clever dramatic construction. L'Embuscade, performed at the Comédie-Française in 1913 and revived there in 1934, is a good museum piece of its kind. It tells the story of the thwarted love of an illegitimate son for his half-sister, the daughter of the owner of the factory where he works. On the ruins of the factory, which is destroyed by the revolutionary factory-hands, of which he is one, the whole truth comes out and all make their peace.

L'Amour, put on at the Porte-Saint-Martin in 1924, shows, however, an attempt by Kistemaeckers to get away from the frenzied manner he had deliberately cultivated. Though the subject provides the usual mixture of violence and sentimentality, the treatment is different: the characters never come into direct conflict with each other; an ambiguous remark, a letter left lying about, are used to indicate the situation.

The early works of René Fraudet, known as PIERRE FRONDAIE, consist mainly of adaptations of novels by Pierre Louÿs, Maurice Barrès, and Claude Farrère. Frondaie makes some attempt at psychological analysis, but the tradition that he really follows is that of the *pièce bien faite,* judiciously seasoned with violence. In the preface to *La Menace,* performed at the Renaissance in 1925, he defended his conception of drama, which he sees as requiring physical action or an "adventure", against "such worthy playwrights as Henri Lenormand"—that is to say, against the *avant-garde* movement of the twenties—and he actually foresaw many of the pitfalls into which the *avant-garde* playwrights were to fall. Purely introspective drama he declared to be only suitable for small theatres, not for the general theatregoing public. Ideas had to be translated into movement, so that all people could be pleased or moved by them. What he meant by "movement" was exemplified by the beginning of *Les Amants de Paris,* performed at the Théâtre Sarah-Bernhardt in 1927: a white man seizes a Negro by the throat, in front of all his guests, in his sumptuous Paris house.

CHARLES MERE defined his own plays as "action drama", and took as his motto "action and still more action", so earning the title of "our modern Sardou". A dramatist, according to Méré, must know how to tell a story, and most of those he told were violent and romantic. He begins with a plot, never a character, and this plot determines the action and feelings of the characters, who only exist for the sake of the "coups de théâtre". His best play is *La Captive,* performed at the Théâtre Antoine in 1920. It tells of a woman who had been married twice to men of different nationalities and who sees her sons in enemy camps.

At the GRAND GUIGNOL, founded in 1897 in a former chapel in the rue Chaptal, melodrama acquired a specialized form, one which not only successfully survived the First World War, but was in great demand during hostilities, particularly by men on leave and convalescent soldiers. The theatre flourished to such an extent during these years that shortly after the war another, though ephemeral, Grand Guignol theatre, Les Deux Masques, came into being. Later, in 1929, a second Grand Guignol theatre was opened at the Théâtre Saint-Georges, and ran for a few months. The two masters of Grand Guignol, André de Lorde and

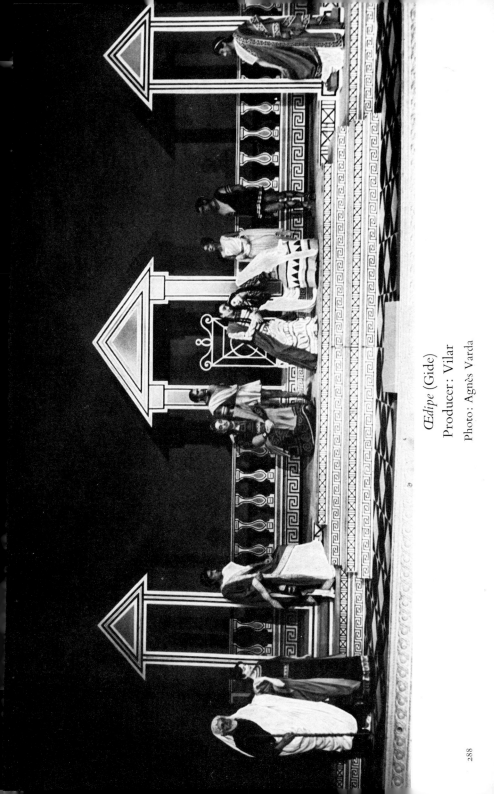

Œdipe (Gide)
Producer: Vilar
Photo: Agnès Varda

The Théâtre du Peuple at Bussang, 1895
By courtesy of Madame Marie-Anne Chan

Encircling Stage, at Dijon, for *Catharsis*, by Michel Parent, 1964
By courtesy of Michel Parent

Henri Duvernois, were staged there as well as at the rue Chaptal. From the inception of the Grand Guignol, de Lorde, the "prince of terror", supplied the horror plays and Duvernois the comic relief. Of the younger generation, Bernard Zimmer tried his hand at de Lorde's speciality, and Jules Romains concentrated on laughter.

Tears and laughter, tragedy and comedy, constitute the Grand Guignol programmes, but unlike the Romantics, who mixed tears and laughter in the same work, the Grand Guignol separates the emotions and presents comedy and "tragedy" alternately, usually three comedies and two "tragedies". After side-splitting farce comes, as a sort of tragic relief, a play like *La Fosse des jeunes filles* (1926), showing life in a licensed brothel and ending with the sickening sound of a razor, which one of the prostitutes draws across her throat when she realizes that she is diseased, or plays like *Le Rapide 13* (1921), by Jean de Sartène. In this play a signalman has a heart attack just as he is about to pull the lever for the approaching express. His daughter, in a panic, pulls the wrong one and sends the express, in which her child is travelling, hurtling into another train.

Strong nerves were often needed at the Grand Guignol. Charles Foley's plays are particularly gruesome. In *Les Nuits au bagne* (1928), for example, a number of convicts, incensed against a brutal warden, force his head into the trap which he had invented to get rid of a rival. The curtain goes down on the warden's shrieks as his head is being crushed in the machine. It was on one of Foley's stories that de Lorde based *Au Téléphone* (1901),[3] which became the chief classic of the Grand Guignol. In it a man listens helplessly on the telephone while his wife and children are being murdered in their home.

Murders, suicide, and tortures are not a feature of all Grand Guignol terror plays. In some physical horror is replaced by anguish of mind, as in *Le Navire aveugle* (1927). Here Max Maurey depicts the distress of the mysteriously blinded crew of a sailing-vessel, as they listen to the siren of a passing ship, which does not hear their frantic cries, and leaves them to drift with the wind.

In others almost scientific studies of certain *milieux*, hospitals, prisons, lunatic asylums, hitherto avoided by dramatists, and pathological cases properly documented, gave the necessary intellectual and nervous stimulus. André de Lorde considered "nature's crimes", madness, cancer, tuberculosis, as no less interesting dramatically than the "crimes of man", though the critic Francisque Sarcey countered by saying that the theatre should be a school of manners and not of medicine. Madness had a peculiar fascination for de Lorde, who wrote plays on it in collaboration with the psychologist and physiologist Alfred Binet; he also consulted the psychiatrist Gilbert Ballet.

In addition to the specialist writers, de Lorde, Max Maurey, Pierre Chaîne, Maurice Level, Robert Francheville, the Grand Guignol billed playwrights like Henri Lenormand, Alfred Savoir, André-Paul Antoine, Léopold Marchand. Between the wars the quality of the comedy at the Grand Guignol began to improve. Tension caused by the terror plays had been relieved by hilarious farces, presenting some burlesque situation, and having little to recommend them beyond their hilarity. Gradually, however, the director, Jack Jouvin, introduced into the repertory one-act comedies, closely observed and humorous, often with a touch of sentimentality. The curtain-raiser profited from this development, but the subsequent shortening of performances gradually eliminated the curtain-raiser from ordinary theatres. Apart from the Grand Guignol, which closed its doors in November 1962, only the Comédie-Française maintains the tradition of the one-act play.

Following the success of the Paris Grand Guignol, a Grand Guignol was opened in London at the Little Theatre in 1920. It lasted two years and drew largely upon the programmes of the French Grand Guignol. Several of de Lorde's plays were seen there, including At the Telephone and The Hand of Death (L'horrible Expérience), and Max Maurey's The Chemist. There was another short season of Grand Guignol at the Granville, Walham Green, in 1945.

NOTES

1. See Dorothy Knowles, The Censor, the Drama and the Film, pp. 140–142.
2. Performed in English in 1936 as Mademoiselle.
3. Comédie-Française repertory, July 20th, 1920.

XII

Towards a People's Theatre

Romain Rolland—Jean-Richard Bloch—Maurice Pot-
techer and the Théâtre du Peuple at Bussang—
Firmin Gémier—Léon Moussinac and the Théâtre
d'Action International—Théâtre du Peuple 1937—
Henri Ghéon and the Compagnons de Notre Dame—
Henri Brochet and the Compagnons de Jeux—Léon
Chancerel and the Comédiens Routiers—Attempts at
Tragedy: Albert Boussac de Saint Marc—Saint-Georges
de Bouhélier—Paul Demasy—Philippe Fauré-Fré-
miet—Paul Raynal—The Chronicle Play: Paul Fort
—The Verse Play: François Porché.

THE Boulevard theatre caters for upper- and middle-class
audiences. Interesting attempts have been made for some time
to write for working-class audiences, and they have been particularly noticeable since the fifties. The difference of class is not a
difference of intellectual level; there is nothing particularly cultured about the Boulevard theatre; the difference is one of outlook
and interest. The recent rapid development of this movement includes the creation by the Government, shortly after the last war, of
a number of *centres dramatiques* in the provinces, and also the
work of Jean Vilar, as director of the Théâtre National Populaire,
in the Palais de Chaillot in Paris, where he sought for twelve years
(1951–63) to build up a repertory catering for audiences drawn
from all classes of society. He was succeeded in 1963 by Georges
Wilson. A similar experiment made with working-class audiences
in mind was started at the Théâtre de la Cité at Villeurbanne
(Lyon), by Roger Planchon in 1957, and a number of attempts at
the creation of a people's theatre, also with a strong political bias,

have been made in certain working-class areas round Paris like Aubervilliers, Saint-Denis, and Villejuif. In fact, the popular theatre movement has been the most striking phenomenon of French theatrical activity for some time, and it is taking the place of the sorely weakened *avant-garde* theatre. The widening of the theatre audience seems to be stimulating the creation of a new type of drama, firmly integrated into social history, and as far removed from the psychological studies, or the tragic or comic variations on the theme of the eternal triangle, which so often form the subject-matter of plays to be seen on the ordinary commercial stage, as it is from the drama of the absurd.

The idea of a "people's" theatre dates back to the eighteenth century, and an attempt to implement it was made at the time of the French Revolution, when the Théâtre-Français was renamed Le Théâtre du Peuple, and the poets were called upon to drama-tize the principal events of the Revolution. All this came to an end with Thermidor. It was not till over a hundred years later that a vast dramatic epic on the French Revolution, comprising a dozen or so plays, was embarked upon by ROMAIN ROLLAND, who called it *Théâtre de la Révolution*. In his book *Le Théâtre du peuple*, published in 1903, which he subtitled "essai d'esthétique d'un théâtre nouveau", Rolland expresses his hope for the creation of a people's theatre which would set against the flabby refinements of Parisian entertainers a manly, robust art, capable of expressing the collective life of the people and preparing, provoking even, the rebirth of the nation. "The people's theatre is not an article of fashion, a sport for dilettantes. It is the compelling expression of a new society, of its voice and ideas, and it is, by the very nature of things, its weapon in moments of crisis, against an ageing, out-worn society" (Preface). Rolland discovered, however, in 1900, that any attempt to establish a people's theatre to counter the "senile lethargy that had come over the middle-class theatre in France" was premature, "because the people did not as yet exist, it had not yet become fully conscious of its destiny or power". But, by 1936, when Rolland made this statement in *Comœdia* (July 14th), he considered that the people had come into their own and that the time was ripe to found a people's theatre. So he cast his eyes towards the site of the Trocadéro, where the new Théâtre du Palais de Chaillot was eventually to be built.

Rolland's *Théâtre de la Révolution* belongs to the beginning of

the century, but in 1926 he added *Les Pâques fleuries*, which was
to serve as an introduction to the series, with its picture of a fête at
the house of the Prince de Conti disturbed by the presence of
Rousseau. In 1927 he wrote *Le Jeu de l'amour et de la mort*, based
on an incident during the Terror, and in 1938 *Robespierre*, depicting the tragedy of those men of the Revolution who accepted the
necessity of the Terror because without it the cause of the Revolution would have been lost. These plays are all historical, but the
dramatist always intended that a present-day significance should be
read into them, and in France they have always had a political
import. They have usually been played on special occasions, such
as the textile workers' strike in the Nord *département*, in 1900,
when a lecture by Jean Jaurès preceded the performance of *Danton*,
or a pacifist campaign in 1933. Certain performances of his plays
have had the character of public festivals on the lines laid down
in 1794 by the Committee of Public Safety. *Le Jeu de l'amour et de
la mort*[1] was staged at the Comédie-Française on July 5th, 1939,
to celebrate the 150th anniversary of the French Revolution. Earlier
in 1936 a performance of *Le Quatorze juillet* was organized to
commemorate the formation of the Government of the Popular
Front. Firmin Gémier had already staged the play in a Boulevard
theatre in 1902, as one of his first attempts at popular theatre, but
it was a premature attempt, and the play had only twenty-nine
performances, despite a good press. In March 1945, Rolland's
Danton was staged in the Lutèce arena in Paris, to mark the liberation of the city. Twenty years later, in June 1965, it was put on in
the courtyard of the Hôtel Sully for the Festival du Marais, but it
was clear that the play was not in line with what the public had
become accustomed to at the T.N.P., where Vilar had already
staged Büchner's drama on the same subject. Oratorical exchanges
between picture-book images of Danton, Robespierre, and Saint-
Just failed to convince, though when the play was staged at the
time of the Front Populaire they had had a certain resonance.
Despite his shortcomings as a dramatist, Rolland was quoted in
1961 by Jean Vilar,[2] alongside Brecht and Sean O'Casey, as a
dramatist who could appeal to vast, popular audiences. Vilar added
that ten years previously he would never even have thought of
staging a play by Rolland, but times had changed, and indeed the
popular theatre, which opened in the industrial Paris suburb of
Villejuif in 1964, was named after Romain Rolland, and gave, as

its first production, his *Le Temps viendra* (November 25th). The play, which was written in 1902 and is based on the Boer War, had been staged in 1927 by Erwin Piscator, assisted by Brecht, but had not been seen in France. At Villejuif the critics generally noted the continued topicality of the play, but remained divided about it. For some it was an excellent dramatic work and even had a prophetic note; for others it was as theatrically dusty as its theme was commendable. It is not, however, unusual for plays of this type to be roughly handled by the critics, particularly when produced outside the normal Paris theatre-land.

In 1937, for the opening of the Universal Exhibition in Paris, the Popular Front Government, going back to the idea of the public festival, commissioned a collective play, *Vive la liberté*, presenting the history of France as a prelude to the Popular Front. Fourteen well-known dramatists, including Henri Lenormand, who was an active supporter of the cause of popular theatre, Jean-Jacques Bernard, Charles Méré, and Jean-Richard Bloch, wrote various scenes, ranging in time from Rabelais (meeting the "1937 Panurge") through to the assassination of Jean Jaurès, with intervening scenes dealing with the Paris Commune and the Confédération Générale du Travail. Artistically, such a venture could not succeed, nor did it serve to present the democratic ideal. It played to thin middle-class audiences. In November the same year, at the Velodrome d'Hiver, JEAN-RICHARD BLOCH's play *La Naissance d'une cité*, symbolizing the different phases in the development of the life of a "collective", was presented. It was not a good play, but it gave Bloch the chance to learn how to write for mass audiences. His *Toulon*, written after the scuttling of the Toulon Fleet during the German occupation of France, is infinitely superior. It offers a study of the collective life of a nation during the Occupation: the various attitudes adopted by the public, collaboration, resistance, or opportunism. As it was designed for popular audiences it was a mistake to stage it at the Odéon (December 13th, 1945), a family theatre frequented by middle-class season-ticket holders. In any case the condemnation of the Vichy policy contained in the play inevitably provoked opposition at the staid Odéon. *Toulon* conforms to the formula of popular drama expounded by Romain Rolland in his *Théâtre du peuple*; such drama must concern itself with the people's desires and hopes; to quote his well-known statement: "Le théâtre du peuple sera *peuple* ou il ne sera pas." The form of the play was original. At a time when writers like Anouilh, Camus, and Sartre turned to myth or history in order to put forward their own ideas on life, Bloch presented a straightforward fresco in a dozen tableaux, enacted by representative characters (the collaborator, the man of the Resistance movement, the denouncer), without any personal "message". His "message" was a public one. The hostile reception given by the critics and the Odéon audience offered no encouragement to others to write in the same vein, and it is only recently that playwrights like Armand Salacrou, Arthur Adamov, Armand Gatti, and the producer-playwright Roger Planchon have taken up the challenge again. Alongside the political movement has existed a regional one. Over a period of sixty years, beginning in 1895, MAURICE POTTECHER wrote some twenty plays for mass audiences, and staged them in a theatre of his own founding, Le Théâtre du Peuple, at Bussang, in the Vosges. The plays are of a local character or are based on folk-lore. The public is mainly a regional public which assembles on August Sunday afternoons in a large wooden theatre containing 1200 seats. Until 1908 the audience sat in the open air, watching the actors on a wooden stage of traditional design but of which the back could be removed, so as to use as a setting, if so desired, the wooded slope of the mountain behind. This stage is still in use, and, as in the past, the actors, mainly local workers, but excellently trained, perform anonymously, thereby helping to bring out the character of a collective effort, which stamps the whole enterprise. Though Pottecher's political sympathies were with the Left, he did not aim at founding a theatre for the poorer and usually less cultivated classes of society—such a venture would, he considered, best be called a *théâtre populaire*. Instead, he opted for a *théâtre du peuple*, in which spectators from all social classes would mix, for their mutual benefit.

FIRMIN GEMIER, who was to become, in 1920, the first director of the Théâtre National Populaire, newly created by the Government in the old theatre of the Trocadéro in Paris, was also opposed to the idea of the creation of a purely working-class theatre. He was just as opposed to the continuance of theatres for the privileged classes. The standards by which he measured the modern theatre were the ancient Greek theatre and the medieval theatre. His ideal was a theatre for all classes of society, neither *national* nor *popular*, but *collective*, bringing about the communion of the spectators with each other and with the author, in a kind of social religion of which Democracy and Pacifism were the main articles of faith. The notion of "communion", which was central to his conception of the theatre, led him to considerable scenographic innovations. As early as 1917, in his production of François Porché's allegorical war-play *Les Butors et la Finette*, on the Boulevard, at the Théâtre Antoine, he suppressed the barrier of the footlights between the stage and the auditorium, and linked the two together by steps, just as Jacques Copeau was to do two years later in his experimental theatre, the Vieux-Colombier. During the course of the play, when the fête given by the princess was interrupted by the sound of guns, crowds of supernumeraries bearing flags surged up from the auditorium, giving the impression that the audience itself was rushing to the rescue of the princess. This was in 1917, and the princess represented France. Gémier considered that it would not be possible to stage truly popular plays in any other way in the future. The essence of people's theatre was the illusion of being intimately connected with the characters and their fate.

Gémier was keenly critical of the layout of the modern theatre, with its auditorium in separate compartments, isolating various categories of spectators. He advised a return to the architecture of the ancient theatres, with their semi-circular terraced auditorium (roofed over in the rainy north), to allow people of all social conditions to mix together.

In 1919 Gémier decided to stage plays in the Cirque d'Hiver, and chose for his first production *Œdipe, roi de Thèbes*, by Saint-Georges de Bouhélier, a playwright who believed that the highest form of theatrical activity was the popular spectacle. Indeed, Gémier's contact with Bouhélier served to confirm him in his attitude towards the theatre. Bouhélier's play is a very free arrangement of the Oedipus story, much nearer in form and spirit to the medieval Mystery play than to ancient tragedy. It is written in octosyllabic verse and is familiar in style. In his production Gémier developed the spectacular element to the limit, and turned Bouhélier's popular tragedy into an "Olympic show" by adding to it an athletic performance on the massive staircase leading up to the walls of Œdipe's palace, which filled one end of the circus. Some two hundred javelin and discus throwers and high-jumpers, who served as the king's guard, participated in the production, which attracted an enthusiastic audience, but the critics were divided about it. The "Olympic show" was followed by a similar production of a Provençal nativity play, *La grande Pastorale*, by Charles Hellem and Pol d'Estoc, with dancers and animals instead of athletes. Gaston Baty was Gémier's assistant producer. Despite the success which attended this, his third attempt to found a popular theatre, it became clear to Gémier that such an undertaking needed Government or municipal support. His preceding attempt was made in 1911–12, with the Théâtre Ambulant, with thirty-seven caravans drawn by eight traction-engines, which took to the road like a giant circus, carrying productions given in the capital to the public in the provinces. The cost was crippling, but forty years before the Government's creation of the Dramatic Centres, Gémier, with his Théâtre Ambulant, pointed the way to the decentralization of the theatre. He showed himself to be well ahead of his time in this and on most aspects of theatrical development. Seven months after his experiment at the Cirque d'Hiver the Government founded the Théâtre National Populaire and nominated him as its director, but the hall allotted to him, the Trocadéro, in one of the most elegant parts of Paris, together with the conditions laid down by the Government for running it, prevented Gémier from creating the truly popular, or "collective", theatre of which he had dreamed.

In his turn, some ten years after he took over the Théâtre National Populaire, in 1951, Jean Vilar declared that the siting of the theatre in such an elegant part of the town, so far from the working-class districts, accounted to a great extent for the low percentage of working-class people—7 per cent. at most—in his audience. While the present Théâtre National Populaire exists as a theatre, having its own company of actors, Gémier had no troupe, and the theatre was little more than a supplementary building where the repertories of the national theatres could be seen at reduced prices. Consequently, Gémier campaigned to obtain the management of the Odéon, so as to have a permanent company with which to continue his theatrical experiments. He succeeded in getting it in 1922. But the Odéon was too far removed in spirit from a popular theatre, such as Gémier had created for a time at the Cirque d'Hiver, and anything like the "Olympic shows" he had put on there were unthinkable in its precincts. When he began to lose interest in the Odéon it was because he had come to realize the pointlessness of presenting programmes cut to measure for the

Odéon audiences at the Théâtre National Populaire, whose audiences they did not suit. Nor was he able, as director of the Théâtre National Populaire, to organize the great civic festivals which he considered to be the culminating point of theatrical activity. "Each festival", he said, "will be one act of an immense play which will dramatize the life of the people and which will be performed by the people themselves."[3] Gémier had already proved himself a master of this type of theatrical activity—for example, in 1903, at the festival held in Lausanne to mark the 100th anniversary of the entry of the canton of Vaud into the Swiss Confederation. On that occasion he handled some 2400 actors, and also drew the audience into active participation in the drama that was being enacted. After his disappointment with the Odéon (he resigned the management in 1930), and with the Théâtre National Populaire, Gémier pursued his plans for the Société Universelle du Théâtre which was to bring together all people concerned with the theatre and so help to promote international understanding and goodwill. It was to organize each year, in some large town in Europe, a theatrical congress and an international festival of dramatic art. The first of these festivals was held in Paris in 1927, the last in London in 1938. Gémier himself died in 1933. During some forty years of active work in the theatre he proved himself to be a tireless pioneer. Many of his technical innovations, considered scandalous at the time, are now commonplace. Jean Vilar was clearly conscious of having taken over from where Gémier left off, and perhaps the international theatre festival, which has been held every year in Paris in May and June since 1954, owes something to Gémier's inspiration.

As far as theatre for the working-class is concerned, the most interesting experiment between the two World Wars was the Théâtre d'Action International, in 1932, with LEON MOUSSINAC as its artistic director. For the Théâtre d'Action Internationale group, which looked to Erwin Piscator for inspiration, the term "popular theatre" meant "political theatre", always provided that it was at the service of a great idea and not a mere programme or policy, and that it was real art. The declared aim of the group was to reveal to the French public the most representative works of the new revolutionary literature from outside France, and thus act as a stimulus for the creation of a similarly revolutionary literature within the country. Of several productions proposed, only three were actually carried out: *Miracle à Verdun*, by Hans Chlumberg, *Le Train blindé No. 14–69*, by Vsevolod Ivanov, which Stanislavsky had staged in 1927 at the Moscow Arts Theatre, and *Acide prussique*, by Friedrich Wolf. These were put on at the Bouffes-du-Nord, in a working-class area of Paris, before audiences drawn from the intelligentsia as well as the working-class. But the intelligentsia stayed away after the second production. They deemed Ivanov's play, which presents an incident in the partisan war in East Siberia in 1919, to be too frankly political, and the experiment came to an end. A theatrical venture requires more than a clearly defined doctrine to assure its future; it requires a stable public, and an initial series of plays of domestic social criticism might well have attracted the public more readily to the Théâtre d'Action International and provided a better preparation for the viewing of foreign revolutionary works of this kind.

In 1937 an organization called Le Théâtre du Peuple, which was linked with the trade unions, staged three works in six months at the Renaissance Theatre, before moving into the large municipal theatre, the Théâtre Sarah-Bernhardt, to play Victor Margueritte's dramatic version of Gorky's novel, *The Mother*, to trade-union members. But the experiment came to an end when the Town Council withdrew the concession allowing the free use of the theatre, earlier made by it to the theatrical group on whose invitation Le Théâtre du Peuple had moved into the theatre. Henri Lenormand, who gave the venture his active support, deplores, in his *Confessions*, the fact that even under a Popular Front Government the notion of a people's theatre should meet with such strong opposition.

A type of popular theatre which differed entirely from deliberately working-class theatre, and also theatre that is directed to large audiences formed from all social classes mixed together, is to be found in the work of HENRI GHEON. After his conversion to Roman Catholicism during the First World War, in which he served as a surgeon, Ghéon had the idea of Christian drama for a Christian public, and proceeded to write a large number of plays for performance by Catholic charity organizations and in modest open-air theatres. The collective title, *Jeux et Miracles pour le peuple fidèle*, given by Ghéon to two volumes of his plays, published in 1923 and 1924, defines not only their type but also their aim. The preface states clearly Ghéon's intention of using the theatre to make the Christian faith "more concrete", and to incorporate it into the daily life of the faithful by revealing the humanity of the saints, who, like ordinary men, had been subject to temptation. The popular Christian repertory which he proposed to constitute was to be addressed to all Christians, without distinction of age or culture, from the man in the street to the man of letters, and was intended in the first place for performances arranged by Church societies. Ghéon also founded, in 1924, Les Compagnons de Notre Dame, a group of some thirty men and women, all practising Catholics, and for the most part non-professional actors, who rapidly established themselves as a body of players capable of holding a Paris theatre audience by the performances of Mystery plays, farces, and pageants, written along medieval lines by modern authors. The majority were by Ghéon himself and by HENRI BROCHET. The Compagnons' technique—their stylized settings and acting, the introduction of music and dancing into their performances—showed the influence of Jacques Copeau's ideas. Under Ghéon's direction the Compagnons gave numerous performances in the provinces and Belgium as well as in Paris. After their last performance in 1931 Ghéon concentrated on writing plays for religious communities, religious festivals, and for groups like the Compagnons de Jeux, which followed on from the Compagnons de Notre Dame and was directed by Henri Brochet. Their performances included Ghéon's Le Mystère du feu vivant sur les apôtres, in the Arènes de Lutèce, at Whitsuntide, 1935, and his Suzanne et les vieillards, at the Paris Exhibition in 1937. Another group to aim at raising Catholic drama above the usual amateur level of the Church guilds was LEON CHANCEREL's Comédiens Routiers. This group arose within the French Scout movement in 1929, and was constituted on the lines followed by Copeau, with his "Copiaus", and later by la Compagnie des Quinze. It had a similar training, and, unlike the Compagnons de Notre Dame and the Compagnons de Jeux, did not concentrate on religious drama (nativity plays and passion plays), but turned its attention mainly to medieval farce, mime, spoken choral work, and Molière plays, such as Le Mariage forcé and Les Fourberies de Scapin. Two years before he started the Routiers' work Chancerel published a remarkable letter in Le Journal (April 2nd, 1927), in which he suggested something similar to what Roger Planchon has recently achieved at the Théâtre de la Cité, at Villeurbanne, and others at Aubervilliers and Saint-Denis. Chancerel suggested that factories, or groups of factories, should provide fully equipped theatres, with resident companies and playwrights working in them on the same terms as workers in the factories. He hoped for the day when the "Citroën Theatre" would compete for the first prize with the "Peugeot Theatre". Even Planchon has not tried anything quite so ambitious as this.

Of Ghéon's own plays the best is Le Pauvre sous l'escalier, which Copeau staged at the Vieux-Colombier on January 24th, 1921. It tells the story of Saint Alexis, who felt the call to the vocation of poverty on the day of his marriage, and who returned seventeen years later, unrecognized, to beg a humble place under the stairs of the rich household of which he was the lawful master. The effect of his presence on his "widow", whom he still cherishes, forms the theme of the play, but the perfect sanctity of the hero and Ghéon's failure to show the hero's struggle against the temptations of the world detract from the dramatic effect of the work. Le Comédien et la grâce ou le comédien pris à son jeu, published in 1925, tells the same story as Rotrou's Saint Genest (1646), but aims at studying the man as well as the actor, and also the effect of grace. According to Ghéon, he had been inspired to write the play by seeing certain actors, who had taken part in the plays he had written for a popular Christian theatre, being brought, like Saint Genest, from indifference in religious matters to belief and prayer. Among the plays written to commemorate a special occasion are Le Triomphe de Saint-Aquin, celebrating the 600th anniversary of the canonization of Thomas Aquinas, and Le Jeu des grandes heures de Rheims, which was performed in front of the cathedral to mark its restoration in 1938. A number of Ghéon's plays have been seen on the professional stage; they include Le Damné pour manque de confiance, which was put on in 1944 at the Palais de Chaillot by the Théâtre National Populaire, then under the direction of Pierre Aldebert, and the performance by the Compagnie des Quinze at the Vieux-Colombier on February 22nd, 1933, of Violante, adapted by Ghéon from Tirso de Molina's La Villana de Vallecas. It is a non-religious play and provides a curious contrast to his other work.

On June 14th–16th, 1935, in front of Notre Dame Cathedral, a shortened version of an authentic Mystery play, Le vrai Mistère de la Passion, written about 1452 by Arnoul Gréban, was produced by Pierre Aldebert. As might have been expected from a disciple of

Gémier, there was a marked insistence on the visual element in the production, and the 500 performers were made to mingle with the audience, to bring about the "communion" of public and actors which Gémier saw as the essential element in every true theatrical experience.

Attempts at Tragedy

At the Odéon, in addition to continuing the experimental work which he had begun as director of the Comédie-Montaigne in 1920–21, Gémier aimed quite clearly at exploiting the popular vein he had opened up at the Cirque d'Hiver. He staged a number of plays by Saint-Georges de Bouhélier, Paul Demasy, Paul Raynal, and Philippe Fauré-Frémiet, all writers of tragedy, some in verse, some in prose. Each summer, from the 1890's onward, tragedies, particularly neo-classical tragedies by Leconte de Lisle, Jean Moréas, Joséphin Péladan, Alfred Poizet, Alfred Mortier, were staged in the great Roman theatres and arenas of Orange, Nîmes, Arles, Saintes, and modern open-air theatres like Béziers, though Péladan's grandiose verse trilogy, La Prométhéide, written in 1904, was given, virtually, its first performance only in 1949 at the Théâtre National Populaire, under the management of Pierre Aldebert. From the early twenties, when this type of play ceased to be written, Greek sources were used in a totally different way. Writers like André Gide, Jean Cocteau, Jean Giraudoux, Jean Anouilh, or Jean-Paul Sartre, were not interested in ancient stage-craft or poetics, nor in making translations or mere adaptations of tragedies of Aeschylus, Sophocles, or Euripides. They saw in the ancient myths an ideal medium for the discussion of the human predicament and the problems of modern life. Those who made a bid to write tragedy looked elsewhere for their inspiration. SAINT-GEORGES DE BOUHELIER and PAUL RAYNAL represent the two extremes of dramatic procedure. Bouhélier believed in the sacred character conferred on the theatre by its Eleusinian origins, and prophesied in the preface to La Tragédie du nouveau Christ (1901) that "the theatre will shortly become a place for the celebration of sacred rites in which the people may participate". This conception of theatre was near in spirit to Gémier's. On the other hand, with plays like Maître de son cœur and his much dis-cussed war play Le Tombeau sous l'Arc de Triomphe, Paul Raynal was clearly aiming at tragedies of the will on Cornelian lines, bare of all ornament. ALBERT BOUSSAC DE SAINT MARC seems to have believed in both types. He called his first play *Le Loup de Gubbio* (1921), which points by its title to a parallel between his heroine, a mystic, and Saint Francis of Assisi, an "Eleusinian drama". In *L'Amour vaincu* (1925) his Cornelian heroine talks constantly of her *gloire*. His *Moloch* was produced at the Comédie-Française on December 22nd, 1926. Boussac believed in the desirability of heroic figures and elevating subjects in the theatre, but the practical application of his theory was a failure.

There is some of the same straining after greatness in Bouhélier, but Bouhélier's attempt, as a self-styled "naturist", at a compromise between conflicting dramatic theories, the naturalists' and the symbolists', particularly in *Le Carnaval des enfants* (1910) and *La Vie d'une femme* (1919), is interesting. The tableau form used in the latter play was relatively new at the time; it is an architectural conception and not a psychological device, as in the plays of Henri Lenormand. In its original form *La Tragédie du nouveau Christ*— that is, of every thinker or poet whose teaching is scorned and whose suffering is dedicated to the redemption of man—was unplayable: the streets, public squares, and all the people in them would have been needed to provide the setting. A revised version, *Le Roi sans couronne*, was, however, staged in 1906 at the Théâtre des Arts, and this version constitutes a decisive step by Bouhélier towards epic drama. In fact, Bouhélier describes as "dramatic epics" a later series of historical plays, *Le Sang de Danton* (Comédie-Française, June 2nd, 1931), *Napoléon* (Odéon, February 24th, 1933), and *Jeanne d'Arc* (Odéon, November 21st, 1934), which aimed at showing the ordinary humanity of these characters behind the legendary figures. All Bouhélier's plays are in multiple tableau form and require large casts. In his first cycle of modern tragedies, written at the beginning of the century, he attempted to show the struggle of man against machine, a machine of which the very cogs and pinions are men themselves. This view of life is given particularly clear expression in the dramatic parable *Les Esclaves*. Though the hero is a soldier in revolt, the army is intended only as a symbol of society, and the barrack wall behind which are to be heard the bugle-calls is the moral prison of an implacably ordered life. The play was written in 1906 but was performed only in 1920, on April 25th, at the Théâtre des Arts, with

Gaston Baty as its producer. Baty undertook the production immediately after the experiment with Gémier at the Cirque d'Hiver.

However, Bouhélier saw other than social forces shaping a man's destiny. "It seems to me", he wrote in the preface to *La Vie d'une femme* (Odéon, February 8th, 1919), "that a man carries his fate within himself ... that it is ... the spontaneous creation of his own passions, instincts and temperaments." Both this play and *Le Carnaval des enfants*, which was first performed at the Théâtre des Arts in 1910 and later went to the Odéon and then into the repertory of the Comédie-Française, put forward this conception of life. Both are set in very humble surroundings and are an attempt to revive poetic tragedy on the basis of "truth". These are Bouhélier's five best plays. After them ranks *La célèbre Histoire* (Mathurins-Pitoëff, April 24th, 1928), which offers a curious modernization of Hamlet's mentality. It stands midway between Bouhélier's modern tragedies and a subsequent series of verse plays on legendary themes. The series opens with *Œdipe, roi de Thèbes* and includes *La Tragédie de Tristan et d'Yseult*, which was given the same free treatment by Gémier at the Odéon, on February 8th, 1923, as *Œdipe* had received at the Cirque d'Hiver. *L'Impératrice aux rochers*, written for Ida Rubinstein, was performed at the Opéra on February 21st, 1927. It was the second of his works to be performed there, the first being *La Fête triomphale*, a dramatic poem in three parts, with songs and dances to music by Reynaldo Hahn. It was staged on July 14th, 1919, to mark the Peace celebrations. Bouhélier was not the only playwright to attempt the grand manner. The Belgian playwright PAUL DEMASY composed a *Tragédie d'Alexandre*, which was staged at the Renaissance in 1919, a *Tragédie du Docteur Faust*, a *César Borgia*, and a *Jésus de Nazareth*, this last being put on by Gémier at the Odéon in 1924. Gémier also staged his *Dalilah* (1922). Demasy continued until 1933 with his efforts to revive tragedy: *Milmort* (1933) is strongly reminiscent of *The Cenci*.

Both Bouhélier and Demasy understood the revival of tragedy in terms of the revival of well-known tragic themes. Among the dramatists who sought to write tragedy by returning to the dramatic form and the psychological or moral analysis of the French classical masters was PHILIPPE FAURE-FREMIER, son of the composer Gabriel Fauré. He was a disciple of Corneille. Each play is centred on a moral problem. In the one-act play *L'Exilé* (1922), in *Sic vos non vobis* (1924), and in *Le Souffle du désordre*, which Gémier revived at the Odéon on January 10th, 1928, after its performances in 1922 and 1923 by the theatre group La Grimace, the sublime is sought in the triumph over the passions, which was the accepted way of interpreting Corneille at the time. Though *Le Souffle du désordre* closes on the explicit statement that duty comes before love, there are a number of ideas in the play that owe nothing to Corneille. The study of Antoine's jealousy, when he sees his brother enjoying the happiness he had denied himself by mastering his love for a married woman, is a sort of denial of his own thesis. The playwright moves further away from his original model in his war-play *La Grand' geste du monde* (1927), which is a large satirical fresco constructed on a pattern similar to that used in 1932 by Kurt Jooss in his satirical ballet *The Green Table*.

Paul Raynal, Corneille's most authentic disciple, is best known for his controversial war play *Le Tombeau sous l'Arc de Triomphe*. It is significant that Gémier staged it at the Odéon after Raynal had withdrawn it from the Comédie-Française, where, between 1924 and 1927, it was given only thirty-two performances.[4]

His first play, *Le Maître de son cœur* (Odéon, June 25th, 1920),[5] which set the pattern, from the technical point of view, both of *Le Tombeau sous l'Arc de Triomphe* and *Le Soleil de l'instinct*, was considered at the time to be a model of modern tragedy. In retrospect it appears as a model of the pseudo-classical play; it is stilted and artificial. There are three main characters, two friends, Henri and Simon, and a woman, and the theme is the clash between love and friendship. The woman is jealous of the bond that unites the two men and seeks to destroy it, but is ordered by the elder of the two, who remains "master of his heart", to accept the younger man's love. The play ends tragically with the death of the younger man, who believes that he has been betrayed both by his friend and the woman he loves. Raynal uses the same theme in *Le Soleil de l'instinct* and gives it an unpleasant twist. Once again nothing is known about the characters except their names. The emotional conflict alone carries weight, and the dissection of the feelings is so minute as to suggest the technique of a novelist rather than a dramatist. A single setting serves throughout the play, and the style bears little relation to that of ordinary speech.

In *Le Tombeau sous l'Arc de Triomphe* there are again three characters, a soldier, who is never more specifically named, his father, and his fiancée, Aude. The action, which takes place in one house, needs hardly more time than that of the actual performance, since it consists of a rapidly reached crisis. Every word of the dialogue is very obviously "written", and feelings are expressed in tirades of a length quite exceptional in the modern theatre. This rhetorical style came in for keen criticism in France, and also in England, where the play has been staged, with cuts by the censor, at various times between 1928 and 1948, but, despite the rhetoric, English audiences and critics, at the various revivals, have praised the poignancy of the situation. In 1928 Bernard Shaw, in typical fashion, said of the play: "It is far better than anything I have written. It is almost worth having a war to have a play like this."

The story is that of the soldier who accepts his fiancée's gift of herself when he is home on a few hours' leave before undertaking an extremely dangerous mission, and the conflict which subsequently arises with his father, but the theme of the play is the same as Paul Géraldy's in his collection of short stories, *La Guerre, Madame* (1916)—namely, the rift between soldiers at the front and the non-combatants comfortably installed in their homes and profiting from the opportune absence of the young. In the twenties the play was still too unpleasantly topical for it not to encounter strong resistance. It was more successful when it was revived at the Comédie in 1932, but the Second World War, which did away with the distinction between a fighting front line and a safe population behind it, has taken much of the point out of the play. It is easy to question the logic of the characters' actions and arguments, to wonder why Raynal should have invented the "moral incest" of the father in a play intended to pit the soldier against the civilian, but the play stands as a condemnation of the so-called glorious adventure of war.

La Francerie (Comédie-Française, March 21st, 1933) takes the form of a running commentary on the course of the battle of the Marne, by a woman and a boy of sixteen, both French, and a German colonel who is convinced that the fate of mankind is best placed in Germany's hands. All three are in a house behind the German lines. The opposition developed between the French characters and the German is symbolic of the opposition between the two nations.

Napoléon unique (Porte-Saint-Martin, April 26th, 1939), which follows, went into the repertory of the Odéon on March 10th, 1942: the love interest is at the centre of the play, though the fact related is Napoleon's repudiation of Joséphine for political reasons.

A souffert sous Ponce Pilate (Comédie-Française, April 26th, 1939) contains some of the best scenes Raynal had written so far, though the play as a whole is the least satisfactory. The main theme is Judas's betrayal of Christ and the reason for it; Raynal's simple-minded Judas hands Christ over for preventive arrest to save Him from a worse fate. Judas's obvious simplicity of mind leaves no possibility of action in the play, which offers only a psychological study. Pilate is more interesting, and is shown to be strongly attracted by the novelty of Christ's teaching.

Raynal's best play is undoubtedly *Le Matériel humain* (Renaissance, February 14th, 1948). It is based on the story of Corporal Lefèvre, who threatened an officer with his rifle and was ordered to be shot by Pétain. Raynal's theme is the impossibility of stopping the functioning of the military machine once it has been set in motion, even though everybody disagrees with the course it is taking. Raynal also puts the question of the importance of the individual, the "Human material", as against that of the success of a cause, and points to the difficulty of remaining a man while becoming a great leader. The unity of the play is adversely affected by Raynal's attempt to cover so many different aspects of war at once, and also by the discrepancy between the incident which causes the trouble—it is a private's dirty, torn tie which a young officer takes exception to—and the importance of the issue alluded to—the widespread mutinies in the French armies in 1917. However, despite the technical flaws, the play grips. It is also innocent of the rhetoric characteristic of his earlier plays. Though the happy end is not in the tradition of tragedy, the atmosphere which Raynal creates in the play is certainly that of tragedy.

In Raynal's previous works his aim was not drama, with its realistic representation of daily life—for a realistic scene of this kind one must turn to the first and last scenes of *Le Matériel humain*, in which a group of soldiers on the Macedonian front wait expectantly for leave passes. Raynal aims at tragedy, together with all the theatrical convention proper to it. His characters are given heroic proportions and sometimes, as in *Le Tombeau*, they succeed in being extremely moving.

The Chronicle Play

With PAUL FORT's chronicle plays, which he staged at the Odéon, Gémier pursued the line of his "vieille France" production at the Cirque d'Hiver. Paul Fort, who was crowned Prince of Poets in 1912, had been associated with the theatre from the age of eighteen as director of the Théâtre d'Art, a theatre group which he founded in 1890, in reaction against the commercial stage. It was an experimental theatre like André Antoine's Théâtre Libre, but repudiated Antoine's realism. In 1893 Fort deserted the theatre for poetry, but Gémier's work to achieve a national popular theatre gave him the idea for the series of plays he called "Chronicles of France". Le Camp du drap d'or contains a tribute to Gémier. Fort's "chronicles", representing significant moments in the nation's history and consisting of a series of picturesque panels, linked by only the slightest thread of an action, are not true dramatic works. Fort did not know how to create characters or dramatic action, or how to write dialogue, but he did know how to create colourful pictures—Louis XI at the siege of Liège, Louis XI and La Balue in his iron cage, the baptism of the Dauphin. His "chronicles" are not intended to be truly historical; they present events magnified and simplified. The series begins with Louis XI, curieux homme (Odéon, November 18th, 1921), which is an arrangement for the stage of an episode from one of his volumes of Ballades françaises, "Le Roman de Louis XI". Les Compères du roi Louis (Comédie-Française, June 21st, 1926) forms the second panel, and Ysabeau, which Gémier staged at the Odéon, on October 16th, 1924, constitutes the third. Gémier also staged L'Or ou une matinée de Philippe le bel (May 26th, 1927). The series continues with Ruggieri ou les fantômes, Guillaume le bâtard ou la conquête de l'Angleterre, and L'Assaut de Paris, "cantos", to quote Léon Uhl,[6] "of a gigantic national epic, a French Iliad, which was taking shape under Fort's pen". Not all these plays have been performed and others announced were not written.

In his last years at the Odéon Gémier turned for a second time for a play to Romain Rolland, whose book Le Théâtre du peuple had for long been an inspiration to him. He chose Le Jeu de l'amour et de la mort (January 27th, 1928), and in the part of Jérôme de Courvoisier obtained his last, and one of his greatest, successes as an actor. This is Rolland's best play, and the Comédie-

Française revived it in 1939 for the 150th anniversary of the Revolution. A striking moment in the action is provided by Jérôme's description of the sitting of the Convention at which Danton's arrest was voted. The tone of the play is that of the heroic epic, which Rolland believed to be ideally suited to the popular theatre.

The Verse Play

FRANÇOIS PORCHE, whose war play Les Butors et la Finette, well seconded by the originality of Gémier's production, had had such success in 1917 as a patriotic demonstration, was one of the two regular writers of verse plays for the French stage after the First World War. The other was MAURICE ROSTAND, who attempted, unsuccessfully, to repeat his father's popular successes with romantic verse plays written for the Boulevard.

Porché's plays, La jeune Fille aux joues roses (1919), La Dauphine (1921), Le Chevalier de Colomb (1922), follow the tradition of Les Butors et la Finette, which symbolizes the invasion of the land of la Finette (France) by les Butors (the Germans). The subtitle of La Vierge au grand cœur, "La Mission, les Travaux et la Passion de Jeanne d'Arc", underlines Porché's leanings towards festival drama. The plays are all in verse, and so is La Race errante (Odéon, March 15th, 1932), the third act of which takes place, in part, in the New York Stock Exchange. Porché considered the alexandrine too rhetorical for the modern theatre and preferred to mix the verse forms, the alexandrine itself, the octosyllabic line, a still shorter line rhyming irregularly, and also blank verse. He would pass in the same play from verse to prose for unheroic characters. Besides writing verse drama, Porché constituted himself champion of the art of the verse play, writing articles and manifestos and lecturing on the subject. It is ironical that the only play of his which is still performed is a prose play, Un Roi, deux Dames et un Valet, which relates the final eviction of Madame de Montespan from the Court of Louis XIV, in 1691, by Madame de Maintenon. His other prose play, Le Tsar Lénine, an expressionistic piece of which the theme is aptly defined by the title, provoked considerable opposition when Charles Dullin performed it in 1931. A year later Dullin, a believer in popular theatre, staged Porché's version, written in prose with some verse, of Aristophanes' The Peace. It proved as compelling for Dullin's intelligentsia audiences as Jean Vilar's version, with its distinctly topical slant, did for the wider audience of the Théâtre National Populaire, in 1961–62.

To all intents and purposes the verse play ceased to exist after the First World War; the reason, paradoxically enough, was the increased feeling for poetry of the rising generation of play-wrights, who, finding the rhymed verse of the theatre devoid of poetic quality and inadequate for the expression of their aspirations, had begun to look for poetry elsewhere, even in prose. Giraudoux's prose was far more poetic than all the rhymed couplets of Maurice Rostand. This gulf between verse and dramatic poetry, to which Maeterlinck's playlets pointed as early as 1890, became even more obvious with the works of Fernand Crommelynck, Armand Salacrou, Jean Cocteau, Jules Supervielle, and, of course, Jean Giraudoux, whose La Guerre de Troie n'aura pas lieu, it might be added, was one of the last of Jean Vilar's productions for the Théâtre National Populaire, and was given at the Avignon Theatre Festival in 1962, and then at the Palais de Chaillot in Paris.[7]

The weakness of all these attempts at people's theatre made between the wars has two sources. The first is the condescending attitude of dramatists and producers. The second is the confusion between theatre and festivals. Roger Planchon, the director of the theatre at Villeurbanne, commits neither of these errors. He produces drama which is first and foremost drama, in a theatre which is first and foremost a theatre. It is drama which has a working-class bias, openly and deliberately, just as the ordinary Paris theatres have an upper- or middle-class bias in all they do, and it is a theatre where working-people are on their own ground. He also happens to be the cleverest producer at present at work in France, and the playwrights whose work he sponsors are first-rate craftsmen. In a theatre such factors count.

NOTES

1. Revived at the Comédie-Française on January 26th, 1966, to mark the centenary of Rolland's birth.
2. Arts, April 12th–18th.
3. Paul Gsell, Gémier, Le Théâtre, 1925, p. 283.
4. Revived, Comédie-Française, May 23rd, 1932.

5. Revived, Comédie-Française, January 31st, 1937.
6. *Odéon-Magazine*, quoted from "La Petite Illustration" (*Théâtre*, Nouvelle Série No. 131), 1924.
7. In a public discussion at Avignon following his production of the play there for the Theatre Festival, Vilar defended it against the accusation that it was a "purely literary piece of the 1930's"; he insisted that it was extremely "topical" and therefore in its place in a "popular theatre". The actor Alfred Simon pointed out on the same occasion that the war is started by Hector because a weapon happens to be at hand. Nowadays press-button weapons are at the disposal of Governments. Mentioning a flight of wild ducks which, according to the Press, almost precipitated atomic "retaliation" by the Americans, he affirmed the continued topicality of the play which shows the permanent danger accruing from the world's failure to disarm.

Postscript

UNTIL the end of the Second World War the French theatre-land was bounded by the Place de la République, the Place de l'Etoile, Montmartre, and the Latin Quarter. The working-class suburbs were remote from it. Theatrical activity was aimed at supplying what people with money wanted, and they did not want to be annoyed by having things said that did not amuse or flatter them. The *avant-garde* movement was in opposition to "after-dinner drama" but did not establish any contact with a popular audience. It was described by Copeau, in 1941, in an essay entitled *Le Théâtre populaire*, as a "little theatre movement". "Little theatres" were laboratories where new dramatic techniques were experimented with and the best traditions of the stage were revived, but they had no contact with the general public; what they offered to such audiences as they managed to attract was pleasure of a special kind, "luxury pleasures", "egoistic pleasures", as Copeau says, intended for a special kind of consumer. As opposed to this Copeau wanted the drama to be "living" drama, and by that he meant "popular" drama. It had to offer its audiences, composed of ordinary people, a means of giving real significance to their lives. It could only be Marxist or Christian, he concluded. Today, with the T.N.P., the *centres dramatiques*, and theatrical ventures like that of Roger Planchon at Villeurbanne, the theatre appears, indeed, to be finding its meaning. To quote Armand Gatti, a playwright whose works have been produced only by these popular theatre centres: "The theatre is a perpetual means of acquiring freedom." It is also finding its public, a much wider public than hitherto; for example, out of 30,000 season-ticket holders at the Théâtre de la Cité in Villeurbanne, in 1964, 27,000 had never set foot in a theatre until they went to see Planchon's productions. An entirely new phase of theatrical history is at present being lived through in France, but apart from Planchon, who openly declares that he does not belong in any way to the tradition of the Cartel, many of those who are making this new theatrical history owe much to Copeau and the Cartel. Jean Dasté, at the Comédie de Saint-Etienne, and Michel Saint-Denis, formerly at the Comédie de l'Est in Strasbourg, are personally related to Copeau. Jean Vilar (T.N.P.) and Maurice Sarrazin (*Centre dramatique de Toulouse*) were formed by Charles Dullin, and so was Claude Martin, who played his banned *Drame à Toulon* on city squares and village-greens all over France, and even near the prison walls in Brest, where Henri Martin, the hero of the play, was confined. It was also Claude Martin who undertook, in 1962, the production of Arthur Adamov's play on the Paris Commune, *Le Printemps 71*, in the working-class suburb of Saint-Denis. Hubert Gignoux (*Centre dramatique de l'Ouest*), like many others, began his career with Léon Chancerel's Comédiens Routiers, and Georges Douking, once a member of Gaston Baty's company, succeeded Baty at the *Centre dramatique d'Aix-en-Provence.*

In Paris the work of the Cartel was extended between the two wars by Jean Marchat and Marcel Herrand (Rideau de Paris), Raymond Rouleau, Pierre Valde, and André Barsacq, and was continued by them after the last war. Barsacq, who founded, together with Jean Dasté and Maurice Jacquemont, the Compagnie des Quatre Saisons in 1936, took over the Atelier from Dullin in 1940. It is significant that theatre groups such as the Compagnie des Quatre Saisons were particularly active in the late thirties, offering a stage to young authors like Anouilh at a time when the Cartel, with the exception of the ever-eclectic Pitoëff, were limiting themselves to their favourite authors, Dullin to the Elizabethans, the old Spanish masters, and Pirandello, Jouvet to Giraudoux and Molière's *L'Ecole des femmes*, and Baty to his own adaptations of novels. The theatre groups compensated for this growing limitation of programmes resorted to by the established *avant-garde* theatres, so contrary to the spirit of the experimental stage, of which the business must be to discover new authors and new works whatever the risk.

Twenty years of experimentation in the *avant-garde* theatres had produced a number of individual successes, but no particular recipe had been concocted for a good and successful play. Playwrights knew what they did not want. They did not want realism. They did not want narrative. Jean Anouilh declared in 1956[1] that he, along with many fellow-dramatists, from Giraudoux to Achard and Salacrou, had set their teeth ever since the First

World War against the play that merely told a story, they had also aimed at discrediting the notion of the "well-made play". Salacrou, commenting on Anouilh's remark, made it clear that by "well-made play" one had to understand here, plays following the old conventions, and not well-written plays, in a more general sense. A new set of techniques had, in fact, been invented by the *avant-garde* playwrights of his generation, so that a play could very well be skilfully composed without conforming to any one given pattern. As far as the dramatic situation is concerned the old conception of what constituted it had been discarded. It was quite often the mental state of one of the characters, rather than a clearly defined set of material factors to which the various characters were supposed to react, or in which a certain problem was solved, which was taken as the "situation". The new dramatists' use of tableau form, flash-backs, and accelerated time produced a flexibility of structure quite foreign to the pre-1914 theatre. At the same time the oldest of the dramatic themes were used afresh; Greek characters were adapted, as Cocteau put it, to the "rhythm of the times", or, as in *Les Parents terribles*, fundamental Greek themes were used with modern characters and realistic settings. These modernizations were, for the most part, the work of writers who were novelists and poets before they were dramatists. The creation of a *théâtre écrit*, as distinct from a *théâtre parlé*, was consequent on the return to the theatre of the novelists and poets.

The advent of the literati raised again the old issue of the relative importance of literary style and of staging. During the few years preceding the 1939–45 war, however, most producers seemed possessed by a passion for lavish settings and symphonic compositions of lighting effects. Even Jouvet, who sponsored a writer for whom style constituted the basis of drama—namely, Giraudoux—seemed to be affected by this craze. That he should have summoned up all his inventiveness in order to enrich an indigent text like Marcel Achard's *Le Corsaire* is understandable, but it was surprising to see him, shortly afterwards, smother an opulent text like *Ondine* in a similar wealth of stage effects. Pitoëff alone abstained from the orgy, and, in 1938, described staging as a lost soul which, in the previous twenty years, had travelled so far, done so many things, tried on so many garbs, and lived in so many different climates, that it no longer knew what it wanted.

As against the Cartel, which was so much in the public eye,

Antonin Artaud, little known at the time and neglected until recently, can now be seen to have exercised a more subtle and lasting influence than the recognized masters. His influence was negative in the first place and may well explain his friend Arthur Adamov's rejection of psychological analysis at the time when he was a leading figure of the Theatre of the Absurd. At that time Adamov was reacting against what he called *théâtre dialogué*, by which he meant such plays as those of Anouilh and Achard. His opposition was shared by several others, including Beckett and Ionesco, who had similarly come to think of drama in terms of "visible theatrical situations". Just as Adamov's condemnation of theatre which was "reduced to the dimension of language alone" was in line with Artaud's, so was his insistence on the need for inventing a "concrete and physical form" (*concrète et corporelle*) which would "coincide" with the fundamental idea in the drama. Plays like his *La Parodie*, *L'Invasion*, *La grande et la petite Manœuvre*, provide excellent illustrations of such a conception of drama and of Artaud's influence. In Samuel Beckett's *Oh! les beaux jours* (*Happy Days*) every movement, right down to the closing or opening of the eyes, is foreseen and demanded by the playwright, and Jean Vauthier publishes texts in which voluminous stage-directions down one half of the page need to be read simultaneously with the text which is intended to be spoken. If such plays get no further than the printed word they cannot, of course, produce any immediate impact, and Adamov mentions this in reference to his *La Parodie* and *L'Invasion*, but they contribute to critical and theoretical discussion.

Adamov also appreciated Artaud's treatment of theatrical space, his method of peopling the stage and then clearing it as part of the "necessary magical operation" that has to take place on the dramatic stage as on that of opera. Where he was later to differ from Artaud was on the reasons behind this treatment of space. It was after seeing Soviet films like *The Battleship Potemkin* that he had come to believe that it should not be dependent on any purely formal development but should be dictated by specific circumstances, such as a strike which fills the stage with people, and its repression which empties it, and, as far as possible, by a specific ideology.

Recent experiments, unique in France, by Michel Parent, in Dijon (1962–65), during the Festivals of the *Nuits de Bourgogne*,

would seem to link up with Artaud's ideas on the need for abandoning the architecture of present-day theatres, so as to establish a
new form of communication between the audience and the players.
Artaud wanted the audience, which would be seated in the centre
of the hall, to be assailed on all sides by the action, which would
take place round it and up against the four walls of the hall. In
Dijon they preferred to set up four stages round the walls of the
hall, and, with simultaneous actions, force the spectator to choose,
as he does in the real life of which he is a part, those aspects of the
action which were of direct concern to him.

The notion of "total theatre" with which Artaud, Baty, and
Barrault have all been connected, has received its fullest expression
so far in *La Reine verte* (1963), which was the work not of a playwright but of a producer and choreographer, Maurice Béjart, who
wrote the dramatic text himself. His declared ambition was to
write only for the *théâtre total*, because everything could be put
into this form of theatre—speech, dancing, music. The words
themselves do not, in this context, have a logical value; they are
there to create a particular impression on the spectator, "their
effect is that of an incantation".[2] Had the text, which was de-
claimed by the actress Maria Casarès as *la reine verte*, had more
quality, so as to counterbalance the other elements of the production, which included electronic music by Pierre Henry, the
success of this attempt might have been more decisive. Other
elements from the cinema and the circus were also incorporated
into the production, which aimed at a wide audience like that of
the T.N.P.; the reduced price of seats in the orchestra stalls was
indicative of this. But one cannot improvise a "popular theatre"
overnight, and it is doubtful whether "popular theatre" can be
produced according to a simple recipe or abstract formula. Roger
Planchon discovered, as Jean Vilar discovered before him, that the
potential popular audience had to be sought out in its workshops
and canteens before it could be enticed into what had so far been a
stronghold of the middle-class, and that to hold this new audience
the plays had to speak to this new audience of itself—so Vilar put
it. As early as 1945 the experimentalist who was also a Boulevard
playwright, Armand Salacrou, had come round to a similar point
of view; dramatists, he said, should take account of the problems
that are of deep concern to the general public, and should give
expression to the public's feelings about them.

As far as drama itself is concerned, a phase which happens to coincide with the inter-war years was clearly coming to a close already in 1938. The events of war and foreign occupation made the closure more conclusive. Even a dramatist of Giraudoux's stature, given his particular view of the universe and his insistence on literary style, seemed to belong to another era when peace returned. The new times took far more kindly to the "committed drama" of Jean-Paul Sartre than to the rhetorical graces of the stylist Giraudoux. What comes as the most surprising phenomenon of the post-1945 theatre, however, is the violence of the reaction expressed in the "anti-theatre" of the fifties, and the fact that this "anti-theatre" registers the sudden triumph of those elements of the experimental movement which had succeeded least of all in the twenties and thirties, if one is to judge from the limited number of performances and the exiguity of the audiences that the "anti-theatre" plays of the inter-war years could command. The productions of the Dadaists and Surrealists had been of negligible importance at the time, but their complete disregard of dramatic structure, psychological developments, and even of the dramatic story—albeit irrational or "absurd"—and their experiments with language, all combined to provide a sort of pattern for the future exponents of "anti-theatre". Ionesco himself has never denied his affiliation with the Surrealists, but to accuse him and Samuel Beckett of ersatz surrealist productions, as Isidore Isou did at a performance of some of the surrealist plays of the twenties, by the Théâtre Neuf, in 1964, is to close one's eyes to the other elements which have gone into the making of a Beckett or Ionesco play, and which are by no means negligible, even if one joins with Sean O'Casey in his telling condemnation of these playwrights for seeming to set down the history of life as a "Doomsday Book". The Ionesco-Beckett movement and the reaction against it, led by Adamov and Planchon, are as important for the understanding of the present position in the theatre as the Copeau movement was, at the end of the First World War, for the appreciation of the drama of the inter-war years.

NOTES

1. *L'Express*, September 14th.
2. *Arts*, October 16th–22nd, 1963.

INDEX

Lugné-Poë, Aurélien-Marie, 41, 66–
68, 73, 87, 112, 133, 143, 145,
150, 162, 163, 230, 240, 281
Lui, 282, 283

MacArthur, Charles, 284
Macbeth (adapted by Baty), 40
Machin chouette, 187
Machine à écrire, La, 58, 61, 62
Machine infernale, La, 53–56, 58,
63, 213
Ma Cousine de Varsovie, 279
Madame Béliard, 123
Madame Bovary (adapted by Baty),
38, 39, 40
Madame Quinze, 167
Madeleine ou la Pâtissière du
village, 283
Madelon, 165
Mademoiselle, 284–285
Maeterlinck, Maurice, 32, 91, 96,
107, 111, 112, 113, 114, 310
Mains sales, Les, 252
Mais n'te promène donc pas toute
nue, 274
Maison avant tout, La, 272–273
Maison des remparts, La, 101–102
Maison épargnée, La, 116
Maison Monestier, La, 121
Maison natale, La, 272
Maître Bolbec et son mari, 280
Maître de forges, Le, 287
Maître de son cœur, Le, 302, 305
Mal Aimés, Les, 108, 109
Malborough s'en va-t-en guerre,
159, 183, 186–187
Mal court, Le, 243
Mallarmé, Camille, 27
Maman Colibri, 261
Mandarine, 168
Mangeur de rêves, Le, 33, 92, 97
Manière forte, La, 285
Marâtre, La, 25
Marceau, Marcel, 188

Marcel, Gabriel, 178, 247–257
Marchand, Léopold, 271, 290
Marchands de gloire, Les, 159
Marchat, Jean, 313
Marché noir, Le, 140
Margot, 269
Margrave, La, 282, 283
Marguéritte, Victor, 299
Maria, 226
Mariage de Figaro, Le, 32, 268
Mariage d'Hamlet, Le, 163, 165
Mariage de Monsieur le Trouhadec,
Le, 77–78
Mariage forcé, Le, 300
Marie, 283
Mariés de la Tour Eiffel, Les, 49–
50, 88, 223
Mariette, 278
Mari, la femme et l'amant, Le, 276
Marius, 15, 259, 270
Marivaux, Pierre Carlet de Cham-
blain de, 22, 39, 166, 174
Martin, Claude, 313
Martin du Gard, Maurice, 32
Martin du Gard, Roger, 110
Martine, 19, 114–115, 116, 122
Marx, Henry, 247
Matériel humain, Le, 307
Mathusalem, 88
Maulnier, Thierry, 64, 214
Maurey, Max, 289, 290
Mauriac, François, 64, 108–110,
214, 251
Mauvaise Conduite, La, 190
Maya, 106–107
Mazaud, Emile, 18, 70–71, 73
Médée, 174, 176
Médico de su honra, El (adapted
by Arnoux), 188
Meilhac, Henri, 280
Mélo, 264
Menace, La, 288
Menaechmi (adapted by Variot),
190